T0177760

Game Data Science

GAME DATA SCIENCE

MAGY SEIF EL-NASR
TRUONG HUY NGUYEN DINH
ALESSANDRO CANOSSA
ANDERS DRACHEN

OXFORD
UNIVERSITY PRESS

Great Clarendon Street, Oxford, OX2 6DP,
United Kingdom

Oxford University Press is a department of the University of Oxford.
It furthers the University's objective of excellence in research, scholarship,
and education by publishing worldwide. Oxford is a registered trade mark of
Oxford University Press in the UK and in certain other countries

© Magy Seif El-Nasr, Truong Huy Nguyen Dinh, Alessandro Canossa, and Anders Drachen 2021

The moral rights of the authors have been asserted

First Edition published in 2021

Impression: 1

Published in the United States of America by Oxford University Press
198 Madison Avenue, New York, NY 10016, United States of America

British Library Cataloguing in Publication Data
Data available

Library of Congress Control Number: 2021932524

ISBN 978-0-19-289787-9 (hbk.)
ISBN 978-0-19-289788-6 (pbk.)

DOI: 10.1093/oso/9780192897879.001.0001

Printed and bound by
CPI Group (UK) Ltd, Croydon, CR0 4YY

FOREWORD

Intuition vs. analytics

I have worked with some deeply brilliant people, and what amazes me most is the intuitive grace with which they can make the myriad microdecisions that go into building a product. The way our intuition operates on data we have already internalized is amazing.

But intuition is, by necessity, often flawed: it is sometimes myopic, based on past experiences and the people we have spent the most time with, and misses facts that stick out of the data like sore thumbs.

We have all met the designer who refuses to even consider insights from data, because "Picasso didn't need analytics." But art and data are not in opposition, and fighting blindfolded is as foolhardy as it is poetic.

Generosity, collaboration, and tooling

When I came to the games industry nearly two decades ago, my favorite aspect of it was how collaborative all these crazy smart and creative people were. Everyone was sharing best practices from articles in the *Gems* book series, to conferences, to their blogs. Industry legend has it that even competing companies sometimes shared useful bits of code with each other.

This all enabled so many of us to make great games and great game engines and ultimately moved the industry forward at the breakneck pace that has made it so fun and crazy and wild and competitive and innovative and frustrating— and also the biggest form of entertainment by far.

As we grew up and moved online, data started pouring in—data without end, and without meaning. But we are smart and resourceful, and the industry has been adapting and inventing methods to understand and act on this torrent.

Yet, it has been frustrating that the sharing of game analytics methods has lagged behind other areas. Too many wheels got reinvented, and the democratization of methods and tools is not quite there.

I hope that this book inspires a generation of toolmakers to bring the industry forward. Data without code is *just a PowerPoint*.

Get smart

Finally, whether or not you intend to make use of the methods described in this book, you can be sure that they *will* be applied to you. And, in an age where your data is never really only yours, the best way to safeguard your digital identity is to wise up about how it will be interpreted and operationalized.

Game Data Science provides an in-depth overview of the techniques and methods used to extract intelligence from the data that can be gathered from playing games. The authors are all pioneers in the field of game analytics, and they offer their experience and insight to bring anyone up to speed with cutting-edge practices.

That by itself is exciting.

David Helgason
Founder of Unity

PREFACE

This book was developed to give readers an introduction to the practical side of game data science. Before we discuss what that means, let's delve a bit deeper into what "game data science" means. Game data science is a term that we use to denote a process composed of methods and techniques by which an analyst or a data scientist can make sense of data to allow decision makers in a game company to make informed decisions. The type of data used, and stakeholders involved can vary from company to company. For example, analysts at Riot use gameplay data collected from players to make decisions about the design of the game. In such cases, game data scientists will analyze data to come up with patterns that they can communicate to the design team, allowing them to adjust their designs. However, this is not the only reason to analyze data from games. Besides gameplay data, there are many other uses of game data, such as system-level analysis, marketing analysis or segmentation, or adjusting workflow plans. In our earlier book, Game Analytics: Maximizing the Value of Player Data, we discussed some case studies of such different and varied uses. If interested, readers should consult this book for more information on how data from games can be used and the different stakeholders involved. We will cover some aspects of this again in Chapter 1 of this book, but these topics will not be discussed in depth.

When you are a game data scientist looking at game data, you may have many goals and/or questions in mind. Some of these questions may be about the following: engagement (how can we engage new users? How long is an average play session?); retention (how many returning users are there in the game? How much time do users typically stay in the game before they quit?); game design (did players learn the game mechanics or did they struggle with some? Were there any dominant strategies in the game?); game development (are there any apparent bugs in the game?); money (e.g., how much money did the game make? Can I project how much money the game will continue to make in the future?); and so on. All these types of questions are answerable through game data science techniques.

Industry and academic researchers have worked hard (and are still working) to develop a set of methods that can be used to answer these questions. These methods and techniques are borrowed and adapted from many fields of study, including Machine Learning (ML), data mining, Social Network Analysis (SNA), Artificial Intelligence (AI), and visualization. It is important to realize that each of these fields have their own community and are active fields of research with several venues where such research is published and presented. Readers who are interested in the basic and advanced techniques in any of these areas are advised to consult these communities and attend conferences in these areas, such as AAAI (American Association for the Advancement of Artificial Intelligence), InfoVis (Information Visualization), VAST (Visual Analytics Science and Technology), ICML (International Conference on Machine Learning), and KDD (Knowledge Discovery and Data Mining). There are also some game specific conferences that often deal with analytic techniques, such as FDG (Foundation of Digital Games), IEEE COG (Conference on Games), and AAAI AIIDE (Artificial Intelligence and Interactive Digital Entertainment).

In this book, we will discuss basic techniques that have been applied in game data science so far from these fields. But the game data science field is still in its infancy. Researchers and analysts in the field are following such conferences closely to acquire more advanced techniques to use to solve open problems or questions. Thus, once readers get acquainted with the basics, they are encouraged to look at conference papers in the field for more advanced techniques.

It is also important to realize that each one of the methods and techniques that we will discuss in this book is essentially borrowed from different fields. Therefore, understanding them will require some theoretical foundations, which we will introduce throughout the book. For example, machine learning techniques are often based on probability theory and information theory. Thus, the book will include an introduction to these theories. We will discuss them when they are applicable to the methods used, and we will also include a more practical example to show how they are applied. However, the book will not go in depth in all areas, and readers may need to consult further readings and references to get more in-depth knowledge of areas covered. Each chapter will contain several pointers for further readings and references that interested readers can consult.

Intended Audience

The intended readers of this book are students who want to learn about game data science techniques and how they are applied. Additionally, the book is also targeted to the game industry: it can in fact help with the communication across teams, for example, game and systems designers often need to interface with data analysts to formulate appropriate and feasible research questions. There are no prerequisites to understanding the techniques in this book, although many of the methods discussed require some understanding of probability theory or other statistical techniques, which we will be introducing throughout the book. Thus, the book should be self-contained and accessible for any student at the graduate or advanced undergraduate level.

Labs and Supplementary Materials

All labs and data are available as supplementary materials at the book's companion website: www.oup.co.uk/companion/GameDataScience. Please navigate to this website and then register to gain access to the lab and data materials discussed through this book.

ACKNOWLEDGMENT

We are grateful to so many people for their help and support as we embarked on the journey of writing this book. We first want to thank our families, our partners, children, parents, and siblings who have already heard a lot about this book as we tirelessly worked on it.

We are also indebted to the many amazing graduate students who have worked on many chapters of this book, including Erica Kleinman, Sabbir Ahmed, Andy Bryant, Madkour Amr AbdelRahman, Nathan Partlan, Luis Fernando Laris Pardo, Evelyn Tan, Valerio Bonometti and Ozan Vardal. We would like to praise them for their hard work and feedback as well as the continued support and help as we polished the chapters involved. And, we are also indebted to Dr. Paola Rizzo for her review and feedback.

A great thanks to our copy editors who have helped us edit this book and gave us a lot of advice on structure, grammar and vision. Great thanks to Miranda Adkins, Simran Dhaliwal, and Fergus Scott, writing advisors and Master's students in the Computer Science Align Program at Khoury College of Computer Sciences; Ian Magnusson, team leader, writing advisor and Master's student in the Computer Science Align Program at Khoury College of Computer Sciences; last but not least great thanks to Jane Kokernak, senior communications advisor at Khoury College of Computer Sciences.

Further, we would like to acknowledge our colleagues across industry and academia who helped out in numerous ways. We are particularly grateful to Yusuf Pisan and Foaad Khosmood for their feedback and suggested edits for Chapter 11 of the book. We also want to recognize our partners and colleagues at Square Enix, Ubisoft Massive, Ubisoft Montreal, King, Nordeus, EA, ESL, Riot Games, Bungie, Microsoft, and many others, who have championed joint exploration and research in game data science across academia and industry, and across disciplinary fields, for close to two decades now. Game data science has grown into a strongly collaborative domain and we are grateful to everyone who has been part of the journey so far, or who will join the journey in the future.

CONTENTS

HOW TO READ THE BOOK

The book is divided into chapters that follow each other, so readers should be able to start from the beginning of the book and read through. Each chapter will include the following:

- **Theoretical foundations.** As discussed above, all methods used will be preceded with a theoretical discussion of their foundations to allow readers to understand them fully.
- **Practical implementations and Labs.** The book will include practical introductions to all algorithms discussed. Almost all chapters, with the exception of one or two chapters, will include labs to allow readers to follow along and apply the techniques discussed. All labs will also come with game data to allow readers to understand how to apply the algorithms to game data. All labs and data are available as supplementary materials at the book's companion website: www.oup.co.uk/companion/GameDataScience. Please go this website and register to gain access to the lab and data materials discussed through this book.
- **Applicability to game data science.** In some sections we will discuss a general technique or algorithm and then follow with a more in-depth discussion of how these more general algorithms apply to games. It should be noted that game data science is still a growing field, and not all methods discussed in the AI community have been applied to games, some for good reasons. We will discuss these as they come up.
- **Case studies.** It is important to show case studies of the use of the techniques discussed either in the industry or academic research. We will include these through the book chapters. But they will become

more apparent in the later parts of the book when we get to more complex concepts or methods.

- **Exercises.** As any textbook, this textbook will include some exercises at the end of each chapter to help solidify the concepts.

CHAPTER 1

Game Data Science: An Introduction

You may have heard of the term game analytics or game data science. In fact, you may have even picked up this book due to the use of the term in industry or academic circles. Game data science has become a cornerstone of game development in a very short period of time. In fact, back in the 1990s, no one would have thought that game data would become a field of study and innovation in game research and industry. Back in the 1990s, we were still working on developing better graphics, development tools, and design practices. Fast forward to now, game data science is emerging as a very important field of study due to the emergence of social games embedded in online social networks. The ubiquity of social games gives access to new data sources and has an impact on important business decisions, given the introduction of freemium[1] business models.

Game data science is a broad domain covering all aspects of collecting, storing, analyzing data, and communicating insights. It can support any aspect of design and development, and it is not *only* about player behavior, although that is certainly an important part of the process. With a mature data science framework in place, companies have the instruments to gain objective knowledge about workflows and competitors, understand their communities and players, improve development processes, increase retention and revenue,

---

[1] Freemium is a monetization strategy where the barebone service is provided for free but customers are expected to pay for additional elements such as vanity items, in-game currency, and faster cooldowns.

Game Data Science. Magy Seif El-Nasr, Truong Huy Nguyen Dinh, Alessandro Canossa, and Anders Drachen, Oxford University Press. © Magy Seif El-Nasr, Truong Huy Nguyen Dinh, Alessandro Canossa, and Anders Drachen (2021). DOI: 10.1093/oso/9780192897879.003.0001

and build capacity to offer games for free to customers, as we shall talk about more below.

Game data science fundamentally aims to add data-driven evidence to support decision-making across operational, tactical, and strategic levels of game development, and this is why it is so valuable. It allows researchers and the industry to move away from guesswork and make decisions based on carefully collected, curated, and analyzed data.

Game data science is the subject of this book. After reading this book, you should have a clear understanding of the current standard methods and tools used to analyze data collected from games. As the knowledge and practices in game data science are expanding rapidly, the ideas, methods, and tools presented in this book will also likely expand as new solutions become available. This book provides an introduction to the foundational approaches and theories that will help you understand current and future approaches of game data science.

With this introductory chapter, you begin your journey in the field of game data science. In particular, this chapter will provide a high-level panoramic introduction to the processes used to analyze and make sense of game data and suggest actionable information with the scientific method as a base process. Unlike other chapters in this book, this opening chapter does not contain practical labs. The material discussed is conceptual, providing you with the basics as you embark on the journey of understanding and practicing game data science.

1.1 What is game data science?

Fundamentally, game data science is the process of discovering and communicating patterns in data with the purpose of informing decision-making in different domains, such as business or design, in the context of games. As such, game data science includes many types of analyses, such as summarizing the number of active players within a certain time unit, predicting when players will stop playing a game, or evaluating the performance of servers.

In our previous book, Game Analytics (Seif El-Nasr, Drachen, and Canossa, 2013), we used the term game analytics rather than game data science to denote the process of analyzing and applying data collected throughout the development process. Here, we adopted game data science rather than game analytics for several reasons, most importantly, because analytics in many communities relates to business intelligence or making decisions about business aspects using data. Therefore, there is sometimes a confusion about whether game analytics refers only to the application of data science to inform decision-making for traditional business purposes or if it also covers the application of data science to inform design processes. Because the application of data science to inform design is a large part of this book, we, therefore, will use the broader and more inclusive term of game data science. The way we use this term denotes the breadth of the field of knowledge discovery using data collected through the game design, development, and post-launch production processes.

Game data science, thus, overlaps substantially with other data-informed processes in game development, including Games User Research (GUR)[2], business intelligence as it is applied in the games industry, and marketing and brand research. While there is much ongoing discussion in the community about what exactly game data science is and is not, in this book, we will adopt an inclusive viewpoint, rather than trying to set limits around the term.

To summarize, game data science is the term we use collectively for the process of providing data-driven evidence for decisions made at various parts of the game design, development, and production processes. You can apply the tools and techniques of game data science across virtually any aspect of the game design and development processes.

1.2 What is game data?

A great variety of data can be collected, stored, analyzed, and leveraged to gather intelligence throughout the lifetime of a game title or game company. Typical sources of data include behavioral data from games, information from advertising partners and other third parties (i.e., social media platforms), and data collected from infrastructure (such as servers), the development process itself, marketing, and user research.

These varied sources of data can be used in many parts of the production process to inform game design and development, including understanding or optimizing developers' workflow during production, optimizing server performance after release, and testing to identify bugs or player engagement. While evaluation of technical infrastructure and platform compatibility can

---

[2] Games User Research (GUR) is a field of study that focuses on understanding user behaviors, needs, and motivations by analyzing how the design of a certain application or game impacts its audience. As you will see in the history section within this chapter, researchers working in this area are also tightly coupled with game analysts as some of the processes used by games user researchers also use game data.

provide substantial data sets that are important to the operation of a game, in this book, we will not focus on this topic as the intersection between software engineering and data science deserves its own book.

In this book, we will focus on player data. The data examples and practical exercises you will find throughout this book will use player data. This is because player data is, by far, the most commonly used and available source of data in game data science. There are different forms of player data, including behavioral data collected in real time as players play the game, and player preference or statistics, such as how many games they played and their ranks or scores. The behavioral data collected in real time is often called behavioral telemetry.

Behavioral telemetry, in a more general sense, is data that we constantly leave as trails through all the actions we perform in our daily life: borrowing books from a library, visiting websites, purchasing a house, working as a middle manager, or vacationing in Southeast Asia. Whether we drive a car, a motorcycle, or a rickshaw, almost any action we take in the public space can represent a syllable of a longer sentence that contributes to composing the narrative of our lives. The digital trails we leave behind are even easier to collect. The way we use our phones creates a constantly evolving representation of who we are.

Telemetry basically means data collected from afar. In the context of games, as people play a game, we can collect data about what they do in the game, down to the press of a button or movement of a mouse, if so desired. This type of user data is commonly collected across the IT sector. The process of collecting and storing telemetry data is easier than ever due to cheap and large storage solutions, pervasive device connectivity, and instrumentation of software and hardware.

Within digital games, the trails can be so detailed and complex that they reveal aspects of player personalities, motivations, and experiences through the actions and decisions taken when playing, declared or inferred preferences, movement patterns, and the relationships players build. Behavioral telemetry is, within the scope of behavioral data, the most common source of information we have and certainly the most voluminous. Behavioral data allows us to move beyond finding patterns in data to begin drawing inference about the meaning behind digital actions. Understanding why players do particular things or behave the way they do is valuable. It can be readily applied to evaluating and informing design, user experience, and monetization.

The games industry has invested, especially in recent years, considerable efforts to establish expertise, implement tools, and build processes that can leverage the knowledge extracted from analyzing the trails of data that players leave behind. The methods—the toolset of a game data scientist—in many ways leverage the knowledge and methods that already exist, pioneered in the rise of big data, data science, and Artificial Intelligence (AI). However, it is important to realize that game data science often ends up drawing upon knowledge in fields, such as design, psychology, sociology, information systems, user experience, or user research, when it comes to informing what analysis to run on player data, how to interpret the results of such analyses, and, perhaps more crucially, how to translate the results into action.

Though knowledge and analytical approaches have grown rapidly, at the time of writing this book, game data science is in many ways still in its infancy. There are no set standards or definitions of metrics, and much of the available knowledge is locked away due to the inherent (proprietary) value in data. On the positive side, this means that now is an exciting time to work in game data science. It also means that there is an ongoing challenge in developing tools and methods that can leverage expert knowledge to analyze and make sense of such vast amounts of data and ensure that new knowledge informs decision-making that translates into action.

1.3 Advantages of game data science

The benefits and advantages of integrating game data science in game development are many and far-reaching. With a mature data science framework in place, companies have the instruments to gain objective knowledge about workflow and server workload as well as gain knowledge about their players, gather insights into which elements of a certain game are most popular, and figure out at what point players stop playing. In addition to insights into design, the games industry utilizes knowledge gained from data to increase revenue and improve player experience. Together, these two issues drive business and development decisions since the vectors for monetization and player experience are aligned. A better user experience turns into higher sales and higher player retention.

In the realm of academic game research and serious games[3], the application of game data science has gained substantial momentum, as it allows companies

---

[3] A term used to describe games developed for purposes other than entertainment, such as training, promoting health, citizen science, or psychological experiments.

and researchers to analyze the relationship between player or user behavior and the outcomes of such behavior, e.g., increased awareness of a topic, health benefits, or learning. The discoveries being made using data-driven techniques, such as in the field of learning analytics, have major implications for education and health. Citizen science and crowdsourcing games also rely on such methods to increase awareness, retention, and motivation.

1.4 The historical context for game data science

Game data science is in many ways a relatively young domain—especially viewed through the lens of academic research. However, the application of data science methods to data from games or from game companies has expanded so fast and evolved so rapidly that it is easy to overlook the fact that, a decade ago, using machine learning algorithms on game data was largely unheard of. The history of game data science can thus be thought of as being shallow but broad.

In general, there are several challenges to mapping the history of game data science. First, the substantial amounts of knowledge generated are not recorded anywhere that is publicly available. Companies invest resources in business intelligence, and the results are often treated as confidential due to their business value. Similarly, early academic research in the area is published across a dozen or more domains and thus is extremely fragmented. Second, there has been a substantial parallel growth in different sectors and countries, and thus it is hard to say when a specific technology was developed or how it influenced the development of the field. Third, any account of the historical perspective will naturally be biased by the specific area of focus or community that the author comes from.

To highlight the challenges in developing a historical overview of game data science or aspects of it, we have included an exercise specifically on this topic (see exercises below). In this section, we will focus on discussing some of the factors that we think has affected the growth of the field as we see it, acknowledging that we have our own biases.

There are several waves of innovation within the field of technology and games that have facilitated the development of game data science. The obvious technology innovations include the development of personal computers, the Internet, the development of platforms, such as Facebook and Steam, the growth of server and database technologies, computing capacity, and machine learning as well as the recent developments in deep learning. Below, we discuss some of what we think are important landmarks that led to the development of game data science as it stands today.

1.4.1 The rise of the MMOG

There are accounts, from very early game titles, of player data being gathered. However, prior to the introduction of first Multi-User Dungeons (MUDs) and then Massively Multiplayer Online Games (MMOGs), the application of such data as an external process, toward informing design, systems, virtual economies, and other aspects of the game world, has been fragmented at best. With MMOGs, such as *Ultima Online*, there emerged a need for monitoring a persistent game world, its user base, and how that user base might even engage in out-of-game trading (e.g., selling *Ultima Online* characters). MMOG economies were designed and tested, and accounts, such as the one by Simpson (2000), show that game data informed part of such development, albeit at a simpler level than the kinds of economic analyses that are often run on contemporary MMOGs.

On the academic side, early analytical work on MMOGs was developed in parallel with such work in the industry. MMOG economies and their analysis were given substantial visibility by Castronova, who published work about *Everquest* in 2001 documenting how synthetic worlds and their economies operate, concluding that the Gross National Product (GNP) of these early game worlds could rival some real-world countries (Castronova, 2001). From this and other contemporary works—e.g., by Williams et al. (2011), Ducheneaut et al. (2006), Yee (2006), and Dibbell (2006), as well as the release of *Second Life* and other virtual worlds—broad public attention has emerged on the use of game worlds and the opportunities they provide as tools to analyze player behavior. This was turbo-charged with the release of *World of Warcraft* and the impressive subscription numbers it reached, bringing Massively Multiplayer Online Role-Playing Games (MMORPGs) into public consciousness, at least in the Western world; *Lineage* and *Guild Wars*, in Asia and beyond, also deserve credit.

With the emergence of early analytical work on games during the years 2003–2006, suddenly, many researchers realized that virtual worlds provided fertile spaces for research across economics, behavioral science, psychology, network latency, and more. Around these years, some early works surfaced across industry and academia that showcased how in-game player behavior could be analyzed for various purposes. There were also many examples of how players themselves mined the games for data, e.g., to build online guides and sites about quests or resource harvesting. In general, there existed a degree of data access in MMOGs and in other games that was not often seen in other data-heavy IT sectors. It should be noted that the analytical methods at the time were still largely confined to statistics and (simple) economic modeling.

1.4.2 Social network games

Another angle on how game data science emerged is the rise of online social network platforms, such as Facebook. The proliferation of social networks led to the emergence of a new type of game, the Social Network Game (SNG) (Alsén et al., 2016). SNGs could tap into social network data and use free-to-play strategies to drive monetization, breaking with the traditional retail sales models. Due to the abundance of data available from the social network platforms, and the requirement to monitor in-game behavior due to the monetization strategy adopted, SNGs had a built-in imperative for analyzing player data. This urgency brought analytics (Seif El-Nasr et al., 2013) to the forefront of the games industry by around 2007–2010. Terms such as monetization, funnel analysis, onboarding research, First-Time User Experience (FTUE), and others started becoming commonplace. In 2011, one of the first books addressing this market was published, which included a list of important monetization metrics, such as Daily Active User (DAU) and Average Revenue Per User (ARPU) (Fields and Cotton, 2011).

1.4.3 Democratizing data collection

A factor arising by around 2010 onward was the democratization of metrics collection. Thanks to technological innovations outside the games industry and the emergence of numerous start-up companies that provided Software as Service (SaaS) analytics platforms, such as DeltaDNA, Game Analytics, Swrve, Ninja Metrics, and, later on, Yokozuna Data and others. Such platforms provided tools and case studies showing the analytics process, which unpacked the process of collection and analysis of behavioral telemetry. Several articles published in tech magazines discuss how companies, such as Wooga, Zynga, Microsoft, and Ubisoft, use telemetry data, giving us more examples and case studies on how an analytics process is implemented.

1.4.4 Games User Research (GUR)

Around the same time that SNGs made their first appearance, GUR started to become a main part of the game development process. The history of GUR is documented in Drachen, Mirza-Babaei, and Nacke (2018) and Isbister and Schaffer (2008). It is interesting to note that the application of behavioral telemetry to inform game design within the context of AAA[4] games was driven, to an extent, by user research. In the mid-2000s, Microsoft's User Research division took game user testing seriously, adapting techniques from the domain of Human–Computer Interaction (HCI) and developing new ones to specifically work in the user experience-focused game environments. To the new field's benefit, Microsoft, Bungie, and other companies discussed their work and methods, e.g., in Thompson's famous *Wired* article in 2007 (Thompson, 2007). Amaya et al. (2008) notably detailed the work of Microsoft User Research that integrated user research with automated recording of user behavior. Importantly, this research and the ideas it propagated enhanced the role of behavioral telemetry as a useful source of knowledge. Around the same time, leading up to 2010, several key blog posts, white papers, and presentations at the Game Developers Conference showcased how the industry at large was exploring game data science and building new technologies, methods, and ideas.

An important milestone in GUR and its influence on game data science is the start of the International Game Developers Association's Game Research and User Experience Special Interest Group (GRUX SIG) in 2012. This special interest group started organizing and connecting games user researchers across industry and academia, building summits, and facilitating knowledge exchange. This incredibly welcoming community had a significant effect on GUR and, by extension, game data science. The group today counts more than 2,100 members worldwide and hosts multiple annual summits (see GRUX SIG, 2015).

1.4.5 Games as a Service

More games developed in the past few years have focused on being online and persistent, with downloadable content, patches, and updates extending the lifetime of these games. Having a Live Operations (LiveOps) team for

---

[4] AAA titles are games that typically have a higher marking and development budget.

mainline titles is commonplace for such games. This then created a shift in the development model where the design and development process started to incorporate data as an integral part of the process to allow design tuning based on player's behaviors as evidenced in the data. Mellon's (2009) report outlined this need more clearly and described how telemetry is applicable to the development of games, outlining the importance of performance and production as well as player metrics.

1.4.6 Rise of machine learning and game data

With the availability of data from commercial titles, academic researchers started to explore the application and development of different machine learning methods to apply to game data. The years 2007–2012 saw a wave of papers that applied data science and data visualization to behavioral telemetry. Drachen, Canossa, and Yannakakis (2009) and Drachen and Canossa (2009a, 2009b) showcased for the first time in academic research the application of machine learning on AAA titles' behavioral telemetry and geospatial visualization of player behavior beyond heatmaps. The goal was to build behavioral profiles of *Tomb Raider: Underworld* players using machine learning approaches. While behavioral profiling is commonplace today, a decade ago, the technical infrastructure was often lacking and cloud computing was very different. There was also a general challenge to find data scientists who understood games. There is a lot more research that could be highlighted for this period. For a more complete resource, refer to Ben Medler's PhD dissertation that summarized the history of the field at the time and also highlighted how analytics/data science can be applied in AAA productions (Medler, 2012).

The years around 2010–2015 saw a massive upskilling of the maturity of game data science in the games industry. At this point, data is not just collected from players but also from server infrastructure, production, and other aspects of game development. All such data form part of the framework of game data science. At the same time, thanks to distribution platforms, such as Steam, it became possible to analyze player behavior across multiple games for the first time (e.g., Sifa, Drachen, and Bauckhage, 2015). Furthermore, the sophistication of game data science methods evolved rapidly following the appearance of deep learning. The proliferation of academic research in the area also increased sharply around this time.

It is also worth mentioning that the emergence of research on esports, which is stronger than ever now, was based on giving the community open access to data through Application Programming Interfaces (APIs) (see examples from *DOTA, DOTA 2*, and *League of Legends*). Esports data was adopted by the community, and numerous independent services and sites were set up to feed data to the players and audience. To this day, a substantial fraction of research in games is based on freely available data from billions of recorded esports sessions (Block et al., 2018).

However, the data science methods and capacity at the time were unevenly distributed across the industry, with larger companies and publishers having more resources to invest in these new technologies. Companies, such as Zynga, Wooga, Ubisoft, Microsoft, Valve, Blizzard, Nordeus, and others, built up game data science pipelines and showcased their new innovations (apologies to relevant companies not listed here). Around this time, data sets became widely available, driving academic research and competitions, for example, on Kaggle—a platform that is used to hold competitions and challenge data scientists in the hopes of developing new data analysis methods (Unman, 2017). Increased collaboration across academia and industry further drove innovation.

1.4.7 Today

Today, the application of machine learning to analyze player behavior is commonplace, and, while not exactly ubiquitous across the games industry, it is within reach of almost everyone, thanks to a proliferation of new tools. There remains a strong need for expertise to apply data science methods in the context of games. However, the barrier to entry has never been lower, and combined with the availability of data, game data science is now more accessible and useful than ever before. There are regular game data science events organized in the US and Europe, and data science has become a common topic in talks and presentations at events and conferences. This mirrors the general development in big data, analytics, and AI, which have impacted virtually every single sector in the past decade.

Some of the main challenges we face today are not technical, but rather focus on communication, with questions on how to explain the results of analytical processes, visualize, and tell stories with data in a way that cultivates knowledge and enables well-reasoned decisions. This same challenge is recognized across the IT sector and beyond, e.g., in finance, energy, and intelligence.

In summary, while there is much work in academia, innovation and research in this field are happening mostly on the industry side. The number of analysts/game data scientists in the games industry now outnumbers the number of academics working in this area. However, the games industry still faces many constraints, including limitations and constraints in regard to time to do basic research or long-term work on game data, and thus there is a lot that the academic community can undertake and contribute toward, beyond just applying already existing techniques.

1.5 The process of game data science

Switching from history, let's now talk about how you derive knowledge from data. To derive knowledge from data, you can adopt the scientific method—a method that has been studied and discussed for thousands of years. Principles of empirical observation and experimentation have been around at least since the Ancient Greeks. The modern principles of empirical science were born from the natural sciences in the seventeenth century.

The scientific method describes a specific process through which knowledge is generated to ensure that it is testable and falsifiable. It is of paramount importance that the conclusions we draw from data are as valid as possible. If we make guesses or know of biases in data sets, we need to state this clearly. The scientific method prescribes several steps and considerations that must be followed in order for the knowledge that it generates to be valid, falsifiable, and generalizable. Valid broadly means measuring what we are intending to measure, falsifiable means that we should be able to apply the same method to a similar data set and achieve the same result, and generalizable means that we can generalize from a specific data set or sample to the population we are interested in saying something about. These brief definitions simplify many underlying complexities for the sake of brevity here, and any data scientist needs to understand the principles of empirical science in more depth.

In this book, we are making the assumption that you already know about the fundamental aspects of empirical and experimental research. If you have any doubts or would like a review, there are good books on this topic, e.g., Field and Hole (2002); see the bibliography section for more references.

In data science, the scientific method has been adapted to the analysis of data via a framework referred to as the Knowledge Discovery Process. Within the process of knowledge discovery, there is a constant shift between inductive and deductive reasoning and the particular algorithms used throughout the process. In deductive reasoning (top-down), a particular conclusion is reached from a general set of rules or a theory. In inductive reasoning (bottom-up), the conclusion is reached from specific observations that can then be generalized to abstract rules or theories. Both approaches are necessary. Inductive reasoning is more open-ended and exploratory, useful especially at the beginning of the knowledge discovery process, during exploratory analyses. Deductive reasoning, on the other hand, is narrower and more concerned with testing or confirming hypotheses, useful later on in the process as a confirmatory analysis. Throughout this book, several methods will be introduced for both types of processes.

Figure 1.1 shows both processes within the context of the scientific method. As the figure shows, this method comprises several important steps. For deductive reasoning, you start from theory deriving some hypotheses (in the order of Steps 7, 1, 2, and then 3). This process is where you use theory from psychology, sociology, or other disciplines to define some variables and collect data. These are observations you see at Step 1. You then run analysis to generate some questions that will allow you to generate some hypotheses, going from Steps 2 to 3. Once the hypotheses are generated, you can collect data and run analysis to accept, reject, or refine such hypotheses (Steps 5 through 7). For inductive reasoning, you start with some observations of the data (Steps 1 and 2), which help you frame questions that formulate hypotheses. As you can see from the figure, this is an iterative process, where you can derive new hypotheses that you can then try to validate through experimentation and so on.

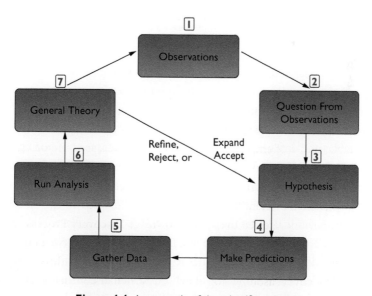

Figure 1.1 An example of the scientific process.

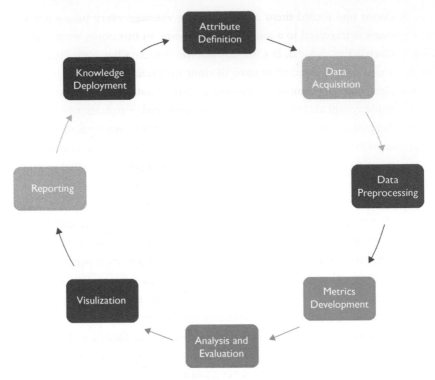

Figure 1.2 Applied process of Knowledge Discovery through game data. The figure is reproduced from Seif El-Nasr et al. (2013) with permission from Springer.

In 2013, we reformulated the knowledge discovery process for game data science (Seif El-Nasr et al., 2013), as shown in Figure 1.2. Specifically, the method consists of the following:

- Attribute definition consists of defining the objectives of the discovery process, framing the observation, and deciding where to direct, what we think of as, the inquisitive gaze. This initial step consists of selecting variables and defining tracking strategies: for example, monitoring the number of times players die. Later, these variables will inform the creation of metrics and Key Performance Indicators (KPIs), which we will discuss later.
- Data acquisition denotes the process by which data is collected through a game telemetry system, i.e., a system that collects all gameplay logs or system logs. Typically, code has to be written to collect the relevant variables defined in the attribute definition step and store it locally or remotely in a database or data file (formats can differ, but common formats are JSON and CSV). For example, one can track all death

events and record them by adding a log message every time a death event is triggered to a log file or a database. In this book, we will not discuss this process, but we will assume that data has been collected and concentrate on other parts of game data science.

- Data preprocessing is the process by which data is checked for consistency and cleaned before it can be analyzed. For example, we will need to get rid of empty values or erroneous values that may have been entered or logged. Some of these issues may arise because of errors in the game system or players performing an unexpected action. Sometimes, empty values can also occur due to unexpected lags or inactivity. Chapter 2 details this part of the process.
- Metrics development is the process where we can construct meaning or abstractions from data. Low-level action data is thus transformed into features and metrics. If you are using a deductive approach, you can formulate these metrics using your hypotheses. For example, the calculation of a metric for death ratio and kill ratio, as well as performance metrics, can help inform a hypothesis about kill ratio and performance. Chapter 4 will delve deeper into this process discussing knowledge-based construction of such metrics (as denoted by the example) as well as algorithmic abstractions through dimension reduction techniques, also defined in Chapter 4.
- Analysis and evaluation are used to accept, reject, or refactor hypotheses. In this part of the process, it is possible to develop a predictive model and even generalize it into a theory. It is also possible to develop several models from data using an inductive approach. This process is a lot more involved, and many techniques can be used, such as inferential statistics (see Chapter 3), machine learning (Chapters 6, 7, 8, and 9), and exploratory visualization approaches (Chapter 5).
- Visualization is concerned with visualizing data. This can be done as an exploratory step to understand the data or as a summative step to present results for the purpose of communication or presentation to stakeholders. Visualization provides the most efficient way to immediately convey information to the widest possible audience with little prior knowledge. Thanks to tools, such as *Tableau*, or libraries, such as *D3*, creating interactive visual reports has evolved beyond bar charts. Some of these techniques are discussed in Chapters 3 and 5.
- Reporting/knowledge deployment. The discovered knowledge is presented to the relevant stakeholders. Reports need to be immediate, understandable, interpretable, and actionable. Reports are being

substituted more and more by interactive dashboards that are fed with live data. This phase is often the beginning of a new discovery cycle. We will aim to use visualization in each chapter to show how one can report results and communicate them.

This model of knowledge discovery has a series of steps for both creation and evaluation of a theory (or model). Creating a model (bottom-up) entails finding information, extracting meaning, schematizing, building a case, and subsequently communicating that information. Evaluating the model (top-down) involves re-evaluating, finding supporting evidence, finding relations in the information, or finding basic information. Each stage can loop back or move forward in the chain.

1.6 Game data science: A glossary

The terminology around game data science is a bit confusing. For many terms and concepts, the field still doesn't have an agreed-upon standard definition. Hence, in this section, a brief glossary is introduced to denote some of the concepts utilized across this book. We must emphasize that these are *our* definitions. While they are based on terminology used in the industry and the field, there is substantial variance in how they are used, so be prepared for these differences as you engage more broadly in game data science. Furthermore, ours is not an exhaustive list of terms, and we anticipate that these terms and metrics will evolve as the field evolves.

1.6.1 Telemetry, metrics, and KPIs

Telemetry data refers to data collected by a system that collects, transmits, and stores it over a distance. Telemetry data is usually collected in a raw form, before it has been manually or computationally processed, and thus called raw data.

Game metrics are interpretable quantitative measures of in-game attributes or objects. If telemetry data is the information in its most raw form, metrics imply some interpretation. An example is a player's total playtime as 15 hours and 30 minutes.

Key Performance Indicators (KPIs) are strategically selected metrics that demonstrate quantitatively how an objective has been achieved. KPIs usually require contextual information to draw conclusions from them and also entail some sort of ground truth to compare with. For example, knowing that a game has 100 Daily Active Users (DAU) is fine, but is it more or fewer than yesterday? Last week? Last month? And what is the reason for any drop/increase? While KPIs are adequate for forming a quick impression, analysts should be cautious on their use and resist drawing conclusions from KPIs that they cannot support.

1.6.2 Player, performance, and process metrics

According to Mellon (2009), there are three classes of metrics and KPIs: player, performance, and process metrics (see Figure 1.3).

Player metrics are related to the people who play games. It is possible to view players as part of a community (relation to other players), as customers (sources of revenue), or as gameplay generators (agents of behavior). Examples of player metrics are total playtime per player, average number of in-game friends per player, or average damage dealt per player. Common analyses include time-spent analysis, trajectory analysis, or social networks analysis.

Performance metrics are related to the performance of the technical infrastructure behind a game. Examples include client frame rate, server stability, client crashes, number of bugs, and concurrent users (CCUs). Performance metrics are heavily used in Quality Assurance (QA) to monitor the health of a game. It is also one of the most mature areas of game data science, because the methods employed are derived from traditional software performance and QA techniques and strategies (Seif El-Nasr et al., 2013).

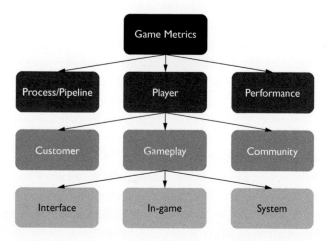

Figure 1.3 Different types of behavioral metrics for the categories player, performance, and process. The figure is reproduced from Seif El-Nasr et al. (2013) with permission from Springer.

Process metrics are related to the actual process of developing games and managing the creative process through development methods. In order to monitor and assess the development process, project managers utilize a combination of task-size estimation and burn-down charts or measure the average turnaround time of new content being delivered to the development pipeline.

1.6.2.1 COMMUNITY METRICS

Community metrics capture the social dimension of players at all resolution levels, from forum activity to number of friends or groups created or joined. These metrics are not only useful to community managers but also to the whole business of games, especially given some recent developments brought about by games that require a constant online connection.

Games as a Service (GaaS), or live games, refers to games that offer an evolving, long-term entertaining experience (as the service) for players. They often have a focus on online competitive multiplayer experiences, but they can also include other types of game experiences. "Live" refers to all the activities and interactions created for the game community, including pre- and post-launch as well as regular updates, new content, and events both in-game and out-of-game, throughout the game's lifespan. With the rise of the GaaS paradigm, designers and producers alike plan games with lifespans of several years. Such games are kept alive by community engagement activities, managers, and players.

Social network analysis provides some useful tools for studying both the structure (modularity) and the sources and distribution of power (centrality and prestige) in communities by examining the relations of players' attributes to other players. Centrality measures give us a way to quantify the different ways that a node can be important for the whole network. In other words, it helps identify the nodes occupying advantageous positions in networks of relations. Prestige is a version of centrality applicable to directed networks. Further, three basic sources of advantage are degree, closeness, and betweenness, which describe the locations of individuals in terms of how close they are to the "center" of the action. Degree is the number of links an actor has with other actors. The more ties an actor has, the more power they have. Actors with more ties have greater opportunities because they have choices. This autonomy makes them less dependent on other actors and hence more powerful. Closeness measures how accessible an actor is to all other actors. Power can be exerted from acting as a "reference point" by which other actors judge themselves, and by being a center of attention, whose views are heard by larger numbers of actors. Actors who are able to reach other actors at shorter path lengths, or who are more reachable by other actors at shorter path lengths, have favored positions. Betweenness measures the number of shortest paths from an actor to all other actors. Being between other actors is equal to a structurally advantaged position and is another measure of actor power in a network.

Modularity is used to examine a network's structure by detecting the sub-communities (Newman, 2006). Modularity measures divide the network into clusters (also called groups or modules) based on whether the number of edges within clusters exceeds the number expected on the basis of chance. Cluster, or module, is a region of the network that is strongly connected within (i.e., dense connections among the nodes within a cluster) and sparsely connected to the rest of the network (i.e., sparse connections among nodes in different clusters).

1.6.2.2 CUSTOMER METRICS

Customer metrics is a category of measurement that covers all aspects of the user as a customer, encompassing all forms of financial transactions. These types of metrics are notably interesting to management, producers, and marketing teams. Example metrics in this category are as follows:

- Active user: An active player is the one who had a session with a game and made some actions within that session (hour/day/week/month). DAU, WAU, and MAU refer to daily, weekly, and monthly active users. The definition of what constitutes an active user can vary and can range from users active in the last day to a full month.
- Inactive user: A player who has not recently interacted with the game but is not considered churned, where churned here means left the game. The specification of what constitutes an inactive user is variable and can range from users active from a month to date to three months to date.
- Churn rate: A measure of the number of users moving out of a collective group over a specific period. The collective group is often the active user group. The length of the window of time to examine for churn differs per game and genre, and developing this measure therefore requires further work with the design team.
- Average Revenue Per User (ARPU): For a game, this is calculated as the revenue divided by the active users of a certain, specified period. If it

is calculated per day, the revenue is divided by DAU producing ARP-DAUs (Average Revenue Per Daily Active Users); if it is calculated per week, the revenue is divided by WAU producing ARPWAU (Average Revenue Per Weekly Active Users); if it is calculated per month, the revenue is divided by MAU producing ARPMAU (Average Revenue Per Monthly Active Users). While ARPU divides the revenue for all users, Average Revenue Per Paying User (ARPPU) divides it only by users who made a payment in the period, showing how much a loyal, paying user is willing to pay.

- Paying share: This is the percentage of users that have made payments.
- Average Margin Per User (AMPU): This profitability metric is focused on profit. It is considered a better metric for management as it formulates pricing and marketing strategies and budgets cost items to maximize the bottom line.
- User Life-Time Value (ULTV): This metric is predictive, attributing the net profit or revenue, at a moment in time, to the entire future relationship with the average customer. This projection is based on previous purchasing behavior in order to deliver the most accurate result.
- Conversion rate: This is the percentage of users who complete a desired goal (a conversion) out of the total number of users. The desired goal could range from trying the demo of a game to purchasing the game, or from playing for free to making a micropayment.
- Repeaters/whales/premiums: With many games that involve micro-transactions, it is often observed that the top 10% of an app's spenders drive 60% of its total revenue. These high-spending players are often referred to as either repeaters or whales. Repeaters are generally 5% of spenders (0.1% of the whole population), and they are identified by both a large number of transactions and a high amount of money spent in their lifetime. Knowing how to find and manage high-spending players is crucial for a game company.

1.6.2.3 GAMEPLAY METRICS

Gameplay metrics include any variable related to the actual behavior of a player inside the game. Examples include interacting with objects, trading items, leveling up, navigating in the environment, and combating with Non-Player Characters (NPCs) and other players. Gameplay metrics are most salient when evaluating a game, level, and system design; they are fundamental for iterating on the initial work by designers and, together, with qualitative insights and direct observation, are the basis of user experience research. Gameplay metrics are particularly useful to stakeholders studying players' reactions to the design to inform design choices and decisions, such as those made by game designers, user researchers, and quality assurance managers.

Five types of information can be logged whenever a player does something— or is expected to do something—in a game:

- What is happening?
- How is it happening?
- Where is it happening?
- When is it happening?
- Whom is it happening to?

For example, during ranged combat, we want to log the event (what: shooting), the weapon used (how: sniper rifle), the location where it happened (where: level 3), the time it happened (when: 7 minutes from the start), and who was involved in the fight (whom: a heavy NPC). Players can easily generate thousands of behavioral measures over the course of a single game, since accurate measures of player activity can include dozens of actions measured per second, flowing from the game client to the collection servers. From a practical perspective, it can be useful to further subdivide gameplay metrics into the following three categories:

- In-game gameplay metrics cover all in-game actions and behaviors of players, including navigation, combat, dialogue choices, inventory, crafting, and difficulty level.
- Interface gameplay metrics include all interactions that players perform with the game interface and menus. This includes setting game variables, such as mouse sensitivity, monitor brightness, and graphics details.
- System gameplay metrics cover the actions performed by game engines and their sub-systems (e.g., AI system, automated events, and NPC actions) initiated to respond to player actions. An example of such an event is an NPC attacking a player character if it moves within range.

To sum up, the sheer number of potential measures from the users of a game (or game service) is staggering. Analysts, trying to manage the data size, will often identify the most essential pieces of information to log and analyze. This selection process imposes a bias but is often necessary to avoid data overload and ensure a functional workflow in the data science process. Each of the metrics described above can be tracked adopting one of these three strategies:

- Triggered event: A log is created any time a prespecified event occurs, such as these: a user starts a game, a designer submits a bug fix request, a unit of a game is sold, a player fires a weapon, or buys an item. Any action initiated by a person or system can form an event. Telemetry built on triggered events is based on tracking such actions and transmitting the generated information to a collection server.
- Sampled events (frequency): Continuous variables, which do not have a clear "on" or "off" state, could benefit from a different strategy of collection. Such information can, in fact, be recorded continuously according to a specific frequency or sampling rate. For example, when tracking the movement of players through virtual environments, we could place triggers in front of every room (triggered event) and record when players enter or just record the x, y, z coordinates of the players' locations once per second, as a compromise between precision and bandwidth constraints. A frequency-based strategy is often used when the attribute of the object being tracked is always present, e.g., a player character always has a position in the world.
- Analyst-initiated event: Sometimes, the game analyst wants to dynamically enable and disable the tracking of specific attributes, rather than record an attribute constantly or never at all. For example, it may not be necessary to record player avatar trajectories all the time, but only when updates or patches are pushed to the users. Having the ability to turn on and turn off the recording of specific attributes can be useful in these situations.

Gameplay metrics are dependent on the individual game, but there are some KPIs that can be generalized and abstracted across all games and all genres, independently from the uniqueness of each game. These KPIs are engagement, acquisition, retention, progression, and player profiles.

1.6.2.3.1 Engagement   Engagement refers to the player's commitment to a given game. Both the definition and operationalization of engagement vary widely in the literature, so much so that it is often confused with or identified as attention, immersion, presence, flow, effort, or enjoyment. A general conceptualization of engagement is the notion of presence or a sense of "being there."

Traditionally, the measures used to gauge engagement are self-reports, questionnaires, physiological, and behavioral measures. For the purpose of a data-driven approach, we define engagement as the degree of activity or attention someone gives to a game over some period of time. For this reason, playtime is the key metric. Playtime indicates the duration of time that the players spent actually playing. It is up to the game designers to define what playing the game means, as it typically depends on the type of gameplay. Idle time is not counted, i.e., whenever the player is not using the controller for a given amount of time. Playtime can be operationalized in different ways.

Days played measures the number of days players played since they started playing the game for the first time. Days where the player is inactive are ignored. A day played is a day where the player logged in or played for at least one session.

Average daily playtime is the average number of hours played each active day. It is computed by taking the sum of total playtime of each player divided by the number of days played and the number of players.

Average total playtime is the average number of hours played since the launch of the game. It is computed by taking the sum of total playtime of each player divided by the number of players.

Distribution of total playtime shows the distribution of total playtime over increasing size intervals, from minutes to hours.

Evolution of average total playtime shows, on a graph, the evolution over time of the average total playtime. Each point on the graph is computed by taking the sum of the total playtime of all players divided by the total number of players.

Evolution of average daily playtime is the average number of hours played each active day over time. Each point on the graph is computed by taking the playtime of all active players on a given day divided by the number of active players for that same day.

Social media engagement can be gauged through community or forum posts. Nowadays, it can also be computed as a ratio between broadcasters and viewers of content on platforms, such as Twitch or YouTube.

Session length and frequency are also important to understand engagement patterns: for how long did players engage in an individual session, how frequent are the sessions, and what time of the day or day of the week do they play more often?

1.6.2.3.2 Acquisition Acquisition is a KPI focused on new players; it accounts for the total number of players on all platforms who started the game at least once since its launch (Life to Date (LTD)). This number includes every player, regardless of the time they actually played. Acquisition can also be measured yearly (Year to Date (YTD)) referring to the period beginning the first day of the current calendar year or fiscal year up to the current date. YTD information is useful for analyzing business trends or comparing performance data. The main currency for acquisition is new players. As we have seen above, a new player is created any time a user starts a play session for the first time.

The first concept to understand in terms of acquisition is the cohort: a group of new players who share a defining characteristic. In this particular case, that characteristic is the fact that they all started the game for the first time on the same day.

Cohort analysis is a subset of behavioral analytics that takes the data from a given data set and rather than analyzing all users as one unit, creating averages and means for each variable, it breaks them into cohorts that share common characteristics within a defined timespan. By analyzing these temporal patterns, a developer can adapt and tailor its service to those specific cohorts.

Returning user is a user who returned to the game after being considered as a churned, or discontinued, user.

Conversion rate measures the proportion of people who completed a process after starting it. It is important to pay attention to what events are considered as the "start" and "end" of the *conversion* process defined based on the product. Typically, for AAA games, the beginning of the process is marked by players downloading a game demo, while the end is the act of purchasing the full game. For free-to-play games, the beginning is installing the game, and the end is marked by the first in-game purchase.

1.6.2.3.3 Retention   Retention is a KPI focused on maintaining active players by assessing how many players remain active within a game and for how long. It is operationalized as the number of players still active for some N or more days after starting to play a game for the first time. It represents the number of days between the player's first and last session; the first session date is considered as "Day Zero." All players with the same Day Zero belong to the same cohort. The time period examined for retention can be days, or as long as weeks or months.

Churn or Churn Rate (CR) is the percentage of players who have been lost over a specific period of time. In other words, these are the players who have stopped playing and, thus, have become inactive. It is calculated as the number of active players at the beginning of a period (usually a month) minus the number of active players at the end of the period; the result is divided by the number of active players at the beginning of a period.

Retention Rate (RR) is the percentage of customers staying in the game over time. This metric provides the clearest picture of how well the retention strategy is performing. It is calculated as the number of active players at the end of a period (usually a month) from which the number of new players acquired throughout the period is subtracted, and the result is divided by the number of active players at the beginning of a period.

1.6.2.3.4 Progression Progression metrics are used to gauge the progress of players through a game. In order to assess progression, designers need to identify meaningful progression check points more or less evenly distributed. It could be the end of each mission or every time players reach a milestone, such as increasing a level or obtaining specific items. Progression points are highly game-dependent, and designers should be involved when they are defined. Representing progression can be done in different ways, but the most used is a chart showing the cumulative number of players who reached each of the progression steps. A progression step is defined as an interval between progression check points; this interval is referred to as a *bin*. For example, bin 1 is between levels 1 and 5, bin 2 is between levels 6 and 10, etc. The chart in Figure 1.4 shows the number of players in each progression bin. The calculation is done on the latest progression event received by each player, with each progression ordered sequentially.

1.7 Applications of metrics to game data science

As you can see, with such an extensive list of metrics, you can do many things from modeling player behaviors, profiling players, predicting win/loss, or predicting churn, to mention a few examples.

Let's take player profiling as an example. Given the metrics in the preceding text, it is not a surprise that different groups of players react differently to the same stimulus and behave very differently in the same game. It is important to understand how players differ and in what way they are similar, because a one-size-fits-all approach to development is not often effective.

Player profiling is the practice of dividing players into groups who are similar in specific ways relevant to different stakeholders, such as brand, live operations, or designers. The similarities can be based on the following attributes:

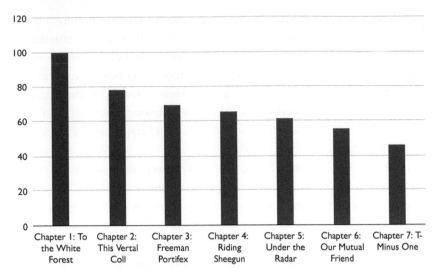

Figure 1.4 Progression bins for the levels of the game *Half-Life 2: Episode Two* showing the percentage of players that completed each level. The figure is reproduced with permission from https://www.jesperjuul.net/ludologist/2007/11/16/half-life-2-episode-two-stats/.

- Socio-demographics: age, gender, education, occupation, income, marital status, ethnicity, language, and religion.
- Geography: country and urban/rural areas.
- Psychographics: motivations, personality, needs, values, attitudes, and interests.
- Behavior: spending habits, frequency, consistency, and duration of playing behavior.

Different stakeholders have different needs. For example, marketing departments are interested in socio-demographics, geography, and psychographics; game and system designers are more interested in behavioral and psychographics; and monetization designers could be interested in all of the above. The end goals for any profiling efforts are relative to the stakeholder. For example, marketing efforts can be tailored to specific groups based on their player profiles. Designers can shape players' experience better if they have a deeper understanding of player profiles, explicitly factoring in their preferences, needs, and values.

Historically, there have been three approaches to profiling: segmenting, clustering, and modeling.

Segmenting is the process of putting customers into groups based on similarities. Groups are derived as archetypes or personas through both qualitative and quantitative research. Then, players are assigned to such groups based on the group and players' attributes. For example, the segment "soccer mom" is defined as a suburban mother who spends a lot of time taking her children to several activities. This segment is composed of geographic and demographic properties: married women with children aged 5–15 years who do not live in cities.

Clustering is the process of finding similarities among players through statistical methods. This process is more data driven and statistical. We will discuss clustering more at length in Chapter 6.

Modeling aims to predict the value of unseen data based on current available data. Player modeling attempts to infer cognitive, affective, and behavioral patterns by creating computational models of players to gain detailed descriptions of their state. These descriptions help detect, model, predict, and express the behavior, thoughts, and feelings of players and personalizes games to their preferences. Furthermore, player models are built on dynamic information obtained during game–player interaction and are able to account for ever-changing playstyles. Methods to use in modeling will be discussed further in the book, especially Chapters 7–11.

Player profiles are extremely useful for contextualizing information. For example, the average death rate for the whole player population in a certain area of the game is just a number. But if we split the player population into "risk takers" and "conservative players" and compare death rates, the results can provide immediately actionable information: if the two death rates are too similar, for example, perhaps the game in that area does not provide enough cover or challenge. The problem is that different stakeholders require different profiling strategies. To provide the most topical context for data intelligence, it is advisable to plan for several profiling sets to coexist. For example, a game could profile players based on their preferred activities if it is an open-world game; based on their effectiveness at performing tasks and challenges the games offer; or based on playtime patterns, social activities, money spent, or progression.

Profiling is just one example application of game data science. There are many other applications and modeling techniques developed by the industry that display the utility of such a discipline. But in order for you to know how to make use of game data, first you will need to learn the processes of game data science, which is what this book is about. Later chapters in the book will include case studies where you will see how to apply these methods in practice, which will facilitate understanding the utility and advantages of player profiling, modeling, and other analytical methods, as well as know the steps to actually construct such models or apply it to your practice.

1.8 Your journey begins

You are ready to begin your journey of learning more fully about the different parts of the game data science process and practice it with game data. The next chapter, and each of the subsequent chapters, will be supplemented with labs in which you will be practicing all the concepts discussed. Make sure to have a laptop or computer ready to begin your practice. Don't worry about getting game data or installing R. We will walk you through these practicalities as we go through the chapters in the book. We will be using several types of data sets, so you can get a variety of different types of game data to play with. Each chapter will also include a bibliography section, as well as exercises that you should read and try out before you move on to the next chapter, as they will only help crystalize your knowledge and practice.

1.9 Takeaways and important terms

This chapter provided an overview of game data science and contextualized the field from a historical perspective to understand the evolution of methods and techniques presented in the book. Further, we examined how game data science generates new knowledge and insights following the scientific method.

Finally, we present a glossary here, to disambiguate nebulous terminology and to foreshadow key concepts that will be recurring throughout the book. Key terms are repeated here:

Game data science is the process of applying methods, practices, and techniques from existing relevant fields such as data science, business intelligence, geographic information systems, or social network analysis to the specific context of games for the purpose of informing and supporting decision-making.

Game analytics is historically related to business intelligence, and hence, it represents a subset of the methods and techniques that collectively form game data science.

Game telemetry is data logged from game clients and/or servers.

Behavioral telemetry is the specific type of game telemetry that deals with the second-by-second behavior of players and the interaction between players and the game.

Knowledge discovery process is a process of finding actionable knowledge from data. It is achieved using data mining methods (algorithms and visualization tools) to extract nontrivial knowledge from a large amount of data.

Inductive reasoning is a method of deriving general principles from specific observations, often called *bottom-up logic*.

Deductive reasoning is the process of reaching a certain conclusion by analyzing evidence refuting or solidifying a hypothesis, often called *top-down logic*.

Game metrics are interpretable quantitative measures of in-game attributes; a metric always implies some level of abstraction from raw data.

Key Performance Indicators (KPIs) are special game metrics that have been strategically selected to demonstrate how effectively a player can achieve an objective.

Community metrics are game metrics that deal with the social dimension of players at all resolutions, from forum activity to number of friends or numbers of groups created or joined.

Customer metrics are game metrics that deal with the user as a customer, taking into consideration all forms of financial transactions.

Gameplay metrics are metrics that deal with the actual behavior of a player within a game.

Acquisition metrics are a set of KPIs focused toward new players and how they become engaged with a game.

Retention metrics are a set of KPIs focused on maintaining active players by assessing how many players remain active within a game for a certain period.

Progression metrics are a set of KPIs focused on the progress of players through a game.

Player profiling is the practice of dividing and grouping players into sets that are similar in specific ways.

Segmenting is the process of assigning players to preexisting groups that were derived from both qualitative and quantitative research.

Clustering is the process of finding similarities and differences among players based on objective quantifiable measures through statistical methods.

Player modeling is the process of creating computational descriptors that can account for differences and similarities in players and also can predict the value of unseen data based on current available data.

• •

EXERCISES

1. What is game data science, and what is its significance?
2. Develop a historical timeline demonstrating the evolution of the field of game data science. You can take a specific perspective, such as esports or player modeling.

3. Given a game that you are designing or playing, can you think of what metrics from the list above or new metrics you would use to understand player engagement or success of your game? Discuss these metrics with a collaborator to see what metrics you had in common and what others did your collaborator think of that is different or can be augmented to your current list?

4. What is the difference between inductive and deductive reasoning given the game data science process? Would you classify player profiling methods as inductive or deductive?

5. Given the process of game data science outlined in this chapter, can you develop a flow graph showing the process you would apply to analyze data from a game you are currently developing or playing? Be specific on the type of variables you would collect, processes you would use, and why.

6. How did Steam and Facebook change the way we develop games, and what is the role of data in this process?

• •

BIBLIOGRAPHY

Alsén, A., Runge, J., Drachen, A., and Klapper, D. (2016, September). Play with me? Understanding and measuring the social aspect of casual gaming. In *Twelfth Artificial Intelligence and Interactive Digital Entertainment Conference*, Vol. 12, No. 1, AAAI. Retrieved from https://ojs.aaai.org/index.php/AIIDE/article/view/12904.

Amaya, G., Davis, J. P., Gunn, D. V., Harrison, C., Pagulayan, R., Phillips, B., and Wixon, D. (2008) Games user research (GUR)—our experience with and evolution of four methods. In Isbister, K. and Schaffer, N. (eds), *Game usability: Advice from the experts*. San Francisco: Morgan Kaufmann.

Block, F. O., Hodge, V. J., Hobson, S. J., Sephton, N. J., Devlin, S. M., Ursu, M., Drachen, A., and Cowling, P. I. (2018). Narrative bytes: Data-driven content production in Esports. In *TVX '18 Proceedings of the 2018 ACM International Conference on Interactive Experiences for TV and Online Video* (pp. 29–41). ACM.

Bonnie, E. (2017). Cohort analysis: The key to improving user retention for your app. *CleverTap*. URL: https://clevertap.com/blog/cohort-analysis-user-retention/

Castronova, E. (2001). Virtual worlds: A first-hand account of market and society on the cyberian frontier. Available at SSRN: https://ssrn.com/abstract=294828

Dibbell, J. (2006). *Play money: Or, how I quit my day job and made millions trading virtual loot*. Basic Books, AZ.

Drachen, A., and Canossa, A. (2009a, September). Towards gameplay analysis via gameplay metrics. In *Proceedings of the 13th International MindTrek Conference: Everyday Life in the Ubiquitous Era* (pp. 202–9). ACM.

Drachen, A., and Canossa, A. (2009b, September). Analyzing spatial user behavior in computer games using geographic information systems. In *Proceedings of the 13th International MindTrek Conference: Everyday Life in the Ubiquitous Era* (pp. 182–9). ACM.

Drachen, A., Canossa, A., and Yannakakis, G. N. (2009, September). Player modeling using self-organization in Tomb Raider: Underworld. In *2009 IEEE Symposium on Computational Intelligence and Games* (pp. 1–8). IEEE.

Drachen, A., Mirza-Babaei, P., and Nacke, L. E. (Eds.). (2018). *Games user research.* Oxford University Press.

Ducheneaut, N., Yee, N., Nickell, E., and Moore, R. J. (2006). Building an MMO with mass appeal: A look at gameplay in World of Warcraft. *Games and Culture, 1*(4), 281–317.

Field, A., and Hole, G. (2002). *How to design and report experiments.* Sage.

Fields, T., and Cotton, B. (2011). *Social game design: Monetization methods and mechanics.* CRC Press.

GRUX SIG. (2015). IGDA games research and user experience special interest group. URL: https://grux.org/#1. Accessed 2019.

Isbister, K., and Schaffer, N. (2008). *Game usability: Advancing the player experience.* CRC Press.

Kotler, P., Armstrong, G., Harris, L. C., and Piercy, N. (2014). *Principles of marketing* (4th European Edition). Financial times/Prentice Hall.

Marriott, K., Schreiber, F., Dwyer, T., Klein, K., Henry Riche, N., Itoh, T., Stuerzlinger, W., and Thomas, B. H. (Eds.). (2018). *Immersive analytics.* Vol. 11190. Springer.

Medler, B. (2012). *Play with data-an exploration of play analytics and its effect on player experiences* (Doctoral dissertation, Georgia Institute of Technology).

Mellon, L. (2009). Applying metrics driven development to MMO costs and risks. White paper. URL: http://maggotranch.com/MMO_Metrics.pdf

Newman, M. E. (2006). Modularity and community structure in networks. *Proceedings of the National Academy of Sciences, 103*(23), 8577–82.

Pirolli, P., and Card, S. (2005). The sensemaking process and leverage points for analyst technology as identified through cognitive task analysis. In *Proceedings of International Conference on Intelligence Analysis* (Vol. 5, pp. 2–4).

Seif El-Nasr, M., Drachen, A., and Canossa, A. (Eds.). (2013). *Game analytics.* Springer Publishers. 800 pp. ISBN: 978-1-4471-4769-5. URL: http://www.springer.com/computer/hci/book/978-1-4471-4768-8.

Sifa, R., Drachen, A., and Bauckhage, C. (2015, September). Large-scale cross-game player behavior analysis on steam. In *Proceedings of Eleventh Artificial Intelligence and Interactive Digital Entertainment Conference* (AIIDE). AAAI, Santa Cruz, USA.

Simpson, Z. (2000). The in-game economics of *Ultima Online.* Paper presented at The Computer Game Developer's Conference, March 2000, San Jose, CA.

Smith, W. R. (1956). Product differentiation and market segmentation as alternative marketing strategies. *Journal of Marketing, 21*(1), 3–8.

Thompson, C. (2007). Halo 3: How Microsoft labs invented a new science of play. *Wired Magazine, 15*(9), 15–22.

Unman, Z. (2017). What is Kaggle, why I participate, what is the impact? Getting started. Kaggle.com. URL: https://www.kaggle.com/getting-started/44916. Accessed 2019.

Williams, D., Contractor, N., Poole, M. S., Srivastava, J., and Cai, D. (2011). The virtual worlds exploratorium: Using large-scale data and computational techniques for communication research. *Communication Methods and Measures*, 5(2), 163–80.

Yankelovich, D., and Meer, D. (2006). Rediscovering market segmentation. *Harvard Business Review*, 84(2), 122.

Yee, N. (2006). The psychology of massively multi-user online role-playing games: Motivations, emotional investment, relationships and problematic usage. In Schroeder, R. and Axelsson, A. (eds), *Avatars at work and play* (pp. 187–207). Dordrecht: Springer.

CHAPTER 2

Data Preprocessing

As you collect data from your game, you will receive a stream of event logs, sometimes with the location and/or timestamps of all the actions that players have performed. You may also receive contextual data from game clients, platforms, or servers. Data preprocessing is the action you need to take before you can analyze the data. It is defined as the process of preparing data for analysis. This means improving the quality of the data and removing any inconsistencies. Preprocessing can be performed before or after the feature definition stage, which is covered in Chapter 4.

Preprocessing is absolutely vital. Data analysis is only as good as the data that is being analyzed, and most algorithms assume the data to be noise-free.

Data collected remotely from game clients, servers, or elsewhere are historically problematic. This is due to many reasons, including network issues, buffer outages, buggy code, misspellings, missing information, and inconsistencies between database updates and game updates. All these issues result in data that is not ready for analysis. Furthermore, most often, you may be integrating data from multiple sources or different databases or across different game updates. In such cases, careful data cleaning is extremely important and necessary.

Performing data mining on low-quality data (or what is called dirty data), with, for example, missing or duplicate information, can compromise the validity and accuracy of the results or even lead to results that are simply incorrect. As a consequence, data cleaning and data transformation (commonly referred to as preprocessing) are vital.

Although it may seem preliminary, and can be tedious, data preprocessing is crucial and can make or break your analysis and results. Therefore, make sure

Game Data Science. Magy Seif El-Nasr, Truong Huy Nguyen Dinh, Alessandro Canossa, and Anders Drachen, Oxford University Press. © Magy Seif El-Nasr, Truong Huy Nguyen Dinh, Alessandro Canossa, and Anders Drachen (2021). DOI: 10.1093/oso/9780192897879.003.0002

to perform it for every dataset you have before you move on to the next step in the data science analysis process outlined in Chapter 1.

2.1 Data preprocessing overview

Imagine that you have all your data in a CSV file. You have built your features (metrics), and you now need to check the quality of the data. There are three basic steps in preprocessing:

1) Data cleaning is formally defined as the process of converting raw data into technically correct data. Technically correct data is data that has a consistent format, where rows and columns have a specific meaning and each column or variable in the data has a consistent data type (defined below).

2) Data consistency processing is defined as the process used to make sure the data is in the right format or is consistent. Consistency here means that the data is correct—that is, with no missing values or impossible values (e.g., negative age). It is unfortunately fairly common to have missing data from telemetry logs because of errors in the system, or congestion in internet traffic, or simply because a user turned off a console in the middle of a play session. These corrections should be straightforward to identify and correct. Another process that is important to complete during the data consistency process is identifying and dealing with outliers. Outliers are defined as data that appears to be largely different from the observed data. The presence of such outliers can skew the calculations and analysis you will need to perform later. For example, the average and standard deviation of a set of values, 10, 15, 10, 12, and 1 (1 here can be considered an outlier), will be significantly different if we remove 1 from this data. Removing outliers is not the only acceptable solution. In fact, for the example above, it is recommended not to remove the 1 but to calculate the median rather than the mean. However, identifying outliers is not simple and must be done through a clear and documented process. You also need to have enough data in order to be able to clearly identify such outliers. If you make decisions on a very small dataset, you increase the chances of identifying valid values that just appear as outliers because you have an incomplete or biased sample. For example, if we continue to collect data in the example above, we may find the following values: 3, 2, 1, 1, 4, 2, 3, 5, 10, and 12. In such a case, 1 is no longer an outlier.

Unfortunately, estimating the exact number of samples needed for us to model the phenomenon we are interested in is not a very simple process and is often impossible.

3) Finally, we will need to perform normalization and standardization to enable statistical analysis. This step is important to make sure that your data is comparable—that is, that all values of a variable are in between 0 and 1. This is especially important when you are comparing two different quantitative variables, as it is easier to compare them if they are in the same scale. In addition, it may be necessary to standardize the types of data in your dataset to run specific types of machine learning or data mining algorithms. In reality, your dataset will probably contain different types of data, such as text, Boolean (e.g., *win* = true/false), categorical (e.g., *hero type*), and numerical (e.g., *XP*). Thus, you may want to convert such data into numerical type in order to run certain algorithms. This can be considered within the normalization or standardization stage, as we will discuss in this chapter.

2.2 Chapter overview

This chapter is focused on the above steps and how to perform them. We will go through these processes in more detail and use examples throughout. The labs will also provide a step-by-step introduction to effectively perform these steps. Completing these labs and following the examples will give you a clearer picture of how the steps in the process are conducted and applied and their utility within the analysis process. You can follow the labs through the materials provided online.

This chapter includes four labs:

- **Lab 2.1:** Focuses on data types in R.
- **Lab 2.2:** Focuses on how to parse a text file within R to get at a data representation that can be used for analysis.
- **Lab 2.3:** Focuses on checking types of data upon import.

Please note that we assume some statistical knowledge. The chapter is not written as a statistics manual, and there may be some methods that are not discussed in detail due to space and our choice to limit the focus of this chapter. If you feel you need more statistical background to understand the materials in this chapter, please consult Chapter 3, which is a primer for statistical techniques that are important for data science. We have also included a bibliography section, which can give you suggestions for where to go to explore preprocessing further.

You may remember that, in Chapter 1, we discussed metrics that you can derive from raw telemetry data. The subject of developing metrics from telemetry data—for example, combining multiple data points to a specific metric, such as *kills+assists/deaths* ratio, or abstracting low-level data into higher-level data, is covered in Chapter 4.

2.3 Programming languages and libraries for data preprocessing

There are many useful programming languages that can be used for preprocessing data. In this book, we will use R primarily due to the fact that R currently includes many useful libraries for data science that we will be using throughout the book and such libraries are not available in other languages or platforms. This is not to say that other languages, such as Python, cannot give you similar advantages, but at the time of writing this book, R is more popular for dealing with data and also has more functionalities, in terms of libraries needed for the various chapters in the book.

R has many different functions to handle data. In fact, R is a very extensible language allowing developers to create their own libraries and distribute them as add-ons to R. Most libraries developed under R used in the book are also very well maintained. It is important to note that R is currently used by many research groups and analysts from different disciplines, including psychology, social science, statistics, and also game data science, to mention a few. R was created as a statistical language, while other languages, such as Python, have much broader uses. This means that, in some professional contexts, R is mostly used to explore the data and experiment with analysis, while Python is used to automate data-driven solutions, such as feeding dynamic dashboards.

Of course, given how rapidly the field of game data science is evolving, the state of such programming languages and libraries used here will inevitably change. Nevertheless, all the concepts in this book are discussed in an abstract manner, thus allowing you to apply them in your selected language for analysis.

When data is collected from games, it is often, but not always, distributed into several CSV or JSON files or located in a database, such as SQL or MongoDB. Therefore, before you start, you will need to collate this data from different sources into one source that you can then use for the steps described here.

Since the practices of data acquisition vary significantly, we will skip the discussion of how such a process is established or how this data is collated. Instead, for the purposes of this book, we will assume that the data exists in a single file in a CSV format. In reality, the data can be in a JSON format, or stored in a MongoDB, or in an SQL database. If you encounter data in these formats, we refer you to the many resources for handling and converting data in these formats, such as MYSQL Reference Manual (see the entry in the bibliography for "MYSQL") and MongoDB resources (see the entry in the bibliography for "MongoDB"). There are also available resources for handling JSON files through Python or R. For instance, one common approach that we employ in our own work is to store our data in MongoDB servers and use a Python library called pymongo to triangulate and join the data from different datasets, which can then be exported into a CSV or JSON file for further analysis.

It is important to note that due to the constant changes in such tools and their availability, we will not suggest a specific set of online resources here, but instead we encourage you to search for them online.

2.4 VPAL data: A data example

Throughout this chapter, we will use an example dataset for illustration. The dataset is extracted from a game we developed at the PLAIT (Playable Interactive Technologies) lab at Northeastern University, funded by the National Science Foundation. The game is called VPAL: Virtual Personality Assessment Lab. It is an instrumented modification of the *Fallout: New Vegas* game (Obsedian, 2010). The dataset, a description of the game, and screenshots can be found in Appendix A of the book.

Figure 2.1 shows an example snapshot of data from VPAL. The instrumentation of the data and storage of all game actions within the game were done through .txt files that are stored on the client side per participant. For each participant, we created a file named [*participantNumber*].*txt*, which includes all session data for that participant. If the participant has more than one session, a folder is created, and multiple files are created for that participant. When the duration of the game test ends, the files are transferred from the client to our server for further processing.

As discussed above, this is not the only way to collect gameplay data. Often, game data will be packaged in CSV files or a database. However, it should be

Position Introhouse, 101, 0.6, 450.19, −132.86, 0.60, 0.00, −0.00, 256.03, 1.00

Position Introhouse, 101, 0.8, 450.19, −132.86, 0.62, 0.00, −0.00, 256.03, 1.00

Quest,101, 21.77, AAAPaulDia, 10

Quest,101, 21.77, AAAPaulDia, Started

Dialogue, 101, 38.77, 1, AAAPaul, Where am I?.

Dialogue, 101, 67.97, 2, AAAPaul, I'll have to thank your parents for helping me then. Where are they?

Position Introhouse, 101, 85.0, 450.19, −132.86, 0.62, 14.39, −0.00, 266.17, 1.00

Position Introhouse, 101, 85.2, 450.19, −132.86, 0.62, 14.39, −0.00, 266.17, 1.00

Position Introhouse, 101, 85.4, 450.19, −132.86, 0.62, 14.39, −0.00, 266.17, 1.00

Position Introhouse, 101, 85.6, 450.19, −132.86, 0.62, 14.39, −0.00, 266.17, 1.00

Position Introhouse, 101, 85.8, 450.19, −132.86, 0.62, 14.39, −0.00, 266.17, 1.00

Position Introhouse, 101, 86.0, 450.19, −132.86, 0.62, 14.39, −0.00, 266.17, 1.00

Position Introhouse, 101, 86.2, 450.19, −132.86, 0.62, 14.39, −0.00, 266.17, 1.00

Position Introhouse, 101, 86.4, 450.19, −132.86, 0.62, 12.20, −0.00, 255.67, 1.00

Position Introhouse, 101, 86.6, 450.19, −132.86, 0.62, 14.81, −0.00, 241.64, 1.00

Position Introhouse, 101, 86.8, 450.19, −132.86, 0.62, 14.56, −0.00, 230.63, 1.00

Position Introhouse, 101, 87.0, 450.19, −132.86, 0.62, 15.23, −0.00, 232.39, 1.00

Position Introhouse, 101, 87.2, 450.19, −132.86, 0.62, 15.73, −0.00, 247.85, 1.00

Position Introhouse, 101, 87.4, 450.19, −132.86, 0.62, 15.73, −0.00, 258.61, 1.00

Position Introhouse, 101, 87.6, 403.77, −142.37, 0.66, 17.92, −0.00, 257.94, 1.00

Figure 2.1 Snapshot of data from a VPAL log file for one player.

noted that most of the techniques discussed here are applicable regardless of the format by which the data is stored or organized.

Figure 2.1 shows several data types stored in the log file, with the following format:

- For movement data [labeled "position" in Figure 2.1]: Location name; subject number; timestamp (every one-fifth of a second/or 20 milliseconds, so steps proceed from 0.0, 0.2, 0.4, etc.); position in x, y, z; orientation of the camera in x, y, z; and health. As an example, the first line says that subject 101 is in *Introhouse, time step* = 0.6 seconds from the beginning of the session, with position: $x = 450.19$,

$y = -132.86, z = 0.6$ and orientation: $x = 0.0, y = -0.0, z = 256.03$, and *health* = 1.00.

- For quest data [labeled "quest"]: Quest keyword, subject number, timestamp, name of quest, and number of steps within the quest or whether it started/ended. For example, in the third line in Figure 2.1, it says that subject 101 started AAAPaulDia quest at timestamp 21.77 with the quest steps of 10, which denote how many steps are needed to complete a quest.

- For dialog data [labeled "dialog"]: Dialog keyword, subject number, timestamp, name of the character the user is talking to, and what the user said. For example, line 5 in Figure 2.1 says that subject number 101 made a dialog action at timestamp 28.77 to an in-game character named *AAAPaul* and said: "Where am I?" The number before the statement told is the number of that dialog choice.

A complete list of events and logs are found in Appendix A.

2.5 Measurement types

A dataset like VPAL's dataset will naturally contain many different types of data. Understanding these data types is important, as it gives you an understanding of how to process such data and what techniques to use for statistical analysis.

We differentiate between the different data types used for statistical analysis vs. variable types defined by database schemas and programming languages.

In statistics, the term *data types* is used to identify how an observation is measured. Depending on the measure used, an observation (data point) can be classified as nominal, ordinal, interval, or ratio. Each type imposes different limits on the statistical analyses we can apply to them. These are statistical terms that help us identify which types of statistical analyses to use for different types of measures.

While the term *data type* is often used to describe the type of measure used, we will instead use the term measurement type here to avoid confusion with programming languages or machine learning.

In addition to the four measurement categories introduced earlier, you will also find that some people describe data as continuous or discrete, where continuous data can be divided into fractions, e.g., *health*, while discrete data cannot, e.g., *gender*. This difference is important, as there are operations that can be done on continuous data, such as average, distance, frequency, and distribution histograms, that cannot be done on discrete data.

In database schemas and programming languages, variable types, also discussed in some books as data types, describe a specific kind of data item, as defined by the value it can take and also what operations can be performed on it. Examples include integer, string, and float. An integer is a whole number, not a fraction. It can be positive, negative, or zero. A float conversely stores floating-point values—that is, values with potential decimal places. A string is a section of text.

It is important to be aware of both of these categorization systems: measurement types and variable types. One tells us about the nature of how we measure something, and the other discusses how this data is represented in a computational system. They are easy to confuse. To take an example, you might have measured the quest completion time in a game. You use seconds as your measurement scale, which means you have ratio data. When you transfer the data into a database for analysis, you would select the integer data type. So here, "integer" was used as a way to represent the data in the computer system and "ratio" is how the data is measured.

Now, let us discuss these different measurement and variable types in detail.

2.5.1 Nominal/Categorical data

Nominal or categorical data describes discrete data that represents categories of things, such as *gender*, *blood type*, and *hero type*. For this measurement type, it is not easy to put it in any particular order. For example, being a "Rogue" type is not necessarily better than being a "Warrior" type, and one does not carry a higher weight than the other. A typical example is the numbers on the backs of football players. A player with the number 1 is not necessarily better than the one with number 2 on their back. The only type of analysis we can apply on nominal data is frequency analysis.

2.5.2 Ordinal data

If there is an order to which these categories fit, then this type of data is ordinal. An example here could be the order in which cars finish a race. The first car is before the second, but the measures do not say anything about how much distance or time there is between the first and second car. This type of measurement is similar to the nominal type, but it describes variables that have a clear order. Good examples of this type of data are *economic status*, *educational experience*, and *game experience* (e.g., "newbie," "casual gamer," and "core gamer").

For this type of data, there is a clear order, but it is not clear if dissimilar values between data points signify any consistent difference measure. For example, suppose we represent the players' skill levels as ordinal values "1" (for a new player), "2" (experienced), and "3" (veterans). In this case, although there is a value difference, because of our chosen scale, the difference between new and experienced players is the same as that between experienced and veterans—that is, "1." This number may not signify an actual difference of "1." The variable *game experience* in this case is represented with a Likert scale. A Likert scale is a psychometric assessment tool used to collect data through surveys by having respondents select one out of several options along a horizontal axis. Thus, the range captures the intensity of their feelings for a given item. Almost any data collected through Likert scales is considered ordinal.

You should be careful about the statistical methods that you use with these variables. In Chapter 3, we will discuss some statistical methods that can or cannot be used for this type of data. For example, for these variables, it does not make sense to compute averages since we are not sure if the spaces between the categories are consistent, and thus, as it will be discussed more in Chapter 3, mode is often used.

2.5.3 Ratio and interval data

Interval and ratio data are data types that are quantitative and continuous. Interval data is like ordinal data, but with consistent spacing. A "2" is twice as much as "1," but there is no true "0" point on the measurement scale. Temperature is an example, where "2" degrees is twice as warm as "1" degree, but "0" does not indicate the absence of temperature.

Ratio data, on the other hand, can be multiplied or divided, because not only the spaces are consistent but the multiples are consistent as well. In other words, the difference between "1" and "2" is one, but "2" is also two times "1." In such measurement types, the "0" measure has a meaning.

The ratio measurement type is by far the most common type of measure in behavioral telemetry from games. In general, we strive to have as much of our data in ratio form as possible. An example of this type of data is continuous game data, such as *health*, *XP*, *position*, and *score*. This means that, for such variables, you can compare participants or values over time quantitatively, and the size of the difference between these variables is consistent among the population or within one participant record. You can also multiply or divide these numbers, and the meaning will make sense. For these types of variables, you can compute average and can use variance and other statistical techniques.

2.6 Data representation

2.6.1 Variables

All of these data types are represented in programming languages as variables. Variables have different types or representations. Interval data due to its continuous quantitative nature is often represented as numbers. Numbers in a programming language can be represented as integers, floats, or doubles. The decision of whether to use integers or floats, for example, varies depending on the importance of representing fractions and the precision needed. Nominal data can be represented as characters, strings, Booleans, or numbers—for example, *gender* can be represented as "0" for male, "1" for female, or as a string, where *gender* can be "male" or "female." Some programming languages allow you to specify an enumeration type, enums or factors, which allows you to specify specific terms as a set of values for the variable. We can also have other special types of representations, such as date information for timestamps, which we will describe later.

2.6.2 Special data

When you start collecting data, you will find that you may have cells of data containing: "NAN" (Not A Number), "NA" (Not Available), and Empty cell or "NULL" (an empty set). This may happen for several reasons. For example, there may be missing data, or you may have done some computation that resulted in a division by zero, which then resulted in a "NAN." Dealing with these types of data can be challenging, depending on the root cause. We will discuss some methods to deal with these data types in this chapter, but this is also an active area of research, and there are many approaches to handle these issues. Readers are encouraged to read the bibliography at the end of this chapter or to explore other online resources on approaches to handling special data types.

2.7 Process for preprocessing, cleaning, and normalizing data

Once you get a log file as described for the VPAL dataset (Figure 2.1), you will need to go through several steps to prepare such data for analysis. These steps are outlined in the diagram depicted in Figure 2.2.

2.7.1 Step 1: Data cleaning

In general, data should be read, parsed, checked for type and range, and added into a standardized structure. To do that, you will have to read the data into variables represented by the programming language of choice. To go through an example of how this is done, we will first introduce R variable types in a simple lab.

2.7.1.1 DATA STRUCTURES: REPRESENTING DATA IN R

We will be using R for data preprocessing. To show you a step-by-step process of parsing and processing data, we will first introduce R and then use it to parse

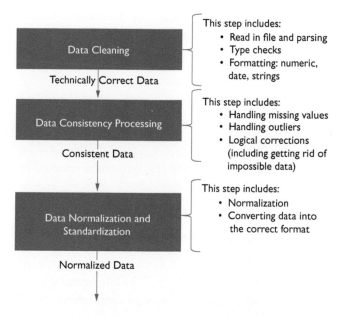

Figure 2.2 Data cleaning and processing steps.

files from VPAL participants. Please consult lab 2.1. In R, you can represent different measurement types using different variable types, including numeric data and character data. You can use R functions to operate on this data. When working with datasets, such as gameplay data, you will often work with variables in terms of vectors or lists or dataframes; see Lab 2.1 for more details on these types of variables.

Practical Note

Getting the VPAL Data

The data files can be accessed from the book's supplementary resources. You can download the data and follow the lab exercise through R scripts discussed in this section.

Installing R

Please note that we do not cover the installation of R, because there are many good resources to do this (please see https://www.r-project.org for R installation). We also recommend that you install and use RStudio (see https://www.rstudio.com/products/rstudio/download) for downloading and training. There are also a lot of online resources and tutorials on YouTube and other venues that can give you a quick introduction on R and RStudio. Please make use of such valuable resources.

Practical Note: Lab 2.1

Lab 2.1

Please see the supplemental materials for the book.

Goal of Lab 2.1

The lab introduces variable types in R. It is meant to supplement the theoretical discussion in the following text with some practical examples using R code that you can follow and replicate.

Other Resources

To get more introduction of variables types and their representation in R, please search through the various online resources on introduction materials on R. The link https://swcarpentry.github.io/r-novice-inflammation/13-supp-data-structures/ is a good one on data structures. But you can find more recent ones if you search for introduction to data structures in R.

Vectors are a sequence of values of the same measurement type. In Lab 2.1, we have an example of a script that creates a vector of 11 values and then computes some descriptive statistics for these values using functions such as *max*, *min*, *quantiles*, *mean*, and *standard deviation*. See the lab for exact R syntax. We will discuss the meaning and importance of these functions for statistical analysis in Chapter 3.

List, on the other hand, is a type of data structure that can hold variables of different measurement types. For example, you can make a list that is composed of a vector for scores of a player, and the players' names. See Lab 2.1 for an example.

Dataframe is a list composed of rows and columns, like a table, where each row in the list has the same length. This type of data is what we will use to read in the game data.

In addition to the simple variable types, such as character, string, and integer, R provides a type for handling called TimeStamps. Timestamps are of interest to us since game events are stored by timestamp. In R, you can represent time and date through the data type POSIXct (where "ct" is calendar time), which stores number of seconds since start of January 1, 1970. Another data type that also stores time data is POS1Xlt (where "lt" is local time). This data type is composed of a vector of seconds, minutes, hours, date: day, month, and year. You can then represent time steps and can manipulate time steps, compare them, etc.

In some cases, as is the case for VPAL, game data may represent time steps in simulation time. In such case, the time of a session starts at "0" and is incremented from there. Each session restarts the time count from "0." Different game companies will assume different standards for collecting and timestamping its data, so consult the data manual provided by the company before processing the data.

2.7.1.2 UNDERSTANDING YOUR DATA

To get a feel for what your data looks like, you can plot the distribution through counts or frequencies of different data points. You will see more on that in Chapter 3. R libraries provide different functions to address this.

What are libraries? As discussed above, R comes with many libraries that provide many functionalities that you can use. A library is a collection of pre-compiled routines that we can use. Routines in a library, which are sequences of actions regularly followed to achieve particular goals, are also called modules, and are stored as objects. Libraries are useful for storing routines that we use repeatedly and do not need to be linked to every program that utilize them. Thus, for R, rather than building your own routines, you can use existing libraries, provided there is one that contains the module you need.

For example, to get a frequency count, you can use the *count* function within the dplyr library. It should be noted that R libraries are in constant change as we write this book, and hence, you should consult the bibliography and see if there are any updates for the libraries used here. You should aim to use the libraries that are most recent, as they will be the ones that are maintained by the developers.

Plotting distributions. In Lab 2.1, we go through an example of plotting a distribution. You can draw a histogram of the data values to see how data is distributed. For this, you can use the *hist* function. Figure 2.3 shows an example histogram for the *Quests Completed* variable in the VPAL data; this is computed per participant. By inspecting the histogram, you can see that this variable follows a normal distribution (see Chapter 3), where most players complete 4–6 quests and less players complete 0–2 or 8–10 quests (tails of the histogram shown in Figure 2.3). Normal distributions, in this case, can be useful because they basically say that most people completed many of the quests, but fewer players completed many or very few quests. This means that the quests are balanced and not so hard that many players finished small number of quests or so easy that all players finished all of them.

You can start to look at distributions like this for the different variables in your game data to get a feel for the different game mechanics exhibited in the data and how they affect players' performance or activities. Once you start playing with the VPAL data, you can start thinking of what type of histograms you want to create, for what variables, and what these histograms tell you about the game and the players. A tool like histogram can give you a way to look into the data; more tools such as these will be discussed in Chapter 3.

2.7.1.3 READING AND PARSING FILES

Now that you know about some basic data structures, we will move on to look into how to parse data and format it into a dataframe. Most of the time, you are interested in a cross-section of the data. For example, you may want to look into how players completed quests, and thus, quest data would be very important or

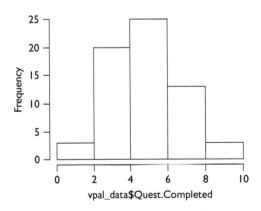

Figure 2.3 Histogram of quests completed.

you may want to organize the data in a specific way. To do that, you will need to write a script that parses your data and formats it in the way that you want into a dataframe that you can then use to analyze the data. Note that R, as any other programming language, has functions that allow you to read in data from different types of files. Depending on how your data is stored, you may need to use different methods to get the data into a dataframe to do more processing on it.

If your data is in a database format or a CSV, where it is organized into rows with columns of consistent data, then it is easy to just call one function in R, such as *read.table* or *read.xls* or *read.csv*, to get the data into a dataframe that you can use for analysis. However, if your data is stored, like VPAL (Figure 2.1) in a log file per player, where each line represents different actions, such as dialog actions and quests, then you will need to write a script to parse and process the data and then convert it into a dataframe. This requires some programming knowledge.

Lab 2.2 shows an example of how to perform such parsing in R. We basically go through the file and take each line and separate the different elements in the line (in VPAL, all elements are separated by commas, and thus, this can be used to separate the elements in each line). Through this process, you can also filter important data you want to keep for the dataframe and discard the rest. You can also summarize some of the data so that you will not have to deal with many variables during analysis.

Coming back to our example, in VPAL, we used the first word in each line to tell us what kind of action we are parsing—for example, quest, position, etc. Based on that action, we have a consistent stream of variables that we can read into different variables. You can then create a different dataframe for each part of the dataset. For example, one dataframe can contain all quest data, another can contain dialog data, etc.

Practical Note: Lab 2.2

Lab 2.2

Please see the supplemental materials for the book.

Goal of Lab 2.2

The lab introduces text parsing in R. It goes through an example of using the VPAL data and showing you how to parse out important information about quests that you can later do more analysis on. The lab will show R code to supplement the discussion below.

As an example, in Lab 2.2, we included the code to parse an example VPAL file 103. In the lab, we go through a step-by-step documentation of the parsing process. We only accumulated quests. As an exercise, you can go through and parse all the dialog utterances or actions related to each quest (see Exercise 3).

The purpose of data cleaning is to make sure the data is correct. It is rarely the case that once data is collected through the game and transferred to the server, it is automatically ready for analysis. Often, the data is incomplete, has wrong entries, or contains outliers. Thus, it is important to check and, when possible, correct data to prepare it for analysis. For example, given VPAL data, each row follows a certain format with variables in certain order and type. *Position* and *orientation* variables are all expected to be integers within certain ranges, timestamps are expected to follow a specific order with increments of "0.2" seconds, and *scores* and *health* are supposed to follow certain ranges and order. To ensure the data is correct, the data needs to go through a series of checking procedures. This can be easily done through the process of parsing and reading. When errors are encountered, we can just use "NAN" or "NA" to signify an error. This process can also be done after reading and parsing content into a data table (or dataframe). Below, we discuss different methods used for type checks, range checks, etc.

2.7.1.4 DATA TYPE CHECKS

There are many ways to check data format. When parsing the data, you can check type or restrict the data to be of a different type, and if that fails, you can generate an exception. In R, we can use different functions to check types after you read in the data. For example, *is.numeric* is a function that will return "TRUE" or "FALSE" based on if the variable is numeric or not (see R documentation online). In most cases, you would want to introduce an "NA" for cells that do not contain the right format or type. If you are looking at numeric data, for example, you can use the *as.numeric* function, which checks if a variable or a column in the dataframe contains numeric values (i.e., real numbers) or not, and for the cells that are not, it will introduce an "NA"; see Lab 2.3. There are also functions to check other types of data: *as.logical, as.factor, as.character*, and *as.integer*.

2.7.1.5 DATA FORMAT CHECKS AND CONVERSIONS

In addition to the type issue discussed above, you may also have data that is dirty, meaning that the ranges or values may not be right. This is not just an issue of a quick type check but requires more involved checking on ranges, given the measurement type and actual variable. This also requires some knowledge from designers about the ranges for the different variables represented in your data.

Practical Note: Lab 2.3

Lab 2.3

Please see the supplemental materials for the book.

Goal of Lab 2.3

The lab shows some examples of using *as.numeric* and *as.character*. We will leave experimentation with the rest of these functions as an exercise for you to do (see Exercise 4). The lab also goes through examples of the time data type to show how you can represent it and check for its validity, in case your dataset does not use simulation time (see discussion above).

For categorical data, this can be as simple as a scenario where you have a value that is not in the right category. When you have a categorical type of data that you want to constrain to be within a specific list of categories, you can enforce that constraint. In R, we use factors to denote that type, and within R, you can enforce a variable of type factor to have specific categories. If a variable shows a value that is not in the right categorical type, a "NaN" or "NA" will be generated in the cell. Please see Lab 2.3 for more details.

For numeric data, you need to encode manual checks on values based on specified logical values or designers' designated value per variable. For example, *health* cannot be negative or cannot go above "100," etc. Similar to the categorical variables, if a value is not right, a "NaN" or "NA" is introduced in that cell and the process continues.

Timestamps can be represented in several ways. One way is to store simulation time as discussed above. This is, in essence, how it is represented in VPAL. However, most other games use standard time. Lab 2.3 shows examples of reading in time and date into a POSIXlt object, as with other type conversions, an "NA" is used if the value cannot be converted.

Once the data is checked for type and for consistency in terms of its range and values, the data is deemed technically correct and ready to be passed onto the next step.

2.7.2 Step 2: Data consistency processing

After we have data that is converted to the right type and is technically correct, the next step is to check for consistency. In this step, we must develop strategies to deal with missing values, or special values: "NAN" (Not-A-Number), "NA" (Not-Available), "INF" (Infinite), and "NULL" (no value). We also will need to figure out a plan to identify and deal with outliers and impossible data, such as negative age.

2.7.2.1 REMOVING "NA"

If we have cells with "NA," it means one of two things happened: the data was dirty or noisy, and thus we had to replace it with an "NA," as we discussed in Step 1 (above), or the data was originally missing. In any of these cases, we will need a strategy to deal with it. A simple way to deal with "NA" cells is to remove the entire row from the dataframe. This can be done using the *na.omit* function. In addition to these techniques discussed above, there are more advanced methods to deduce a value for "NA" cells using a model-based technique, such as imputation.

2.7.2.2 REMOVING "NA" BY IMPUTATION

Imputation refers to a process by which a missing data is substituted by an estimate. For example, a simple imputation technique can be substituting the missing data with an average from the known data or using a data cell from a very similar record. Estimation techniques can vary from very simple to very complex requiring model development to estimate missing values. Owing to complexity and the variety of such techniques, we refer the reader to this chapter's bibliography, which have some entries that discuss these methods in more detail. In practice, with game data, most of the time, we have enough context and knowledge to allow us to deduce values for "NA" cells that are more relevant to the concept we are investigating. It is also possible that we are collecting so much data that it is okay to omit the few rows with "NA" values that we cannot deduce. However, at times, when such techniques fail, one can use simple averages as substitutes for numerical missing values. While there are several packages to automatically compute statistically valid values for the missing values, we would usually inspect the missing values and the suggested statistical values manually to make sure they make sense. Of course, with a large dataset, this may be a tedious process, and thus, a package like mice in R or other libraries provided by other languages or tools can help with this.

2.7.2.3 IDENTIFYING AND DEALING WITH OUTLIERS

We often have outliers in the data. For example, in the VPAL game, we had someone who knew the game well and so he entered in God Mode as soon as he came in, and thus his play data was so different from all other players. As an

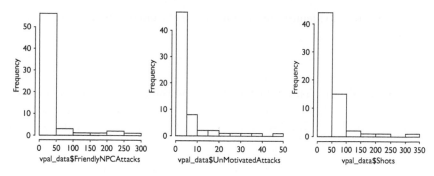

Figure 2.4 Histogram of some variables to detect outliers.

exercise, you may want to look through the files to see if you can pinpoint this participant (see Exercise 7).

The first step to deal with such outliers is to identify them. We can identify outliers in the data through histogram plots or boxplots. For example, we plotted several variables: *friendly NPC attacks, unmotivated attacks,* and *number of shots*, aggregated per participant and plotted as histograms in Figure 2.4. As you can see from these figures, one or two participants seemed to be a bit more extreme: attacking more friendly NPCs, doing more unmotivated attacks, and firing more shots than all others. If you have access to game videos, you can inspect the gameplay videos for these participants to see what they did that may not be logged in the data. But you can also use quartiles to figure out how the data spreads and use that as a way to identify outliers.

Once we have identified who the outliers are, we will need to figure out ways to deal with them. A simple way to deal with them is to remove them. However, in some cases, especially if you do not have much data, it is hard to say if the outlier is an outlier or is a real case of a group of participants whom you may have just not seen yet. So, having more data in this case before determining what to do with an outlier is important.

2.7.2.4 IDENTIFYING AND DEALING WITH SPECIAL TYPES

For "NaN," "NA," "Inf", etc. that were introduced in Step 1, it may be worthwhile to look through the data to see if there is a specific operation causing this issue. If it is logical, you can perhaps adjust your computation to allow the result to be a valid number, and, thus, dodge the whole problem. For example, when computing averages or ratios, you may introduce a "NAN" due to a division by "0." In such cases, it may be worthwhile to go through your computation and check if it is possible logically to divide by "0." If so, you may be able to adjust your functions to avoid this situation.

If the situation is unavoidable or if there is no way to trace out the reasons for these special values, then you can convert these special values to "NA"s and then handle "NA"s as you would, based on the discussion above.

2.7.2.5 IDENTIFYING AND DEALING WITH OTHER TYPES OF INCONSISTENCIES

You will need to check ranges to make sure they make sense. For example, player's *age* should not be negative. *Scores*, depending on the game, may also be greater than "0" but less than a specific number that designers can set. For checks on such ranges, we can use R's editrules package. In this package, you can identify specific rules, like *age*> 0, *score*>= 0, and <=170. Once you have identified some violations, you can then treat them as an NA and deal with them as discussed above.

With temporal data, such as the ones we get with gameplay data, we can get other kinds of inconsistencies. For example, we can find participants who completed a quest that they never started or had very low health without any cause for that change. For these types of inconsistencies, you need to go back to the design to check if these are actually possible or are issues with the logging and instrumentation process. In some cases, it can be a valid route in the design. For example, falling from a certain height can cause a health decrease without an apparent cause, since falling may not trigger an event.

2.7.3 Step 3: Data normalization and standardization

Normalization can be defined as the process of transforming the data into a dataset that is roughly normally distributed. This is important because many statistical analysis techniques (see Chapter 3) assume normal distribution, and thus, if your data is not normally distributed, you can use different transformations based on how the data is skewed to turn it into a normally distributed data, as we will discuss below.

Normalization is also a term used to define the process of applying a transformation on the data to produce a dataset in the range "0–1" so as not to allow ranges to dominate in some calculations. To differentiate between these two different forms of normalization, we will call the process of converting the numerical data to a range "0–1" standardization or scaling (see below on how it is done). Standardization is important because features that have larger ranges can dominate the results of statistical analysis, which you will see later as you embark on labs and examples in Chapters 6–9.

2.7.3.1 SCALING

One way to transform the data to a value between "0–1" is to perform feature scaling using Equation 2.1:

$$\frac{x_j - min(x)}{max(x) - min(x)}$$

(Equation 2.1)

2.7.3.2 STANDARDIZATION

Standardization, also a type of transformation, is done by subtracting the mean and dividing it by the standard deviation (explained in Chapter 3), which will transform the data to have a "0" mean and a "1" unit variance, as follows:

$$\frac{x_j - \mu}{\sigma}$$

(Equation 2.2)

This method works best if the data is normally distributed.

2.7.3.3 DATA TRANSFORMATION FROM SKEWED TO A NORMAL DISTRIBUTION

In many cases, you will need to do some more data transformation to get your data to fit a normal distribution. It should be noted that in some cases you may lose interpretability by doing such a transformation, so you should keep that in mind as you apply the methods discussed here.

In cases where you need to transform the data, you need to inspect the data first by plotting histograms for the different variables, and then decide how it is skewed and what type of transformations you would want to use based on how the data is skewed. For example, you can apply the square root or log transformation to normalize right skewed distribution and square transformation to normalize left skewed distributions. More discussion on how to normalize different types of distributions can be found in the bibliography section. Specifically, consult Mangiafico (2016) for more details. This reference is great for data transformation as well as other R functions and statistical functions, which we will discuss in Chapter 3.

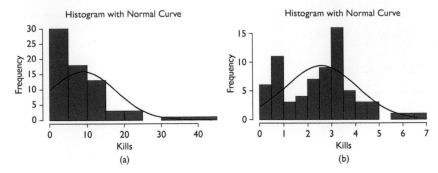

Figure 2.5 Histogram of kill data from VPAL participants. The graph shows the frequency of kills: (a) the distribution before the transformation was applied to normalize the data; (b) the distribution after the transformation was applied.

As an example, see Figure 2.5(a), where the number of kills for all participants are plotted as a histogram. As you can see from the figure on the left, the original data was left skewed, because the bulk of the data is on the left part of the scale. We applied the square transformation to transform the data into a more normally distributed sample, see Figure 2.5 (b). In the lab in Chapter 3, we will go over this example in more detail.

2.8 Data transformation

In addition to these steps, we also need to ensure that the type of data is handled properly for the analysis needed. For example, there are operations that can only be done on quantitative variables, and thus, discrete variables need to be dealt with accordingly.

One way to convert categorical variables to numerical is to use one-hot encoding. One-hot encoding is a technique whereby one categorical variable is converted into several columns in the database such that the values are binary. R and Python both have libraries to convert data into one-hot encoding. Let us take an example to make this clearer.

For example, the *gender* column (see Figure 2.6) has only two values: Female "F" and Male "M." The one-hot encoding will then convert the column of *gender* into two columns: *Female* and *Male*. The data within the columns will then be "0" for False or "1" for True, depending the original value. R has a package called onehot that allows you to convert the data into this format through two simple calls: *encoder <- onehot(<dataset_variable>)* and then *x <- predict (encoder,*

	Gender	Quest.Started	Quest.Completed	DialogNumber	TakeHits
1	F	9	4	47	9
2	M	7	5	68	3
3	F	8	3	64	0
4	F	6	5	27	0
5	F	9	5	79	9
6	F	12	6	83	3

(a)

	Gender = F	Gender = M	Quest.Started	Quest.Completed	DialogNumber	TakeHits
[1,]	1	0	9	4	47	9
[2,]	0	1	7	5	68	3
[3,]	1	0	8	3	64	0
[4,]	1	0	6	5	27	0
[5,]	1	0	9	5	79	9
[6,]	1	0	12	6	83	3

(b)

Figure 2.6 One-hot encoding using R on aggregate data with gender.

<dataset_variable>). An example of this is shown in Figure 2.6 that shows two screenshots of tables from R: (a) the data before one-hot encoding and (b) with the one-hot encoding. As you can see, the gender column was split into two to show the binary value split. Of course, these functions have a lot more parameters that can be used. You may consult the library for more information on these parameters.

Why can we not just have one *gender* column and just use "1" for Female and "2" for Male? This is called label encoding for categorical variables. This may be okay for some processing, but for most Machine Learning algorithms, order and distance are important. Thus, if we assume values of "1" and "2" for Female and Male, respectively, we are assuming that there is an order and that the distance of "1" between these variables has a meaning. For such type of encoding, we cannot use it as a distance metric or to calculate averages or variance. Therefore, it is more correct to use one-hot encoding, where such distances or relations between the numbers are not assumed.

If you have many discrete variables, using one-hot encoding will increase the number of dimensions of your data. Further, another complication is that your data will become sparser. Therefore, there are other types of techniques that you may want to use instead of one-hot encoding. An example of one of the most popular techniques in data science today is mean encoding. In mean encoding, the target variable is taken into account to compute a number per category that represents the mean of the target variable given that category. You can consult online sources for more information on the subject.

2.9 Summary

In this chapter, you learned how to process data, specifically how to represent raw data, clean it, and prepare it for further processing. The main learning objectives for this chapter are to give you the following:

- Understanding the need for preprocessing in the analytics process.
- Understanding the differences between different measurement types (e.g., ordinal, ratio, and interval data).
- Understanding how data is represented through variables in an application like R and understanding the different types of variables that exist.
- Ability to format the data in a consistent fashion for the next stage of processing.
- Ability to process and clean the data, removing empty values and wrong values.
- Ability to deal with outliers or inconsistent data.
- Ability to normalize or standardize the data.

••

EXERCISES

1. What is the difference between measurement types and variable types? Given the VPAL dataset, name all different measurement types you see in the data.
2. In the VPAL dataset, there are several textual data types, such as *Dialog*. Name all variables of types in the VPAL dataset. Identify the character and string types. Can these data types be converted to numbers? If so, how?
3. Using the VPAL data, extend the parsing to include parsing of:

   a Dialog utterances into a dataframe with columns: character and utterance.

   b Attack-related actions into a dataframe with columns: who attacked first, what is the object attacked, and player health.

4. Using the VPAL file, design a dataframe that captures the types of actions within the game. Then, extend your parsing algorithm in Exercise 3 to include all the different actions that are not captured in your algorithm already. Iterate over all players, resulting in one dataframe that contains all players (rows) and all actions they did aggregated over time (columns).

5. Given the VPAL data, check for consistency. What type of consistency issues did you find with the data? Please show your work and all types of inconsistencies that you found in the data.

6. For all inconsistencies you can find in the data, please develop ways to handle them. Show your work.

7. Using the VPAL data, we have identified several outliers. Using movement data, quest data, and dialog data, can you identify outliers and describe why you think they are outliers? Show your work visually.

8. For quest data, develop an R function that parses the VPAL file to collect all quest data. Check if the data distributions per variable is normal. Normalize any non-normalized distribution, and scale all the variables to values of "0–1."

9. Identify any and all nominal or categorical variables. Use one-hot-encoding to transform the variables into dimensions in the data.

10. Examine the DOTAlicious data in Appendix A and discuss a plan for data preprocessing that would allow you to analyze this data per participant and compare their actions.

• •

BIBLIOGRAPHY

Jonge, E. d., and van der Loo, M. (2013). *An introduction to data cleaning with R*. Statistics Netherlands.

Onehot Encoding Library. URL: https://cran.r-project.org/web/packages/onehot/ onehot.pdf. Last accessed December 28, 2017.

MySQL. MY SQL Reference Manual. https://dev.mysql.com/

MongoDB. http://docs.mongodb.com

Mangiafico, S. S. (2016). Summary and Analysis of Extension Program Evaluation in R, version 1.15.0. (PDF version:rcompanion.org/documents/RHandbookProgram Evaluation.pdf.)

Osborne, J. W. (2013). *Best practices in data cleaning: A complete guide to everything you need to do before and after collecting your data*. Los Angeles, CA: Sage.

Squire, M. (2015). *Clean Data*. Bimingham, UK: Packt Publishing.

Yeo, I., and Johnson, R. A. (2000). A new family of power transformations to improve normality or symmetry. *Biometrika*, *87*, 954–9.

CHAPTER 3

Introduction to Statistics and Probability Theory

Exploring gameplay metrics can be done in different ways, but it is fundamentally performed either via analysis or synthesis, two different angles of the scientific method described in Chapter 1. Analysis is defined as the process by which we break down an intellectual or substantial whole into parts or components. For example, we break down a play session into time spent on each activity. On the other hand, synthesis is defined as the opposite process, where we combine separate elements or components to form a coherent whole. For example, a chart showing the number of daily active users is a synthesis of time, number of users, date, etc. Every synthesis is built using results from some analyses, and every analysis requires a subsequent synthesis to verify and correct its results. Although analysis and synthesis go hand in hand, they complement one another. There are important situations when one method can be regarded as more suitable than the other.

Further, there are two types of analyses used to address both synthesis and analysis processes. Such processes can be initiated by fairly open-ended questions, such as "do our players cheat?", or specific questions, such as "does that player cheat by using the inverse-shield duping method?" These define two different approaches in scientific inquiry: explorative and hypothesis-driven inquiry. These are important concepts, because they give you a clear method and a set of principles to approach your examination of game data and the analysis processes you adopt. In other words, such concepts provide you with guidance to plan your analysis work and a set of methods to apply, as we will

Game Data Science. Magy Seif El-Nasr, Truong Huy Nguyen Dinh, Alessandro Canossa, and Anders Drachen, Oxford University Press. © Magy Seif El-Nasr, Truong Huy Nguyen Dinh, Alessandro Canossa, and Anders Drachen (2021). DOI: 10.1093/oso/9780192897879.003.0003

discuss below. They also provide you with a means for classifying methods and terminology to be used when discussing gameplay analyses with your peers.

In a nutshell, most of the analytical methods you will learn throughout this book and your practice with game data fall into one of the two types:

(1) Hypothesis-driven analysis, also referred to as Confirmatory Data Analysis (CDA): In this analysis, you are looking to confirm some idea or a hypothesis you may have or have formulated after an explorative analysis. For example, we can hypothesize based on observation of gameplay sessions that "zombies are way too powerful in level 10 of our game." This is then turned into a hypothesis or a set of hypotheses that we can investigate using game data. CDA allows researchers to move from a general principle toward special cases; hence, it is a perfect example of deductive reasoning. This type of analysis involves testing hypotheses and quantifying to what extent the patterns seen in the data could have been produced by chance. The most common tools look at significance, confidence, and variance.

(2) Explorative Data Analysis (EDA): In this analysis, you usually do not assume anything about the data and do not have well-defined hypotheses, but probably have a general idea about what you are looking for. This analysis is concerned with discovery, exploration, and empirically detecting patterns in the data. In essence, you need to know more about the data or the problem before you can build more concrete hypotheses, and this type of analysis helps you in this process toward formulating the questions you want to ask and the way you are going to frame them. A good example for this is exploring which items or package deals are the most popular among your players, and thus allowing you to know what deals are important to drive the conversion from a nonpaying user to a paying user. EDA allows researchers to formulate general principles, starting from special cases and individual observations; hence, it is a perfect example of inductive reasoning. The most common procedures are identifying key variables and establishing models that are able to explain the data with the fewest variables.

In our experience, explorative questions are usually more time-consuming to answer and often require more time to process than hypothesis-driven questions, which can often be handled using synthesis (or very simple statistical analysis) of the relevant data.

Furthermore, purely exploratory questions, in our experience, are rare— a game developer usually does not have the luxury of time or resources to indulge in such type of analysis. This is not to say that purely explorative analysis of gameplay telemetry cannot be useful, but it is often hard to justify the expenditure of resources that would be needed to implement it.

The book will go through many different methods you can use to do explorative and hypothesis-driven analysis, as well as methods that fit within the synthesis or analysis processes defined above. This chapter introduces the important foundations for the work you will be doing for the rest of the book.

There are two core types of statistical approaches that you should be aware of: descriptive and inferential. Descriptive statistics is often used to understand the data itself, how it is distributed or spread. It is an important step to know what techniques from the tools of statistical analysis methods to use, based on the shape and structure of the data. It is also the first step for both hypothesis-driven and explorative analyses. Through descriptive statistics, you can describe the basic features of a dataset and develop simple summaries and graphs. This is similar to what you did following the labs in Chapter 2.

Inferential statistics, on the other hand, attempts to reach conclusions that are not self-evident in the dataset alone. While descriptive statistics is completely focused on the data in question (observed data), the assumption in inferential statistics is that we are looking at a sample of data derived from a larger population (unobserved data). Inferential statistics is focused on creating a pathway toward inferring something about a population by examining a sample. For example, if you have a sample of 1,000 players, but want to be able to say something about the 1 million players in your game, you would use inferential techniques to evaluate patterns in the sample and estimate the probability of these patterns occurring in a larger population of players. Inferential statistics is also used to test and confirm hypotheses.

This chapter introduces these two groups of methods in detail, providing you with some labs where you can practice these concepts. However, the chapter is not meant to be the only resource you need for statistical analysis. Several important books cover statistics that you should probably read further to gain a deeper understanding of the different statistical approaches discussed in this chapter. These resources are listed in the bibliography section. In particular, please refer to Field, Miles, and Field (2012) for a thorough introduction to statistical analysis. The book is a very good resource to go beyond this chapter and get a deeper understanding of both descriptive and inferential statistics.

In this chapter, we will go through the following concepts:

- Descriptive statistics (Section 3.1)
- Inferential statistics (Section 3.2)
- Introduction to probability (Section 3.3)

The chapter also includes two labs, which go through methods for descriptive and inferential statistics:

- **Lab 3.1:** Descriptive statistics
- **Lab 3.2:** Inferential statistics

3.1 Descriptive statistics

Descriptive Statistics is often heavily used in the game data science pipeline to:

- Understand how the data is distributed and what further statistical methods to use.
- Derive some questions that can be used for hypothesis-driven analysis.
- Develop aggregate measures of game data; such measures form the metrics discussed in Chapter 1. Some examples of such metrics are Daily Active Users (DAUs) and Average Revenue Per User (ARPU).

Typically, there are three general types of methods you would want to use for that purpose: measures of centrality, measures of spread, and correlation analysis. Correlation analysis is specifically used to understand relationships between variables. Using these methods, you can then derive measures for the three goals described above. We will go through some examples to clarify this process.

Practical Note: Lab 3.1

Lab 3.1

Please see the supplemental materials for the book.

Goal of Lab 3.1

The lab goes over descriptive statistics of the data using VPAL data.

3.1.1 Measures of centrality

Now that you have already played with some game data in Chapter 2 labs, we will use this data here. Assuming you have gone through the lab to parse the Virtual Personality Assessment Lab (VPAL) data and have some quest data for all players, you can generate a histogram for different variables, such as *Kills*; see Figure 3.1a. As you can see from the figure, the data in this variable is not normally distributed. This is an important step to understand what methods to

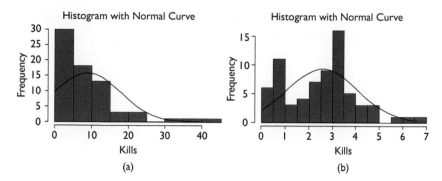

Figure 3.1 Histogram of kill data from VPAL participants. The graph shows the frequency of kills: (a) the distribution before the transformation was applied to normalize the data; (b) the distribution after the transformation was applied.

use on your data. As discussed in Chapter 2, many statistical techniques assume a normal distribution, and thus you may need to apply a transformation on this variable to normalize it. Chapter 2 discussed different types of transformations that you can perform on the data based on how the data is skewed. In the example below, it looks like the data is left-skewed. In the lab, we will go through an example to show you how to normalize this data through square transformation, as it was suggested in Chapter 2. The resulting data is shown in Figure 3.1b.

The measure of centrality is a measure of the centrality for a distribution, like the one shown in Figure 3.1. There are multiple ways to calculate the centrality of such a distribution, including *Mean*, *Median*, and *Mode*.

3.1.1.1 MEAN

The *mean* is the average, which is calculated given the formula shown below:

$$\hat{x} = \frac{\sum_i x_i}{n} \qquad \text{(Equation 3.1)}$$

where n is the number of items you are averaging, x is the variable you are averaging, and i is a counter from "0" to "n."

Sometimes, you may *not* want to use mean as a measure of centrality. Why? You may remember that mean is not an appropriate measure for categorical or nominal measures, as discussed in Chapter 2. Additionally, simple averages are susceptible to outliers. Also, when the raw data is skewed or not normally distributed, as shown in Figure 3.1a, the mean will not give you a good measure of centrality. For example, Figure 3.1 shows some participants who are exceeding 30 kills, while most of the participants are between "0" and "10."

When you compare the *mean* of *Kills* to other measures, such as *mode* and *median*, described below, you will understand the differences between these functions and which measure would be better for variables that do not have a normal distribution such as *Kills*. Follow Lab 3.1 for this example.

3.1.1.2 MEDIAN

Another measure of centrality is *median*, which is defined by the following equation:

$$median(x) = x_j \qquad \text{(Equation 3.2)}$$

where *j* is the middle of the dataset, defined by *n/2*, with *n* being the number of elements in the set. The assumption here is that the data is sorted from low to high. This value is not affected by data that may be skewed or contains some outliers. Lab 3.1 will illustrate the robustness of the *Median* against outliers and data skewness.

3.1.1.3 MODE

Another operation that you can use to define centrality of the data is mode. *Mode* is defined by the following equation:

$$mode(x) = Freq(x) \qquad \text{(Equation 3.3)}$$

where *Freq* is a function that calculates the most frequent value. As discussed in Chapter 2, *mode* is often used for categorical data.

Some problems arise with using mode with quantitative or continuous data. For example, what happens when you have a lot of very frequent values, which one do you choose? It also may not yield a real good measure of centrality of the data depending on how the data is skewed, and thus the results may be misleading. Lab 3.1 goes through examples of *Kills* and *Quest Completed* as two variables to show the differences depicted with these variables in terms of mean, median, and mode.

It is important to note that the more skewed your data is, the greater the difference would be between the *median* and *mean*, as you can see in Lab 3.1. Thus, you should try to use the median in such cases or transforming the data into a normally distributed data before applying the centrality measure (see Lab 3.1 for an example of how to do that). In general, we usually report *median* and *mean* in our analysis results.

3.1.2 Measures of spread (dispersion)

A measure of spread or dispersion is often used to describe how the data is varied within the sample. This measure is important because it allows us to understand how the different data points are laid out within our distribution for a particular variable. We can use various methods to compute this measure: *range*, *variance*, and *standard deviation*.

3.1.2.1 RANGE

Range shows how the variables vary from min to max values, as defined by the following equation:

$$Range = Min(x) : Max(x)$$ (Equation 3.4)

3.1.2.2 VARIANCE AND STANDARD DEVIATION

Variance is a measure of how much each point deviates from the mean. A formula for calculating that is as follows:

$$variance = \frac{\sum_i (x_i - mean(x))^2}{n}$$ (Equation 3.5)

where n is the number of items you have, x is the variable you are investigating, and i is a counter from "0" to "n."

Standard deviation is a measure of dispersion computed as the square root of the variance. Figure 3.2 shows the calculations of the *variance* and *standard deviation* on *Kills* and *Quests Completed* within the VPAL data. See Lab 3.1 for more information.

3.1.3 Relationships between variables

It is important to know how your variables are related to one another to understand how to normalize these variables and the results when you run inferential statistics described in Section 3.2. Two types of relationships are important to highlight here: (a) *correlational* and (b) *causal*, where one variable causes an effect in another. A correlational relationship simply states that two variables are synchronized. For instance, you can have a relationship between the amount of NPC (Non-Player Character) interaction and the number of dialog lines a player exhibits in the VPAL game. This relationship is positive,

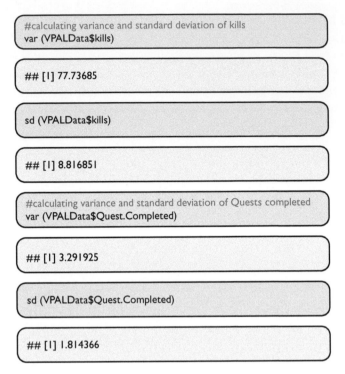

```
#calculating variance and standard deviation of kills
var (VPALData$kills)
```

```
## [1] 77.73685
```

```
sd (VPALData$kills)
```

```
## [1] 8.816851
```

```
#calculating variance and standard deviation of Quests completed
var (VPALData$Quest.Completed)
```

```
## [1] 3.291925
```

```
sd (VPALData$Quest.Completed)
```

```
## [1] 1.814366
```

Figure 3.2 *Variance* and *Standard Deviation* for VPAL data variables: *Kills* and *Quest Completed*.

meaning, the more NPCs you interact with, the more dialog lines you have. You can also imagine a negative correlation, such as the bigger the difference between *Quests Taken* and *Quests Completed*, the more the *unmotivated attacks*. This basically means, we hypothesized that people who could not complete the quests they have taken on may become frustrated, which results in a higher probability of them going on a rampage attacking NPCs or objects unmotivated. Notice that we do not have a means to measure *frustration*, but we can look at the relationship between *unmotivated attacks*, *Quests Taken*, and *Quests Completed*. Without directly measuring *frustration*, however, we cannot predict causation even if a relationship between the variables exists.

We ran an analysis on the VPAL data by plotting the variables and trying to fit a line through it. Figure 3.3 shows these two examples. As the figure shows, our hypothesis that more quests left uncompleted would lead to more unmotivated attacks was not confirmed given the data. As you can see from Figure 3.3(a), the line is not in the right direction (i.e., if the relationship sought holds, we would see an incline in the line as we go from left to right, which would say when quests completed increases so does the unmotivated attacks) and also the

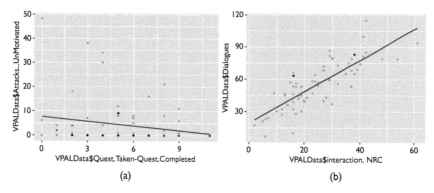

Figure 3.3 Looking at relationships between variables from VPAL data. (a) the relationship between unmotivated attacks and quests remaining (= quests taken − quests completed); (b) the relationship between dialogues and NPC interaction.

points are spread and do not specifically fit on the line. This indicates that there is no strong correlation, at least linear correlation, between the two variables.

Further, as described above, it is important to note that correlation does not imply causation, as one variable may not have **caused** the other. For example, there may be a correlation between *gold* and *kills* as the player explores the game and kills more NPCs; they may be collecting more gold. However, the fact that such a correlation exists does not mean that collecting more gold, in this case, **caused** more kills or that more kills caused the collection of more gold.

This leads to the consideration of what is often termed as the third variable problem. In this example (see Figure 3.3a), we see that the more the quests completed, the less the unmotivated attacks—although, as discussed above, this is not significant. But if we assume that there is a relationship, although weak, there may be a third variable that is causing us to see this correlation; this variable can be time spent in the game or player expertise. Specifically, the more experienced the player is, the less the remaining quests, because they should be able to complete many quests in the game. This then leads to more quest-related kills and more gold collected and probably less time spent on unmotivated attacks. Because of such a direct, causal relationship with this third variable, the two variables you are observing may fluctuate in a similar manner—that is, correlate.

In general, the third variable problem arises when we see a correlation between two variables not because they are related to one another, but rather due to some causal relationship between each of them with a third, unobserved variable.

The key lesson here is that you have to be careful when you interpret correlations. If you observe a correlation between the number of hours players use a certain item in a game and their hit accuracy, you cannot assume that the relationship is causal (i.e., that item causes high hit accuracy). You may want to think more deeply about what that third variable may be.

3.1.4 Correlation analysis

Correlation analysis is one of the most useful types of analysis you can use with game data. It allows you to understand how the variables are related to one another. This is very useful for the methods we will talk about later in the book, such as dimension reduction or machine learning methods. It is also important, as we discussed above, for inferential statistics, which we discuss in the next section.

You can first start by understanding how some variables are related to one another. In general, there are different methods in statistics that allow us to understand the relationship between variables. Correlation analysis is a bivariate analysis—that is, an analysis between two variables that measures the strength of an association between two variables. In such an analysis, positive and negative are used as ways to indicate the type of association. A correlation of "0" means no relation, and usually the values go from "-1" to "+1," where "+1" is a perfect positive association and "-1" is a perfect negative or opposite association.

In R, you can use three kinds of correlation measures: Pearson, Kendall, and Spearman correlations. Pearson correlation is the one most widely used to measure linear relationships between variables. It assumes that both variables are normally distributed, and the relationship can be linearly modeled. Kendall correlation is a nonparametric test that measures the strength of the connection between two variables. We will define parametric and nonparametric methods in Chapter 7. For now, a simple definition is that they represent two different types of modeling: one assumes a function and tries to find parameters to fit that function (parametric) and the other does not (nonparametric). Spearman correlation is, similar to Kendall, a nonparametric method, used to measure how the variables change together monotonically. Nonparametric methods do not assume a particular shape for the model produced and can be used for non-normally distributed measures. It is also an appropriate correlation to use for ordinal data.

Lab 3.1 walks you through an application of correlation measures between the two variables discussed above: *Kills* and *Shots*. We used Spearman

##	Quest.Taken	Quest.Completed	Dialogues	Loots	Loots.Items	Loots.Dead	Shots	Kills
## Quest.Taken	1.00	0.64	0.72	0.46	0.55	0.14	−0.10	0.00
## Quest.Completed	0.64	1.00	0.66	0.40	0.48	0.30	0.05	0.20
## Dialogues	0.72	0.66	1.00	0.47	0.47	0.22	0.09	0.22
## Loots	0.46	0.40	0.47	1.00	0.92	0.43	0.17	0.37
## Loots.Items	0.55	0.48	0.47	0.92	1.00	0.23	0.10	0.20
## Loots.Dead	0.14	0.30	0.22	0.43	0.23	1.00	0.01	0.34
## Shots	−0.10	0.05	0.09	0.17	0.10	0.01	1.00	0.46
## kills	0.00	0.20	0.22	0.37	0.20	0.34	0.46	1.00
## Interaction.NPC	0.61	0.69	0.81	0.49	0.49	0.25	0.21	0.31
## Interaction.Container	0.25	0.42	0.41	0.44	0.47	0.35	0.34	0.27
## Attacks	−0.13	−0.15	−0.10	0.12	0.00	0.11	0.60	0.68
## Attacks...Quest.rRelated	−0.09	0.04	0.06	0.18	0.10	0.08	0.51	0.21
## Attacks...Friendly.NPC	−0.24	−0.57	−0.42	−0.21	−0.32	−0.13	0.23	0.23
## Attacks...UnMotivated	0.06	0.22	0.22	0.14	0.07	0.27	0.32	0.63
## Attacks...SelfDefense	0.10	0.22	0.23	0.27	0.17	0.34	0.21	0.65

Figure 3.4 Correlation table between eight different variables within VPAL data.

correlation, because we did not want to assume a normal distribution. The lab also goes through using R to develop a correlation table between each two variables within the VPAL data (see the table in Figure 3.4). This table shows the correlation values between every two variables. Again, we are using Spearman correlation here since we did not want to assume a normal distribution.

It is important to note that a correlation value of 0–0.19 is very weak, 0.2–0.39 is weak, 0.4–0.59 is moderate, 0.6–0.79 is strong, and 0.8–1 is very strong. In the lab, we also printed out the p-values for these correlations.

The p-value is an important measure in statistics, which states the significance of the test you are running. P-value is the level of marginal significance within a hypothesis test, which represents the probability of the occurrence of this event. If the p-value in this table is below a small number, such as "0.05," then we can assume that the relationship outlined by the correlation value is significant.

It is important to note here, however, that while we note weak and strong relations and that a p-value of 0.05 is considered significant, these are highly arbitrary values and labels that have historically been used. In any experimental context, we suggest that you should decide on an individual basis whether a given value is good enough for the purpose, rather than just use 0.05 as a principle in the case of p-value. Interested readers should see Morrison and Henkel's book (2006) in the bibliography section for more information.

3.1.5 Modeling

Another task you can do is try to fit the data into a model. An example of a simple model is a line. The process of line fitting given several variables is called linear regression and is part of a class of modeling techniques called: Generalized Linear Models (GLMs). By modeling, we mean fitting the data into a particular computational or statistical structure that can be used to explain the relationship between the variables involved. In the context of GLMs, it is a linear function. We will discuss this further in Chapter 7, where we will also review other types of modeling techniques to understand the relationship between variables, in addition to constructing a model to show how these variables interact or predict a target variable.

Figure 3.5 shows an example plot showing the relationship between *Kills* and *Shots*. The line drawn in the figure is the best line that fits this data. As you can see, the data is far more spread and not exactly on that line, while the example shown in Figure 3.3b shows a much better fit. This means that the relationship between the variables shown in Figure 3.3b is a lot more linear than the variables in 3.5. However, fitting the line too close to the data may cause an overfitting problem—that is, the model (line in this case) fits the data too well, but since your data is never complete, once you get unseen examples, they may deviate from the very well-fit model you have created. We will talk more about overfitting in later chapters. For more discussion on modeling, readers can refer to later chapters in the book. We will proceed to discuss inferential statistics, which also uses modeling techniques to draw inferences about the differences between experimental groups.

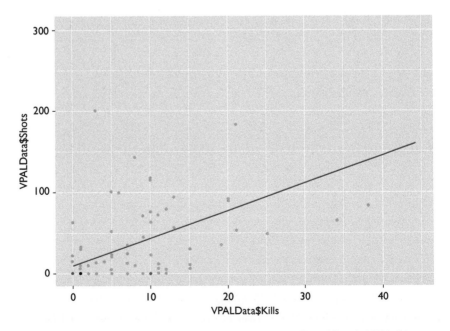

Figure 3.5 Linear model to fit the relationship between *Kills* and *Shots* in VPAL data.

3.2 Inferential statistics

In inferential statistics, you are looking for conclusions beyond the immediate data, such as inferring how version A, of a game you are working on, can impact players as compared to version B; in other words, performing simple A/B testing and comparing the effect of a simple game design change on engagement, retention, or performance. In such cases, you are not just describing what the data is like, but you are using statistics to make inferences about which version is better using the data.

Many popular inferential statistics methods can be used here—for example, when comparing between groups: t-tests, Analysis of Variance (ANOVA), regression analysis; and when trying to understand grouping or clustering of participants or features: factor analysis or cluster analysis. Chapters 6, 7, and 8 will go into a lot more details discussing techniques, such as regression, clustering, and classification. Chapter 4 will introduce Principal Component Analysis (similar to Factor Analysis) mostly used for feature extraction. This chapter will focus on t-tests and ANOVA, leaving the rest for other chapters to delve deeper into.

Practical Note: Lab 3.2

Lab 3.2

Please see the supplemental materials for the book.

Goal of Lab 3.2

The lab goes over inferential statistics of the data using VPAL data.

3.2.1 Dependent and independent variables

When discussing inferential statistics, it is important to differentiate between dependent and independent variables. An independent variable is what you manipulate—a treatment, a program, or a cause. The dependent variable is what is affected by the independent variable or in effect what you are measuring or predicting. For example, if you are studying the effects of a new game mechanic on player experience or retention, the features of the new game mechanic you are developing are all independent variables and player experience or retention are/is the dependent variable. Thus, before you embark on such analysis, you need to be very clear about:

- Your goals: What are you trying to accomplish through this analysis?
- Your hypotheses: What are the clear and distinct hypotheses you are testing through this analysis?
- Your variables and groups: What are the dependent and independent variables? Do you have one group or more groups to compare?
- Distributions: Are your variables all normally distributed?
- Clean data: Is your data clean and normalized for analysis?

You can use the above list as a checklist to verify if you are ready to run some analyses on the data. The data needs to be cleaned (see Chapter 2). You also need to know what the variables and groups are and the types of variables as well as their distributions (see Chapter 2 and also Section 3.1). You also need to make sure you have a clear goal and hypotheses set for your analysis.

Once you have answers to all these questions or you have performed all the necessary steps, you are ready to choose a method for your analysis. Below, we discuss two analysis methods.

3.2.2 t-tests

t-test is a method used to compare two groups. The method specifically compares the means of the two groups and determines if the means are statistically different. This type of analysis will involve understanding the spread of the data in the two populations and then determining how close they are, based on the mean and the spread in the data.

To illustrate how this works, we will use, again, VPAL as an example, but we will split the data by game experience. We can then compare the two groups. Please follow through the Lab 3.2 to understand more effectively how such a test is applied. As an example, see Figure 3.6 showing *Quests Completed*

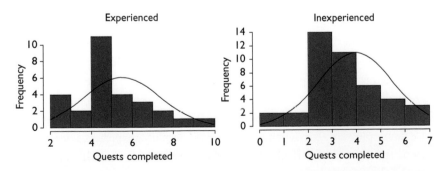

Figure 3.6 Histogram of *Quest Completed* shown for experienced and inexperienced players.

compared by two groups: *inexperienced* and *experienced* participants. The means calculated for these two groups are "5.5" (for experienced) and "3.9" (for inexperienced). The question is, given the spread and variance within the two groups, is this difference statistically significant? It makes perfect sense that we would expect experienced players to get further in the game and so they should have significantly more quests completed than inexperienced players. The question is, are the means significantly different? You would use a *t*-test to answer this question.

There are two types of t-tests used to compare two groups: paired *t*-tests and unpaired *t*-tests. Paired *t*-tests are used if the samples or the groups are related. A good example of this would be if you are looking at a before and after effect on the same population. Since the group tested is the same, the samples are related. To give you a concrete example, suppose you are looking at the time a player would take to solve a puzzle in version A vs. version B of a game. You would use paired *t*-tests to compare means in this case. In contrast, unpaired *t*-tests do not assume that the samples are related.

For paired 2 sample *t*-tests, *t-value* and *p-value* are computed. *t-value* is computed as follows:

$$t = \frac{mean\,(X - Y)}{\frac{sd(X-Y)}{\sqrt{n}}} \qquad \text{(Equation 3.6)}$$

where *mean* is the mean function and $X-Y$ is the difference between the pairs in the data. For example, for person 1, you would find the difference in the variable of interest between the version A and version B. *sd* is the standard deviation considering all pairs in the data, and *n* is the size of the data.

In order to calculate the *p-value*, which will give us an idea of the significance of the mean difference, we need to understand how much degrees of freedom we have. Degrees of freedom is a measure of how much parameters vary, given the constraint imposed by the hypothesis. For a 1-sample *t*-test, it is generally: $n-1$, where *n* is the sample size. For a 2-sample *t*-test, it is generally $n_1 + n_2 - 1$. This is because all observations can vary, except the last one.

Given the degrees of freedom and the *t*-values, we can then use the *t*-table (not included here, but you can look it up online) to estimate the *p-value*. The *p-value* here would represent the area under the distribution to the right of the value of the *t* statistic. The t-table usually will have the area (which is the *p-value*) as the columns and a list of degrees of freedom as the rows. You would then want to go to the right row given the degrees of freedom and find the *t-value* you calculated and see which area it corresponds to. As discussed above, a *p-value* of less than or equal to "0.05" means the observed difference is statistically significant. This basically states that we are 95% confident that these two mean values are different. See the note earlier, however, about the choice of this value, it is important that you are mindful of the purpose and what the values mean for the context you are applying these tests for.

The *t-value* for unpaired *t*-tests is computed, as follows:

$$t = \frac{mean(X) - mean(Y)}{\sqrt{\frac{(n_X-1)sd^2(X)+(n_Y-1)sd^2(Y)}{2}}\sqrt{\frac{1}{n_X}+\frac{1}{n_Y}}}$$ (Equation 3.7)

With unequal variances, however, another equation should be used, as follows:

$$t = \frac{mean(X) - mean(Y)}{\sqrt{\frac{sd^2(X)}{n_X}+\frac{sd^2(Y)}{n_Y}}}$$ (Equation 3.8)

where n_X and n_Y are the numbers in sample X and sample Y, respectively.

The *p-value* is calculated as discussed above. You would usually use R, or other statistical package, to calculate *t-values* and *p-values*. Thus, you would not really have to calculate it by hand, but this section went through the details of the formulae, so you can understand how it is internally calculated in R.

Figure 3.7 shows the results of running the *t*-test in R for the example discussed above, given the experienced and inexperienced groups and looking at the variable *Quest_Completed*. As shown in the figure, the *p-value* is around "0.0005." As discussed above, a *p-value* of "0.05" or lower is usually considered statistically significant. Therefore, it looks like our mean difference between

```
##
## Welch two sample t-test
##
## data: Experienced$Quest. Completed and Inexperienced$Quest. completed
## t = 3.6883, df = 50.628, p-value = 0.0005515
## alternative hypothesis: true difference in means is not equal to 0
## 95 percent confidence interval:
##   0.7050864 2.3901517
## sample estimates:
## mean of x mean of y
##   5.500000 3.952381
```

Figure 3.7 Results of T-tests operated on *Quest Completed* between *Experienced* and *In-Experienced Players*.

these two groups for *Quest_Completed* is significantly different. The mean values calculated are "5.5" and "3.95," which is congruent with our hypothesis.

3.2.3 ANOVA

t-tests are constrained to calculating differences between two groups. If you want to do more, such as if your dataset includes more than one group to compare or more than one independent variable, then you would want to use a different test. A good test to run is ANOVA. ANOVA is used to understand the sources of variation in the dependent variable—that is, which independent variables have how much impact on the variance as observed in the dependent variables. There are several types of ANOVAs that can be used in different circumstances. For example, there is a one-way ANOVA used when you have one independent variable, while a factorial ANOVA can be used when you have more than one independent variable.

Like *t*-tests, ANOVAs belong to the GLM family. Both ANOVAs and *t*-tests assume normality in the data. Thus, before you build your ANOVA model, you would want to boxplot the variables involved to check on normality visually. You can also check for normality using Levene's test (Levene, 1960). Also, ANOVA is mostly used with categorical dependent variables rather than continuous ones, and thus you would want to make sure that the dependent variables you are using in the model are categorical.

As you can see from VPAL data, much of the data is actually continuous rather than categorical. With such variables, one would use regression or other types of models to try to model the data. However, for the sake of example here, we will partition our data to look into some examples to show you how you would apply ANOVA.

Let us take the example of determining how *expertise* can be explained by *gender*. In this example, we will use two variables, the dependent variable here is *expertise* and independent variable is *gender*. We will then use ANOVA since we have more than one group of expertise; in particular, we have three groups (levels "1," "2," and "3").

In this sense, we are using *expertise* as our target variable—that is, the variable you want to explain with your data. In a general case, ANOVA will follow a similar logic to regression, in that you will have an equation as shown in Equation 3.9, whereby you are given a list of independent variables, x, and you are trying to understand how these variables can explain the variance in the outcome of the dependent variable (y). In case of one independent variable, we will be using one-way ANOVA, but for the general case with more than one independent variable, we will use factorial ANOVA. Note that this is very similar to linear regression, which we will talk about in more depth in Chapter 7.

$$Y = \beta_0 + \beta_1 X_1 + \cdots + \beta_n X_n \qquad \text{(Equation 3.9)}$$

where Y is the target or the dependent variable, X_i are the independent variables, n is the number of independent variables, and β, as described above, are the parameters that this algorithm tunes to fit the data to a line.

For our example discussed above, we only have one dependent variable: *Game Expertise*. Using R to perform ANOVA given *gender*, see Lab 3.2 for details. In particular, we first test for homogeneity of the data by running Levene's test. The results show a P value of "0.0017," indicating that the groups are actually not homogenous, and there is a statistical significance in the difference of the variance between the groups. For this reason, we cannot adopt a simple ANOVA, instead we can do a Welch F test or Robust ANOVA test. See the lab for more details on how to apply these tests. After performing these tests, it looks like the results are showing that there is a significant effect of *Gender* on *Expertise*, with all tests showing a very low *p-value*, well below 0.05.

In addition, the lab goes through an example of using a two-way ANOVA, or a factorial ANOVA with two independent variables: *Gender* and *Quest.Completed*. In this case, we are trying to figure out the effect of these two-independent variables on the dependent variable of *Game Expertise*. The results show an effect of *Gender* and *Quest.Completed*, both significant but no effect of the combined variable of *Gender+Quest.Completed*. This variable was included in the test to test for the interaction effect between *Gender* and *Quest.Completed*.

The lab also goes further to calculate effect size by calculating the *R-squared* value. The *R-squared* value is the proportion of variability in the dependent variable that can be accounted for by the model, which is discussed in detail in Chapter 8.

It is important to note that it really matters what independent variables you use in the ANOVA analysis because of the interaction effect between variables. In our case, we controlled for the interaction effect by adding the combined variable *Gender+Quest.Completed*. Luckily, the model shows there is no effect from that combined variable. But that may not always be the case. It is important to understand that, in some cases, there may be a latent variable (see the third variable discussion above) that explains the results you are seeing.

Further, it is important to note that our example is not set up as an experiment, as would be the case with an A/B test, for example. However, the field of Game User Research has ample of examples where such statistical methods are used to test the effect of a design change or an introduction of a mechanics on game behaviors. Such data will be richer than the example discussed here and may require more post hoc analysis. For more discussion on that aspect, readers are referred to the book by Field et al. (2012). In their book, there is a larger discussion on experimental setups and the use of variations of ANOVA.

Of course, there is always the question of what if our data does not really fit a linear model? How do we deal with that situation? In Chapter 7, we will discuss linear regression and other classification methods that go beyond the linear model assumption. You will learn more about how to use machine learning techniques to run methods and build models to predict a dependent variable or variables. This chapter provided a brief introduction to statistical analysis, which is the basis for many machine learning techniques that you will learn more about in the coming chapters.

It should be noted that, throughout this section, we discussed *p-value* as a measure of statistical significance. However, as we noted above, there are also many cases where you can get a significant *p-value* just by accident or by virtue of trying so many tests. Please see the discussion by Morrison and Henkel (2006). Further, in 2014, Nuzzo (2014) discussed the term p-hacking, which denotes the conscious or subconscious process by which researchers may try many tests until they get the desired, also called *data-dredging, snooping, fishing, significance-chasing*, or *double-dripping*. In her article, Nuzzo stated, "the irony is that when UK statistician Ronald Fisher introduced the *P* value in the 1920s, she did not mean it to be a definitive test. He intended it simply as an informal way to judge whether evidence was significant in the old-fashioned sense: worthy of a second look." In the last chapter of the book, we will conclude with a discussion on the issue of reproducibility and replicability, which expands on this issue further. **The lesson here is that you should be very careful about what you report and make sure to test the effect size and the validity of the results you are reporting.**

3.4 Introduction to probability

This section discusses some basic concepts on discrete probability, which are also the basis for many of the techniques you will learn about in Chapters 6–8.

Readers are highly recommended to refer to the textbooks by Walpole et al. (1993) and Bishop (2006) for further readings on probabilities, as this section just briefly touches on the concepts used in the subsequent chapters.

3.4.1 Probability

Probability is used to capture the chances, in numerical terms, of how likely it is that a certain event happens. For instance, if the probability that a player purchases an item G in some game is 0.7, this can be denoted as, in which *purchases item* $G = True$ is an event (in contrast with the event *purchases item* $G = False$) and 0.7 (or 70%) is the chance of it happening.

Formally, an event is often denoted as a random variable X taking a specific value in a set of values, which could be discrete or continuous. In the above example, *purchases item* G is considered a random variable, as its value is not known, but can be either "True" or "False" for any player. The probability that X takes a specific value "x," written as $P(X = x)$, is a real value between "0" and "1"—that is, $0 \leq P(X = x) \leq 1$. Furthermore, the sum of the probabilities of all outcomes must be "1"—that is, $\sum_x P(X = x) = 1$.

For the purpose of brevity, we are going to refer to P as $P(x)$.

3.4.2 Joint probability

Given variables $X_1, X_2, \ldots, X_n$, the joint probability of these variables taking on a specific combined outcome $X_1 = x_1, X_2 = x_2, \ldots, X_n = x_n$ is written as $P(x_1, x_2, \ldots x_n)$, or $P(x)$, in which x represents the combined outcome $(x_1, x_2, \ldots, x_n)$. Similar to the probability of single variables, $0 \leq P(x) \leq 1$ and $\sum_x P(x) = 1$.

Note that the order of variables shown in a joint probability is not important.

3.4.3 Conditional probability

Given variables X_1 and X_2, the conditional probability of $X_1 = x_1$ given $X_2 = x_2$ is denoted as $P(X_1 = x_1 | X_2 = x_2)$ or $P(x_1 | x_2)$, and is computed as

$$P(x_1 | x_2) = \frac{P(x_1, x_2)}{P(x_2)} \qquad \text{(Equation 3.10)}$$

That is the joint probability of $X_1 = x_1$ and $X_2 = x_2$ divided by the probability of $X_2 = x_2$. It can be proven that $P(x_2)$ is indeed a probability—that is, satisfying

1. $0 \leq P(x_1|x_2) \leq 1$ and
2. $\sum_{x_1} P(x_1|x_2) = 1$

Similarly, we can also compute the conditional probability of X_2 given X_1 as

$$P(x_2|x_1) = \frac{P(x_1, x_2)}{P(x_1)} \qquad \text{(Equation 3.11)}$$

Note that from Equation 3.10 and 3.11, we can obtain:

$$P(x_1, x_2) = P(x_1|x_2) P(x_2) = P(x_2|x_1) P(x_1) \qquad \text{(Equation 3.12)}$$

3.4.4 Independence

Two variables X_1 and X_2 are called independent, if $P(x_1, x_2) = P(x_1) P(x_2)$ for all values x_1 and x_2. It can be shown that in such case, $P(x_1|x_2) = P(x_1)$ and $P(x_2|x_1) = P(x_2)$ for all values x_1 and x_2.

You should be careful not to confuse this concept of probabilistic independency with the dependent/independent variables discussed in Section 3.1. To make it clear which notion you are referring to, you can call this probabilistic independency, or that "X_1 and X_2 are probabilistically independent from one another" instead of just "X_1 and X_2 are independent variables."

3.4.5 Chain rule

The chain rule is a generalization of Equation 3.9, allowing the joint probability of a set of variables to be computed as the product of their conditional probabilities, as follows:

$$P(x_1, x_2, \ldots, x_n) = P(x_1) P(x_2|x_1) \ldots P(x_n|x_1, \ldots x_{n-1}) \qquad \text{(Equation 3.13)}$$

3.4.6 Bayes' theorem

Bayes' theorem, or Bayes' rule, combines Equations 3.10 and 3.11 and is based on Equation 3.12, stating that

$$P(x_1|x_2) = \frac{P(x_2|x_1) P(x_1)}{P(x_2)} \qquad \text{(Equation 3.14)}$$

in which

- The conditional probability $P(x_1|x_2)$ is also called the likelihood of event $X_1 = x_1$ given that event $X_2 = x_2$.
- The conditional probability $P(x_2|x_1)$ is also called the likelihood of event $X_2 = x_2$ given that event $X_1 = x_1$.

Bayes' theorem provdes a principled rule to update the likelihood of an event (X_1) given observation of some related events (X_2).

3.4.7 Some common probability distributions

Note that it is sometimes important to understand how a probability is distributed, which then gives us the term probability distributions. This basically gives us a mathematical function that provides us with probabilities of occurrence of a possible outcome over a number of trials. Table 3.1 depicts some common probability distributions, namely Bernoulli, Gaussian (a.k.a. normal), and categorical distributions. A Bernoulli distribution is a distribution of the occurrences of binary variable of 1 or 0; this is similar to a coin toss of heads vs. tails. Gaussian distribution, or the normal distribution, is usually referred to as the layman term *bell curve* due to its shape. Categorical distributions are generalized Bernoulli distributions where the number of outcomes is fixed and more than two—for example, colors or grades (i.e., A to F).

Table 3.1 *Popular distributions.*

	Bernoulli distribution	Gaussian distribution	Categorical distribution
Applicable variable type	Discrete, binary (e.g., value $x \in \{0, 1\}$)	Continuous (i.e., value $x \in R$)	Discrete, multivalued (e.g., $x \in \{1, \ldots, k\}$)
Parameter(s)	$0 < p < 1, p \in R$ (probability of $x = 1$)	$\mu \in R$ (mean) $\sigma^2 \in R$ (variance)	$k > 2, k \in N$ (number of categories) $p_1, p_2, \ldots, p_k \in [0, 1]$, s.t. $\sum_{i=1}^{k} p_i = 1$ (probabilities of categories)
Probability function	$p(x = 1) = p$ $p(x = 0) = 1 - p$	$p(x) = \frac{1}{\sqrt{2\pi\sigma^2}} . e^{-\frac{(x-\mu)^2}{2\sigma^2}}$	$p(x = i) = p_i,$ $\forall i \in \{1, \ldots, k\}$

There are many other types of distributions; interested readers can refer to the two books we referenced above on probability to read more about such probability distributions. Table 3.1 lists popular distributions that are frequently encountered in practice.

3.5 Summary

In this chapter, we discussed descriptive statistics as well as different types of inferential statistics, including ANOVA and t-tests. We discussed that ANOVA is based on GLMs, which will be discussed in further detail in later chapters. We also introduced probabilistic measures and distributions, which will be used in future chapters.

• •

EXERCISES

1. Taking the VPAL data you created through the labs in Chapter 2, develop some histograms for all quests to see how many participants have completed these quests.
2. Using VPAL data, run some correlation analysis between the different variables you parsed. Are any of the variables linearly correlated? Which ones are significantly positively or negatively correlated? Explain your answers.
3. Using VPAL data, select a target variable such as *gender*. Perform ANOVA on that variable to see what independent variables can predict it. Describe your answer and results.
4. Given VPAL data, add a new set of variables: time spent in different locations. Then, compute the ANOVA scores for experience as a target variable using the full variable set (current variables + time spent variables you developed). Are your results different from what was discussed above? Why?

• •

BIBLIOGRAPHY

A good course on Statistics, http://www.cuclasses.com/stat1001/

Bishop, C. M. (2006). *Pattern Recognition and Machine Learning*. New York, NY: Springer.

Dalgaard, P. (2008). *Introductory statistics with R*. Springer Science & Business Media.

Field, A., Miles, J., and Field, Z. (2012). *Discovering statistics using R*. Sage Publications.

Levene, H. (1960). Robust tests for equality of variances. In Olkin, I. (ed). *Contributions to Probability and statistics* (pp. 278–92). Palo Alto, VA: Stanford University Press.

Morrison, D. E., and Henkel, R. E. (Eds.). (2006). *The significance test controversy: A reader.* New York, NY: Transaction Publishers.

Nuzzo, R. (2014). Scientific method: statistical errors. *Nature News*, 506(7487), 150–2.

Olshausen, B. A. (2004). A Probability Primer. http://www.rctn.org/bruno/npb163/probability.pdf

Walpole, R. E., Myers, R. H., Myers, S. L., and Ye, K. (1993). *Probability and statistics for engineers and scientists* (Vol. 5). New York: Macmillan.

CHAPTER 4

Data Abstraction

When you start working with behavioral telemetry data from games, you will see that the raw data collected is often in the order of 50+ features or independent/dependent variables that are measured continuously throughout the duration of a play session. On top of this, there will usually be many play sessions associated with each player. Often, each data point also relies on other data points—for example, quest completion relies on being in the right location, having the right items, etc.

Analyzing such high-dimensional data can be challenging. Especially, if you also need to take into account the temporal dimension, for example, in a time-series analysis. As you saw in Chapter 3, there are many interactions and interdependencies between these variables that would also have an effect on the statistical analysis you will be performing.

Furthermore, it is important to remember that behavioral telemetry is collected from players as they play. The more information you collect, the sparser the data will likely be across those dimensions, because not all participants actually go through all the game spaces, especially in open world games. This sparsity can make it hard to develop accurate models for specific problems: for example, it will be hard to analyze player movement patterns in an area that few players have visited.

For all these reasons, we have to be strategic about the information we are collecting. Instead of attempting to deal with such high dimensional data, a very common strategy is to develop an abstraction from the raw variables to a higher level fewer variables, which reduces the dimensionality of the data and provides useful information about player behavior. We refer to these variables as

Game Data Science. Magy Seif El-Nasr, Truong Huy Nguyen Dinh, Alessandro Canossa, and Anders Drachen, Oxford University Press. © Magy Seif El-Nasr, Truong Huy Nguyen Dinh, Alessandro Canossa, and Anders Drachen (2021). DOI: 10.1093/oso/9780192897879.003.0004

features or metrics. We use these two terms interchangeably to mean a variable of interest (or an independent variable, as we called them in Chapter 3) from the abstracted, raw data/measures.

Abstractions can have several purposes. For example, using abstraction methods, you can condense time but keep the sequential nature of the measures; aggregate over the temporal dimension (i.e., removing time as a dimension); or develop new abstract variables that are functions of the variables in the raw data, thereby condensing the number of variables into a more manageable set. To take an example, the kill/death ratio is a common feature/metric developed for shooter games. Other good examples of abstractions over raw data points are provided in the list of game metrics discussed in Chapter 1. Please review this list as it is extensive and can give you an idea of what we are trying to achieve in this chapter.

In this chapter, we will introduce the process of creating such features and metrics from raw data. There are many different strategies to accomplish this. These strategies can be summarized into three processes:

a) Feature engineering refers to the process of using domain or expert knowledge to aggregate data and develop new features. Examples of this process are metrics, discussed in Chapter 1. Other examples can include "averaging kills per match per player" and "time spent on each location," where location is defined as an area in the game map.

b) Feature extraction refers to the process of developing new features using statistical techniques from raw measures reducing the number of variables by obtaining a set of principal variables. Therefore, feature extraction derives new features $F_1, \ldots, F_m$, which are new variables obtained statistically from the raw variables $X_1, \ldots, X_n$. Some methods that allow us to perform such extraction is Principal Component Analysis (PCA), which we will discuss in detail in this chapter. It should be noted that these types of techniques produce features that may not be interpretable by humans. This is an important note that we will discuss later in this chapter.

c) Feature selection refers to the process of filtering the raw measures and selecting a few that are of interest, thus reducing the number of variables that can be used for further analysis. This process is usually done through statistical methods that allow us to rank or score the importance of features given a prediction or outcome variable, such as whether the player won or not. As opposed to feature extraction, feature selection selects specific variables from the raw variables, $X_1, \ldots, X_n$, owing to their importance for modeling a particular relationship with a target variable: Y. Therefore, the new variables are a subset of the raw variables, while the feature extraction technique develops new variables from the raw variables.

In this chapter, we will discuss these techniques in detail. We will present some of the algorithms used and explain how such algorithms can be used through labs in R. We will focus on the latter two techniques, feature extraction and selection, rather than feature engineering. This is due to the fact that feature engineering is a technique that is often game dependent and requires expert knowledge. Further, for feature engineering, you mostly use scripting to develop aggregate measures, using similar functions to what we have discussed in Chapters 2 and 3. Therefore, we will keep it as an exercise for you to use Virtual Personality Assessment Lab (VPAL) data to engineer some features that may be useful for your analysis goal.

This chapter includes the following labs:

- **Lab 4.1:** Focuses on feature extraction with PCA.
- **Lab 4.2:** Extends the techniques used in the previous lab to include mixed data: qualitative and quantitative.
- **Lab 4.3:** Focuses on feature selection showing forward and backward feature selection methods with example game data.

It should be noted that some of these algorithms are based on machine learning techniques, which we will introduce in more detail later in the book. For such cases, we will not delve deeply into the techniques, but just introduce them and show you how to use them, referring to the relevant chapters for more details. When such algorithms are discussed in later chapters, we recommend coming back to this chapter and considering how this added knowledge impacts your understanding of data abstraction.

Before we delve into the subject of this chapter, we will first discuss the dataset we will be using throughout this chapter for examples and labs.

4.1 Dataset

We chose to use data from Multiplayer Online Battle Arena (MOBA) games in this chapter. For more information on the datasets and the games used in the book, please see Appendix A. These types of games have become very popular, with millions of players playing them at any given time. They have been adopted in e-sports tournaments. MOBA games are real-time strategy games, where each player assumes a hero type and joins a team competing against another team. Each hero type has different capabilities, which allow players to perform different actions in the game. Each hero will then engage in different types of actions that may include assisting, killing, moving around, etc. The objective of the game is to destroy the other team's base. The duration of each match varies, but mostly average about an hour of play. Example games in this genre are *League of Legends* developed by Riot and released in 2009 and *DOTA 2* developed by Valve and released in 2013.

There are several options to get data from MOBA games. One is to use the Application Programming Interface (API) provided by the developers to crawl and collect data of different matches. Another is to use publicly available replays or data, of which there are many, including from services, such as Kaggle (see Chapter 1).

In this chapter, we will use a derivative data from the one publicly distributed through the Game Trace Archive by TU Delft (Guo and Iosup, 2012). We accessed this data in 2016 and developed our own algorithms to derive the dataset included in the lab. This data represents "data collected from *DOTAlicious* Gaming, which is a *DOTA* platform, with servers geographically distributed over North America and Europe. For each match, information such as: the nicknames of the players, the countries from which they are playing, the start and end times, the match results, and friendships between players are included" (Guo and Iosup, 2012). In this section, we will discuss the data in sufficient detail as to allow you to follow through the examples used in this chapter.

We have about 84,000 matches. We have preprocessed the dataset, removed missing data, and selected the variables of interest (following techniques discussed in Chapter 2). Further, we selected a subset (1,000 players) of the total number of players. Moreover, we scaled each of the columns in the dataset, and then converted the data into a CSV file with the following aggregate variables:

- *PlayerID*
- *GamesPlayed*
- *GamesWon*
- *GamesLeft*
- *Ditches*
- *Points*

- *SkillLevel*
- *Kills*
- *KillsPerMin*
- *Deaths*
- *Assists*
- *CreepsKilled*
- *CreepsDenied*
- *NaturalsKilled*
- *TowersDestroyed*
- *RaxsDestroyed*
- *Character Gender*
- *TotalTime*

Most of the variables here are numeric with the exception of *SkillLevel*, which is ordinal, and *Gender*, which is nominal, and thus both were not scaled. Most often, in game data, you will have a mix of measurement types (see Chapter 2), including ratio, ordinal, or nominal.

4.2 Feature engineering

In Chapters 2 and 3, we discussed some techniques to abstract raw data through aggregations, such as averages or summations. Developing such features from the data can be as simple as an aggregation of a raw variable, such as total number of lines of dialog, or can involve calculations over several variables. Most such aggregations can be done using standard statistics software, depending on dataset size, or by using R via the mean or mode functions over specific columns in the data. Please refer to Chapters 2 and 3 to review how to use such functions in R.

In some domains, such as medicine, there exist specific time windows or standard aggregations of variables based on biological principles or expert knowledge. In such a domain, there are standard methods for abstraction over time, called knowledge-based temporal abstraction techniques (Moskovitch and Shahar, 2005). The methods acquired from experts typically use various scripting techniques developed in the form of rules applied over temporal data. This then creates an abstracted data model where the abstracted variables are often discrete rather than continuous over time.

Unfortunately, standard methods similar to these do not exist for games—as the field of game data science has yet to agree on standards for metrics/features. However, while the specific definitions can vary from company to company, there are temporally abstracted metrics that are broadly understood at least in principle. These are also commonly game agnostic. Examples of these metrics are included in Chapter 1 and include:

- *Monthly Active Users (MAU)*
- *Daily Active Users (DAU)*
- *Average Revenue Per Paying User (ARPPU)*
- *Life Time Value (LTV)*
- Conversion Rate (*CVR*)

See exercise 3 for an exercise on this part of the chapter.

In addition to these broad metrics, game user researchers and game data scientists often develop a set of metrics based on the game and the variables of interest. Some of these variables may be abstracted per level, thus diminishing the time dimension to the level unit, or they may be abstracted given a time window. The choice of which variables to aggregate is still an art at this point and mostly depends on what you are interested in measuring. For example, if you are interested in player types, you may want to abstract time spent per location, since locations may give you different affordances that can differentiate between players. You can also aggregate the time spent in conversation with NPCs or the number of dialogs initiated, etc. You may also aggregate over performance metrics, such as quest-completion rate or deaths/kills ratio. We have attempted to develop a process for abstraction using visualization and data analysis; please see Javvaji, Harteveld, and Seif El-Nasr (2020) for more details on the process.

Here, we present a concrete case study to showcase feature engineering applied to game activity (see Table 4.1). The table shows the activity pattern for two players. Both players display 4 days of activity in the past week. The two players had the same cumulative number of days active in the game. However, looking at the time spent per day over the course of a week, we can see that the players are different. While the first player shows increased engagement later in the week, the second shows a decreased engagement toward the end of the week. One way of capturing this pattern of engagement is by defining three types of patterns: *increasing*, *stable*, and *decreasing*. We can then divide the whole period into three parts (Monday–Tuesday, Wednesday–Thursday, and Friday–Saturday–Sunday), adding the number of active days in the third period divided

Table 4.1 *Player activity per day.*

	Monday	Tuesday	Wednesday	Thursday	Friday	Saturday	Sunday
Player 1	×	—	—	×	—	×	×
Player 2	×	×	×	—	×	—	—

by the number of days in the third period, and dividing it by the total number of active days for the three periods divided by the total number of days. For the first player, we have $(2/3)/(4/7) = 1.15$; for the second player, we have $(1/3)/(4/7) = 0.58$. We can posit that values between 0 and 0.9 show a decreasing activity engagement; values between 0.9 and 1.1 show a stable activity engagement; and values above 1.1 show an increasing activity engagement. For more resources on this type of abstraction process, please refer to Chapter 13 of the *Game Analytics* book (Seif El-Nasr et al., 2013).

4.3 Feature extraction

Feature Extraction is usually employed when you do not have an idea how to reduce the dimension space from the raw data or when you think the raw data sits in a smaller dimensional space than what you currently have represented in your data. In such cases, a statistical approach to extract different dimensions from the raw data is applied. There are several algorithms used to extract features from raw data. In this chapter, we will discuss *Principal Component Analysis* (PCA).

It should be noted that traditionally statistically based feature extraction techniques are often used with ratio or interval measures. Ordinal or nominal measures need special handling, which we will discuss in Section 4.3.2.

4.3.1 PCA: Principal Component Analysis

PCA is a statistical technique used to reduce the dimensionality of data to a smaller set of dimensions that can better explain the data. It is possible that in some cases you may be collecting a high dimensional dataset with variables representing all user actions within the game. But, in reality, because of how the data is structured, there may be fewer variables that can explain variations between players. Discovering these fewer variables or metrics is the goal of PCA.

4.3.1.1 HOW DOES PCA WORK?

The basic idea behind PCA is to develop new dimensions, given the data, in the direction of the greatest variance. We take three specific data points from the *VPAL* dataset, specifically *Kills*, *Quest Completed*, and *Dialogues*. The three variables are shown in 3D in Figure 4.1 with colors denoting *gender*. Using PCA, we can reduce the dimension space from three dimensions to 2D or 1D but still group the points in a way that captures the variance.

PCA is a technique that computes n dimensions that fit the highest variance. Why the highest variance? Because the n dimension space with the highest variance represents dimensions that capture the highest separation for the points. See Figure 4.2.

Algorithm for PCA

Compute the covariance matrix $C = \frac{1}{n} \sum_{i=1}^{n} (x_i - \mu)(y_i - \mu)$. This matrix tells us the relationship between the variables in our data. μ is the mean, n is the number of data points, and x and y are points in our data.

Compute the eigenvectors for the given dimensions:
solve the equation: $\det(C - \lambda I) = 0$

find eigenvectors, i, by solving: $C\vec{e_i} = \lambda_i \vec{e_i}$

Using the eigenvectors, project the data to each eigenvector: $(\vec{x} - \mu)^T \cdot \vec{e_i}$

The algorithm for computing PCA is shown above. The algorithm relies on finding eigenvectors (Strang, 2016), because eigenvectors are vectors in the direction of the greatest variance in the data, which is what is useful to reduce the dimensionality of the data. The equation for computing eigenvectors is shown above; it relies on computing the covariance matrix. After computing all the eigenvectors, you would then select the eigenvectors that explain the most variance.

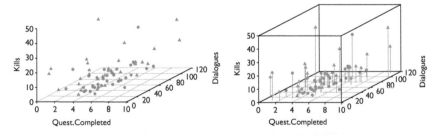

Figure 4.1 Plot of different points in 3D for VPAL variables: Kills, Quest Completed, and Dialogs. The orange- and gray-colored dots represent different genders.

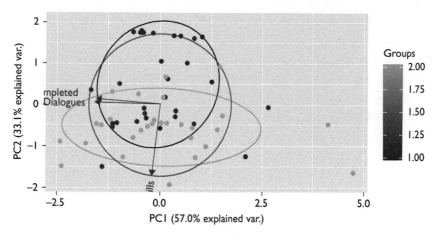

Figure 4.2 The data displayed in Figure 4.1 is projected here in 2D, PC1 and PC2, where PC1 explains 57% of the variance and PC2 explains 33.1% of the variance. Together, they account for 90.1% of the variance, reducing the space from 3D to 2D as shown. The colored dots differentiate between genders as in Figure 4.1.

Practical Note: Lab 4.1

Lab 4.1

Please see the supplemental materials for the book.

Goal of Lab 4.1

The lab goes over how you would go about using PCA on your dataset. For this lab, we will use the *DOTAlicious* dataset, which is available publicly as discussed earlier. The following discussion discusses the theory of the results, and the lab specifically takes you through the steps of how to perform PCA through R.

4.3.1.2 A PRACTICAL EXAMPLE OF APPLYING PCA

In order to understand how PCA is applied in practice, let us look at an example. Please also follow Lab 4.1 for all the details on using R. For the lab and the examples in this chapter, we will use the data described in Section 4.1. Remember that PCA works with ratio and interval measures, so if your data has any nominal or ordinal measures, these variables will need to be removed before performing PCA. We will discuss various solutions for dealing with nominal or ordinal measures in Section 4.3.2.

There are many libraries that can be used to perform PCA on data, and thus you will not be implementing the algorithm discussed earlier. However, it is important to understand the internal mechanics of the function you are about to use. In R, we use the *princomp* function, which is a standard function for performing PCA.

In the lab, we start with the data containing 15 features or variables; our aim is to use PCA to reduce this data into a smaller, more manageable number of variables. We use the *princomp* function on the dataset, which then results in a total of 15 Principal Components (PCs). However, the first six PCs account for 99% of the variance, as you can see from the output shown in Figure 4.3.

We can also plot the amount of variance explained per component using a scree plot, as shown in Figure 4.4. Using this plot, we can then use the Elbow method to identify what number of PCs we can use. The Elbow method is one of the most frequently used approaches to select parameters. It does not have an official definition. It is a heuristic that is interpreted as a rule of thumb in picking a parameter: given a chart that shows how a parameter (to be selected) affects a performance metric, the transition point in the chart between drastic and gradual changes is often the one that balances between the two conflicting objectives. In cases when there are more than one Elbow, further investigation is needed to decide which one is better, which is often done with some external or expert knowledge. From the figure, we can see that a solution with three or four PCs explain most of the variance in the data. These PCs are named *Comp. 1*, *Comp. 2*, *Comp. 3*, and *Comp. 4*.

```
## Importance of components:
##                            Comp.1          Comp.2          Comp.3          Comp.4
## Standard deviation         0.2490061       0.1498776       0.07757663      0.07397600
## Proportion of variance     0.6122428       0.2218080       0.05942452      0.05403629
## Cumulative proportion      0.6122428       0.8340508       0.89347533      0.9475162
##                            Comp.5          Comp.6          Comp.7          Comp.8
## Standard deviation         0.05490239      0.03434227      0.020597646     0.018707702
## Proportion of variance     0.02976366      0.01164560      0.004189277     0.003455769
## Cumulative proportion      0.97727528      0.98892089      0.993110164     0.996565934
##                            Comp.9          Comp.10         Comp.11         Comp.12
## Standard deviation         0.011669192     0.0092777855    0.0069625219    0.0061120547
## Proportion of variance     0.001344576     0.0008499483    0.0004786709    0.0003688743
## Cumulative proportion      0.997910510     0.9987604582    0.9992391291    0.9996080034
##                            Comp.13         Comp.14         Comp.15
## Standard deviation         0.0049497745    0.0032049407    2.219682e-03
## Proportion of variance     0.0002419216    0.0001014247    4.865028e-05
## Cumulative proportion      0.9998499250    0.9999513497    1.000000e+00
```

Figure 4.3 Resulting principal components and the variance explained.

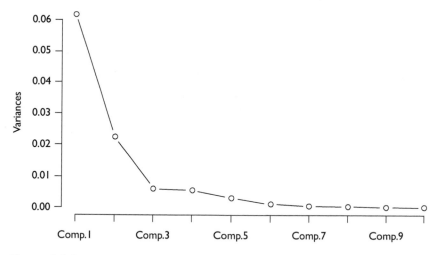

Figure 4.4 Scree Plot on the components to show how much variance each component explains.

So, what are these new variables, *Comp. 1* through *Comp. 15*? These components can be seen as linear combinations of the old variables, such as:

$$P_i = \lambda_{i1}x_1 + \lambda_{i2}x_2 + \cdots + \lambda_{in}x_n \qquad \text{(Equation 4.1)}$$

where x represents the old variables and P is the PC, n is the number of dimensions for the old variables, and λ is the loading or the coefficient for each variable.

As you may be able to see from the previous equation, PCA creates new dimensions or variables that are, in essence, linear combinations of the old dimensions/features. Thus, we can interpret the semantics of the new dimensions or variables as coefficients (called *loadings* in PCA) of the old variables. Figure 4.5 shows the components as proportions of the old variables; notice that we only use the quantitative variables, so *PlayerID* and *SkillLevel* are not included in the loadings.

By inspecting Figure 4.5, we see that:

- *Comp. 1* is composed of a vector of all the old variables.
- *Comp. 2* is composed of a vector of *Ditches*, *Points* (-ive), *KillsPerMin* (-ive), and *Deaths*.

```
##
## Loadings:
##
```

	Comp.1	Comp.2	Comp.3	Comp.4	Comp.5	Comp.6	Comp.7	Comp.8
## GamesPlayed	−0.253		0.106				−0.215	
## Gameswon	−0.257		0.104					−0.138
## GamesLeft	−0.243			−0.175	0.941	−0.126		
## Ditches	−0.272	0.107	−0.917	−0.142	−0.130	0.171		
## Points	−0.185	−0.102	−0.128	0.957	0.124			
## kills	−0.245		0.126			0.240	0.155	−0.184
## killsPerMin	−0.255	−0.952		−0.145				
## Deaths	−0.268	0.105				−0.287	−0.369	
## Assists	−0.250		0.110				−0.312	−0.162
## Creepskilled	−0.202		0.137			0.287	−0.108	
## CreepsDenied	−0.162		0.163			0.336	−0.548	
## Neutralskilled	−0.262						0.164	0.912
## TowersDestroyed	−0.260		0.111			0.352	0.361	−0.181
## RaxsDestroyed	−0.251		0.117			0.352	0.309	−0.165
## TotalTime	−0.422	0.151			−0.232	−0.591	0.330	−0.118

Figure 4.5 Loadings for each principal component.

- *Comp. 3* is composed of a vector of *GamesPlayed, GamesWon, Ditches* (-ive), *Points* (-ive), *Kills, Assists, CreepsKilled, CreepsDenied, Towers-Destroyed,* and *RaxsDestroyed.*
- *Comp. 4* is composed of a vector of *GamesLeft* (-ive), *Ditches* (-ive), *Points,* and *KillsPerMin* (-ive).

It is important to note that before you perform PCA or other feature extraction techniques on your data, you need to normalize the data as well as preprocess it using the steps discussed in Chapter 2. This is very important, especially scaling the data, because in the absence of scaling, you may end up with some features dominating others.

4.3.1.3 HOW TO USE THE PRINCIPLE COMPONENTS

Once the PCs are computed, you can then use them in place of the raw variables for statistical analysis or machine learning. For example, in the previous data, we had 16 original variables. Figure 4.6 shows the first 10 of them for the first 10 rows of the data. Alternatively, Figure 4.7 shows the four PCs we chose to use based on the previous discussion with their computed values. Given the dataset we have, we are only showing the first 10 rows of the data (same rows as in Figure 4.6). Thus, the two figures are showing the same dataset, but computed on different dimensions. Therefore, as you can see, using PCA would be very advantageous, because you can greatly reduce the dimensions of the data, and thus produce better ways to understand and visualize the data.

GamesPlayed <dbl>	GamesWon <dbl>	GamesLeft <dbl>	Ditches <dbl>	Points <dbl>	Kills <dbl>	KillsPerMin <dbl>	Deaths <dbl>	Assists <dbl>	CreepsKilled <dbl>
0.141362916	0.140589569	0.150	0.33333333	0.3502400	0.095653273	0.2857143	0.111196138	0.122157604	0.104006703
0.020602219	0.022108844	0.000	0.00000000	0.2624290	0.015710555	0.3095238	0.026489287	0.021663274	0.012018230
0.000633914	0.000000000	0.000	0.00000000	0.2697428	0.000463314	0.2619048	0.001648222	0.000523408	0.000475358
0.031378764	0.033446712	0.125	0.05555556	0.4348863	0.045446887	0.6190476	0.026371556	0.027159058	0.037421680
0.000000000	0.000566893	0.000	0.00000000	0.2841999	0.000379075	0.6666667	0.000117730	0.000290782	0.000077900
0.006339144	0.004535147	0.000	0.00000000	0.2413425	0.005601887	0.3095238	0.008476572	0.005815644	0.005518986
0.005071315	0.003968254	0.000	0.00000000	0.2110585	0.002990481	0.2380952	0.008241111	0.003634778	0.002255936
0.006656101	0.006235828	0.000	0.05555556	0.2667610	0.005475529	0.3571439	0.007652461	0.006106426	0.004608555
0.000633914	0.001133787	0.000	0.00000000	0.2697428	0.000758150	0.3571429	0.001000706	0.000872347	0.000410903
0.066561014	0.047619048	0.125	0.05555556	0.2159248	0.043551512	0.2619048	0.091770662	0.053125909	0.036226571

Figure 4.6 10 rows and 10 variables of the original data, which contains 41 variables.

	Comp.1	Comp.2	Comp.3	Comp.4
[1,]	−0.41249901	0.143095317	−0.176733531	−0.008830656
[2,]	0.05100857	−0.006979332	0.031466185	−0.001347351
[3,]	0.12116385	0.019770953	0.009566420	0.016809997
[4,]	−0.15454314	−0.297185679	−0.028702629	0.086350598
[5,]	0.01635120	−0.367585540	0.004088132	−0.028069785
[6,]	0.09634421	−0.017203135	0.019134450	−0.018880620
[7,]	0.12727492	0.051855242	0.020803130	−0.036761888
[8,]	0.06271613	−0.058896690	−0.034552857	−0.009426720
[9,]	0.09507808	−0.070520587	0.009556620	0.002915397
[10,]	−0.08630858	0.088631221	0.015590612	−0.080802234

Figure 4.7 10 rows for the four principal components that explain most of the variances in the data.

4.3.2 How do we deal with nominal and ordinal measures?

As discussed earlier, PCA works mostly for ratio or interval measures. So, what happens if your data is categorical (nonparametric, i.e., measured using an ordinal or nominal scale) or mixed? There are different methods to use for different types of data:

- PCA for ratio and interval measures.
- MCA (Multiple Correspondence Analysis) for categorical data.
- MFA (Multiple Factor Analysis) for ratio, interval, or categorical data but the data needs to be of the same type for any given group. There is an R package called MFAmixdata that includes a function called *MFAmix* to perform this type of analysis but with mixed data.
- PCAMIX for mix of categorical and ratio and interval measures. There is an R package called PCAmixdata that includes functions for handling mixed data as well as PCA and MCA.

The R package PCAmixdata provides us with different functions to deal with different types of measures. *PCAmix* is a function that allows us to perform feature extraction on quantitative and qualitative data. Lab 4.2 will go through an example showing you how to apply this method.

PCAmixdata uses a mixture of standard PCA used for numerical data and MCA used for categorical data (Chavent et al., 2017) to find loadings for both measures that can explain or model the data. "The procedure finds transformations of variables using the method of alternating least squares to optimize properties of the transformed variables' covariance or correlation matrices" (Chavent et al., 2017), or correlation ratios in case of categorical values. Similar to standard PCA, the result of the PCAmix procedure is a set of components to be used with loadings over all variables, as shown in the example used in the lab.

Practical Note: Lab 4.2

Lab 4.2

Please see the supplement materials for the book.

Goal of Lab 4.2

The lab goes over how you would go about using PCAmix on data that contains both categorical and numeric data.

4.3.3 Pros and cons of using PCA or PCAMix

As discussed earlier, using PCA, you can reduce the dimension space of your data. However, the new dimensions produced may not be interpretable since they combine many variables, and thus interpreting results using these dimensions can be problematic. Also, as shown in the previous section, PCA does not deal well with categorical data, and thus if you have many variables that are nominal or ordinal, PCA may not be a good option.

4.4 Feature selection

Feature selection is the process by which we select specific variables from the raw data and remove others from the analysis, because the variables chosen may be the most salient. So, how can you determine which features to keep and which to throw out? There exists some research to guide us with this question.

There are two main methods to determine which features are important, and therefore, you would want to keep. One way to do this is through a measure of information gain, which is a technique based on a statistical method called entropy, which we will define in more detail later. The other technique widely used for feature selection is to treat the problem as a search problem, in which you search for the best possible features to model the data. A good set of algorithms to use is greedy search algorithms. Greedy search algorithms are algorithms that use heuristics to calculate a solution that is locally optimal, where locally optimal means that the solution found may be best given all the solutions tried around it, though it may or may not be the best possible solution (i.e., global optimum). In this case, the greedy algorithm will add or remove a feature, and then assesses the current solution to determine how good it is, given the previous solutions.

Many different algorithms have been developed for searching a space of possibilities to find the best local optimal answer. One such search algorithms is Forward search, whereby you start with no features and continuously add a new feature, measuring how much better or worse the model is with the new feature set compared to without it. If the model is better with the new feature, then this feature is selected and the algorithm then moves on to add another feature, evaluates its utility, and so on. If not, it will try to select another feature to add and so on. A greedy *sequential forward selection* algorithm is shown as follows.

Algorithm for sequential forward feature selection

Start with empty set of features Y
Select a feature x that maximizes the following equation:

$$f(m(Y+x))$$

where f here is an evaluation function and m is the model developed given $Y+x$ features—m can be any kind of model, such as linear regression (LR; described in more detail in Chapter 7). Add that feature to the set Y

---

f in this algorithm is a way of scoring how well the data is modeled using the feature set. As we will see later, one can use many different modeling or prediction methods. In the example in the Lab 4.3, we chose to use LR (this method is defined in more detail in Chapter 7), but you can use any of the models discussed in Chapter 7. For now, we will just define a model m, which can be derived from the data given the features $Y+x$, and a function, f, which can evaluate how good that model is. Evaluation methods will be discussed in more detail in Chapter 8.

An advantage of this algorithm is that it is simple, and because it is greedy, it is also fast. However, a drawback is that it cannot remove features that may have become obsolete when other features are added. This is important to note as it can be a downside of a greedy approach.

Backward search is another search strategy, whereby you start with the full set of features and remove them one by one, checking to see if your model using these features produce similar results to the one before removing the set. If it is, then the feature was probably not as important. If not, then the algorithm will not remove that feature and will pick another feature to remove, and so on. A *sequential backward selection* algorithm is shown as follows.

Algorithm for sequential backward feature selection

Start with full set of features Y
Select a feature x that maximizes the following equation (note that we are maximizing the value after removing the feature in question):

$$f\left(m\left(Y - x\right)\right)$$

where f here is an evaluation function and m is the model developed given $Y{-}x$ features. Like with sequential forward search, m can be any kind of model, such as LR (described in more detail in Chapter 7).
Remove that feature from the set Y

This algorithm works well if you expect the final features to be large since it is initialized with the full set. The drawback of the algorithm, similar to the *sequential forward selection* algorithm, discussed earlier, is that when it discards a feature, it will not be able to re-evaluate it.

There are also other algorithms that have been used and proposed. For example:

- *Bidirectional search* is an algorithm that performs forward as well as backward selection with the constraint that the features selected by the forward process are not removed by the backward process, and features removed by the backward process are not added by the forward process.

- Other types of search. You can also imagine using other search algorithms to select features, given a heuristic function that tells us how well the feature is doing.

It should also be noted that backward and forward searches as well as other greedy search algorithms can ultimately result in different models as they find the local optimal solution rather than global optimal.

As you can see from the previous discussion, most of the algorithms for feature selection will rely on a measure of fitness for the feature or the model produced given the feature subset we have, and this corresponds to the function f, introduced earlier. There are generally several ways to estimate the fitness of the model. One way is based on a measure called Akaike Information Criterion (AIC), using a modeling method—for example, LR. Another is to use entropy, as briefly mentioned earlier.

4.4.1 AIC

AIC is a measure that compares the quality of several models to each other, determining the best model given the data. The basic formula for this measure is as follows:

$$AIC = 2k - 2ln(\hat{L}) \qquad \text{(Equation 4.2)}$$

where k is the number of parameters and $\hat{L}$ is the maximum value of the likelihood function, given the model. The likelihood function is a function that statically models the data, which is a measure of the model fit. We will discuss the likelihood function in more detail when we discuss machine learning algorithms in Chapters 6 through 9, where we will discuss in more detail how to model data for prediction or for exploratory analysis.

In the previous equation, we want to minimize the AIC, so the features with the lowest AIC will be best. As you can see from the equation, the measure of AIC is a mix of parameter numbers, k. The more the parameters, the worse the AIC value. The better the max likelihood you have given the model, the smaller the AIC is. As such, an optimal set of features according to AIC is one which balances the number of features (not too large) and its ability to capture the essence of the data.

In order to show how this will work with a dataset, we will need to use a function or process to develop a model—that is, a method to derive the likelihood function. In this example, we will use LR. *LR*, as we discussed earlier, will be discussed in more detail in Chapter 7. For the purposes of this section, we will provide a very simple introduction.

LR is a modeling technique in which you attempt to fit the data into a linear model of the form:

$$Y = AX_1 + BX_2 + \cdots + AAX_n + C \qquad \text{(Equation 4.3)}$$

Thus, the goal of the algorithm in this case is to find values for $A, B, \ldots, C$ given the data $X_1, \ldots, X_n$ that can give us the outcomes Y.

Given this modeling technique, we can then use the feature selection algorithms described earlier to select a subset of the features X_1 through X_n that minimizes this *AIC* values.

Practical Note: Lab 4.3

Lab 4.3

Please see the supplemental materials for the book.

Goal of Lab 4.3

The lab shows you how to use R to compute forward and backward feature selection using the league of legends dataset we used in the previous labs.

4.4.2 Information entropy

Another approach for understanding the importance of various features is the measure of entropy. Entropy is a measure developed in information theory, which can be used to estimate a measure of event predictability. An event with high entropy is one that is hard to predict, while one with low entropy is easy to predict. To give you an intuitive understanding of this concept, let us consider a coin toss where the coin has a 50/50 chance of landing on heads vs. tails. This event will have a high entropy, because there is no way to predict what the outcome will be with better than a probability of 0.5. If the coin was biased with heads 90% of the time, then the entropy would be lower, as the probability of us predicting heads is greater. Given this example, note that high entropy features split the population of observation roughly in half, while low entropy features split the population in a much more skewed manner.

Let us look at another example. Table 4.2 shows an example of a discrete dataset. Our target here is to figure out if the player will win or lose the game. Win/loss depends on several variables: Experience of the group (*Experience*), Playing Solo, with Friends or with Strangers (*Team*), Difficulty of the Game (*Difficulty*), and whether the team has played before together or not (*Played-Before*). In the data shown in Table 4.2, we have *Outcome* (your target variable): 9 Wins and 5 Losses. We can calculate the entropy for these outcome variables without taking into account any other factors, given the following equation:

$$-\left(\frac{P}{P+N} log_2 \frac{P}{P+N} + \frac{N}{P+N} log_2 \frac{N}{P+N} \right) \qquad \text{(Equation 4.4)}$$

where P is the number of positive cases and N is the number of negative cases. In our example, we can compute the entropy of the *outcome* variable, given the dataset in Table 4.2 as:

$$Entropy_{Outcome} = -\left(\frac{9}{14} log_2 \frac{9}{14} + \frac{5}{14} log_2 \frac{5}{14} \right)$$

$$= -(0.64 \cdot -0.64 + 0.36 \cdot -1.47) = 0.94 \qquad \text{(Equation 4.5)}$$

Table 4.2 *Example of discrete data for playing a game.*

Experience	Team	Difficulty	PlayedBefore	Outcome
Mixed	Solo	Normal	T	Win
Mixed	WithFriends	High	F	Win
Mixed	WithFriends	Normal	F	Win
Mixed	WithStrangers	High	T	Win
Newbies	Solo	Normal	T	Loss
Newbies	WithStrangers	High	T	Loss
Newbies	Solo	Normal	F	Win
Newbies	WithStrangers	High	F	Win
Newbies	WithStrangers	Normal	F	Win
ExperiencedGroup	WithFriends	High	F	Loss
ExperiencedGroup	WithFriends	High	T	Loss
ExperiencedGroup	WithStrangers	High	F	Loss
ExperiencedGroup	Solo	Normal	F	Win
ExperiencedGroup	WithStrangers	Normal	T	Win

For each of the variables, we can calculate its entropy as follows:

- *Experience* has three values: "Newbies," "ExperiencedGroup," and "Mixed."

We can calculate the entropy for each one as follows.
For "Mixed," all *Outcome* variables are a "Win":

$$-\left(\frac{4}{4}log_2\frac{4}{4}\right) = 0$$

For "Newbies," 3 "Win" and 2 "Loss"

$$-\left(\frac{3}{5}log_2\frac{3}{5} + \frac{2}{5}log_2\frac{2}{5}\right) = 0.97$$

For "ExperiencedGroup," 2 "Win" and 3 "Loss," similar to "Newbies" entropy:

$$-\left(\frac{2}{5}log_2\frac{2}{5} + \frac{3}{5}log_2\frac{3}{5}\right) = 0.97$$

$$Entropy_{Experience} = \frac{4}{14} \cdot 0 + \frac{5}{14} \cdot 0.97 + \frac{5}{14} \cdot 0.97 = 0.69$$

- *Team* has three values: "Strangers," "Solo," and "WithFriends."

We can calculate the entropy for each one as follows.
For "Solo": 3 "Win," 1 "Loss"

$$-\left(\frac{3}{4}log_2\frac{3}{4} + \frac{1}{4}log_2\frac{1}{4}\right) = 0.81$$

For "WithFriends," 2 "Win" and 2 "Loss"

$$-\left(\frac{2}{4}log_2\frac{2}{4} + \frac{2}{4}log_2\frac{2}{4}\right) = 1$$

For "Strangers," 4 "Win" and 2 "Loss"

$$-\left(\frac{4}{6}log_2\frac{4}{6} + \frac{2}{6}log_2\frac{2}{6}\right) = 0.92$$

$$Entropy_{Team} = \frac{4}{14} \cdot 0.81 + \frac{4}{14} \cdot 1 + \frac{6}{14} \cdot 0.92 = 0.91$$

- *Difficulty* has two values: "Normal" and "High"

For "Normal": 6 "Win" and 1 "Loss"

$$-\left(\frac{6}{7}log_2\frac{6}{7} + \frac{1}{7}log_2\frac{1}{7}\right) = 0.59$$

For "High," 2 "Win" and 5 "Loss"

$$-\left(\frac{2}{7}log_2\frac{2}{7} + \frac{5}{7}log_2\frac{5}{7}\right) = 0.86$$

$$Entropy_{Difficulty} = \frac{7}{14} \cdot 0.59 + \frac{7}{14} \cdot 0.86 = 0.725$$

- *PlayedBefore* is "T" or "F"

For "F," 6 "Win" and 2 "Loss"

$$-\left(\frac{6}{8}log_2\frac{6}{8} + \frac{2}{8}log_2\frac{2}{8}\right) = 0.81$$

For "T," 3 "Win" and 3 "Loss"

$$-\left(\frac{3}{6}log_2\frac{3}{6} + \frac{3}{6}log_2\frac{3}{6}\right) = 0.88$$

$$Entropy_{PlayedBefore} = \frac{8}{14} \cdot 0.81 + \frac{6}{14} \cdot 0.88 = 0.84$$

Then, we can calculate *information gain* for each attribute, which denotes a decrease in entropy and in essence defines how much information is in each variable. This is calculated as entropy of the *outcome*—entropy of the *variable*, as follows:

- For *Experience* = Entropy of *outcome*—Entropy of *Experience* = 0.94 − 0.69 = 0.25
- For *Team* = Entropy of *outcome*—Entropy of *Team* = 0.94 − 0.91 = 0.03

- For *Difficulty* = Entropy of *outcome*—Entropy of *Difficulty* = 0.94 − 0.725 = 0.215
- For *PlayedBefore* = Entropy of *outcome*—Entropy of *PlayedBefore* = 0.94 − 0.84 = 0.1

Once we get the *information gain* for the different features or variables, we can then deduce the importance of the feature, given others. The feature with the highest *information gain* is the one you would want to choose. Thus, from the previous information, we would want to choose *Experience* as the important feature. You can then repeat the process by selecting the next most-important feature, and so on.

Later, in Chapter 7, we will discuss decision trees, a data modeling technique that uses entropy to develop a tree to model how different features factor in the *target* prediction. There, we will return to *information gain* and show a different example, as well as experiment using different datasets.

4.5 Summary

In summary, we have discussed different ways to reduce the dimensionality of game data:

- Feature engineering: The process by which an expert develops a set of features or metrics based on his/her own knowledge of the game or domain. It is important to note that many industry groups use the metrics we discussed in Chapter 1 (for more examples, see Seif El-Nasr et al., 2013). This is due to the amount of control one can have in developing such a set of metrics. Also, such metrics provide parallels to many business metrics that have been developed by other industries. This makes it easier to use these metrics in reporting and general communication.
- Feature extraction: The process where statistical models are used to develop new dimensions from the features in the raw dataset as a way to reduce dimensionality. This technique is popular; however, as you can see, it is hard to integrate different measurement types. Often, the low dimensional space is not as explainable, meaning that the new dimensions do not have a clear meaning to the designer, thereby limiting the explainable power of the models that use them.

- Feature selection: A set of techniques where a search is used to select the best features that represent the space. The technique is easy, but as with any search algorithm, it is often the case that it is difficult to converge on a global optimal. Thus, the different search methods used may provide different solutions. Further, the technique depends on the existence of a way to measure the quality of different variables or models produced, and this measure typically depends on the model produced and may be different based on what the designer or researcher is modeling.

Further, we have also covered detailed examples of how to perform these methods on game data. We used *DOTA* data, but you can use other datasets as an exercise.

● ●

EXERCISES

1. What is dimensional reduction? Why is it useful?
2. What is the difference between feature engineering, feature selection, and feature extraction techniques?
3. Using the *VPAL* data and the metrics discussed in Chapter 1, select three appropriate metrics for the data. Use R to develop simple functions that would derive these metrics given the *VPAL* data.
4. Given the *VPAL* dataset, perform dimension reduction to produce some meaningful data that would allow us to understand how players are different based on the time they spent in different areas. Explain the dimensions of the data and detail the algorithms or the equations you would use to reduce the logs to get the dimensions needed for this task.
5. Given time spent data from the *VPAL* dataset you produced for exercise 4, perform PCA on the data to see if the dimensions can be reduced. Explain your results.
6. Given the *VPAL* data, use feature selection techniques to reduce the dimensionality of the data given that the outcome is to predict *Extroversion* scores for players in the data. For this exercise, you need to use personality scores for players. Note that we did not use this data before. Therefore, please familiarize yourself with these scores, see the dataset included with the book, it contains a file explaining the different measures. The scores of the personality survey comes from the IPIP-NEO which ranks players based on five traits: openness, conscientiousness, extroversion, agreeableness, and neuroticism. There is a file documenting a key to variable names for each variable collected.
7. We discussed two techniques for feature selection: backward and forward searches. But there are other search techniques, such as best-first, etc. Select a technique that is

not discussed in the chapter, implement it, and compare the results with the backward and forward search results for *VPAL* (Exercise 7) and *DOTA* data (in the labs).

• •

BIBLIOGRAPHY

Chavent, M., Kuentz-Simonet, V., Labenne, A., and Saracco, J. (2017). *Multivariate analysis of mixed data: The R package PCAmixdata*. arXiv preprint arXiv:1411.4911.

Guo, Y., and Iosup, A. (2012). The game trace archive: A technical report. *TU Delft*. URL: http://gta.st.ewi.tudelft.nl/

Javvaji, N., Harteveld, C., and Seif El-Nasr, M. (2020). Understanding player patterns by combining knowledge-based data abstraction with interactive visualization. *CHI Play*.

Lavrenko, V. (2015). Dimensionality reduction and PCA. *YouTube*. URL: https://www.youtube.com/watch?v=6Pv2txQVhxA&list=PLBv09BD7ez_4InDh85LM_43Bsw0cFDHdN&index=7. Last accessed October 2, 2017.

Liao, T. W. (2005). Clustering of time series data—A survey. *Pattern Recognition*, 38(11), 1857–74.

Mailolo, A. (2017). Principle component analysis using truncated SVD. URL: https://antonio-maiolo.com/2016/03/02/principal-component-analysis-using-truncated-svd/. Last accessed October 2, 2017.

Moskovitch, R., and Shahar, Y. (2005). Temporal data mining based on temporal abstractions. In *ICDM-05 Workshop on Temporal Data Mining*.

Seif El-Nasr, M., Drachen, A., and Canossa, A. (2013). *Game Analytics: Maximizing the Value of Player Data*. London, UK: Springer.

Shahar, Y. (1997). A framework for knowledge-based temporal abstraction. *Artificial Intelligence*, 90(1–2), 79–133.

Strang, G. (2016). *Introduction to linear algebra* (5th Edition). Wellesley, MA: Wellesley Cambridge Press.

## CHAPTER 5

Data Analysis through Visualization

One of the most effective methods for exploratory analysis is *visualization*. Game data analysis and communication of results of such analysis are not easy processes. The sequential and contextual nature of gameplay actions makes it hard to understand user behavior and infer the user's goals, intent, plans, and preferences. In this chapter, we will discuss how visualization can be used to allow analysts to make such inferences. However, to be able to do this, the visualization system itself needs to be capable of handling multidimensional spaces. Therefore, when discussing how visualization can be used as part of the analysis process, we will also discuss visualization systems and tools that have been proposed and are currently used for this purpose.

Throughout this book, we used different types of visualization tools to communicate analysis or compare results. For example, in Chapters 2 and 3, we used bar charts and line graphs to show data distributions. In Chapter 10, we introduced the TraMineR package, which enabled us to see sequential and temporal data through charts and colored sequences or actions. In this chapter, we will discuss other tools and systems and their uses. In particular, it should be noted that we will focus our discussion here on visualization tools and systems that are used for analysis of player behaviors. We will not focus on communicating aggregate results or distributions of data since these were covered in other chapters.

Game Data Science. Magy Seif El-Nasr, Truong Huy Nguyen Dinh, Alessandro Canossa, and Anders Drachen, Oxford University Press. © Magy Seif El-Nasr, Truong Huy Nguyen Dinh, Alessandro Canossa, and Anders Drachen (2021). DOI: 10.1093/oso/9780192897879.003.0005

With this focus, we will discuss the following:

- Heatmaps: Heatmaps are aggregate[1] visualizations on top of game maps that use color coding to show high density regions in the map. The visualized variables can be *kills, deaths, gold collection*, or other variables of interest to the designer/analyst.
- Spatio-temporal visualization systems: Spatio-temporal visualization systems are systems that show game actions over time overlaid on the game map. They usually allow designers and analysts to zoom into a specific time window or play a specific segment within the game to better understand sequences of behaviors within a game for multiple players across multiple playthroughs.
- State-action transition visualization systems: State-action transitions are basic elements of problem-solving behaviors, showing a game state and an action that a player or group of players took. Using such visualizations, analysts and designers can more deeply understand the problem-solving strategies that their players took or where players failed to deduce design problems in terms of puzzles or mechanics.

We will introduce different labs that focus on these types of visualizations. Therefore, the chapter will be composed of the following labs:

- **Lab 5.1:** This lab specifically looks at how to generate heatmaps. For this, we will use Tableau—a visualization tool that is very handy for visualizing different types of data.
- **Lab 5.2:** This lab specifically looks at spatio-temporal visualizations. For this visualization, we will use a tool developed in the Game User Interaction and Intelligence (GUII) lab.
- **Lab 5.3:** This lab focuses on state-action transition visualization systems. For this type of visualization, we will use a tool also developed in the GUII lab.

5.1 Heatmaps

5.1.1 What are heatmaps?

First, let us define what a *heatmap* is. A heatmap is a 2D graph representing data using colors that signify hot (red/orange) and cool (blue) areas. The use of color

---

[1] Where variables are aggregated over time (e.g., total kills over time).

can signify the frequency of that particular variable visualized. This is appealing to game analysts because it is intuitive. The use of hot and cool colors makes it very easy to use as a communicative tool. There are many examples of the use of heatmaps with game data that was published in many venues, including academia and industry. Examples include Drachen and Canossa's (2009) use of heatmaps with *Tomb Raider*'s data to look at areas that are lethal, signifying a very high number of deaths, circled in red. Another good example is the use of heatmaps to see congestions in the maps of *Assassin's Creed* (see Dankoff, 2014).

5.1.2 Heatmaps—Practical guide

To give you a better idea of how these heatmaps are generated, we will explore the generation of heatmaps from a dataset publicly available on kaggle. In particular, the research team, composed of students in Dr Seif El-Nasr's class, was interested in analyzing data from *PlayerUnknown's Battlegrounds* (*PUBG*). *PUBG* is an online, multiplayer, battle royal game developed by *PUBG* Corporation. The game takes place on an island, in which 100 players are parachuted when they log in. The last player standing is the winner of the game. As players enter the game, they start by looking for weapons within the island that they can use to fight each other or defend themselves from getting killed. The game area decreases over time. Through this game, the team wanted to explore kill ratios and weapons used for kills given different game areas within the game. For example, the team hypothesized that there may be specific advantage locations for sniping where we see more kills with a sniper rifle.

Practical Note: Lab 5.1

Lab 5.1

Please see the supplemental materials for the book.

Goal of Lab 5.1

The lab introduces the process of creating a heatmap from game data using Tableau as a visualization system.

The team then created a heatmap to show where the most kills by rifle happened, shown in Figure 5.1. The map showed areas where some kills by rifle happened in green, but the most significant areas for kills by rifle were the ones highlighted in orange/red. Through this visualization, it is then easy to see if the hypothesis was valid or not by inspecting the areas highlighted in red/orange.

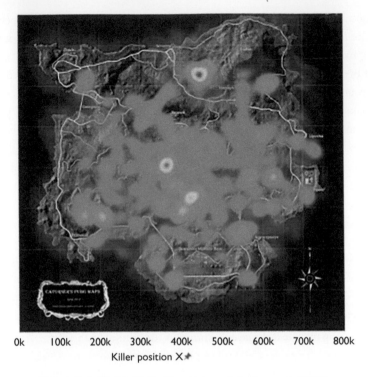

0k   100k   200k   300k   400k   500k   600k   700k   800k

Killer position X ✦

Figure 5.1 Kills by rifle for *PlayerUnknown's Battlegrounds (PUBG)*.

5.1.3 Heatmaps and their use

The games industry has been using this technique to understand issues with level design. For example, Bungie used heatmaps to show player deaths and to balance the design of their multiplayer maps in *Halo 3* (see Thompson, 2007). There are many visualization tools and add-ons that have been proposed by both researchers and industry analysts. For example, *Unity Analytics* now provides methods to show heatmaps of player movements through the level.

5.1.4 Current state of the art of heatmaps

A very good review of heatmaps, overlays, and operations on heatmaps, as well as trajectory visualization can be found in Drachen and Schubert (2013). For example, there has been some work done in integrating binary operators and aggregations over heatmaps. Since these are more advanced topics, we will not discuss them here, but interested readers are encouraged to read more on this topic and look into the Game Developers Conference talks or academic conferences, such as CHI Play, Foundations of Digital Games (FDG), or Conference of Human Factors in Computing conference (CHI) for more work in this area.

However, it should be noted that heatmaps, while useful for shedding light on level design issues and navigational problems, they fail to deliver a more granular look at issues with game content or level design mechanics, such as navigational problems. They also do not give us a good idea of the users' experiences, including users' preferences, immersion, engagement, breakdowns, and emotions. For example, it is hard to see problem-solving issues or breakdowns in such an aggregated view. Other systems discussed next were developed to remedy these shortcomings.

5.2 Spatio-temporal visualization systems

Spatio-temporal visualization systems are visualization systems that are concerned with viewing game variables over time within the game map. A literature review of relevant visualization systems proposed by academia and industry can be found in Wallner and Kriglstein (2013). We will discuss some example systems here.

5.2.1 Visualizing flow

One of the very early systems developed for looking at player traces through time and space is the VU-Flow (Chittaro, Ranon, and Leronutti, 2006). In this system, the idea is to show the traces of players as they navigate within the 3D environment as paths through a 2D overhead representation of a map (see Figure 5.2). The system views aggregated and non-aggregated data. In the non-aggregated view, a user color is chosen and a path for the user is shown as a line. Figure 5.2(a), for example, shows multiple users navigating through a specific game level. The system will generally allow filtering users, color coding users, and zooming in and out of the map. Because such graphs can become cluttered very quickly, VU-Flow allows for several ways to aggregate paths. They developed four ways to aggregate the data:

- Density maps based on time spent. Figure 5.2(b) shows an aggregation by factoring in time (i.e., color density in the graph represents how much time users spent in a certain area).

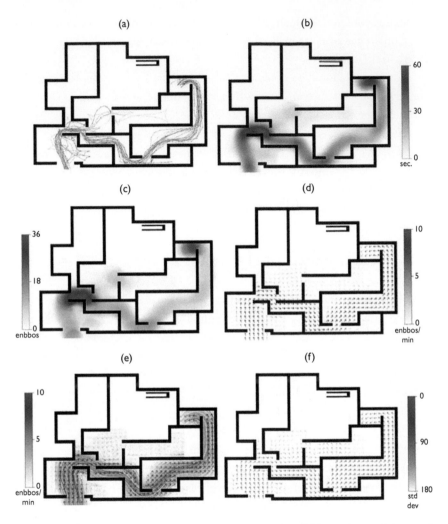

Figure 5.2 This figure shows the different systems for *VU-Flow* (Chittaro, Ranon, & Leronutti, 2006): (a) different user paths through the game environment; (b)–(f) different types of aggregations of movement and time. Figure reproduced with permission from IEEE. Original figure appeared in Chittaro, L., Ranon, R., and Ieronutti, L. (2006). Vu-flow: A visualization tool for analyzing navigation in virtual environments, *IEEE Transactions on Visualization and Computer Graphics*, 12(6), 1475–1485.

- Density maps based on how many users went through the same paths. Figure 5.2(c) shows a visualization of the number of users as the aggregate measure for color density.
- Flow visualizations. Figures 5.2(d–f) show aggregations of user flow. In these visualizations, the direction of each arrow is calculated as an

aggregate sum of all directions of movement from the considered area. Color is used to show the intensity of flow (d) or standard deviation (f).

Such visualizations provide a great advantage for game developers as they can allow them to explore the style and preferences of their players and perhaps build better player profiles. They can also allow them to test navigational aids and level design issues for better design tuning.

Building on this approach, there are several systems proposed to understand how players move and navigate in game spaces. Each of these systems explores a new approach or angle adding to the VU-Flow described earlier. For example, Gagné, Seif El-Nasr, and Shaw (2011) developed a visualization system using a similar approach to VU-Flow where the visualization shows user movement traces, but they split the visualization into two panels denoting win/loss. Such a split allowed designers to compare loss and win patterns and understand how players learned to win.

Another system developed by Moura, Seif El-Nasr, and Shaw (2011) extended this visualization approach to allow for more scalable data visualization, where multiple different player actions are displayed and not just movement. So, instead of just showing player movement traces as lines, the visualization uses circles of varying width to depict different actions, such as talking to nonplayer characters (NPCs) (in red) and interactions with items (in blue). The visualization also uses green to show player traces; however, instead of just showing a trace of moment-to-moment movement, it shows a different line-based chart that visualizes lines between the different game zones, to show the traces. Further, the visualization also uses different charts displaying different information, such as how many items the player interacted with and at what point in time and how many times they visited or revisited different areas. It should be noted that this is a more complex visualization showing very granular interactions per player. However, the work did not address how to scale such visualizations for many players to investigate cumulative effects or patterns across different player types. This was left as future work.

While all these systems present great work to show players' movement and how they interact with different parts of the game, they are often developed for research purposes and are not publicly available, making them hard to use without further investment in recreating them. To give you a sense of what these systems are like and how to interact with them, we will discuss a related system called Stratmapper.

5.2.2 Stratmapper

Stratmapper is a spatio-temporal visualization system developed in the GUII lab. StratMapper, similar to the systems described earlier, visualizes players' movement as well as game variables over time and over spatial maps. Using such visualization, you can see how players played the game in a more granular way. Further, Stratmapper incorporates several features that make it easier to interact with the visualization for further analysis of players' strategies. Figure 5.3 shows a screenshot of the interface. One noteworthy feature is the space–time constraint modifiers, which allows users to impose a specific spatial and temporal constraint on queries, effectively limiting the amount of data visualized to a small set. This improves the analysts' capability of honing down to specific action and decreases visual overload. In the timeline (shown in the figure), users can select a temporal period of interest with the brush component, which places a start and end time for the data query. Figure 5.4 shows screenshot of such interaction mechanisms. Events listed on the timeline can also be filtered using a mute function, which removes that particular event type from the timeline and map.

It is easier to show the functionality of this system using a video—please see this link to view the video: https://vimeo.com/385250946)—which discusses the features of the interface and how the data is visualized. As you can see from the video, there are several functionalities provided by the system to allow users to control and filter what they see. This can be very effective for analyzing specific actions or following strategies as they evolve within a team match.

Another functionality that we found useful to add to StratMapper is labeling or annotating the action. In particular, see the following video to see how users can select units, event types, and time to identify and abstract higher order events on the map from the returned selection (video link: https://vimeo.com/385251490). The system then includes a labeling or annotation component, which enables users to save these selections of units, event types, and time as singular abstractions. These labeled higher order events can then be recalled and visualized automatically in StratMapper or exported for use in other applications. Further, they can also be shared among a group of analysts for discussion and collaborative analysis.

Lab 5.2 includes practical steps of how to use Stratmapper to look through various scenarios. In the lab, we provide a set of behavioral labels that have already been applied to the data. We will walk you through navigating the interface and understanding what these labels mean, how to read them, and

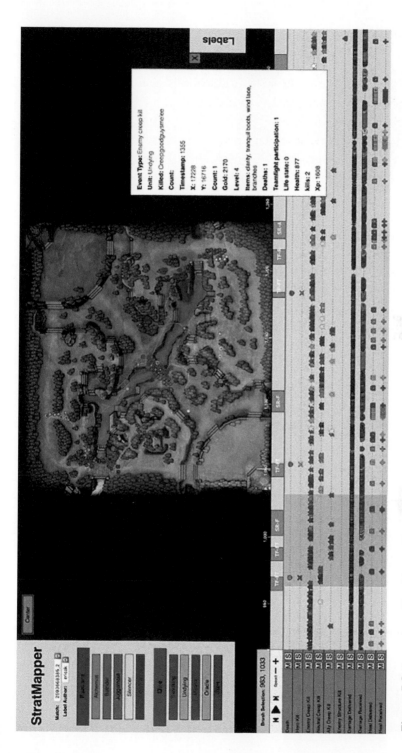

Figure 5.3 Screenshot of StratMapper: The interface shows the map in the center, which can be zoomed in and out, as well as shifted in two dimensions. In the top left, selection tools are available for matches, label authors, teams, and individual players. Pictured on the right is a tooltip that displays relevant event statistics on icon hover. At the bottom is the timeline with a list of events in this match, all of which can be toggled in and out. This component can be zoomed and shifted as well. The colors in the timeline correspond to different player icons visualized on the map.

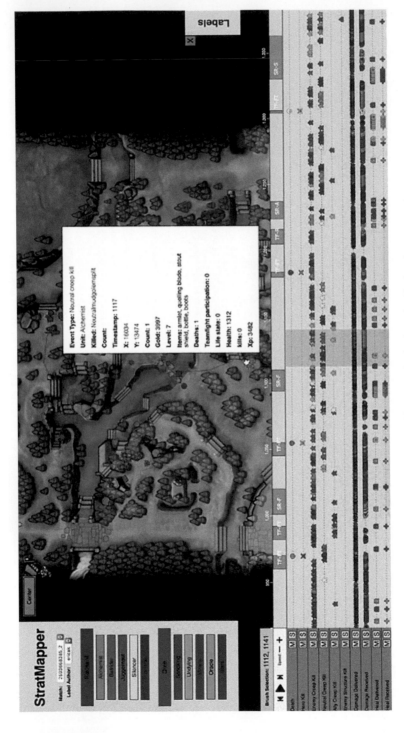

Figure 5.4 Screenshot of *StratMapper* showing the timeline with temporal selection using the brush component.

how to derive meaningful information from them. For a refresher on unit and event selection, as well as how an analyst might explore players' behaviors using Stratmapper, please review this video: https://vimeo.com/385251490. Further, a link for working with Stratmapper can be found at https://sm-dota-v2-ro.herokuapp.com/.

Practical Note: Lab 5.2

Lab 5.2

Please see the supplemental materials for the book.

Goal of Lab 5.2

The lab introduces the *Stratmapper* interface and walks you through looking at labels for player behavior and deriving meaning from them.

5.2.3 Current state of the art of spatio-temporal visualization systems

The work in this area is still ongoing. We discussed some work to show how some game variables or events can be filtered and visualized through a spatio-temporal visualization. There are several systems that have been proposed to aggregate other playtesting data beyond just game logs and visualize them on the game map. Interested readers are invited to continue exploring this work as it is an active area of research. Most of this work is published in conferences such as Game Developers Conference, Conference on Human Factors in Computing Systems, CHI Play and Foundations of Digital Games, among other game specific conferences.

An interesting example of this ongoing work is the work of Wallner, Halabi and Mirza-Babaei (2019). In their work, they aggregated various variables such as survey responses of the player, player's physiological measures, and game log data. They investigated various ways to integrate this data on the game map. They used the *DBSCAN* clustering algorithm (review Chapter 6) to cluster events happening in the same space and placed them on the game map. They then partitioned the game space into smaller cells based on player movement and colored these cells based on the arousal values collected from physiological measures. They also aggregated movements showing varying thickness of lines indicating the amount of movement. They conducted studies with designers to evaluate their visualizations. Game designers liked this visualization as it was integrated and less cluttered than a non-aggregated view of the same data. However, there is still room for improvement as designers raised issues with extracting information due to the overlays used to mask some of the game-level details.

5.3 State-action transition visualization systems

State-action transition type visualizations are more concerned with how players made decisions given the game's state. This is often useful because it allows designers to understand players' strategies. Designers can also use such analysis to understand how to tune difficulty or to determine how to best balance or pace the game content and skills. Further, such analysis can also shed light on dominant strategies found by players or other unexpected solutions to game obstacles.

5.3.1 Representing states and actions

Game state is the virtual context which would typically include the factors inside the game that directly or indirectly relate to the actions that players make. This is similar to Jasper Juul's (2004) definition of game state using the metaphor of state machines, where a player performs an action, and the game calculates a response. These responses trigger an update to the game state (the state describes the global state of the game), and the player is then confronted with new choices to perform a new action. We can envision game playing as a cyclical process of players performing actions, followed by updates to the game state.

To visualize and understand players' decision-making processes through the game state, one must define players' actions and the game state as well as identify how the game state changes as the player makes decisions within the game. Such information is not usually recorded within the log file but can be computed from the log data. For example, by knowing the players' position, we can deduce the spatial context, such as how many team members are around them, how many enemies are around them, and whether they are hidden by trees or other spatial elements in the level.

To give you a clearer example of how this state representation can be calculated from game actions, let us take a simple puzzle game. The game is called

WuzzitTrouble, developed by BrainQuake Games to teach algebraic math to middle school students. The game is composed of a simple screen showing a creature called "Wuzzit" behind the bars, which the player needs to set free. The game screen is composed of a big wheel with several items on it at different steps. The player can interact with the game by rotating the cog found at the contour of the big wheel (see screenshots in Figure 5.5). The cog can be turned clockwise or counterclockwise in some increments per turn. The player needs to collect keys and bonus items in order to clear the level and to free the Wuzzit. Figure 5.5 shows two players starting in one start state shown in blue performing actions signified by edges taking them to intermediate game states in yellow to finally get to the end state in red.

When choosing a representation for game states, however, one can imagine that defining such a game state can include previous game states, players' game states, goals, and how far each player is from their goals. Therefore, we can add more information to the game state to get a better picture of what the player was confronting as they made their decisions. A question that arises is as follows: is all this information necessary? The more information we add to the game state, the bigger the dimensions for our visualization and analysis space. Therefore, most often, we will need to be strategic about how much information we want to use for the game state to constrain our visualization space and make our analysis tractable. One can also use dimension reduction techniques (discussed in Chapter 4) to define states or clustering algorithms (discussed in Chapter 6) to cluster states, similar to what was done in Wallner and Kriglstein (2012).

5.3.2 Visualizing state-actions in games

Most visualization systems proposed to visualize game state-action transitions use node-link visualizations (similar to what is shown in Figure 5.5). In the GUII lab, we developed a similar visualization, called "Glyph." Glyph has an added feature of a window showing clustered patterns. This window is shown alongside the state-action transition graphs. When one selects a pattern from this window, the corresponding state-action transitions are shown. This allows analysts to navigate similar patterns and identify different ones. We will discuss this interface in more detail later. It should be noted that Glyph has been published in Nguyen, Seif El-Nasr, and Canossa (2015); we refer the readers to this article for more information.

Glyph visualization has two components: a state window and a sequence window, as shown in Figure 5.6. The state window (on the left) displays a

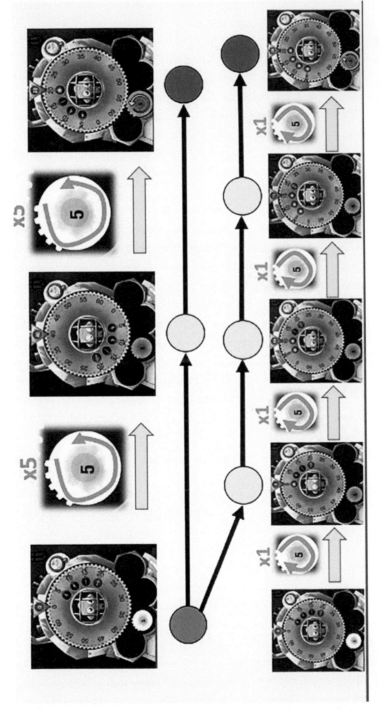

Figure 5.5 Two traces through the *Wuzzit* trouble game. One player (on top) did two actions to get from start (blue node) to end (red node). Other player (bottom) performed four actions to make the same transition. Nodes in these graphs show different game states.

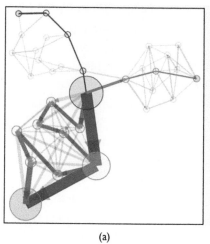 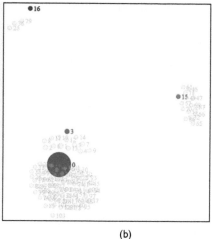

(a)   (b)

Figure 5.6 *Glyph* two-window visualization of game action: (a) state graph and (b) sequence graph. The graph shows a user highlighting four patterns, one from each cluster and two from the biggest cluster in the bottom left of the sequence graph.

graph visualization represented in a node-link diagram, where a path through the game will be composed of different nodes; one node (in blue) represents the start of the game, another (in red) represents the end of the game, and others are intermediate nodes. Each arrow from one node to another represents a transition—a decision or an action made by a player or a team. On the other hand, the sequence window (on the right) represents different sequences represented as nodes. Each node represents a corresponding pattern of state-action transitions from start of the level to the end of the level represented in the state graph.

   Therefore, as players engage with the game, they navigate within game states represented in this visualization. In general, a game state captures all information associated with in-game entities that affect players' choice of actions. For instance, in a shooter game, a game state could consist of information on the player's current position, health level, wielded weapon, carried item, and similar information of surrounding NPCs.

   To facilitate the comparison of individual action sequences, analysts use and interact with the sequence graph, which shows the popularity and similarity of sequence patterns exhibited by users (Figure 5.5). As mentioned earlier, each node in the sequence window represents a full play trace. The node size implies popularity. The distance between each node in this sequence window provides a visual representation of how dissimilar corresponding action sequences are. We used *Dynamic Time Warping (DTW)* (Berndt and Clifford, 1994) to compute the similarity measure. *DTW* (see Chapter 10) is a dynamic programming algorithm that computes the difference of sequences by comparing items between the involved sequences. *DTW* takes as input a metric function d (s1, s2) that returns the difference (i.e., dissimilarity) between any pair of items (or states) s1, s2 in the sequences. This measure is similar to optimal matching, a method discussed in Cornwell (2015; see Chapter 10). When using Glyph with a new dataset, defining a suitable metric function is extremely important as it will greatly affect how the nodes are arranged in the graphs and thus how clusters form.

Utilizing synchronized visual information presentation, the interface provides multiple perspectives on the same data at different levels of granularity, allowing instant examination of play data at different scales.

5.3.3 Using state-action transition visualization to compare players' dialog choices

Let us take an example to show you the power of this system. For this example, we will be using dialog data collected from the *VPAL* game used in the previous chapters. For more information on the game, please refer to Appendix A. Figure 5.7 displays 48 players' branching dialog choices from one conversation with a quest giving NPC within *VPAL*. There are closeup screenshots in Figures 5.8 and 5.9. Upon speaking with the NPC, players will receive some information about their surroundings and have a number of dialog options to choose from to converse with the NPC. These dialog options can reveal more information about the area and ultimately result in the player receiving a quest to chase away a group of bikers. To complete the quest, the player needs to return to the NPC to report that the bikers are gone.

In this example, each state in the state graph represents the quest giver's dialog that the player "heard," while the transitions between the states represent the player's chosen dialog options. For example, "Howdy stranger, you look like the capable sort" is the first node and something the NPC says. One transition line from this node to an adjacent node is "I always have a minute to talk," which represents one of several response options the player has. The other transitions to adjacent nodes represent other response options. Representing the data like this allows us to identify the flow of the conversation between the player and the NPC, such as how long they spoke for, whether they were friendly or rude, and what information they were most interested in hearing from the NPC (e.g.,

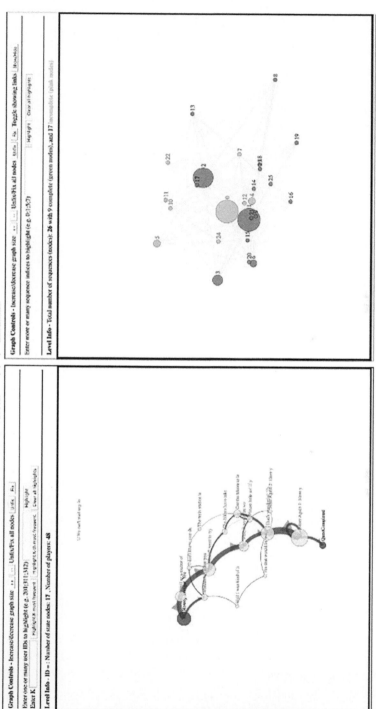

Figure 5.7 *Glyph* visualization system of VPAL data. The state graph is on the left and sequence graph on the right. There are many interactions and features available for highlighting sequences to make sense of the data, as shown in the panels above the graph.

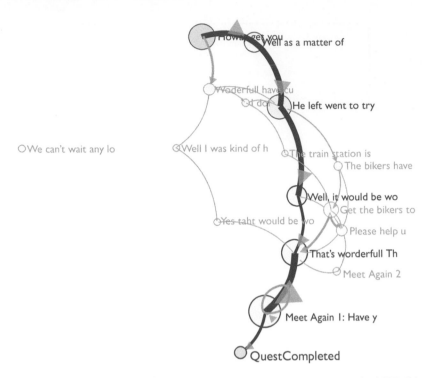

Figure 5.8 State graph of VPAL data. In this example, the nodes represent the NPC dialog that the player encountered. The lines between the nodes (transitions) represent the player's chosen dialog option. The highlighted trajectory (in red) in this particular example is the most popular sequence of dialog, representing a relatively direct path through the conversation. The paths that are faded are state transitions that do not belong to this sequence—that is, players with this trajectory never chose those dialog options.

information about the town or the location of the bikers). The sequence graph on the right represents each state sequence as a single node. The size of the node represents how many people followed that sequence, while the distance between nodes represents how similar they are. The coloring of the nodes, in this particular example, indicates whether that sequence completed the quest that was given by the NPC (green) or not (pink).

We can use the interactive element of the visualization to examine the different patterns. Figure 5.10 shows the dialog pattern of sequence 0, one of the most popular sequences, and Figures 5.11 and 5.12 compare that pattern to the pattern of sequence 5, a less popular sequence. To compare the two patterns, one can put sequence numbers into the highlight box on the top right. Examining the figures more closely, it can be observed that sequence 0 represents a very direct path through the dialog with the NPC, in which the

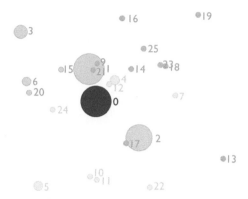

Figure 5.9 Screenshot of the clusters of patterns shown in the state graph. As discussed, each node is a full sequence from start to end. The distance between the nodes is how similar they are, and the size represents how many players had that sequence. Sequence 0 corresponds to the trajectory shown in Figure 5.8. It is one of the most popular sequences, as indicated by its size. Only one other sequence was pursued by the same number of players (sequence 1), which can be seen next to sequence 0 in the figure, at the exact same size.

player follows the prompts through to accepting the quest without asking for any other information. By contrast, the two players who followed sequence 5 asked more questions about the environment, such as where the bikers came from and why it was a problem. This analysis allows us to identify different player types, those who want to get straight to the point, and those who wish to explore and learn more about their environment.

Lab 5.3 allows you to go through the visualization to identify different patterns of playing in this level of *VPAL*. In this lab, you will just use Glyph and will not be able to adjust the abstraction or state representation. Since Glyph is not yet packaged as an open-source software to be used to adjust the state and action representation, such experimentation will not be available. However, you can develop your own visualization of the data provided and develop your own state representation to experiment and understand players' strategies and decision-making actions.

Practical Note: Lab 5.3

Lab 5.3

Please see the supplemental materials for the book.

Goal of Lab 5.3

The lab introduces the *Glyph* interface and walks you through looking at two different patterns within the game.

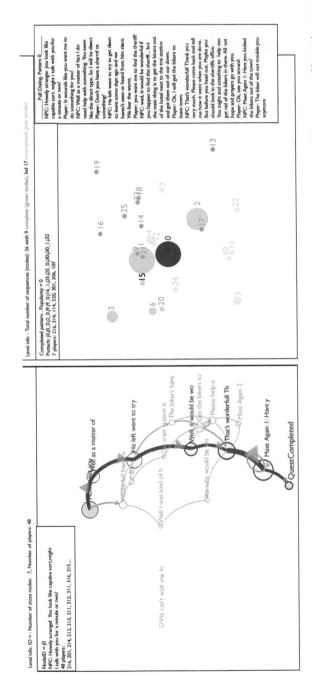

Figure 5.10 Sequence 0 is highlighted in both graphs side by side in *Glyph*. The popup on the right side shows the entire dialog sequence (the entire trajectory in the state graph on the left) between the player and the NPC.

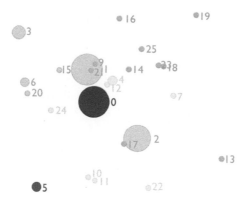

Figure 5.11 Using *Glyph* to compare sequence 0 (one of the most popular, in blue) to sequence 5 (a less popular sequence, in orange). The distance between the two nodes in the sequence graph represents how different they are as determined by the different dialog options that were chosen (see Figure 5.12 for more details on the trajectories).

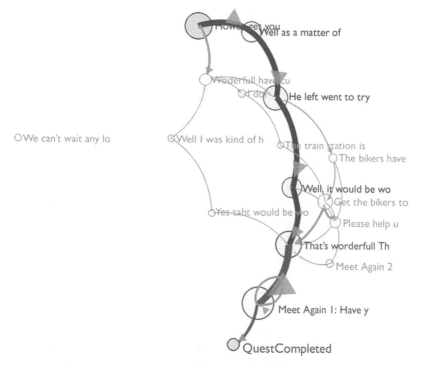

Figure 5.12 The appearance of the state graph with sequences 0 (blue) and 5 (orange) highlighted. Here, one can see how the dialog choices made by the different players varied, as the two trajectories visit different state nodes before converging toward the end of the conversation.

5.4 Summary and takeaways

In this chapter, we discussed visualization systems of in-game behavioral data that can be used, or augmented by analysts and designers, to help tune the development process. Of these different in-game visualization systems, we discussed heatmaps and showed how you can develop one. We also discussed spatio-temporal visualizations and state-action transition visualizations. Heatmap type analysis has been around a lot longer than the other two types of visualizations, and therefore, there are more tools and systems that you can use to develop these heatmaps. Unfortunately, this is not true for the other visualization types. We have provided links to two visualization systems that we have developed within the GUII lab: Stratmapper and Glyph.

Research is still ongoing for these types of visualization systems. There is more work proposed through conferences such as CHI Play, FDG, and CHI, and we advise readers to continue exploring these sources for new systems.

• •

EXERCISES

1. Using the heatmap you created in Lab 5.1, look at where kills by rifle occurred most frequently. What can you conclude about the game environment based on this heatmap? What would you change about the environment if you wanted rifle kills to be more evenly distributed?

2. Use the heatmaps to examine which gun types were used more frequently in different parts of the map. What can you conclude about the map based on the distribution of kills from different types of guns? What can you conclude about the strengths and weaknesses of the different guns from this distribution?

3. Look at the labels provided in StratMapper. What conclusions can you draw about the game's design based on when and how often labels were placed and who they included? If you were a developer working on *DOTA 2*, how would you use this information to inform your work?

4. Stratmapper can be used in tandem with domain knowledge to extract player behavior from data and derive behavioral labels. In the chapter and lab, we provided a list of example behavioral labels. Using the Stratmapper link provided, examine the *DOTA 2* data and develop three new labels based on what players appear to be doing in the data. What elements of player behavior or strategy that you see in Stratmapper are your labels capturing?

5. In the chapter and lab, we talk about how different player types can be recognized from the sequence data. We identify players who explore their narrative context and players who try to get to the point as quickly as possible. Explore the data at https://truonghuy.github.io/glyph-vpal-dialogue/ and identify two more player types.

How are their state graphs similar or different from each other and from the existing types? What can you conclude about their approaches to narrative gameplay and NPC interaction based on their dialog choices?

6. In the Glyph visualization provided, look at the sequences that finished the quest (green) and the sequences that did not (pink). Do you see any patterns in how their sequences are similar or different? Can you draw any conclusions about the kinds of interactions that players who did not finish the quest had? How do they differ from those who did finish the quest?

ACKNOWLEDGMENTS

This chapter was written in collaboration with Riddhi Padte and Varun Sriram based on their work in Dr. Seif El-Nasr's Game data Science class at Northeastern University. The chapter was also written based on the work of Erica Kleinman, PhD student at University of California at Santa Cruz, and Andy Bryant, Software Engineer at GUII Lab. Both Erica and Andy worked on the development of the visualization systems, *Glyph* and *Stratmapper*, used in this chapter.

We would like to acknowledge Northeastern University for funding the work that resulted in the development of Glyph and G-Player (earlier version of StratMapper). This was funded under internal grant (Tier 1). We also would like to acknowledge and thank BrainQuake for their support and for providing us with data for *Wuzzit Trouble* that stimulated the development of Glyph. We would also like to acknowledge Defense Advanced Research Projects Agency for funding the subsequent work on the visualization systems developing StratMapper based on G-Player as well as some minor adjustments in Glyph. We further would like to acknowledge Soar Technology, Inc., and the Army for funding the work on *DOTA 2* data abstraction that resulted in the visualization of *DOTA 2* in Glyph under for Phase II Small Business Innovative Research Grant, contract W56HZV-17-C-0012. We also would like to acknowledge the work done under this contract by Soar Technology in scrapping the *DOTA 2* data for us from the public replays.

BIBLIOGRAPHY

Aung, M., Demediuk, S., Sun, Y., Tu, Y., Ang, Y., Nekkanti, S., Raghav, S., Klabjan, D., Sifa, R., and Drachen, A., (2019, August). The trails of *Just Cause 2*: Spatio-temporal player profiling in open-world games. In *Proceedings of the 14th International Conference on the Foundations of Digital Games* (p. 41). ACM.

Bauckhage, C., Sifa, R., Drachen, A., Thurau, C., and Hadiji, F. (2014, August). Beyond heatmaps: Spatio-temporal clustering using behavior-based partitioning of game levels. In *2014* IEEE *Conference on Computational Intelligence and Games* (pp. 1–8). IEEE.

Berndt, D. J., and Clifford, J. (1994). Using dynamic time warping to find patterns in time series. *KDD workshop*, 1994, 359–70.

Canossa, A., Nguyen, T., and Seif El-Nasr, M. (2016). G-player: Exploratory visual analytics for accessible knowledge discovery. *Foundations of Digital Games*.

Chittaro, L., Ranon, R., and Ieronutti, L. (2006). Vu-flow: A visualization tool for analyzing navigation in virtual environments. *IEEE Transactions on Visualization and Computer Graphics*, 12(6), 1475–85.

Cornwell, B. (2015). *Social sequence analysis: Methods and applications* (Vol. 37). Cambridge, UK: Cambridge University Press.

Dankoff, J. (2014). Game Telemetry with DNA Tracking on *Assassin's Creed*. *Gamasutra*.

Dixit, P. N., and Youngblood, G. M. (2008, August). Understanding information observation in interactive 3D environments. In *Proceedings of the 2008 ACM SIGGRAPH Symposium on Video Games* (pp. 163–70). ACM.

Drachen, A. and Canossa, A. (2009, September). Analyzing spatial user behavior in computer games using geographic information systems. In *Proceedings of the 13th International MindTrek Conference: Everyday Life in the Ubiquitous Era* (pp. 182–9). ACM.

Drachen, A. and Schubert, M. (2013, August). Spatial game analytics and visualization. In *2013 IEEE Conference on Computational Intelligence in Games (CIG)* (pp. 1–8). Niagara Falls, ON, Canada: IEEE.

Gagné, A. R., Seif El-Nasr, M., and Shaw, C. D. (2011, October). A Deeper Look at the use of Telemetry for Analysis of Player Behavior in RTS Games. In *International Conference on Entertainment Computing* (pp. 247–57). Berlin, Heidelberg: Springer.

Hoobler, N., Humphreys, G., and Agrawala, M. (2004, October). Visualizing competitive behaviors in multi-user virtual environments. In *Proceedings of the Conference on Visualization '04* (pp. 163–70). IEEE Computer Society.

Houghton, S. (2013). Investigating balance maps in *Transformers: War for Cybertron*. URL: https://gameanalytics.com/blog/balance-and-flow-maps.html. Accessed December 2019.

Juul, J. (2004). Introduction to game time/time to play: An examination of game temporality. In Wardrip-Fruin, N. and Harrigan, P. (eds). *First Person: New Media as Story, Performance and Game* (pp. 131–42). Cambridge, MA: MIT Press.

Miller, J. L., and Crowcroft, J. (2009, November). Avatar movement in *World of Warcraft* battlegrounds. In *Proceedings of the 8th Annual Workshop on Network and Systems Support for Games* (p. 1). Paris, France: IEEE Press.

Moura, D., El-Nasr, M. S., and Shaw, C. D. (2011, August). Visualizing and understanding players' behavior in video games: discovering patterns and supporting aggregation and comparison. In *Proceedings of the 2011 ACM SIGGRAPH Symposium on Video Games* (pp. 11–15). ACM.

Nguyen, T.-H. D., Seif El-Nasr, M., and Canossa, A. (2015). Glyph: Visualization tool for understanding problem solving strategies in puzzle games. In *Foundations of Digital Games*.

PsychoStats. Heatmaps. URL: http://www.psychostats.com/doc/Heatmaps. Accessed July 2012.

Seif El-Nasr, M., and Yan, S. (2006, June). Visual attention in 3D video games. In *Proceedings of the 2006 ACM SIGCHI International Conference on Advances in Computer Entertainment Technology* (pp. 22-es).

Sifa, R., Srikanth, S., Drachen, A., Ojeda, C., and Bauckhage, C. (2016, September). Predicting retention in sandbox games with tensor factorization-based representation learning. In *2016 IEEE Conference on Computational Intelligence and Games (CIG)* (pp. 1–8). IEEE.

Thawonmas, R., and Iizuka, K. (2008). Visualization of online-game players based on their action behaviors. *International Journal of Computer Games Technology, 2008,* 5.

Thompson, C. (2007). *Halo 3*: How Microsoft Labs invented a new science of play. *Wired* URL: http://www.wired.com/gaming/virtualworlds/magazine/15-09/ff_halo. Accessed December 2019.

Wallner, G., and Kriglstein, S. (2013). Visualization-based analysis of gameplay data—a review of literature. *Entertainment Computing, 4*(3), 143–55.

Wallner, G., Halabi, N., and Mirza-Babaei, P. (2019, April). Aggregated visualization of playtesting data. In *Proceedings of the 2019 CHI Conference on Human Factors in Computing Systems* (p. 363). ACM.

Wallner, G., and Kriglstein, S. (2012, May). A spatiotemporal visualization approach for the analysis of gameplay data. In *Proceedings of the SIGCHI conference on human factors in computing systems* (pp. 1115–24). ACM.

CHAPTER 6

Clustering Methods in Game Data Science

O ne of the central challenges in game data science is dealing with high
dimensionality of behavioral telemetry which varies from genre to
genre. Consider, for example, a typical Massively Multiplayer Online
Game (MMOG); there are literally thousands of potential features that can
be captured for each individual player, nonplayer character, mobs, systems,
and economies. This then makes it hard to find behavioral patterns that can
help us gain insights to derive design, business, or marketing. The existence of
such high-dimensional datasets is a common problem within the field of game
data science. Game data scientists deal with this problem in several ways. One
way is to abstract the data as discussed in Chapter 4 using techniques such as
feature extraction, feature selection, or feature engineering. However, feature
engineering can be problematic if we do not have a good idea of how the data is
structured. One way to address this problem is to use clustering methods, which
brings us to the focus of this chapter.

Clustering methods offer a way to explore datasets and discover patterns that
can reduce the overall complexity of the data. In particular, clustering refers to
the task of grouping elements in a set to form subsets of closely related elements,
called clusters. Using clustering methods for analysis is formally known as
cluster analysis. The outcome of this analysis is cluster models. Such models
are used when running exploratory analysis, defined in Chapter 1. They can
also be used for hypothesis testing. However, classification methods, which we
will discuss in the next chapter, are more commonly used for hypothesis testing
and prediction analysis.

Game Data Science. Magy Seif El-Nasr, Truong Huy Nguyen Dinh, Alessandro Canossa, and Anders Drachen, Oxford
University Press. © Magy Seif El-Nasr, Truong Huy Nguyen Dinh, Alessandro Canossa, and Anders Drachen (2021).
DOI: 10.1093/oso/9780192897879.003.0006

One popular usage of cluster analysis, within games, is to group players together, based on some descriptive characteristics about them. For example, players can be grouped based on their behavior or performance in games, or their activities within games, such as purchase history, etc. Such a practice is often referred to as player profiling, discussed in Chapter 1.

To contextualize this discussion, let us take a quick look at an example. Consider you are working on a team-based first-person shooter game and want to investigate how the game is being played by focusing on various gameplay metrics and retention. You collect many variables including *kill/death*, *movement* data, *vehicle mount* events, *stop* events, *item pick up* events, and *dialog* events. This dimension space can explode rapidly, as you can see. With all these variables, you can use the techniques discussed in Chapter 4 to derive metrics, such as *kill/death* ratios and time spent in particular modes (on foot, driving, being a passenger, etc.). However, these variables alone will not give you much insight. By using clustering, you can examine groupings of players who share some behaviors or values. For example, by running a cluster analysis, you can find different clusters. One cluster could be a grouping of players who churned early in the game. Investigating this cluster further, you may find that these players spend all of their time in vehicles and they also *only* play the few maps where vehicles are used. Given this analysis, it would be reasonable to suspect that this group of players prefers vehicle-based combat, but that the low availability of vehicles in the game caused them to churn early. The solution could be to add more maps with vehicles, or more things to do with vehicles. More detailed analysis, using other analysis methods, could be performed to uncover further details. Further, you could survey some of the players in the different clusters you found to shed more light on their game experience and reasons for churn, etc. You can then derive different solutions and test them. In either case, clustering can be used as a way to understand your players and how they are grouped in relation to game elements.

In this chapter, we will discuss some commonly used clustering techniques, specifically:

- K-means: A simple yet effective clustering method. Practical lab that shows how the technique can be applied is shown in **Lab 6.1.**
- Fuzzy C-means: An extension of K-means with fuzzy membership for clusters. Practical lab that shows how the technique can be applied is shown in **Lab 6.2.**

- Density-based spatial clustering and application with noise (DBSCAN): A density-based clustering algorithm. Practical lab that shows how the technique can be applied is shown in **Lab 6.3.**
- Hierarchical clustering (HC, single- and complete-link): Clustering methods that construct, not one set of clusters, but a hierarchy of clusters. Practical lab that shows how the technique can be applied is shown in **Lab 6.4.**
- Archetypal analysis (AA): A clustering method based on shapes of convex polygons created by plotting the data. Practical lab that shows how the technique can be applied is shown in **Lab 6.5.**
- Advanced method: Model-based clustering. Since this method is advanced, we will not go through the details of showing a lab to apply it. But interested readers are referred to the MClust library in R for relevant functions to apply this method.

For the labs in this chapter, you will be using the *DOTAlicious* dataset introduced in Chapter 4.

It is important to note that clustering methods do not have ground truth. Ground truth is a concept of having a standard known measure or model that you can compare your results to in order to determine if your results are correct. Therefore, it is hard to validate the results from clustering methods. Different clustering algorithms, or even the same algorithm, can be run with different configurations or parameters and may result in a wide variety of valid ways to group data points.

So how do we know which is the correct groupings? In this chapter, in addition to discussing the clustering methods mentioned above, we will also discuss some principled methods to evaluate a clustering result. These methods mostly measure how stable or robust a cluster is against data perturbation. The more stable the clusters are, the stronger relationships among data within the same clusters, which makes it reasonable to conclude that the data points are indeed similar to one another in those clusters. Of these methods, we will discuss:

- *Within-Cluster Sum of Squares (WSS)*
- *Average silhouette width*
- For *Agglomerative Hierarchical Clustering (AHC)*, agglomerative coefficients

It should be noted that there are many papers and books on clustering methods, and there is a wealth of information available online on the topic. Therefore, for further readings, readers are referred to the bibliography section and are encouraged to browse books on data science and, specifically, clustering.

6.1 What is cluster analysis?

Cluster analysis fundamentally refers to the process of grouping sets of objects in such a way that objects assigned to the same group, called a cluster, are more similar (in some sense or another) to each other than to those in other clusters. In game data science, the objects can be players, agents, quests, etc. Each of these is described via a finite set of variables, as you have seen in previous chapters. For example, for a player, there can be many variables, such as number of kills or deaths, their character level, their XP, and movement patterns. As discussed in Chapter 4, we often call these variables features.

The term cluster analysis is then a process describing an algorithm used to develop clusters. There are many algorithms developed for this task, each with different strengths and weaknesses and with different traditional application areas in different fields. Therefore, the definition of what a cluster is also varies between algorithms. While all of these algorithms somehow refer to a group of objects in a data space, understanding the different cluster models is vital to be able to correctly apply the algorithm to the data.

Objects are generally represented as points (vectors) in the multidimensional space defined by the data. Each dimension is one feature (or variable). Conceptually, data for clustering is represented as an $m \times n$ data matrix, where there are m rows (one per object) and n columns (one per feature). The alternative to the data matrix is a proximity (or distance) matrix, which is an $m \times m$ matrix containing the pairwise similarities or dissimilarities. More complex data structures can also be used (e.g., graphs or text strings). One of the first operations necessary in a game context is the scaling and transformation of the features, as discussed in Chapter 2. This normalizes the data, brings them into the same scale, and reduces the number of dimensions.

Importantly, across all algorithms, the assigning of objects to clusters can be either hard or soft. Hard assignment means that an object is placed within a cluster completely (e.g., *k-means*), whereas soft assignment means that the model provides information about the degrees to which an object belongs to different clusters. The exact process of assigning objects to clusters depends on the clustering algorithm chosen and will be discussed in more detail later.

6.2 Clustering for exploratory analysis

As discussed in Chapters 1 and 3, data analyses can be loosely categorized into two types: exploratory and confirmatory (i.e., hypothesis-testing) analyses. With exploratory analyses, you examine the data with few, if any, preconceptions or hypotheses about the data. For instance, given players' play traces in a game level, an exploratory analysis may be used to check whether there are any patterns exhibited in the ways players experience the game. Confirmatory analyses, on the other hand, start with some hypotheses in terms of patterns or underlying structures that are probably embedded in the data, and the goal is to confirm or reject such hypotheses. As you can see, confirmatory analyses are, therefore, more directed than exploratory ones.

As discussed above, cluster analysis belongs to the first kind, which is conducted during the exploratory phase of the knowledge discovery process (Chapter 1). Clustering is an iterative process of knowledge discovery where you can use several algorithms to examine how the data is grouped. When you use the clustering algorithms discussed in this chapter, you will need to set some parameters for the algorithms used. Care must be taken when you modify these parameters, because the same dataset can lead to different outcomes depending on how the parameters are set. As discussed above, there are no right or wrong answers here, but rather the whole process is iterative, and you will need to try out different algorithms as certain algorithms are designed to work with specific kind of groupings and thus may result in better or worse fits. Therefore, the process of applying cluster analysis is a user-dependent process, where the first task focuses on iteratively working with algorithms and tuning parameters to get different models that you can then compare to give you some insight about how the underlying data can be grouped. As we will discuss throughout the chapter, most of the time, you can use statistical methods to estimate good values for the parameters you use for the different algorithms. You can also use cluster cohesiveness measures to see how well the clusters are formed. However, most often, for game data science, inspecting the data points within each cluster can give you more insight on what qualitative label you can use to understand these groupings. In this chapter, we will discuss all these approaches.

The goal of such analysis is to discover a clustering structure that puts data points into groups of similar characteristics. Such grouping helps to partition the data into smaller closely related data subsets that enables further in-depth analyses. For instance, as an immediate follow-up step, hypotheses can be formulated on the groups and validated via confirmatory analyses.

6.3 Clustering models

Because of the usefulness of clustering in exploratory analysis across a vast number of domains including health, finance, information technology, etc., there have been thousands of clustering algorithms and approaches proposed over the past half a century or so (Jain, 2010). Such methods can be generally grouped into two types of clustering approaches based on how the underlying model operates, namely partitional and hierarchical, as depicted in Figure 6.1.

Partitional clustering approaches aim to partition the data into disjoint subsets, each of which makes up a cluster. There are three types of partitional clustering: centroid, distribution, and density. Some experts argue that these should be treated as individual groups, creating four basic groups of clustering methods. Hybrids also exist, which makes classification even more tricky. HC

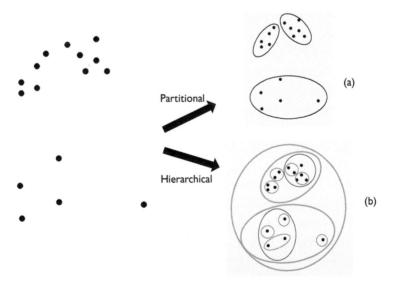

Figure 6.1 Input data and output of (a) partitional clustering and (b) hierarchical clustering. In (b), each eclipse corresponds to one cluster in the partitioning hierarchy.

approaches aim to construct a partition tree, each node of which corresponds to a subset of the data. In this tree, the root node comprises the whole dataset. There are nesting relationships between the clusters (or nodes in the tree), with child nodes nested within parent nodes. We will provide a bit more detail on each group below.

6.3.1 Hierarchical clustering

Hierarchical Clustering (HC), also called connectivity-based clustering, is based on the idea that objects are more related to nearby objects than those further away. Clusters are thus developed based on distance between objects in the data space. HC models were among the earliest techniques developed, and care must be taken with respect to outliers that can cause cluster merging (chaining). Furthermore, these models do not scale well to big datasets. In general, the models can be either agglomerative (beginning with individual objects and aggregating them) or divisive (beginning with all observations in the dataset and partitioning them). Hierarchical models are further differentiated based on the distance function used. When applying these models, the analyst needs to decide which distance function to use, as well as decide which linkage criterion to employ, and finally, which distance to use. Given the hierarchical nature of the algorithms, there is no single partitioning provided, but rather a hierarchy of clusters, which expand or shrink in number based on distance, the choice of distance function, and linkage criterion.

6.3.2 Centroid clustering

Centroid-based clustering is often used in game data science, primarily due to popularity and widespread use of *k-means* clustering, which forms the basis for centroid clustering techniques, and is conceptually easy to understand. Centroid-based models represent clusters by a central vector, which does not need to be an actual object (the term Archetypal analysis denotes when centroids are restricted to objects in the dataset and k-medians denotes when medians are used; fuzzy assignment of clusters is also common, i.e., *Fuzzy C-means*). For these methods, the analyst needs to define the number of clusters in advance (the number can be defined via initial exploration of the dataset). *K-means* clustering then targets the optimization problem of finding k centers and assigning objects to the nearest center, in a way that minimizes the squared distances. *K-means* finds local optima, not global optima, and is therefore typically run multiple times with randomized initializations. Modifications of the *k-means* algorithm, such as *k-medoids* and *spherical k-means*, use other distance measures than Euclidean distance.

6.3.3 Distribution clustering

Distribution-based clustering directly relates to the use of distribution models (e.g., Gaussian/Normal), see Chapter 3. Fundamentally, clusters are defined based on how likely the objects included belong to the same distribution. Distribution-based models can provide information beyond the cluster assignments of objects (e.g., correlation of object attributes), but suffer from overfitting problems if the complexity of the model used is not constrained (e.g., defining a specific number of Gaussian distributions, Gaussian mixture models). Importantly, these models do not work if there is no mathematical model inherent in the dataset for the model to optimize.

6.3.4 Density clustering

In this group of models, clusters are defined based on identifying areas of higher density. These approaches apply a local cluster criterion. The resulting clusters (regions in data space) can have an arbitrary shape and the points within can be arbitrarily distributed. Density clustering is able to handle noise if the results of the noise are objects in areas of the data space that is sparse. Density-based models can discover clusters of arbitrary shape and are optimized in one scan. However, these models require the analyst to define density parameters as termination condition. Among the commonly used methods are *DBSCAN*, *OPTICS*, *DENCLUE*, and *CLIQUE*. These methods vary substantially in how they operate and come in numerous variations. Density-based models have rarely been used on behavioral data from games but might be used in the future due to their ability to handle noise, which is a common feature in behavioral game telemetry.

6.4 The clustering process

The general process of data clustering comprises of five steps, as depicted in Figure 6.2:

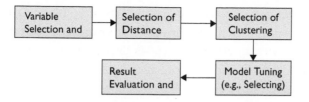

Figure 6.2 Clustering process.

Step 1: Variable selection and/or transformation. This is when you decide which data features or variables you want to use as input into the algorithm; what variables to use for clustering; and, in cases when the data variables are too low level, what new, possibly higher level variables should be generated to better represent the data and get you closer to the kinds of clusters of interest? Having too many variables, especially irrelevant ones, may degrade the quality and dilute the meaningfulness of the clusters you get. As such, determining the right abstraction is critical to not only clustering but also machine learning tasks in general. In such cases, some data transformation or feature engineering is needed to get the right set of variables for the analysis. This task is often highly domain specific, especially if done manually. See Chapter 4 for more details on this step.

Step 2: Choice of metric (or similarity measure). This metric defines the notion of "similarity" in your data. There are some popular choices, such as Minkowski distance functions[1] for data represented as numeric vectors. This choice of metric is also domain- and purpose-specific. For example, assume that you are trying to cluster players based on two of their in-game behavior statistics, namely *Deaths* (number of deaths) and *Kills* (number of kills). One simple similarity metric to compare players is the *Euclidean* distance, defined as:

$$d(x, y) = \sqrt{(x_{Deaths} - y_{Deaths})^2 + (x_{Kills} - y_{Kills})^2} \qquad \text{(Equation 6.1)}$$

where x_{Deaths} and x_{Kills} represent total *deaths* and *kills* for player x, and y_{Deaths} and y_{Kills} represent total *deaths* and *kills* for player y. You can compute these variables by aggregating over death events per player. Note that Euclidean distance here only works for continuous numerical measures. Later, we will discuss how to compute similarity metrics for different types of measures discussed in Chapter 2, such as categorical and ordinal measures.

[1] Minkowski distance is the generalization of Euclidean and Manhattan distances.

Step 3: Selecting a clustering algorithm. There are many clustering algorithms and variants existing in the literature, and each comes with a specific set of assumptions, including the target type of clusters. As such, when selecting a clustering algorithm, you need to not only consider its computational demand and ease of use but also be aware of the limitations (e.g., its inability to discover certain cluster types). This will become a lot clearer when we discuss the particular algorithms and apply them.

Step 4: Determining the values for hyperparameters. Some clustering algorithms require the number of clusters, K, as an input. As such, you may need to determine or hypothesize a suitable number of clusters to feed into the algorithm. Alternatively, K can be treated as a hyperparameter—that is, a parameter that the user can change to compute several models. Following this, the user can use a validation technique to compare between the models (see Chapter 7 for more details on hyperparameter tuning). Note, however, as mentioned above, we do not have a clear ground truth for clustering. The optimal number of clusters is defined as one that is small yet produces high-quality data clusters or ones that make sense to the eye of an expert. This turns out to be a problem with multiple but conflicting objectives.

As such, for selection of the number of clusters to use, we will rely on a heuristic principle that you have seen before in Chapter 4, called the *Elbow* method. This method often yields reasonable results in practice, despite having no theoretical guarantee. Figure 6.3(a) depicts a scree plot used to determine an optimal number of clusters. The "Elbow" points at $K = 4$ and $K = 8$ are good candidates for the number of clusters.

Step 5: Evaluating and interpreting the results. This is the postprocessing step of clustering. Once the final clusters are obtained, you need to apply evaluation metrics to assess the quality of the resultant clusters. This can be done through various measures. One of these measures is known as *Within-Cluster Sum of Squares* (*WSS*), also referred to as *Within-Group Sum of Squares*, a metric that captures how tightly knitted the resultant clusters are. This measure is often used to denote how well the data was clustered. Another approach is *qualitative assessment*, where an expert looks at the data points per cluster and tries to meaningfully assign a label that explains their similarity.

Additionally, you may consider applying visualization to summarize the clusters in ways that allow domain experts to examine, interpret, and help determine whether the clusters are reasonable from their perspectives. For example, Figure 6.3(b) depicts how the clusters can be visualized to present to experts, showing each cluster as a colored shape encompassing data points belonging to that

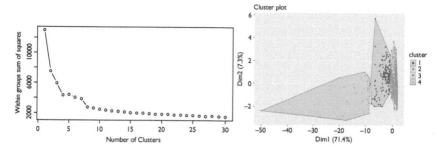

Figure 6.3 Approaches for tuning clustering models and visualizing clusters: (a) is a scree plot showing the WSS scores with respect to varying number of clusters; (b) is a 2D visualization of resultant clusters; x-axis is the first component and y-axis is the second component, as resulted from applying PCA on the data.

cluster. In the case of multidimensional data, it can be hard to develop such visualizations, and thus you can either (a) use methods for dimensionality reduction, such as Principal Component Analysis (PCA) (see Chapter 4) so that clusters can be visualized in a 2D representation or (b) summarize the clusters in text and allow experts to review. Figure 6.3(b) shows the visualization of the data after PCA has been applied to reduce the dimensionality to 2D. In the labs for this chapter, you will also learn how to examine and summarize the clusters and interpret the results. It should be noted that for the labs in this chapter, we opted to use PCA and visualize the data as you see above; we left it as an exercise for you to examine the points per cluster and see what groupings you get.

The outcome of this step may lead to two next steps. If the results are deemed reasonable and reliable, you can conclude this cluster analysis and utilize the new-found insights on downstream tasks. Otherwise, you may need to go back to one of the previous steps to try something else.

6.5 Challenges in applying clustering

When applying clustering, there are some key challenges that users usually face.

6.5.1 Cluster definition

First, how do you define a suitable cluster given a dataset? This is problematic because at this stage you are exploring the data, and thus you may not necessarily know what a cluster looks like or how the points can be grouped

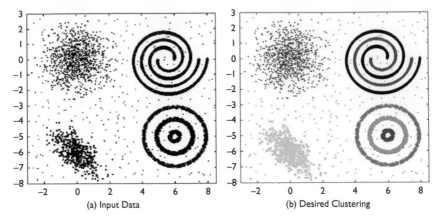

Figure 6.4 Different kinds of clusters. Reprinted from Jain, A. K. (2010). Data clustering: 50 years beyond K-means. Pattern Recognition Letters, 31(8), 651–66. Copyright (2010), with permission from Elsevier.

together. When we discuss clustering algorithms below, you will see that each algorithm imposes certain assumptions on the kinds of clusters it is looking for. For example, *K-means* is optimized to search for clusters that are in the form of convex, blob-like shapes. Accepting such assumptions when applying a specific clustering algorithm means that you may not find all clusters existing in the data, or worse, clusters discovered may be wrong.

Specifically, clusters may take vastly different forms in real life, as illustrated in Figure 6.4. Besides being blob-like, round, or elliptical, clusters may also be elongated entities that encompass one another. Note that there is no single clustering algorithm able to detect all these kinds of clusters. Therefore, knowing beforehand the types of clusters you are looking for is critical to the success of your analyses. To overcome this issue, you can apply different clustering algorithms on the same dataset to make sure that you are not missing out any particular type of clusters.

6.5.2 Similarity definition

The second challenge is related to how you define similarity between points that form a cluster. This is crucial as it is a key piece of information required by all clustering algorithms. When clustering, the user sets out to find groups of "similar" data points, so this concept of "similarity" needs to be defined concretely through a similarity metric function, or a pairwise distance matrix. Fortunately, unlike the first challenge, this is comparably easier to define given the right domain knowledge. For instance, if the data of interest is concerned with players' game experiences, and each data point takes the form of a numeric vector characterizing a player's in-game performance statistics, such as *number of attacks*, *purchases*, or *deaths*, your definition of similarity can simply be the Euclidean distance. In cases when a mathematical function fails to capture the similarities satisfactorily, a distance matrix that encodes pairwise dissimilarity values can also be used. Further, in cases where you cannot define a good metric like when you are comparing movement trajectory or action patterns, such as the case in sequence data, you may use other methods, discussed in Chapter 9, such as time wrapping or optimal matching.

6.5.3 Cluster tendency

Cluster tendency refers to the degree to which there exists meaningful clusters in the data, which sometimes can only be determined with domain knowledge. Even random data sometimes appear to have structures embedded in them due to randomness in the artifacts studied. This means you are guaranteed to get some clusters forming on any dataset, which could be misleading as there is no ground truth to validate such results. As such, before applying cluster analysis, you may need to determine whether your data has cluster tendency to make sure that you are not trying to retrieve patterns out of random artifacts.

6.5.4 Outliers

Outliers (see Chapter 2 for more details on this topic) refer to data points that do not contribute to the main structures or relationships underlying the data. Outliers distract the algorithms and are problematic to machine learning in general as well as clustering. As such, before trying to apply clustering, you need to answer the following questions: Are there any outliers in the data? If so, what is their impact on the clustering result? Due to the exploratory nature of clustering, we may hesitate to exclude such data points. However, this also means there could be outliers affecting the quality of the resultant clustering.

6.6 Evaluation and tuning

After you perform clustering and obtain some clusters, you will need to evaluate the results. Since there is no ground truth in clustering, this process is tricky.

Therefore, we will discuss some methods here before we discuss how you would cluster your data. For clustering, the goal is to maximize intracluster similarity and minimize intercluster similarity. The metrics that capture such criteria are called internal evaluation metrics, since the evaluation is done on the data itself. In addition to internal evaluation, you can also conduct an external evaluation of the results (see Section 6.6.1). During external evaluation, external resources, such as expert-defined labels, are used (see Section 6.6.2).

In some cases, you may need to tune the hyperparameters that are used as parameters for tuning the algorithm's output. More generally, different algorithms may have different parameters that you can hypertune. Usually, this is achieved by first computing several clusters, each corresponding to a different hyperparameter configuration, then plotting a graph that shows how good the clusters are (using one of the evaluation metrics). The hyperparameters with the most reasonable result would be selected. "Reasonable" here often means a good balance between the goodness of clusters and their generalizability and/or simplicity.

We will first discuss some popular evaluation metrics, before detailing tuning methods.

6.6.1 Internal evaluation metrics

To assess the quality of resultant clusters using the data itself, we can use *WSS metric* computed as:

$$WSS = \sum_{i=1}^{K} \sum_{d \in d_i} (d - \mu_i)^2 \qquad \text{(Equation 6.2)}$$

Where,

- $i = 1 \ldots K$ is the index of a cluster,
- D_i is the data subset containing data points belonging to cluster i, and
- μ_i is the centroid of cluster i, computed as the mean of all data points in D_i.

WSS is a real value in the range $[0, +\infty)$. The smaller it is, the better the clusters. This measure captures the distances between every data point (d in Equation 6.2) to the center of the cluster it belongs to, μ_i, thus signifying how close-knit the clusters are.

Intuitively, given the same number of clusters K, having a smaller *WSS* means that the data points are closer to the center of the clusters they are assigned to, which is an indication that the resultant clusters are tighter grouped, or better clustered. It is worth noting, however, that as the number of clusters K increases, WSS will grow smaller. In the extreme case, when $K = |D|$, that is, the number of clusters is equal to the number of data points, WSS could be equal to 0 when each data point is in a cluster on its own. As such, you should only compare the WSS measures of two clustering results with the same K.

Another method to use is *average silhouette width* or just *silhouette*, $s(x)$ of a data point x. This defines a measure of cohesion, that is, how similar an object is to its own cluster compared to other clusters, and computed as follows:

$$s(x) = \frac{b(x) - d(x, C_x)}{\max\{b(x), d(x, C_x)\}} \qquad \text{(Equation 6.3)}$$

where

- $d(x, C_x)$ is the distance between x and its assigned cluster C_x, defined as the average distance between x and all other points in C_x, that is, $d(x, C_x) = \frac{1}{|C_x|-1} \sum_{y \in C_x, y \neq x} d(x, y)$, with $d(.)$ being the distance measure on data.
- $b(x)$ is the smallest distance between x and all other clusters, that is, $b(x) = \min_{C_{-x}} d(x, C_{-x})$, with C_{-x} denoting clusters not containing x.

As such, silhouette width takes a value between -1 and 1, with values close to 1 signifying good clustering (i.e., x is very close to other points in its cluster and far from points in other clusters) and values near -1 signifying bad clustering. Usually, the silhouette width is interpreted as shown in Table 6.1 (Kaufman and Rousseeuw, 2005). Silhouette width of less than 0.25 means that the found structure is not substantial enough and might be random.

There is another approach to show the silhouette widths of a clustering on a dataset, which is to plot the silhouette plot (see Figure 6.5). This plot shows all data points' silhouette width verbatim, sorted in decreasing order and grouped

Table 6.1 *Interpretation of Silhouette Width.*

Range of Silhouette Width	Interpretation
0.71–1.0	A strong structure has been found
0.51–0.70	A reasonable structure has been found
0.26–0.50	The structure is weak and could be artificial
< 0.25	No substantial structure has been found

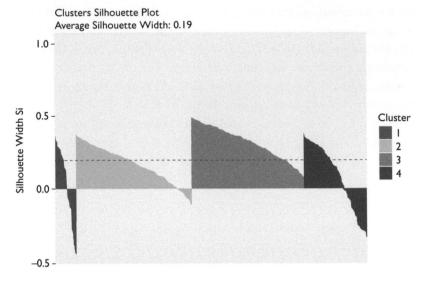

Clusters Silhouette Plot
Average Silhouette Width: 0.19

Figure 6.5 Figure from silhouette calculation generated in Lab 6.2. The figure shows silhouette width of each datapoint within a particular cluster calculated using Equation 6.3 on four clusters that emerged from Lab 6.2.

according to clusters (encoded as different colors). From the chart shown in Figure 6.5, we can see that Clusters 1 and 4 are not good, as almost half of their data have negative silhouette widths. Cluster 3 is well separated from the rest of the data, with all points having positive silhouette.

6.6.2 External evaluation metrics

One popular way to evaluate the cluster assignment of data points is to use externally obtained labels and compare them with those assigned by the clustering algorithm. For example, after clustering players using their in-game activity statistics (such as the number of *kills*, *deaths*, and *assists*), we could compare the resultant clusters with players' skill level tiers, such as "Novice," "Beginner," and "Advanced." The intuition here is that players' in-game activities may be heavily influenced by their fluency in the game. As such, players of similar skill tiers may behave similarly and thus are more likely to be grouped in the same cluster. If there is a high overlap or correlation between the cluster assignments and such labels, then this can be considered strong evidence that the clustering algorithm was successful.

Given externally obtained labels of the data points, the task of evaluating resultant clusters is reduced to evaluating how similar they are to the clusters partitioned by the provided labels. This is similar to how classification methods are evaluated, as will be discussed in Chapter 7.

6.6.3 Tuning methods

The *Elbow* method (discussed above and in Chapter 4) is one of the most frequently used approaches to select hyperparameters for clustering. It is often adopted in cases when we try to optimize a multi-objective function with conflicting objectives. For example, finding the optimal number of clusters K is one such problem, as we are trying to get the smallest number of clusters, but also want the clusters to be of high quality (i.e., low *WSS*). More specifically, we know that as K increases, *WSS* will almost always monotonically decrease. As such, one easy way to get clusters with low *WSS* is to increase K. This is, unfortunately, not desirable as large K values result in fragmented data clusters that may provide little insight into the structure of the data.

Figure 6.6 shows how the *Elbow* method can be used to select the optimal value for the number of clusters K in *K-means*. The charted scree plot shows the relationship between the quality of clustering results, in terms of *WSS* and K. In this plot, $K = 4$ and $K = 8$ are two Elbows of the plot, and both can be considered as candidates for the best K values. To decide which one is better, we can run *K-means* for both values, visualize the resultant clusters, and then check the clusters, possibly with a domain expert, to decide which clustering makes more sense.

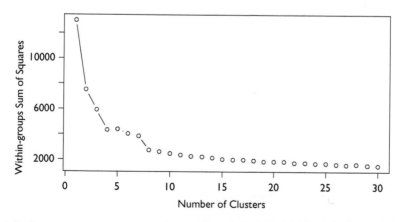

Figure 6.6 Scree plot for K-means clustering, with two potential candidates for K being four or eight.

6.7 Partitional methods

In this section, we are going to discuss the first clustering approach, partitional clustering, and its three subtypes: density, centroid, and distribution-based partitioning, as outlined above. This approach aims to partition the data into disjoint subsets, each of which makes up a cluster. Methods adopting this approach include *K-means*, *Fuzzy C-means*, *DBSCAN*, and *model-based cluster learning using Expectation-Maximization (EM)*.

6.7.1 K-means

K-means' goal is to find a set of centroids, each of which represents the center of a cluster and is characterized by the mean vectors of data points belonging to that cluster. Based on the provided distance metric, each data point is then assigned to the centroid closest to it.

6.7.1.1 ASSUMPTIONS AND TARGET CLUSTER TYPE

K-means searches for clusters that are spherical in shape. Note that this algorithm will not perform well in cases where we have elongated or intertwined clusters, such as those appearing as spiral and nested circles in Figure 6.4. *K-means* expects data in the form of continuous, numeric vectors, since it uses the mean vector (i.e., computed on all attributes) as the representation of clusters.

6.7.1.2 METHOD

The inputs of *K-means* are

- The input dataset, D
- (optional) The distance function $d(x, y)$ with x, y being data points in D
- The number of clusters, K

The second input is optional, because, by default, *K-means* implementation uses Euclidean distance. In theory, *K-means* can work with other metrics as well, for instance, the use of kernel in *Kernel K-means* (Dhillon, Guan, and Kulis, 2004).

K-means follows the following steps:

Step 1: Initialization. Select K initial centroids, represented as mean vectors $c_1, c_2, \ldots, c_K$. These centroids can be selected randomly or with prior knowledge.

Step 2: Cluster assignment. Each data point in D is assigned to the centroid closest to it. The distance is computed using the distance function d, which is the Euclidean distance by default.

Step 3: Centroid update. Cluster centroids are recomputed to be the means:

$$c_j = \frac{1}{|D_j|} \sum_{x_i \in D_j} x_i, \qquad \text{(Equation 6.4)}$$

where

- c_j is the mean vector of cluster j,
- $D_j \subset D$ is the data subset containing all data points currently assigned to cluster j, and
- $x_i \in D_j$ are data points assigned to cluster j.

Step 4: Cluster reassignment. Each data point in D is assigned to the centroid closest to it.

Step 5: Stability checking and termination. If there is no change in the cluster assignment, the algorithm terminates. Otherwise, go back to Step 3.

6.7.1.3 HYPERPARAMETER TUNING

K-means expects the number of clusters K as input, but you often do not know K apriori. As such, K needs to be tuned, starting with a small K to a large one. Cluster evaluation metrics will be used to assess the quality of the clusters, and the Elbow method (Thorndike, 1953) is used to select the best K. Later, we discuss the example used in the Lab to give you an intuition about how this is applied.

Practical Note: Lab 6.1

Lab 6.1

Please see the supplementary materials for the book.

Goal of Lab 1

The lab shows how to apply K-means to discover clusters in the *DOTA* dataset courtesy of DOTAlicious Gaming and the Game Trace Archive (Guo and Iosup, 2012).

6.7.1.4 A PRACTICAL EXAMPLE OF APPLYING K-MEANS

In Lab 6.1, we applied *K-means* to cluster players from the *DOTAlicious* dataset. You are strongly encouraged to follow the lab. As discussed in Chapter 1, you will first need to load and preprocess the data. Next, since *K-means* assumes clusters of spherical shape, it is important to scale or normalize the data, following the process outlined in Chapter 2, to put the variables into comparable scales. Optionally, you may want to see if there is any correlation among the attributes to consolidate the features. To do so, please follow the steps discussed in Chapters 3 and 4. It is important to do this, because you do not want to introduce bias into the distance computation. In general, using dimension reduction techniques, such as *PCA*, is useful to eliminate such correlations in your data, before running cluster analysis.

Next, as discussed earlier, to select an appropriate number of clusters, we use a scree plot to examine how the *WSS* metric changes with the number of clusters (see Figure 6.7). We can observe clearly that the improvement on *WSS* slows down after $K = 8$, with $K = 4$ and $K = 8$ being the two "elbows" of the plot. We can also use the silhouette width to see how cohesive the clusters are, given the number of clusters chosen; see the lab for more details.

Finally, with K determined through this *Elbow* method, we run the *K-means* algorithm to obtain clusters. The output of *K-means* will show you how points in the data are grouped into clusters. Following this, you can inspect the cluster centroids given the different variables or features used or you can also inspect the data rows and what cluster they were assigned to.

Visualizing the results is very useful for communication and discussion with experts. However, visualizing the results of 12-dimension cluster space is not useful. Therefore, as you can see in the lab, we used *PCA* to condense the space into two dimensions and then visualized the clusters. Note that using this method forces the cluster results into a 2D space which was not used to construct the clusters to start with, and thus may not be a good way to visualize how

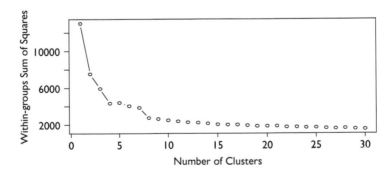

Figure 6.7 Scree plot showing WSS with respect to the number of clusters.

well the algorithm have clustered the data. This is because the data points that appear near each other in a 2D space may not be in a higher dimensional space.

6.7.1.5 AN EXAMPLE FROM THE WILD: TERA ONLINE

To contextualize the use of the *K-means* method within game data science, we adopt an example of using *K-means* clustering to develop player profiles from *TERA*[2] *Online* behavioral telemetry. This work was published in Drachen et al. (2012). It is a straight-forward, simple example of how cluster analysis can be utilized to build behavioral profiles in games. *TERA Online* is an MMORPG that was released by Enmasse Entertainment in South Korea, January 2011. The game was released in North America/Europe the following year. The game is currently free-to-play. It is, at the time of writing, still an active game. It has typical MMORPG features, such as a questing system, crafting, player vs. player action, as well as an integrated economy. Players generate one or more characters, which fall into one of seven races (e.g., Aman, Baraka, or Castanic). In addition, players choose a class (e.g., Warrior, Lancer, or Berserker), each tuned to specific roles in the game (e.g., having a high damage output or being able to absorb high amounts of damage).

6.7.1.5.1 Dataset   The dataset from *TERA Online* is from the game's open beta (character levels 1–32 only) and contains the following behavioral variables (or *features* in data mining terminology):

- *Quests completed*: Number of quests completed
- *Friends*: Number of friends in the game
- *Achievements*: Number of achievements earned
- *Skill levels*: Level in the Mining and Plants skills, respectively
- *Monster kills*: Number of Artificial Intelligence (AI)–controlled enemies killed by the character (combining small, medium, and large monsters in one feature)
- *Deaths by monsters*: Number of times the character has been killed by AI-controlled enemies
- *Total items looted*: Total number of items the character has picked up during the game
- *Auctions house use*: Combined number of times the character has either created an auction or purchased something from an auction

---

[2] TERA stands for *The Exiled Realm of Arborea*.

- *Character level*: Ranges from level 1 to 32. In this example, we will focus on level 32 players (if we just used all possible players, the cluster analysis would neatly give us clusters that are level dependent, given how the values of the different variables change with character level, that is, a level 32 character will have completed, say 1000 quests, where a level 1 character will have completed 2).

6.7.1.5.2 Data preparation and analysis Behavioral telemetry can suffer from quality problems. Incomplete records were removed, and various types of analyses were performed on the data to find any outliers and to check the distribution of the data for each feature.

6.7.1.5.3 Normalizing and scaling input data As discussed in Chapter 2, a common issue in game data is that it usually contains a mix of different types of measurements. Cluster analysis can be sensitive to different measures, and thus we adopt normalization/scaling strategies (as discussed in Chapters 2 and 3). This is a step in the analysis process that is often overlooked; doing so can produce potentially disastrous results. For example, if we had a collection of variables that ranged in value from "3" to "10," with one variable ranging from "0" to "1," the latter can have a disproportionate impact, because it is a binary value. In this case, it can be an advantage to normalize all variables into a "0"–"1" range. The data mining literature is brimmed with ways of normalizing data. For example, standardization (see Chapter 2) transforms the data according to the mean and the standard deviation values. Another example discussed in Chapter 2 is min-max normalization, which transforms the data into a defined range normalized min value and max value. While the choice or normalization strategy is case dependent, we find that min-max normalization is rather sensitive to outliers, so we recommend variance normalization when you are dealing with datasets with outliers. Below, we present the results using variance normalization (for the purpose of this example, it should be noted that there was not much difference in the results using the two techniques).

6.7.1.5.4 Performing clustering on TERA Online data As discussed above, a key element of human decision-making in a cluster analysis is deciding how to determine the number of clusters. There are ways to obtain an idea about the best number of clusters in an analysis (see below), but essentially, deciding how many clusters there are in a dataset is ultimately up to the human running the analysis. In practice, we normally try out different numbers of clusters to see what gives us the best and most interpretable results, as shown in the lab and above. For *TERA Online*, irrespective of which level range we looked at, we found that 6–7 clusters provided the best fit. These clusters do not adhere to character classes but rather to specific behavior ranges. This is perhaps not surprising given how much freedom you have as a player to impact the play style of any character class. We will discuss more on this below.

The *K-means* analysis resulted in six clusters. One cluster has the highest values across all or most of the behavioral variables, and another has abysmal values across the board. The remaining four clusters contain players who perform averagely but have different sets of high or low scores—that is, different things they emphasize in the game.

These clusters are as follows: (a) Elite players (6%): These had the highest scores across all features but were not killed often by AI opponents. Also, these players had very low skill levels in Plants and Mining. This indicates players focused on performance, without interest in skills not impacting their performance (Plants and Mining provide access to resources and equipment; however, resources can also be obtained via solving quests or auctioning off found items). These players are of direct interest not only because they are dedicated but also because of their strong social networks (high number of friends). Retaining these players assists with ensuring a sustainable community. (b) Stragglers (40%): the players with the lowest score for all features (including deaths from monsters). These players, even though they have reached level 32, perform rather badly in the game and are a group that is potentially at risk of churning.

Next to these interesting clusters, there are two clusters with successively better scores: (c) Average Joes (13%) and (d) The Dependables (19%). The latter of these two groups possesses the highest scores except for the Elite. Investigating other features, such as playtime, in connection with this cluster might help in gaining insights into how we can coach these players to progress up to the Elite profile. Both of these groups of players exhibit low Plants and Mining skills.

However, they are matched by the last two groups, the (e) Worker I (16%) and (f) Worker II (8%). These groups have scores similar to the Average Joes and The Dependables, respectively, but with high Mining and Plants skills, and comparably higher loot values (i.e., they have looted more items).

The fact that only two of six clusters of players appear to spend time on learning noncombat skills could indicate a design problem for *TERA Online*, or they might simply be focused on resource collection (keep in mind these are data from the beta version several years ago, and thus not representative of the current game). Resource-gathering skills like these are fundamental to the economy of an MMORPG. Therefore, the fact that only few of the player clusters are learning skills related to economic mechanics is definitely worth investigating further. Additionally, from a cost–benefit perspective, core gameplay features, such as the noncombat skills, should be utilized by most of the player base.

6.7.2 Fuzzy C-means (FCM)

In *K-means*, the boundaries between clusters are hard or crisp (i.e., a data point either belongs to a cluster or not). *Fuzzy C-means* (Bezdek, 1981), also known as *Fuzzy K-means*, extends *K-means* by fuzzifying the boundaries, that is, allowing data points to simultaneously belong to many clusters with varying degrees of membership. As such, a data point, for example, may have 40% membership with Cluster 1 and 60% membership with Cluster 2. Such clusters are called *soft* or *fuzzy*, as there are no concrete boundary lines between them.

6.7.2.1 ASSUMPTIONS AND TARGET CLUSTER TYPE

The key extension of *FCM* over *K-means* is that it utilizes fuzzy clusters instead of crisp ones. Its assumptions and implications are the same as those of *K-means* (i.e., it still looks for spherical-shaped clusters).

6.7.2.2 METHOD

We will adopt the description of this algorithm from Yen and Langari (1999) on Fuzzy Logic. For more information on how the equations used in this algorithm are derived, please review the theorems in this book, particularly Chapter 13. Similar to *K-means*, the inputs of *FCM* are:

- The input dataset, D
- (optional) The distance function $d(x, y)$ with x, y being data points in D
- The number of clusters, K
- A convergence threshold ε
- The fuzziness parameter $m > 1$, which controls how fuzzy the clusters will be: the higher m is, the fuzzier the clusters (more details follow below).

Usually, d is set to be the Euclidean distance function.

FCM follows the following steps:

Step 1: Initialization. Select K initial centroids, represented as mean vectors $c_1, c_2, \ldots, c_K$. These centroids can be selected randomly or with prior knowledge.

Step 2: Cluster membership computation. For all clusters c_j ($j = 1..K$), the memberships $\mu_{c_j}(x)$ of each data point $x \in D$ is computed as follows:

$$\mu_{c_j}(x) = \frac{1}{\sum_{i=1}^{K} \left(\frac{d(x,c_j)}{d(x,c_i)} \right)^{\frac{1}{m-1}}}, \qquad \text{(Equation 6.5)}$$

where

- j is between 1 and K
- $d(x, c_i)$ and $d(x, c_j)$ denote the distance between x and clusters c_i, c_j
- Note here that m is the exponent fuzzy membership and is a parameter in the objective function. $m > 1$ denotes the fuzziness of the cluster. As m approaches 1, the membership values degrade to either 0 or 1 (i.e., the membership to the closest cluster will approach 1 and others 0).

In Equation 6.5, $\mu_{c_j}(x)$ is proportional to $\frac{1}{d(x,c_j)^{\frac{1}{m-1}}} = d(x, c_j)^{\frac{1}{1-m}}$, with $\sum_{i=1}^{K} \frac{1}{d(x,c_i)^{\frac{1}{m-1}}}$ acting as a normalization term.

When m goes to "infinity," the exponent approaches "0"; thus, the term $d(x, c_j)^{\frac{1}{1-m}}$ approaches "1." This means it does not matter which cluster is closer to x: all memberships will be almost the same. This is what extreme fuzziness looks like: every point has similar membership to every cluster, regardless of their proximity. On the other hand, as m goes to "1," the term grows exponentially with the inverse of the distance toward "infinity." Through normalization, the distance to the closest cluster will greatly outweigh the rest, thus making for very crisp boundaries.

Step 3: Centroid update. Cluster centroids are recomputed as weighted means of their members, taking into account the membership w:

$$c_j = \frac{\sum_{x \in D} (\mu_{C_j}(x))^m x}{\sum_{x \in D} (\mu_{C_j}(x))^m} \qquad \text{(Equation 6.6)}$$

where

- x are points in the dataset D,
- c_j is the centroid of cluster j, and
- $\mu_{c_j}(x)$ is the membership degree of x in cluster j.

Step 4: Cluster membership re-computation. The cluster membership values of each data point in D are recomputed after the centroid update using the Equation 6.5.

Step 5: Stability checking and termination.

$$T = \sum_{i=1}^{C} |c_i^{Previous} - c_i| \leq \varepsilon \qquad \text{(Equation 6.7)}$$

Equation 6.7 checks whether the difference between the centroid of a cluster over all clusters does not change more than a specific threshold ε set as an input. If it is below that threshold, then it is deemed converged and the algorithm terminates. Otherwise, go back to Step 3.

6.7.2.3 HYPERPARAMETER TUNING

The key parameter to tune for *FCM* is the number of clusters K. While the fuzziness parameter m could be a target for tuning, it usually suffices to fix $m = 2$ unless there is some domain knowledge to set it otherwise. The distance metric d is often set to Euclidean distance.

Practical Note: Lab 6.2

Lab 6.2

Please see the supplemental materials for the book.

Goal of Lab 6.2

The lab shows how to apply *FCM* to discover clusters in the DOTA dataset courtesy of DOTAlicious Gaming and the Game Trace Archive (Guo and Iosup, 2012).

6.7.2.4 A PRACTICAL EXAMPLE OF APPLYING FCM

In Lab 6.2, we show how to use *FCM* to cluster the player data in the *DOTAlicous* dataset. The usage of *FCM* here is almost identical to *K-means*, except with a different function: *fanny* instead of *k-means*. Similar to Lab 6.1, in Lab 6.1, we also clean and normalize the data. Then, we will call the *fanny* method. Please

```
# show membership
head (fit$membership)
```

##	[, 1]	[, 2]	[, 3]	[, 4]
## B	0.604786506	0.08649803	0.08289371	0.22582175
## B.1	0.006153275	0.54715172	0.31392755	0.13276746
## N	0.002412201	0.26253301	0.69695848	0.03809631
## B.2	0.048362219	0.16999865	0.15729056	0.62434857
## N.1	0.015887566	0.43841522	0.34646985	0.19922736
## N.2	0.002619130	0.28281458	0.66817862	0.04638767

Figure 6.8 Output of *FCM* showing membership of each point to the cluster.

follow the lab to understand the practical aspect of applying the appropriate methods.

After applying *FCM*, we can inspect the memberships by printing the membership degrees for each centroid. Figure 6.8 shows the result, where each row corresponds to one data point labeled by its unique row name (B, B.1, N, B.2, etc.), and each column indicates the membership to the corresponding centroids (i.e., centroid 1, 2, 3, or 4). The membership values on each row should sum up to 1.

Finally, to assess the clustering result, we can compute and visualize its silhouette widths in the silhouette plot (see the lab for more practical exercise on how to do so with this dataset). We will leave it as an exercise for you to compare the clusters you obtained with *FCM* and *K-means*. Note that every dataset is different, and thus some clustering methods will be better for one dataset than the other, so it is a good exercise to compare the results of different methods on this dataset.

6.7.3 DBSCAN

DBSCAN is a density-based clustering algorithm (Ester et al., 1996) operating on the notion that clusters are highly dense groups of data points separated by low density areas. Figure 6.9 shows the kind of clusters *DBSCAN* targets. Points that do not belong to any cluster are considered noise. *DBSCAN* utilizes two important parameters to determine density, namely a real value $\epsilon > 0$ and an integer *minPts*. Given a data point x, if the number of data points within the radius ϵ surrounding x (i.e., within its ϵ-neighborhood) is greater than *minPts*, the density at x is considered to be high and x is called a core point. Non-core points that are in a core point's ϵ-neighborhood are called border points. The

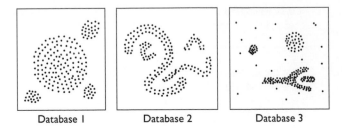

Database I   Database 2   Database 3

Figure 6.9 Clusters based on density; in database 3, points that are located in sparse areas, i.e., with low point density, are considered noise. Figure taken from Ester et al. (1996). Ester, M., Kriegel, H. P., Sander, J., and Xu, X. (1996, August). A density-based algorithm for discovering clusters in large spatial databases with noise. In *KDD* (Vol. 96, No. 34, pp. 226–231). © 1996, Association of the Advancement of Artificial Intelligence.

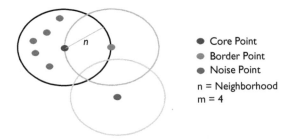

● Core Point
● Border Point
● Noise Point
n = Neighborhood
m = 4

Figure 6.10 Different labels DBSCAN assigns to data points: core, border, and noise. Core and border points end up being part of a cluster, while noise is not part of any cluster. Image used with permission from author Abhijit Annaldas. Appeared in the post: http://abhijitannaldas.com/ml/dbscan-clustering-in-machine-learning.html

rest are outliers and eventually treated as noise, not belonging to any cluster. Figure 6.10 shows how DBSCAN labels the data points, with *minPts* = 6 and the ϵ-neighborhood depicted as circles.

6.7.3.1 CHARACTERISTICS

Because clusters are defined, and thus detected, based on the above notion of density, *DBSCAN* presents several advantages over other methods, such as *K-means* and *FCM*:

- It does not require the number of clusters as input.
- It is not limited to any type of clusters. As long as the clusters are dense and separated by sparse areas, they will be found regardless of their shapes.
- It is robust regarding noise and outliers. *K-means* and *FCM* are susceptible to noise, as their clusters are easily skewed by outliers.

- It is deterministic. While both *K-means* and *FCM* are stochastic and may need to run multiple times with random initialization to avoid falling into local optima, *DBSCAN*'s density-based computation does not depend on randomness.

That said, *DBSCAN* is not perfect; some of its cons are:

- Clusters with varying density are difficult to detect, as density is fixed by ϵ and *minPts*
- *DBSCAN* is sensitive to its hyperparameters: changing ϵ and *minPts* slightly may significantly change the outcome. For instance, in cases where a cluster comprises two large dense regions connected by a thin but dense area (like a corridor connecting two rooms), if ϵ and *minPts* are not set appropriately to capture such connection, we may see two clusters in the result instead of one.

6.7.3.2 METHOD

The inputs of *DBSCAN* are as follows:

- The neighborhood's radius ϵ (epsilon)
- The minimum number of neighbors *minPts* in the neighborhood for the center data point to be considered core
- The distance function $d(x, y)$ with x, y being data points in D (optional)
- As with other clustering algorithms discussed before, such as *K-means* and *FCM*, the distance function d is often chosen to be Euclidean distance

DBSCAN comprises the following steps:

Step 1: Find core and non-core points. For each data point $x \in D$, if the number of ϵ-neighbors is greater than *minPts*, that is, $|N_x| > minPts$, with $N_x = \{z \in D, d(x, z) < \epsilon\}$, label x as "core." Otherwise, if the number of ϵ-neighbors is less than *minPts* but greater than 1, it is "non-core."
Step 2: Find contiguous regions of core points. This is done by grouping together core points that are in the ϵ-neighborhood of each other.
Step 3: Construct clusters. Each contiguous region of core points is set as one cluster. Assign each non-core point p to a cluster c if there exists some point in c that is in the ϵ-neighborhood of p. Otherwise, consider p as noise.

6.7.3.3 HYPERPARAMETER TUNING

Both *minPts* and ϵ are key to the operation of *DBSCAN* and require tuning. Usually, such tuning is done by plotting a K-distance chart that shows the mean distance of every point to its K neighbors. The plot provides an overview of the data's density, which helps us decide which values of *minPts* and ϵ would reasonably split the data into dense regions. We will demonstrate how to use a K-distance chart to tune these hyperparameters in Lab 6.3.

Practical Note: Lab 6.3

Lab 6.3

Please see the supplement materials for the book.

Goal of Lab 3

The lab shows how to apply DBSCAN to discover clusters in the *DOTA* dataset courtesy of DOTAlicious Gaming and the Game Trace Archive (Guo and Iosup, 2012).

6.8 Hierarchical clustering methods

Unlike partitional methods, *HC* methods do not aim to output a single partitioning of the data. Their goal is to construct a tree, called the cluster dendrogram, denoting how data can be merged or split into nesting clusters. See Figure 6.11 for an example tree. In a dendrogram, the x-axis displays all data points, the y-axis captures the distance measure of clusters being split or merged (i.e., height of the tree), and the tree structure shows how data can split/merge to form smaller/bigger clusters.

To construct this dendrogram, there are two approaches:

- **Bottom-up:** Each individual data point starts out as a cluster on its own (i.e., as the leaves of the tree), then subsequently these clusters are merged to form bigger clusters at parent nodes. The root node contains the whole dataset. Algorithms using the bottom-up approach are called Agglomerative Hierarchical Clustering (AHC).
- **Top-down:** The whole dataset is assigned to a single cluster initially at the root node, then split out to smaller clusters until each cluster comprises a single data point. Algorithms using the top-down approach are called Divisive Hierarchical Clustering (DHC).

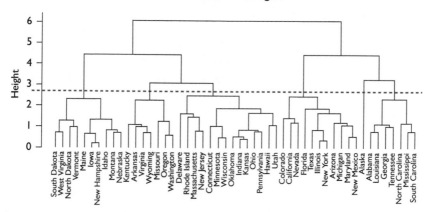

Figure 6.11 A cluster dendrogram resulted from a hierarchical clustering algorithm. The dotted line is a cut through the dendrogram to return a clustering, in this case splitting the data into the six disjoint clusters. Image used with permission from author Bradley Boehmke. Appeared in https://uc-r.github.io/hc_clustering.

In order to return a clustering comprised of disjoint data subsets, a cut line can be applied to the dendrogram (as shown in Figure 6.11). The placement of this line is determined by the height of the dendrogram, which represents the within-cluster distance in each cluster. Low cut lines produce small but compact clusters, while high lines yield larger and sparser ones.

In this chapter, we will concentrate on reviewing *AHC* rather than *DHC* algorithms due to the popularity of *AHC* over *DHC*. However, there has been some work on *DHC*, and interested readers should consult the bibliography section for more about this method.

6.8.1 Characteristics

HC has a number of advantages over other methods we discussed in this chapter so far, specifically:

- It does not require the knowledge of the number of clusters K before running. Users can determine K after the fact. As such, unlike *K-means* or *FCM*, which need to be run anew when you want to try a different K value, *HC* only needs to run once.
- It is easy to use and gives good results in many cases.

That said, there are some weaknesses and challenges associated with *HC* that you need to be aware of:

- It is not very robust against noise and outliers. The outlier points will most likely be well separated from the rest, so they often end up in clusters of their own. In cases when you already know how many clusters to expect, *HC* may give you some clusters that consist entirely of outliers.
- It could be difficult to select the right cut line or right number of clusters.
- While methods such as *K-means* explicitly optimize a loss function (e.g., the *WSS* given the number of clusters K), *HC* does not optimize any such function. It is, therefore, difficult to fairly compare different *HCs*' results to find the optimal one.

The above drawbacks of *HC* are mostly solved by domain expertise, when clusters are visualized and examined by relevant stakeholders to understand their nature and determine if the resultant clusters make sense.

As will be discussed in more detail later, while the outcome can be similar, the main disadvantage of *DHC* as compared to *AHC* is that it requires a method as input to split the clusters. *AHC* does not have such a requirement and thus is more lightweight and popular than *DHC*.

6.8.2 AHC

AHC relies on the idea of merging closest clusters together to form larger clusters. While it is easy to compute the distance between two data points using measures such as Euclidean metrics, computing the distance between two clusters is not as straightforward. There could be more than one data point in each cluster, so, between two clusters, we can obtain many different distance values, depending on which pair of data points we have selected. There are many approaches to computing cluster distance given pair-wise individual distances, some of which are depicted in Figure 6.12:

- Minimum distance (a.k.a. single-link): Cluster distance is the smallest distance between any pair of data from the two clusters—that is,

$$dist(C_i, C_j) = \min_{\forall x_m \in C_i, x_n \in C_j} d(x_m, x_n) \qquad \text{(Equation 6.8)}$$

- where d is the distance between two points, and x is a point in the data.

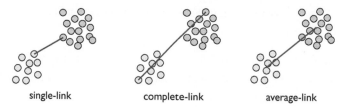

single-link   complete-link   average-link

Figure 6.12 Methods to compute distances. Permission granted from the author. Figure from Guevara (2011).

- Maximum distance (a.k.a. *complete-link*): Taking the largest instead of the smallest distance,

$$dist(C_i, C_j) = \max_{\forall x_m \in C_i, x_n \in C_j} d(x_m, x_n) \qquad \text{(Equation 6.9)}$$

where C is a cluster, d is the distance between two points, and x is a point in the data.

- Mean distance (a.k.a. *average-link*):

$$dist(C_i, C_j) = \frac{1}{|C_i||C_j|} \sum_{x_m \in C_i} \sum_{x_n \in C_j} d(x_m, x_n) \qquad \text{(Equation 6.10)}$$

with $|C_i|, |C_j|$ denoting the respective number of data points in C_i and C_j. C is a cluster, d is the distance between two points, and x is a point in the data.

- Centroid distance (a.k.a. *centroid-link*): Taking the distance between the two centroids, that is, mean vectors, of all data in each cluster.

$$dist(C_i, C_j) = d \left(\frac{1}{|C_i|} \sum_{x_m \in C_i} x_m, \frac{1}{|C_j|} \sum_{x_n \in C_j} x_n \right) \qquad \text{(Equation 6.11)}$$

with $|C_i|, |C_j|$ denoting the respective number of data points in C_i and C_j. C is a cluster, d is the distance between two points, and x is a point in the data.

- Ward's minimum variance method (a.k.a. *Ward*): In this method, a global objective function that represents the within-cluster variance is selected and minimized at each merging step. One common choice for such an objective function is the minimum squared distance $d^2(C_i, C_j)$ with C_i, C_j being the centroids.

Given these distance functions, an *AHC* algorithm will iteratively merge the most similar (or closest) data points together until a stopping condition is met or until a specific number of clusters are created.

6.8.3 Hyperparameter tuning

When using *AHC*, one decision that must be made is the choice of linkage—that is, *single-*, *complete-*, *average-*, *centroid-linkage*, or *Ward's* method. This decision is made based mainly on domain knowledge, depending on whether it makes sense to compare clusters based on the min, max, mean, of distances, or the Ward's method. See the lab for more details.

Practical Note: Lab 6.5

Lab 6.5

Please see the supplemental materials for the book.

Goal of Lab 6.5

The lab shows how to apply *HC* to discover clusters in the DOTA dataset courtesy of DOTAlicious Gaming and the Game Trace Archive (Guo and Iosup, 2012).

6.9 Archetypal Analysis (AA)

AA (Cutler and Breiman, 1994) is an unsupervised learning method which aims to summarize the data not in terms of clusters, but in terms of archetypes. Archetypes are representative data points, which can express a linear combination of the observed data. This is one of the most heavily employed models for building profiles of players because it allows for the expression of profiles with regards to their proximity to behaviors in the extreme (convex hull) ends of the data distribution space. In contrast to centroid-based clustering algorithms, such as *k-means,* for example, the clusters found using *AA* are identified by prototypical points. This means that the contrast between various archetypes is magnified.

AA seeks to identify points whose convex combinations can generally represent the population of the dataset. These archetype points are not necessarily observed but exist as manifestations of extreme behavioral qualities. This means that archetypes typically exhibit more radical values than the typical data points. Each observed data point is then classified to its closest archetype, resulting in clusters. We can also either assign a player to one archetype or to a combination of archetypes, depending on where in relation to different archetype points that player is positioned in the multivariate space.

For example, consider the in-game activity statistics of players, such as number of *kills*, *deaths*, and *assists*. A player can be thought of as an archetype formed by a linear combination of these statistics, such as "Novice," "Beginner," and "Advanced," in which:

- "Novice" archetype has low number of kills, high number of deaths, and low number of assists,
- "Beginner" archetype has medium number of kills, high number of deaths, and medium number of assists, and
- "Advanced" archetype has high number of kills, low number of deaths, and medium number of assists.

A player's in-game statistics can be expressed as, for example, a sum of 20% Novice, 60% Beginner, and 20% Advanced.

6.9.1 Characteristics

AA is not a traditional clustering algorithm, as it does not partition the data. That said, *AA* allows us to understand the data structure using typical, representative data points, similar to how cluster centroids can be used to understand structures in the data.

AA was originally introduced as a dimensionality reduction method, similar to *PCA*, which was discussed in Chapter 4. The output of *AA* also reminds us of the output of *PCA*, that is, principal components into which each data point can be decomposed. However, while *PCA* computes principal components as those that best capture the variance in the data, *AA* finds archetypes that are extreme and sparse, that is, with most data features being close to 0. The rationale is that such extremes, when represented as vectors of features, are easier to interpret and explain for human users than those with many nonzero values.

In geometrical terms, *AA* aims to find extreme points that best approximate the convex hull of all data points in the training data (Figure 6.13).

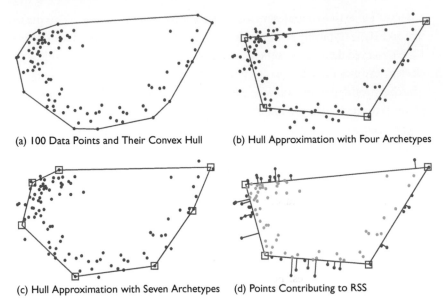

(a) 100 Data Points and Their Convex Hull (b) Hull Approximation with Four Archetypes

(c) Hull Approximation with Seven Archetypes (d) Points Contributing to RSS

Figure 6.13 Archetypes are extreme points that approximate the convex hull of the training dataset in the multi-dimensional space. Image taken from Bauckhage and Thurau (2009) with permission.

6.9.2 Method

The inputs of AA include

- The input dataset, D
- The number of archetypes, K

The technical details of AA can be referred to in Bauckhage and Thurau (2009) or Eugster and Leisch (2009). We briefly summarize the steps here:

Step 1: Initialization. Initialize a set of archetypes $Z = (z_1, z_2, \ldots, z_K)$
Step 2: Find best combinations. Given the archetypes, find the coefficient matrix α and β that minimizes:

$$RSS = min_{\alpha_{ik}} \sum_{i=1}^{n} x_i - \sum_{k=1}^{p} \alpha_{ik} z_k \|^2 \qquad \text{(Equation 6.12)}$$

Where

- x_i is the training dataset in matrix form, of dimension $n \times m$ with n being the number of data points and m the number of data features.
- α is the coefficient matrix of dimension $n \times p$, with p being the number of archetypes. α defines the linear combination that decomposes the data into archetypes. Furthermore, it is enforced that $\sum_{j=1}^{p} \alpha_{ij} = 1$ with $\alpha_{ij} \geq 0$.
- $Z = (z_1, z_2, \ldots, z_K)$ is the matrix of dimensions $m \times K$ representing the archetypes and is represented as $z_k = \sum_{j=1}^{n} \beta_{kj} x_j$ and $\beta_{kj} \geq 0$ and $\sum_{j=1}^{n} \beta_{kj} = 1$

As described in Cutler and Brieman (1994), this optimization problem is trying to find α and β that minimize the *RSS* defined in Equation 6.12. This problem can be solved by constraint nonlinear least squares algorithm. However, it can also be solved by dividing the problem and trying to solve for α first given a set of archetypes, Z, and then β given the αs are derived and stopping when the algorithm converges.

6.9.3 Hyperparameter tuning

AA requires the number of archetypes K as an input, so tuning is needed to select the most appropriate value for K. The Elbow method, to be discussed in Chapter 4 and used in various sections above, can be applied here. See Lab 6.6 for more details.

Practical Note: Lab 6.6

Lab 6.6

Please see the supplemental materials for the book.

Goal of Lab 6.6

The lab shows how to apply *AA* to discover archetypes in the *DOTA* dataset courtesy of DOTAlicious Gaming and the Game Trace Archive (Guo and Iosup, 2012).

6.9.4 Advanced method: Model-based Clustering (MC)

One way to look at clustering is to treat it as a model learning problem, where the term *model* refers to a computational structure that is assumed to have generated the observed data. In this case, the model is the set of distributions that best fits the data, where distributions are input to the algorithm, as we will see below.

In this view, the observed data D are assumed to be sampled from a mixture of distributions $Z_1, Z_2, \ldots, Z_k$ according to the following procedure:

1. Pick a distribution Z_i according to $P(Z_i)$, which defines how probable it is that Z_i will be picked, $i = 1, \ldots, k$
2. Sample a data point d from $P(d|Z_i)$

This two-step procedure is repeated $|D|$ times to obtain the complete dataset D. In this case, the probability of observing the data point d in D is equal to $\sum_{i=1}^{k} P(Z_i) P(d|Z_i)$. Collectively, the probability of observing D will be:

$$P(D|Z_1, Z_2, \ldots, Z_k) = \prod_{d \in D} P(d|Z_1, Z_2, \ldots, Z_k) = \prod_{d \in D} \left(\sum_{i=1}^{k} P(Z_i) P(d|Z_i) \right)$$

(Equation 6.13)

For example, each eclipse in Figure 6.14 represents one distribution from a total of six distributions from which the data might have been sampled. Each such distribution is characterized by a set of parameters. For example, Gaussian distributions are probability distributions in which the data probability is

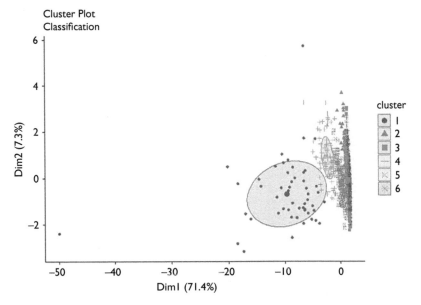

Figure 6.14 The data distribution model learned from *Expectation-Maximization*. Each ellipse represents a Gaussian distribution in the mixture of six distributions, from which the data could have been sampled.

defined as $P(x) = \dfrac{e^{-\frac{(x-\mu)^2}{2\sigma^2}}}{\sqrt{2\pi\sigma^2}}$ with μ defined as the mean and σ the standard deviation. As such, each Gaussian distribution has two parameters: μ and σ.

The goal of *MC* is to find the optimal parameters, denoted as Θ, that define these distributions $Z_1, Z_2, \ldots, Z_k$, such that the likelihood that data was generated from these distributions $P(D|\Theta) = P(D|Z_1, Z_2, \ldots, Z_k)$ is maximal. For example, in the case of *MC* with Gaussian distributions, this set of parameters includes the means and standard deviations of all the distributions involved. This problem, which is called an *optimization problem* since it is trying to find the optimal parameter Θ, is equivalent to solving its log version, that is, the log likelihood. Since log is a monotonic function, it does not change the optimality of solutions. Additionally, log conveniently converts from products into summations, making computation easier, and helps avoid small products, which may be truncated to zeros due to the fixed floating-point representation on computers.

Expectation-Maximization (EM) is an approximate algorithm that can be used to solve this optimization problem. More specifically, *EM* aims to find the Θ^*, maximizing the log likelihood of generating the observed data D:

$$\Theta^* = argmax_\Theta\, L(D|\Theta) = argmax_\Theta \left(\log \prod_{d\in D} P(D|\Theta) \right)$$

$$= argmax_\Theta \left(\sum_{d\in D} logP(d|\Theta) \right) \quad \text{(Equation 6.14)}$$

The log likelihood, $L(D|\Theta)$, captures the quality of fit of the model, M, defined by Θ, as it represents the likelihood that the observed dataset, D, was generated from M. Due to this reason, given the same number of clusters, we prefer the model with higher $L(D|\Theta)$. Note that, generally, more clusters lead to higher evaluation scores, as there is less variation within the clusters. As such, we want to find a balance between maximizing the goodness of fit and minimizing the number of clusters.

The output of this algorithm is then a model (in the form of clusters) and cluster assignments.

6.9.5 Characteristics

MC is considered a more general class of algorithms than, but behaves very similar to, *K-means* and *FCM*. For instance, in *K-means*, each data point, d, is assigned to the cluster, C, whose centroid is closest to it. In probability terms, this is similar to placing the same Gaussian distribution (with the same mean and standard deviation) at each centroid and imposing that the data is most likely generated from the distribution closest to it.

The flexibility of *MC* is that it allows users to set different probability distributions and obtain clusters with elliptical shapes instead of spherical, as in the case of *K-means* or *Fuzzy C-means*.

6.9.6 Method

The input of *MC* includes:

- The input dataset, D,
- The number of distributions (i.e., clusters), K, and
- The parametric form of each cluster (optional). By default, each cluster is set to be a Gaussian distribution.

EM can then be used to estimate the optimal parameter Θ^* defining the clusters. *EM* is a mathematically sophisticated method, the details of which can be referred to in (WikiStat, 2016). At a high level, solving *MC* using *EM* comprises the following steps:

Step 1: Initialization. Initialize the parameters Θ that define set of distributions.

Step 2: Expectation. Fix the model (defined by parameters Θ) and estimate the log likelihood $L(D|\Theta)$.

Step 3: Maximization. Find a new parameter Θ^* that maximizes $L(D|\Theta)$, using Equation 6.14.

Step 4: Termination check. Check the parameters Θ^* to see if they converge, that is, that the change is within a predefined margin. If so, terminate; otherwise, go back to Step 2.

Once Θ^* is obtained, that is, $P(x|Z_i)$ are known for any cluster Z_i, the cluster membership of each data point d belong to cluster Z_i is computed using $P(d|Z_i)$, allowing us to obtain something similar to *FCM*: the membership to each cluster for every data point.

6.9.7 Hyperparameter tuning

The implementation of *EM* in the R package mclust allows for tuning of the clusters' structures, which defines the shapes of clusters to be obtained. More information can be found in the documentation (Fraley et al., 2018).

The best model is selected using the Bayesian Information Criterion (BIC) (Schwarz, 1978). The higher the *BIC* score is, the better the obtained model is in explaining the observed data.

6.10 Advice on applying cluster methods to behavioral telemetry

On a final note, it is worth adding a few pieces of general advice about applying clustering methods in the context of behavioral telemetry.

6.10.1 Time dependency

Players can change their behavior, game communities may evolve, and games themselves can change throughout their lifecycle. Therefore, it is also possible for clusters to change. A traditional cluster analysis provides a static snapshot of behavior, which has a limited shelf life. This means that cluster analyses should be re-run in response to, for example, patch releases, as well as following a regular schedule for persistent games. It is also possible to use time in a more dynamic fashion by including temporal behavioral patterns in clustering—for example, for finding temporal patterns leading to player churn, or conversions from non-paying to paying users. Implementing temporal information in a cluster analysis can be done, for example, via time-series analysis (such as graph-based clustering).

6.10.2 High dimensionality and big data

While the definition of high dimensionality in a dataset is somewhat nebulous, anywhere from a dozen to hundreds or even thousands of dimensions can occur in cluster analysis in games (e.g., player forum mining). High-dimensional data is useful because it is granular and help us to find behavioral features that determine the groupings of players but makes the analysis process more cumbersome. Notably, many of the common clustering algorithms do not scale well to large datasets, or distance functions encounter problems in high-dimensional space—aptly named curse of dimensionality—because the number of grid points increases exponentially with dimensionality. Generally, problems with dimensionality occur because a fixed number of data points become increasingly sparse as the number of dimensions increases. This increases distance/similarity between points. For certain data distributions, the relative difference of the distance of the closest and farthest data points of an independently selected point goes to zero with increasing dimensionality.

This means that, in high-dimensional spaces, distances between points become relatively uniform, which invalidates the notion of nearest neighbor. In recent years, there have been several developments toward improving the performance of algorithms for clustering high-dimensional data or the development of new approaches. For example, pre-clustering methods such as *canopy clustering*, which pre-partitions data and then clusters each partition individually. *Canopy clustering* is often used as a preprocessing step for *k-means* or *HC*. Other examples of algorithms for high-dimensionality datasets include *subspace clustering* and *correlation clustering*.

6.10.3 Finding the right features

Feature selection is a topic that is increasingly relevant in the games industry due to the potential range of behavioral features in games. While many monetization metrics (such as *Daily Active Users* (*DAU*), *MAU*, and *ARPU*) are based on features that extend across games, they can be defined in different ways. For example, *DAU* provides a concrete temporal frame, but what constitutes an active player is still vague. The problems with feature selection usually occur when trying to evaluate player behavior in relation to the actual game mechanics and design. Finding out that players, for example, have a tendency to churn at level "8" is in and of itself not valuable, but drilling down and discovering the underlying causes of churn is. Identifying the features to investigate in these situations can be difficult. Furthermore, due to the often-changeable nature of notably persistent games, predicting which behaviors are valuable to track can be challenging as well. Cluster analysis can be used to assist with identifying important features, but this requires that such behavioral features are present in the dataset in the first place.

6.10.4 Mixtures of qualitative and quantitative data

A typical problem with behavior analysis in games is the mixing of measurement types, as behavioral features are often measured in different ways. For example, ratios (e.g., *kill/death* ratio or *hit/miss* ratio) may be mixed with categorical data (e.g., *character type*). Such data require a careful consideration of data normalization strategies.

6.11 Summary

In this chapter, you learned different methods that aim to divide the data into groups of data points with similar characteristics, that is, clusters. Some important takeaways are as follows:

- Clustering is an inherently exploratory analysis. As there is hardly any ground truth to validate the discovered clusters, it is usually up to the domain experts to examine the results and decide whether the clusters provide any useful insight on the data and how to utilize them in practice. Visualization becomes an important tool to convey the results of clustering to the experts. That being said, cluster analysis is one of the most commonly applied unsupervised machine learning tools in game data science because it allows discovery of patterns of behavior in high-dimensional datasets.

- Although we usually apply clustering with very few preconceptions about the structure of the data, it is important to decide whether the data even has cluster tendency or not. As any clustering algorithm will return some clusters, the fact that we do not yet have any universally reliable way to validate the result makes it very difficult to know whether the newly gained insights are just random artifacts or real, generalizable structures.

- In order to implement the results of a behavioral cluster analysis, the outcome must be presented in a language that is understandable to the stakeholder in question. Professionals in marketing, design, management, and engineering may use different professional jargons which must be taken into consideration when describing results. The use of visualization techniques best suited for the target stakeholder group is critical to ensure acceptance of the results, and thus, implementation of design changes. A cluster analysis, in and of itself, will provide insights into the patterns of players' behavior; however, it will not necessarily show the best way to change a game's design or its business strategy toward modifying those behaviors. Just like in game user research and user testing analytics, results must be communicated to and interpreted by the relevant stakeholders, who can further develop more hypothesis to validate or points to explore. Thus, the process never stops with just one form of analysis. It is iterative, as discussed in Chapter 1.

• •

EXERCISES

1. What are the pros and cons of:

   a. *K-means*?
   b. *DBSCAN*?
   c. *Hierarchical Clustering*?

2. Considering the *VPAL* dataset, apply *K-means* on it. Use the Elbow method to select a suitable value for the number of clusters *K*.

3. Use *FCM* instead of *K-means* for exercise 2 and compare the results. Discuss pros and cons of the two algorithms.

4. Considering the *VPAL* dataset, apply *DBSCAN* on it. Discuss the differences between clusters obtained using this method and those using *K-means* or *FCM*.

5. Consider *VPAL* data, apply *HC* to it and compare the results to the *K-means* and *DBSCAN*.

6. Consider *VPAL* data, apply *AA* to it and compare the results to other methods for clustering you have used throughout this chapter.

7. Consider the *DOTAlicious* dataset:

   a. Apply *PCA* to reduce its dimension.
   b. Choose three cluster analysis methods you have learned in this chapter and run them on the reduced data.
   c. Compare the results and discuss similarities as well as differences in the obtained clusters.

8. Does the *VPAL* dataset have cluster tendency? Show the steps you take to answer this question.

• •

BIBLIOGRAPHY

https://nlp.stanford.edu/IR-book/html/htmledition/hierarchical-agglomerative-clustering-1.htmlhttps://nlp.stanford.edu/IR-book/html/htmledition/hierarchical-agglomerative-clustering-1.html

Ambroise, C., Sèze, G., Badran, F., and Thiria, S. (2000). Hierarchical clustering of self-organizing maps for cloud classification. *Neurocomputing, 30*(1–4), 47–52.

Bauckhage, C., and Christian, T. (2009). Making archetypal analysis practical. In *Lecture Notes in Computer Science (Including Subseries Lecture Notes in Artificial Intelligence and Lecture Notes in Bioinformatics)*. https://doi.org/10.1007/978-3-642-03798-6_28.

Bezdek, J. C. (1981). Objective function clustering. In *Pattern Recognition with Fuzzy Objective Function Algorithms* (pp. 43–93). Boston, MA: Springer US. https://doi.org/10.1007/978-1-4757-0450-1_3.

Cutler, A., and Breinman, L. (1994). Archetypal analysis. *Technometrics.* https://doi.org/10.1080/00401706.1994.10485840.

D'Souza, A. A. (1999). Using EM to estimate a probability density with a mixture of gaussians. *Technical Note.*

Dhillon, I. S., Guan, Y., and Kulis, B. (2004). Kernel K-means: spectral clustering and normalized cuts." In *Proceedings of the 2004 ACM SIGKDD International Conference on Knowledge Discovery and Data Mining—KDD '04* (pp. 551–56). Seattle, WA, USA: ACM Press. https://doi.org/10.1145/1014052.1014118.

Drachen, A., Sifa, R., Bauckhage, C., and Thurau, C. (2012). Guns, swords and data: Clustering of player behavior in computer games in the wild. In *Proceedings of IEEE Computational Intelligence in Games, 2012* (pp. 163–170). Granada, Spain: IEEE Publishers. DOI: 10.1109/CIG.2012.6374152

Ester, M., Hans-Peter, K., Jörg, S., and Xiaowei, X. (1996). A density-based algorithm for discovering clusters in large spatial databases with noise." In *Proceedings of the Second International Conference on Knowledge Discovery and Data Mining* (pp. 226–31), AAAI Press.

Eugster, M. J. A., and Friedrich, L. (2009). From Spider-man to hero: Archetypal analysis in R. *Journal of Statistical Software, 30*(8), 1–23.

Fraley, C., Adrian, E.R., Luca, S., Thomas, B. M., and Michael, F. (2018). Package 'mclust.' URL: https://cran.r-project.org/web/packages/mclust/mclust.pdf.

Guevara, A. P. B. (2011). *Inference of a human brain fiber bundle atlas from high angular resolution diffusion imaging* (Doctoral dissertation, Paris 11).

Guo, Y., and Alexandru, I. (2012). The game trace archive. In *Annual Workshop on Network and Systems Support for Games.* Venice, Italy. https://doi.org/10.1109/NetGames.2012.6404027.

Huang, K. Y. (2002). The use of a newly developed algorithm of divisive hierarchical clustering for remote sensing image analysis. *International Journal of Remote Sensing, 23*(16), 3149–68.

Jain, A. K. (2010). Data clustering: 50 years beyond K-means. *Pattern Recognition Letters, 31*(8), 651–66.

Jiang, D., Pei, J., and Zhang, A. (2003, March). DHC: A density-based hierarchical clustering method for time series gene expression data. In *Proceedings of Third IEEE Symposium on Bioinformatics and Bioengineering* (pp. 393–400). IEEE, Bethesda, MD, USA.

Kaufman, L., and Peter, J. R. (2005). *Finding groups in data: An introduction to cluster analysis,* 1st edition. New Jersy, USA: Wiley-Interscience.

Rousseeuw, P. J. (1987). Silhouettes: A graphical aid to the interpretation and validation of cluster analysis. *Journal of Computational and Applied Mathematics20*(C), 53–65. https://doi.org/10.1016/0377-0427(87)90125-7.

Schwarz, G. (1978). Estimating the dimension of a model. *The Annals of Statistics.* https://doi.org/10.1214/aos/1176344136.

Thorndike, R. L. (1953). Who belongs in the family? *Psychometrika*, *18*(4), 267–76. https://doi.org/10.1007/BF02289263.

WikiStat. (2016). Unsupervised clustering with E.M. URL: https://www.math.univ-toulouse.fr/~besse/Wikistat/pdf/st-m-datSc4-EMmixt.pdf.

Yen, J., and Langari, R. (1999). *Fuzzy logic: intelligence, control, and information* (Vol. 1). Upper Saddle River, NJ: Prentice Hall.

CHAPTER 7

Supervised Learning in Game Data Science

G ame data scientists, whether working in industry or academia, need to find patterns in data. This means extracting generalizable knowledge and insights, summarizing recurring patterns, and identifying similarities and differences from complex data. Pattern finding is central to game data science because it can sort out what is going on in voluminous, volatile, longitudinal, and sometimes sparse datasets.

To take an example, game companies using the freemium revenue model need to understand how players move from nonpaying to paying players. To investigate the path of decisions and events that led a person to make the decision to invest cash in a game requires locating recurring patterns and trends among potentially millions of paths. This is where supervised machine learning methods, such as classification and regression analysis, can be incredibly useful. Such methods are in widespread use across both industry and academia.

Supervised machine learning, together with deep learning methods, are used to classify players into profiles, predict winners in e-sports, predict team strategies, analyze churn patterns, predict purchases in free-to-play games, and predict reactions to new game features. There are hundreds of papers and presentations available on these topics. This area then forms one of the current frontlines in game data science.

Game Data Science. Magy Seif El-Nasr, Truong Huy Nguyen Dinh, Alessandro Canossa, and Anders Drachen, Oxford University Press. © Magy Seif El-Nasr, Truong Huy Nguyen Dinh, Alessandro Canossa, and Anders Drachen (2021).
DOI: 10.1093/oso/9780192897879.003.0007

Classification and regression[1] are two machine learning techniques that belong to the class of supervised learning. Supervised learning is where you have data in the form of a set of input variables and one or more output or target variables, and the goal is to develop an algorithm that learns to predict the target variables from the input. Compare this to the unsupervised learning methods discussed in Chapter 6. For unsupervised learning, you only have the input data with no corresponding target to predict, and the focus is to investigate data groupings or clusters. As discussed in Chapter 6, unsupervised learning methods are typically employed for exploratory analysis rather than prediction tasks. One further note: recall that in Chapter 3, we discussed two types of analysis: exploratory and confirmatory. You would normally use classification and regression to perform confirmatory analyses.

The objective of classification and regression is to discover the correlation between input features and the target variables (also called class variables), so that future data points can be labeled or predicted accordingly. As a simple example, you can try to predict the amount of *gold* or *XP* or an *outcome* of a match in League of Legends given other game variables. In this case, *gold*, *XP*, or *outcome* are the target variables you are trying to predict, and the other game variables are features you use to build the prediction model. Solving such a task results in a classification or regression model[2], which maps from the input features to class value(s). The process of discovering such models is called training or learning.

While classification deals with predicting discrete target variables, regression deals with continuous target variables. Examples of discrete variables you may be dealing with when analyzing player data is win/loss of a game, while a continuous variable can be amount of gold. Note that continuous target variables can be transformed into discrete variables by binning the data into discrete partitions. As an exercise, look at the data you processed in the previous chapters and think of the discrete and continuous variables you have already worked with: are these target variables? Are they continuous or discrete? Can the continuous be converted into discrete?

---

[1] It is worth noting that there is an ongoing debate about whether regression is machine learning or not. This arises because the boundaries between statistics and machine learning are somewhat artificial. For our purposes, it does not matter, as our focus is on understanding data, not arguing semantics. Thus, we will simply treat regression as supervised machine learning.

[2] Note that in other text, you can see terms such as *model-free* and *model-based* methods. In this chapter, we will refer to model-based methods as *parametric* and model-free as *nonparametric* models.

Returning to our conversation about nonpaying users and how they become paying customers, we stated that you can use classification for this task. Here, you would think of it as developing a model to learn if a player will be converted into a paying customer or not, which would be your target variable. You would then aim to predict this variable given several features: game-agnostic features, such as *length of play sessions, frequency of play sessions,* and *spacing between play sessions,* and game-specific features, such as *how often players engage with NPCs* or *how often players use different items.* A classification model can then show which features are important in driving the shift from nonpaying to paying players.

In Chapter 3, we covered the basics of inferential statistics and introduced the generalized linear model, which forms the foundation for regression analysis. We will, therefore, take the discussion in Chapter 3 as our starting point. As discussed in Chapter 3, analysis begins with applying descriptive statistics to understand the structure of the dataset you are working on. Correlation analysis is useful to investigate if there are relationships between input variables (features) and target variables for a prediction analysis. Ultimately, the goal is to find a good method to accurately predict the target variable or variables.

In this chapter, you will learn about some of the most widely used and popular classification and regression methods adopted for game data science. This chapter is aimed to be broadly accessible, and thus minimizes detailed technical discussion, but for interested readers, there are many excellent resources on the market that go into more depth on the algorithms and implementations discussed here, for example, Bishop (2006) or Han, Kamber, and Pei (2011).

The process of supervised machine learning typically involves three steps each with separate datasets. Ideally, you operate with three separate datasets, but it is not uncommon to see the validation step run on the same dataset as the one used in the training step. The use of different datasets here is important because we want to make sure your learned model can be evaluated on a clean dataset that it has not seen before. Therefore, it gives us a good way to estimate how this model generalizes outside of the dataset it used for training. The three steps are:

- **Training step:** This step refers to the process of constructing a classification model from training data, that is, from a subset of the full dataset, typically randomly selected. There are different principles for how much of the dataset to use for this step depending on the properties of the data, the model used, the problem we are trying to solve, etc.

- **Validation step:** In this step, we use a dataset to tune or pick the hyperparameters we need to use for our model. This is typically done using a validation dataset. As discussed in Chapter 6, a hyperparameter is usually a continuous or integer variable, leading to mixed-type optimization problems. It is important to note that the time required to train and test a model can depend upon the choice of its hyperparameters. In some cases, the existence of a hyperparameter is conditional upon the value of another. An example is the size of each hidden layer in a Neural Network (NN), which can be conditional upon the number of layers. Different settings of these parameters may give you different results. We will discuss this more in detail in Chapter 8.
- **Testing step:** In this step, we evaluate how well the model works with unseen data or a subset of the original dataset which was set aside before the training step.

This chapter will focus on the training step. Chapter 8 focuses on the validation and testing steps. While there exists many tools and programming libraries that make machine learning methods widely accessible, it is important that you understand the inner workings of these algorithms and methods so that you can use them correctly and appropriately. Therefore, in this chapter, we will lay out important foundation theories before detailing the techniques themselves. In particular, for classification, we will discuss:

- *K-Nearest Neighbor* (*KNN*; Section 7.3.1),
- *Naïve Bayes* (*NB*; Section 7.3.2),
- *Logistic Regression* (Section 7.3.3),
- *Linear Discriminant Analysis* (*LDA*; Section 7.3.4),
- *Support Vector Machines* (*SVMs*; Section 7.3.5),
- *Decision Trees* (*DTs*; Section 7.3.6), and
- *Random Forests* (*RFs*; Section 7.3.7).

For regression, we will discuss *linear regression* and some popular extensions, including ridge and lasso regressions (Section 7.2).

To help you learn the practical aspect of using these algorithms, we will discuss their technical details. We will also augment this discussion with labs in R, where you can practice using the algorithms and setting their parameters with some game data. We will use *DOTA 2* data in all the labs in this chapter. As with the previous chapters, we have included the data with the book, which you can access through the lab folder. The chapter includes the following labs:

- **Lab 7.1**: *Linear Regression*
- **Lab 7.2**: *KNN*
- **Lab 7.3**: *NB*
- **Lab 7.4**: *Logistic Regression*
- **Lab 7.5**: *LDA*
- **Lab 7.6**: *SVM*
- **Lab 7.7**: *SVM* with Kernel Methods
- **Lab 7.8**: *DT*
- **Lab 7.9**: *RF*

7.1 Predictive model categorizations

There are several ways to categorize prediction models developed under classification and regression techniques. One approach is to categorize them through two dimensions: parametric/nonparametric (discussed in Section 7.1.1) and discriminative/generative (discussed in Section 7.1.2). In general, parametric and generative models are structurally constrained, while nonparametric and discriminative models place less emphasis on capturing the data's structures and more on outcome accuracy. Another approach is to categorize them according to how human interpretable the model is as: black-box or white-box, where white-box models are those easily transformed into human-readable rules, while black-box models are not. Figure 7.1 shows the different classifiers discussed in this chapter along the three categorization approaches. As you can observe from the figure, most classification methods are black-box methods. Only tree-based models, such as *DTs* and *RFs* are white-box methods, and thus interpretable. You will learn more about these methods and their limitations later. However, it is important to note that there have been several approaches developed to interpret some of the black-box methods through explainable Artificial Intelligence methods (see Adadi and Berrada, 2018). Interested readers should refer to articles within this area for more information on these methods and their limitations.

7.1.1 Parametric vs. nonparametric models

Parametric models refer to models that assume that the data follows a predefined structure characterized by a finite set of parameters (e.g., fitting a linear equation of a line). These types of models are usually used to model ratio and

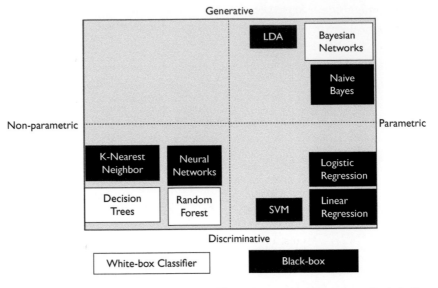

Figure 7.1 Predictive model categorization. Those closer to the bottom are discriminative models, to the top are generative, left are non-parametric, and right are parametric.

interval measures discussed in Chapter 2. Such models assume that our data can fit a predefined structure, and the modeling process is then focused on setting the parameters for the equation that best explains the data given the assumed structure or function (e.g., linear or quadratic). In contrast, nonparametric models do not have any assumptions on the structure of the data. As a result, they are regarded as models with a potentially infinite number of parameters, contrary to a fixed number in the case of parametric counterparts.

More formally, assume that n_p is the size of the training dataset, and n_p is the number of parameters to be learned for a model M. To identify the parametricity of M, examine how n_p changes as n_D approaches infinity, that is, $n_p \rightarrow \infty$:

- If n_p does not change, then M is parametric
- If $n_p \rightarrow \infty$, then M is nonparametric.

For example, as you will learn in greater detail in Section 7.2.1, *linear regression* is parametric, because n_p is equivalent to the number of data features plus one, and thus does not change when $n_p \rightarrow \infty$. In contrast, *KNN* (Section 7.3.1) retains the whole training dataset as a reference set and classifies new data based on how *similar* they are to those in that set. This means with *KNN*, $n_p = n_D$, and thus, $n_p \to \infty$ if $n_D \to \infty$. *KNN* is therefore a nonparametric model.

In practice, determining if a model is parametric, or not, may not be as straightforward as it seems. Take for example *NNs*. On the surface, it seems that *NN* is parametric, since a specific *NN* will have a fixed structure and, thus, a fixed number of parameters. By examining the process more closely, we notice that it is in fact nonparametric. When the data size n_p is small, a small network may suffice, but with big data, the network needs to be expanded in structure to avoid underfitting, a problem with some machine learning methods that we are going to discuss in Chapter 8. Briefly here, underfitting occurs when a model is too simple to capture the intricate relationships in the data and, thus, fails to model the data appropriately. To address underfitting, a model of higher complexity needs to be adopted instead.

7.1.2 Discriminative vs. generative

Generative models are those capable of producing new data that are similar to the ones used to train them. Usually, this is achieved by approximating the global probability distribution of all data points, that is, $P(X, Y)$, where X is the input feature vector and Y is the class variable, and then using this distribution to sample new data. Knowing how data are distributed allows such models to assign probabilities to target class values, given input features. As such, generative models can also be used for other applications than just classification that requires an understanding of the underlying data generation mechanisms. This could be useful in cases such as when game designers seek to understand how game components affect logged in-game behaviors.

An example method is *Naïve Bayes (NB)* discussed in Section 7.3.2. As you will see later, obtaining a *NB* model from data does not only provide a classification model but also informs us of the probabilistic relationship between each input feature and the output variable. For example, a *NB* model that predicts the outcome of a chess game, given input features—for example, players' *skill level* and *play style*—will contain information on how likely a player may win a game given just their *skill level*, or *play style*.

In contrast, discriminative models focus solely on constructing the association relationships between input variables and the target variable. Such relationships are often discovered by solving an optimization problem with the goal of minimizing the overall errors of predicting class values. Since these models directly address the classification problem, they are generally not helpful outside of this task. Most classification models discussed in this chapter are discriminative, including *linear regression, neural networks, DTs*, etc.

Since discriminative methods are more direct than generative ones, they tend to outperform generative models in the same task. This focus, however, leads to the fact that many discriminative methods are opaque and noninterpretable (as shown in Figure 7.1).

7.2 Regression methods

Regression refers to the task of predicting a continuous class variable, given some input features. We will discuss *linear regression* as the main method frequently used for regression, and some other more advanced techniques in this chapter.

For the sake of consistency, we are going to use the following system of naming:

- $X = (X_1, X_2, X_3, \ldots, X_n)$ are the input variables.
- $x = (x_1, x_2, x_3, \ldots, x_n)$ is an input instance, in which input variable X_i takes on value x_i. To denote different input instances, we use $x^{(i)}$, $x^{(j)}$.
- Y is the target/output/class variable and y a value Y
- can take. In case there are many class values to be discussed, we will use subscripts to differentiate them (e.g., y_j or y_k). Similar to the input, we use $y^{(i)}$, $y^{(j)}$ to denote corresponding target values of inputs $x^{(i)}$, $x^{(j)}$.

7.2.1 Linear regression

Linear regression is a regression method that models the relationship between a continuous class/target variable Y, called dependent variable, and a set of input features $X = (X_1, X_2, \ldots, X_n)$, called independent variables. You may recall already seeing these terms in Chapter 3. A dependent variable is what you are measuring (or predicting in this case) and an independent variable is what you are controlling or manipulating (or have as an input in this case). Note that we also call the input features, X, feature vector, since it comprises multiple variables, each corresponding to one dimension in the vector space formed by the features. As such, we are going to use data points and data vectors interchangeably in this chapter.

Back to the method at hand, *linear regression* assumes a linear relationship between the variables. That is, the dependent variable Y can be expressed as a linear combination of independent variables $X_1, X_2, \ldots, X_n$, as illustrated in Figure 7.2.

7.2.1.1 METHOD

Suppose you have training data D with some input features, $X = (X_1, X_2, \ldots, X_n)$, where n is the number of features and X is the class variable. *Linear regression* is formulated to solve the following equation for values of $\beta_0, \beta_1, \ldots \beta_n$:

$$Y = \beta_0 + \beta_1 X_1 + \beta_2 X_2 + \cdots + \beta_n X_n \qquad \text{(Equation 7.1)}$$

in which $\beta_0, \beta_1, \beta_2, \ldots, \beta_n$ are scalar coefficients determining the linear relationship.

Given the training data, D, *linear regression*'s goal is to find the parameter vector $\beta = (\beta_0, \beta_1, \beta_2, \ldots, \beta_n)$ that best fits the data by minimizing the discrepancy between the left- and the right-hand sides of Equation 7.1. Such

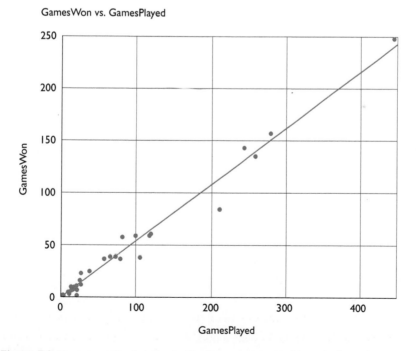

Figure 7.2 *Linear regression* that aims to fit a line as close as possible to the input data points.

discrepancy is often modeled as the sum of squared residuals (Equation 7.2), the minimization of which is referred to as *least squares*:

$$J(\beta) = \sum_{i=1}^{|D|} \left(y^{(i)} - x^{(i)}\beta\right)^2 \qquad \text{(Equation 7.2)}$$

In Equation 7.2, $J(\beta)$ is called the cost function, parameterized by β, with the intuition being that the optimal parameters are able to minimize such cost, and $x^{(i)}, y^{(i)}$ are input features and respective class values in the training dataset.

Note that the sum of squared residuals is not the only possible cost function. Another popular choice is L^1-norm, that is, $J(\beta) = \sum_{i=1}^{|D|} |y^{(i)} - x^{(i)}\beta|$, which is the sum of absolute errors.

In Lab 7.1, you are going to learn how to apply *linear regression* in R.

Practical Note: Lab 7.1

Lab 7.1

Please see the supplemental materials for the book.

Goal of Lab 7.1

The lab goes over how you would go about using *linear regression* on your dataset. For this lab, we will use *DOTA* dataset courtesy of DOTAlicious Gaming and the Game Trace Archive (Guo and Iosup, 2012) to predict the number of points players earn given other performance indicators, such as the number of deaths and kills.

7.2.1.2 GOODNESS OF FIT

Sometimes, the data does not follow a linear relationship, and thus using *linear regression* may not be appropriate. It is, therefore, important for you to develop methods to assess how good the resultant model is to get a sense of how reasonable the resultant model actually is. These methods are discussed in more detail in Chapter 8. For now, note that the most popular measure for assessing *linear regression* is R^2.

7.2.2 Beyond linear regression

In some cases, it is desirable to reduce the number of nonzero coefficients in β (the vector of computed coefficients). For example, if the set of nonzero coefficients is small, it is easier to interpret and understand the main effects of input features on output. Or when the number of data points is small—for example, smaller than the number of input variables—*linear regression* can suffer from overfitting. Overfitting occurs when a model fits the training data so well that it fails to generalize and retain similar performance level on unseen data. We will discuss overfitting and underfitting in Chapter 8. Forcing the coefficients of many variables to be zero directly reduces the dimensionality of the resultant coefficients and thus helps alleviate this issue.

One approach to minimize the number of nonzero coefficients is to use regularization. Regularization is defined as adding a term to the cost function that penalizes the magnitudes of the coefficients. Such addition means that when an optimization algorithm is applied to solve the coefficients, it will need to consider both the optimality of the solution and its simplicity, as represented by the number of nonzero coefficients. This leads to a few different regression methods:

- *Ridge regression*, with the cost function to minimize being

$$J(\beta) = \sum_{i=1}^{|D|} \left(y^{(i)} - x^{(i)}\beta \right)^2 + \lambda \sum_{j=1}^{n} \beta_j^2 \qquad \text{(Equation 7.3)}$$

- *Lasso regression*, with the cost function to minimize being

$$J(\beta) = \sum_{i=1}^{|D|} \left(y^{(i)} - x^{(i)}\beta \right)^2 + \lambda \sum_{j=1}^{n} |\beta_j| \qquad \text{(Equation 7.4)}$$

These extensions of *linear regression* added a second term that penalizes coefficients to varying degrees: *Ridge* penalizes them quadratically (Equation 7.3), while *Lasso* does so in absolute terms (Equation 7.4). As a result, when the cost function is minimized, the resultant β not only minimizes the error in prediction but also is the smallest possible in terms of magnitudes.

The fundamental assumption of *linear regression* is the linear relationship between input and class variables. This is rather constrained, as it excludes nonlinear cases. There are other regression methods that extend the linear constraint to the nonlinear space.

Polynomial regression is a natural extension of *linear regression*, in which the relationship is assumed to take a polynomial form. For example, with input features, $X = (X_1, X_2)$. *Quadratic regression* learns relationship in the form of

$Y = \beta_0 + \beta_1 X_1 + \beta_2 X_2 + \beta_{11} X_1^2 + \beta_{22} X_2^2 + \beta_{12} X_1 X_2$. You can see that when β_{11}, β_{12}, and β_{22} are zero, *polynomial regression* degenerates to *linear regression*.

As the model is more flexible than *linear regression*, it comes at the cost of introducing more parameters. For instance, while a linear relationship has $O(n)$ parameters, with n being the number of input variables, a quadratic relationship requires up to $O(n^2)$ parameters. A high number of parameters causes *polynomial regression* to be more susceptible to overfitting, as having more parameters is equivalent to more degrees of freedom and more complex models. As such, while *polynomial regression* is in theory more expressive than *linear regression*, *linear regression* remains more popular due to its simplicity.

Logistic regression is a regression method that, instead of predicting continuous class values, predicts the *probability* of data belonging to target classes (*class probabilities*). As such, it is commonly regarded as a classification method, instead of a regression method, and thus we will cover it in Section 7.3.

7.3 Classification methods

Moving on from regression models, we will now focus on classification methods. As discussed in the introduction to this chapter, these aim to predict class variables that are discrete, so categorical or ordinal (see Chapter 2 for definitions). An example could be trying to predict the level of skill of a *DOTA* player based on a set of performance features. In the remaining part of this chapter, we will try to predict the variable *SkillLevel* for players in the *DOTAlicious* dataset using the rest of the performance features in that dataset as input features. We will use this as an example in the labs below and show you how to build different classification methods to build predictive models. As you will remember from Lab 7.1 above, *SkillLevel* is a discrete numeric variable that is suitable for classification.

In the following subsections, we will discuss each algorithm. We will first outline the main idea and then delve deeper into each method. We will also discuss the hyperparameters that each method uses or needs to tune. As described above, these are the parameters that are used as input for the algorithm to learn the model, similar to the k value in *k-means* discussed in Chapter 6. More information on hyperparameters is detailed in Chapter 8. Hyperparameter tuning refers to the task of picking values for these hyperparameters to achieve the most suitable model to conduct learning on.

As done previously, each algorithm will be supplemented with a lab describing how you can use the algorithm with game data.

7.3.1 K-Nearest Neighbor (KNN)

KNN is a simple, nonparametric technique that requires no training to build a model, basically a mapping from input to output. *KNN* operates based on the intuition that objects with similar descriptive attributes have a higher chance of belonging to the same class and thus should have the same class labels.

For example, consider the *DOTAlicious* dataset, in which we would like to predict the *SkillLevel* of a player given other performance statistics, such as the *number of kills*, *deaths*, and *assists*. Note that in this dataset, a player's skill level is an integer between "0 " and "3," making it suitable for a classification task. Given the input features,*x*, of a new player, *KNN* looks for players with input feature values similar to *x*. If among these players, there is a majority agreement on *SkillLevel*, for example, most of them are at level "3," *KNN* will label *x* with *SkillLevel* = "3" as well.

In vector space representation, let us assume that each object is represented as a point in the multidimensional space where each dimension corresponds to one input feature. The intuition for *KNN* is then to group objects that are close in proximity and label them with similar class labels.

Based on this intuition, *KNN* estimates a new data point's unknown label based on the K items that are closest to it in distance, that is, most similar to the data point. K takes positive integer values, that is, $K = 1, 2, 3, \ldots, n$ representing the number of reference points the algorithm consults to label new data. As such, K needs to be selected so that it is not too small to avoid lack of information but also not too large to avoid information coming from irrelevant references, that is, points that are too dissimilar.

7.3.1.1 METHOD

KNN is described algorithmically as follows:

Input

1. A training dataset D and
2. A distance function $d : D^2 \rightarrow R$ that returns a real value $d(x^{(i)}, x^{(j)})$ for any two data points $x^{(i)}, x^{(j)}$ from the input training dataset D.

Model *KNN* uses the whole dataset as a model. The provided metric function is used to compute the distance between data points.

Classification approach

> **Step 1:** Obtain the *KNNs*, with "nearest" defined as the shortest distances, as computed using a metric d (defined below).
>
> **Step 2:** Return the majority class label among K neighbors, where K is a parameter also chosen for this algorithm discussed below.

KNN can also be used for continuous class values, that is, regression. Instead of returning the majority class label, in such cases, *KNN* returns the weighted average of class values as observed in the K selected neighbors.

Off the shelf, *KNN* is a black-box model, as it does not generate generalizable classification rules. However, we can understand why one point has a particular label by looking at the labels for the neighboring points, but this does not give us a rule or intuition why this label is the right label for that data point.

7.3.1.2 HYPERPARAMETER TUNING

KNN uses several hyperparameters that require tuning, including a distance metric d and the number of neighbors K. While the choice of d is often domain specific, one of the most popular options for d is Euclidean distance, as discussed in Chapter 6. Note that Euclidean distance is sensitive to scale, since features with values ranging over a large interval will dominate the term. Therefore, data scaling should be applied before running *KNN*.

There are many approaches to select an optimal value of K. One of the simplest and most popular methods is to compute cross-validation errors of different K values and select the one with minimum error. While *KNN* cannot handle big data, there is a class of algorithms called *approximate nearest neighbor*, which have extended *KNN*'s implementation to big data (e.g., see Muja and Lowe, 2014).

Practical Note: Lab 7.2

Lab 7.2

Please see the supplemental materials for the book.

Goal of Lab 7.2

The lab shows how you can use *KNN* to predict a discrete target variable. For this lab, we continue to use the *DOTA* dataset courtesy of *DOTAlicious* Gaming and the Game Trace Archive (Guo and Iosup, 2012).

7.3.2 NB

NB is a classification method based on Bayes theorem (Bayes and Price, 1763), a probability rule that updates probabilities based on evidence. Given observed input features $x = (x_1, x_2, \ldots, x_n)$ and target class variable Y, NB computes the conditional class probability $P(Y = y_i | X_1 = x_1, X_2 = x_1, \ldots, X_n = x_n) \forall i$, that is, the probability that the class variable takes on class values y_i given the observed values of input variables. It then outputs the class value with the highest probability.

As such, NB is a parametric classification method, where the parameters are the conditional probabilities between the class value and input variables and the structure of the adopted model. NB's underlying assumption is that the input features X used for classification have direct probability relationship with the target value, but not with one another. This means any correlation among the input variables' observed values can be completely explained from their relationship with the class/target.

For example, consider the task of predicting the *SkillLevel* of a player in the *DOTAlicious* dataset. Applying a NB classifier in this task imposes an implicit assumption that all input features, such as the *number of deaths* and *kills*, are conditionally independent given the knowledge of the *SkillLevel*. In other words, if you know a player's *SkillLevel*, you do not need the *number of deaths* to infer the *number of kills* and vice versa, that is, they are pieces of information fully inferable from *SkillLevel* alone. On the other hand, if you do not know the value of *SkillLevel*, these two variables may be correlated, due to their indirect relationship through *SkillLevel* as the proxy. Therefore, you need to confirm that your variables conform with this assumption, if not, you may need to do some processing on the data to get a set of features that conform with this assumption; see Chapter 4 for techniques for that.

As compared to other classification techniques, NB is extremely fast and not susceptible to the curse of dimensionality, discussed in Chapters 4 and 6, which is a notorious challenge when dealing with big data. In the context of classification, the curse of dimensionality refers to the situation in which the volume of the data space expands very quickly, that is, typically at an exponential or higher rate, as the number of input features increases, making the available data sparse. As a result, a learning algorithm susceptible to this curse either requires a prohibitively larger amount of computing resources (in terms of space, speed, or time) or cannot yield a good model due to the sparsity of the available data. NB is not susceptible to this curse, because the assumption of independence between features simplifies the relationship among features, breaking the otherwise complex label estimation down to terms of single-dimensional probability. This can also be problematic, however, as some argue that such assumption may be too strong. Moreover, as *NB* estimates the probability terms from the data, in cases of imbalanced data (i.e., when we have very few or no data points for some variables), there could be many probabilities that are close to zero, which affects the overall class estimation. However, in practice, despite the naïveté of the assumption, *NB* has shown to still be a very strong baseline classifier that is worth a try, at least at the early stages of the data analysis process.

7.3.2.1 METHOD

Before delving into the technical details of *NB*, you are encouraged to brush up on probability basics, especially Bayes' Theorem. A good reference is *Machine Learning* (Mitchell, 1997), specifically Chapter 6, Sections 6.1, 6.2, and the beginning of 6.3.

NB formulates the classification problem as a problem of finding the most probable class label given the input features as evidence, that is, solving the optimization equation:

$$y^* = argmax_y P(Y = y|x_1, x_2, \ldots, x_n) \qquad \text{(Equation 7.5)}$$

For any class value y, the probability can be computed as follows:

$$P(Y = y|x_1, x_2, \ldots, x_n) = \frac{P(x_1, x_2, \ldots, x_n|Y = y)P(Y = y)}{P(x_1, x_2, \ldots, x_n)}$$
$$= \frac{P(y)\prod_{i=1}^n P(x_i|y)}{P(x_1, x_2, \ldots, x_n)} \qquad \text{(Equation 7.6)}$$

For the sake of simplifying notations, we write $P(y)$ and $P(x_i|y)$ in place of $P(Y = y)$ and $P(x_i|Y = y)$, respectively. The last equality is derived from the chain rule and independence assumption. Specifically, first, you apply the chain rule:

$$P(x_1, x_2, x_3, \ldots, x_n|y) = P(x_1|x_2, x_3, \ldots, x_n, y)P(x_2|x_3, \ldots, x_n, y) \cdots$$
$$P(x_n|y)P(y) \quad \text{(Equation 7.7)}$$

Under the independence assumption, that is, $x_1, x_2, x_3, \ldots, x_n$ are conditionally independent given y, it follows that

$$P(x_1|x_2, x_3, \ldots, x_n, y) = P(x_1|y)$$

$$P(x_2|x_3, x_4, \ldots, x_n, y) = P(x_2|y) \ldots$$

$$P(x_{n-1}|x_n, y) = P(x_{n-1}|y)$$

Substituting these terms back to the chain rule yields:

$$P(x_1, x_2, \ldots, x_n|y) = \prod_{i=1}^{n} P(x_i|y) \qquad \text{(Equation 7.8)}$$

Since $P(x_1, x_2, \ldots, x_n)$ is constant given the input $(x_1, x_2, \ldots, x_n)$, solving Equation 7.5 is equivalent to solving:

$$y^* = argmax_y P(y) \prod_{i=1}^{n} P(x_i|y) \qquad \text{(Equation 7.9)}$$

While $P(y)$ can be estimated from the training data, that is, by counting the occurrence frequency of records labeled as class y, there are many ways to estimate the conditional probability $P(x_i|y)$, also called likelihood, of each input variable x_i, each of which yields a different variant of NB.

Likelihood estimation. The most popular approach is to assume some parametric form of $P(x_i|y)$, then learn the parameters defining the distributions from data. For instance, *Bernoulli NB*, *Gaussian NB*, and *Categorical NB* are three NB classifiers that, respectively, assume $P(x_i|y)$ take the form of Bernoulli, Gaussian, and multinomial distributions. For more information on the distributions, please refer to Chapter 3. For the sake of reference, Table 7.1 summarizes the applicability of these distribution forms and their parameters. This list is certainly not exhaustive; depending on the nature of the measures for the variables (e.g., continuous or discrete, binary or multivalued), other distributions can be used.

Once the distribution form is determined, their parameters are estimated from the training set. Here is an example with estimating $P(x_i|y_j)$ as a Gaussian distribution, with x_i being the observed input value of the continuous-valued input variable X_1, and y_j being some value the target variable Y can take. Since

Table 7.1 *Popular distributions used with NB.*

	Bernoulli distribution	Gaussian distribution	Categorical distribution
Applicable variable type	Discrete, binary (e.g., value $x \in \{0, 1\}$)	Continuous (i.e., value $x \in R$)	Discrete, multivalued (e.g., $x \in \{1, \ldots, k\}$)
Parameter(s) to learn	$0 < p < 1, p \in R$ (probability of $x = 1$)	$\mu \in R$ (mean) $\sigma^2 \in R$ (variance)	$k > 2, k \in N$ (number of categories) $p_1, p_2, \ldots, p_k \in [0, 1]$, s.t. $\sum_{i=1}^{k} p_i = 1$ (probabilities of categories)
Probability	$p(x = 1) = p$ $p(x = 0) = 1 - p$	$p(x) = $ $\frac{1}{\sqrt{2\pi\sigma^2}} \cdot e^{-\frac{(x-\mu)^2}{2\sigma^2}}$	$p(x = i) = p_i, \forall i \in \{1, \ldots, k\}$

Gaussian distributions are defined by the mean $\mu \in R$, and variance $\sigma^2 \in R$, the following steps are taken to estimate these two parameters:

Step 1: Obtain the data subset D_j that only contains data points labeled as y_j.

Step 2 (compute μ_i): Set μ_i to be the mean of variable X_i with respect to data points in D_j.

Step 3 (compute σ_i^2): Set σ_i^2 to be the sample variance of variable X_i with respect to data points in D_j, that is, $\sigma_i^2 = \frac{1}{|D_j|} \sum_{x_i^{(k)} \in D_j} \left[x_i^{(k)} - \mu_i \right]^2$, with μ_i computed from Step 2. Note that Steps 2 and 3 need to be repeated for all input feature X_i. After this step, since we assume that the input variables are Gaussian distributions, we can obtain the likelihood $P(x_i|y_j) = \frac{1}{\sqrt{2\pi\sigma_i^2}} \cdot e^{-\frac{(x_i-\mu_i)^2}{2\sigma_i^2}}$ for any value x_i that X_i can take.

Step 4: NB classification involves the following steps. Given the input $x = (x_1, x_2, \ldots, x_n :)$

1. For each class value y_j, compute the prior probability $P(Y = y_j)$ by counting its frequency in the training data.
2. For each feature value x_i, estimate likelihoods $P(x_i|y_j)$ with the assumed probability distribution form (e.g., Gaussian, categorical, or Bernoulli) from the training data using the aforementioned steps.

3. Now that we have computed all terms in Equation 7.9, they can be substituted and the target value y^* that is resulted from solving this equation is returned as the output.

In practice, it is common that the above procedure be executed in the log probability space, that is, using log $P(.)$ instead of $P(.)$. Specifically, in Step 3, we compute

$$y^* = argmax_y \left[\log P(y) \prod_{i=1}^{n} P\left(x_i|y\right) \right]$$

$$= argmax_y \left[\log P(y) + \sum_{i=1}^{n} \log P\left(x_i|y\right) \right] \quad \text{(Equation 7.10)}$$

instead of the original form in Equation 7.8. This has a number of advantages. First, in log space, multiplication and exponentiation become summation. When solving an optimization problem, we often have to compute the derivatives of some function. Summations are easier to solve and take derivatives from than terms involving multiplication and exponents. Second, small values represented in log space do not suffer from floating point imprecision when they are computed on computers. For example, 0.0001 in log space is -4.

7.3.2.2 HYPERPARAMETER TUNING

With *NB*, there are no hyperparameters to tune, although there is one decision you need to make—choosing which probability distribution to use for $P(x_i|y_j)$. Oftentimes, with continuous variables, you will use Gaussian, and with discrete variables, you will use categorical distributions. In Lab 7.3, you will learn about training a *Gaussian NB* classifier, since we are dealing with continuous input features with the *DOTA* data we have been using.

Practical Note: Lab 7.3

Lab 7.3

Please see the supplemental materials for the book.

Goal of Lab 7.3

The lab shows how to use *NB* to predict a discrete target variable. For this lab, we continue to use the *DOTA* dataset courtesy of *DOTAlicious* Gaming and the Game Trace Archive (Guo and Iosup, 2012).

7.3.3 Logistic regression

As discussed in Section 7.2.2, *logistic regression*, despite the name, is considered a classification method rather than a regression method. Specifically, its goal is similar to that of *NB*: to estimate the class probabilities of an input datum. The class with the highest probability will be used to label the respective input. We will focus on *logistic regression* with binary class labels, in which the target/class variable can take on one of two possible categorical values. In cases where there are more than two class values, extended versions of *logistic regression*, such as *multinomial* or *ordinal logistic regression* (Hosmer, Lemeshow, David, and Hosmer, 1989), can be used.

Before delving into the technical details, we would like to discuss a function the *logistic regression* uses, namely the *logistic function*, as depicted in Figure 7.3b. This function takes the form:

$$f(x) = \frac{1}{1 + e^{-x}}, x \in R \qquad \text{(Equation 7.11)}$$

As can be observed from its shape, the logistic function maps the range $(-\infty, +\infty) - (0, 1)$, while its inverse, that is, logit function,

$$g(y) = \log \frac{y}{1 - y}, y \in (0, 1) \qquad \text{(Equation 7.12)}$$

maps from $(0, 1)$ to $(-\infty, +\infty)$. *Logistic regression* uses these functions to estimate probabilities, which are valued within $(0, 1)$. This is why the algorithm is called *logistic regression*.

7.3.3.1 METHOD

For the sake of clarity, assume the two classes to be labeled are $\{0, 1\}$. While *linear regression*'s goal is to fit a line *on* the data points, the goal for *logistic regression* is to fit a line *between* the data points. As such, both of them assume a linear relationship between the input features and target variable, but in *logistic regression* case, this relationship is related to the probability that a data point belongs to a specific class. Figure 7.3 demonstrates *logistic regression*'s operation, with blue representing "1," and red "0."

To do this, the algorithm takes on the following steps:

Step 1: It first computes a hyperplane H which linearly separates the points into two sides, each containing data points belonging to only one class (Figure 7.3a). The hyperplane H is computed such that

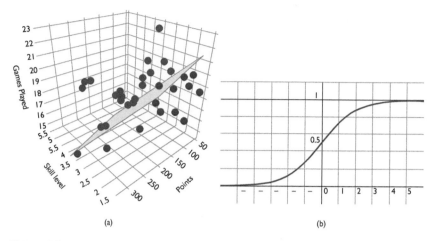

(a)　　　　　　　　　　　　(b)

Figure 7.3 *Logistic regression* aims to find a hyperplane that linearly separates the input data points: (a) the targeted linear decision boundary, which separates data points belonging to different classes; (b) the *Logistic function* that maps from distance to probability.

- For all data points x of class 1, $P(y = 1|x)$ is as close to 1 as possible, and
- For all data points x of class 0, $P(y = 0|x)$ is as close to 0 as possible

Logistic regression takes the following approach to achieve this: First, we obtain H such that the signed distances between data 1-labeled points and H are as close to $+\infty$ as possible, while those between 0-labeled data and H are as close to $-\infty$ as possible. We can then use the *logistic function* to convert these distances into class probabilities.

To obtain H, given the training dataset $D = \{(x_i, y_i), i = 1, \ldots, |D|\}$ with (x_i, y_i) being labeled data points, the following cost function needs to be minimized:

$$J(\beta) = \sum_{i=1}^{|D|} \left[y_i \log h_\beta(x_i) + (1 - y_i) \log(1 - h_\beta(x_i)) \right] \qquad \text{(Equation 7.13)}$$

where

- β is the parameter vector defining the targeted hyperplane H,
- $h_\beta(x_i) = x_i \cdot \beta$ is the dot product of data point x_i and β, capturing the signed distance between x_i and H.

Step 2: Next, given the found hyperplane H parameterized by β and a new data point x, *logistic regression* transforms the distance of x to H into the class probability using the logistic function (Equation 7.11). Specifically, *logistic regression* computes the class probabilities as:

$$P\left(y=1|x\right) = \frac{1}{1+e^{-h_\beta(x)}} \qquad \text{(Equation 7.14)}$$
$$\text{and } P\left(y=0|x\right) = 1 - P\left(y=1|x\right)$$

The idea is that the further away x is to one side of H, the more probable that x belongs to its side's class.

Note that the hyperplane H decides the quality of the classification. If H successfully separates the data into two sets according to their label, the data will be classified correctly. However, if there are many points crossing over to the opposite side, that is, the separation is not distinct, the classification accuracy will be lower. To measure the quality of the resultant hyperplane, one popular measure is R^2 (R-squared), which will be discussed in Chapter 8.

While *logistic regression*'s goal is to find a linear decision boundary that separates data points of different classes apart, it can find nonlinear boundaries using some tricks. The first is to introduce higher-order terms into the set of input variables, for example, artificially adding x^2, x^3 generated from some input variable x. The second is by employing of the *kernel method* (Hofmann, Schölkopf, and Smola, 2008), similar to the case with *SVMs*; see below.

Practical Note: Lab 7.4

Lab 7.4

Please see the supplemental materials for the book.

Goal of Lab 7.4

The lab shows how to use *logistic regression* to predict a discrete target variable. For this lab, we continue to use the *DOTA* dataset courtesy of *DOTAlicious* Gaming and the Game Trace Archive (Guo and Iosup, 2012).

7.3.4 Linear Discriminant Analysis (LDA)

LDA is a parametric method that uses vector space projection to transform the data points before classifying them. Like other projection-based methods, such as *Principal Component Analysis (PCA)* (see Chapter 4), one major step in the *LDA*'s process is to find a lower-dimensional space to project the data.

The motivation and intuition of *LDA* are as follows. Suppose you have a 1000-dimensional dataset, which are labeled with three class values. You suspect that there are about 10 input features (dimensions) that are critical to the classification. How should you go about building a classifier for this dataset? A natural approach would be to apply a dimension reduction routine, such as *PCA*, to reduce the number of dimensions down to a smaller number, such as 10, and then classify data in this new data space. However, *PCA* does not care about class labels, but only the spread of data, that is, in computing eigenvectors. *LDA* was invented for the purpose of making better use of the labels. Similar to *PCA*, it also considers the spread of the data, but selects the new, lower dimensional space, such that

- the scatter of points with different labels (i.e., between-class scatter) is as large as possible, and
- the scatter of points with the same labels (i.e., within-class scatter) is as small as possible

Although *PCA* and *LDA* use similar approach (projection-based), there are some key differences. While *PCA* is unsupervised, focusing on finding a linear transformation that best captures the variance within the data without caring about class values, *LDA* is supervised, which means it needs to know class labels during training. Unlike *PCA*, it aims to maximize the accuracy of class prediction while computing the projection. As such, *LDA* can be used for dimensionality reduction as well, but in a more informed way, as it utilizes the class labels in the process.

7.3.4.1 METHOD

LDA was originally designed for binary class classification problems. Later, multiclass *LDA* was devised to handle the more general case of multiple class values (Rao, 1948). However, this extended version was used mainly as a supervised learning approach to dimension reduction. In this section, we will focus the discussion on the original binary version of *LDA* (herein referred to as just *LDA*) for classification.

Suppose the two class values are y_1 and y_2, and D_i is the data subset containing only data points belonging to class y_i, the method is composed of the following steps:

Step 1: Compute the d-dimensional mean vectors μ_1 and μ_2, averaged from data points belonging to classes y_1 (i.e., belonging to D_1) and y_2, respectively, with d being the number of input features.

Step 2: Compute the estimate of the within-class scatter S_w.

$$S_w = \frac{N_1 S_w^1 + N_2 S_w^2}{N_1 + N_2}, \ with \ S_w^j = \sum_{x^{(i)} \in D_j} (x^{(i)} - \mu_j) \cdot (x^{(i)} - \mu_j)^{\mathrm{T}} \quad \text{(Equation 7.15)}$$

whereby

- S_w^j is the covariance of data points belonging to class C_j
- N_j is the number of data points belonging to class j, that is, $N_j = |D_j|$.
- μ_j is the mean vectors of D_j.

Step 3: Compute the discriminant coefficient vector β. This vector will play the role of the projection function that projects data to the new vector space.

$$\beta = S_w^{-1}(\mu_1 - \mu_2) \qquad \text{(Equation 7.16)}$$

Step 4: Label a datum x as y_1 if the projected value satisfies

$$\beta^{\mathsf{T}}\left(x - \left(\frac{\mu_1 + \mu_2}{2}\right)\right) > \log\frac{P(y_1)}{P(y_2)} \qquad \text{(Equation 7.17)}$$

where $P(y_1)$ and $P(y_2)$ are respective class probabilities of y_1 and y_2, computed from the training data. If the inequality in Equation 7.16 is not satisfied, label the datum as y_2.

You can see that Equation 7.16 captures both within- and between-class scatters in its computation: within-class scatter is represented by S_w while between-class scatter by $(\mu_1 - \mu_2)$. With the above binary *LDA* process, you may wonder where the projection step happens. Indeed, the projection happens implicitly in Equation 7.17, in the left-hand side with β^{T} playing the role of the projection function. More information on *LDA* can be found in James, Witten, Hastie, and Tibishirani (2013).

For using *LDA* for dimensionality reduction, interested readers can refer to the bibliography section, specifically Tharwat et al. (2017).

7.3.4.2 HYPERPARAMETER TUNING

For *LDA*, there are no hyperparameters to tune.

Practical Note: Lab 7.5

Lab 7.5

Please see the supplemental materials for the book.

Goal of Lab 7.5

The lab shows how to use *LDA* to predict a discrete target variable. For this lab, we continue to use the *DOTA* dataset courtesy of *DOTAlicious* Gaming and the Game Trace Archive (Guo and Iosup, 2012).

7.3.5 SVMs

SVM is a discriminative parametric classification method designed for binary problems. Like *logistic regression*, its goal is to compute a hyperplane that separates data points belonging to two classes. However, *SVMs* take one step further by computing, not just any hyperplane, but the optimal one that best separates the data, while *logistic regression* simply searches for some hyperplane that satisfies the separation requirement with no further optimization. The best separating hyperplane is considered to be the one that is farthest away from both sides of the data. For example, in Figure 7.4, although all plotted lines can be used to classify the data points correctly, the dotted line would be the one returned by an *SVM*, since it (1) separates the data well and (2) is farthest away from any point of the two classes. The data points closest to the separating hyperplane returned by SVMs are called *support vectors* (thus the name), because they have a direct effect on the decision boundary.

When given new data to label, depending on which side of the hyperplane the new data falls into, *SVMs* will label them according to the majority class of that

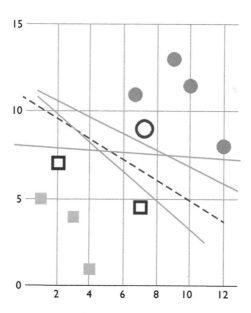

Figure 7.4 Candidate hyperplanes (lines in this case) separating two classes; the dotted line represents the optimal separating line SVMs aim to find, while thick-lined circles and squares are targeted support vectors.

side. Note that *SVMs* can also be used to learn nonlinear decision boundaries by employing the kernel trick (Hofmann et al., 2008). In order to use *SVMs* for multiclass problems (e.g., n classes with $n > 2$), people commonly take the one-against-all approach by training $nSVMs$, each of which learns to distinguish one single class from the rest.

7.3.5.1 METHOD

Without the loss of generality, assume that the two class labels are represented as $\{-1, 1\}$. The objective of *SVMs* is to compute the parameters (β, β_0), which determine the linear hyperplane $Y = \beta^\top X + \beta_0$, by solving the following constraint optimization problem:

$$argmax_{\beta,\beta_0} \frac{2}{\|\beta\|}, subject\ to: y_i(\beta^\top x_i + \beta_0) \geq 1, \forall(x_i, y_i) \in D,$$

(Equation 7.18)

with $y_i \in \{-1, 1\}$ representing the label of each data point x_i in the training dataset D. Equation 7.18 means that when $y_i = 1$, $(\beta^\top x_i + \beta_0)$ should be as close to 1 as possible, and when $y_i = -1$, $(\beta^\top x_i + \beta_0)$ should be as close to -1 as possible. As such, the effect is that we are trying to look for (β, β_0) that best approximates Y given X.

The constraint in Equation 7.18 enforces that all data points be placed on the correct side of the linear separator, that is, the hyperplane correctly separates the points. The function to maximize, that is, $\frac{2}{\|\beta\|}$, corresponds to the distance from the closest points of each class (i.e., the support vectors) to the hyperplane.

The maximization problem expressed in Equation 7.18 is equivalent to the quadratic minimization with the same constraint, that is,

$$argmin_{\beta,\beta_0} \|\beta\|^2, subject\ to: y_i(\beta^\top x_i + \beta_0) \geq 1, \forall(x_i, y_i) \in D$$
(Equation 7.19)

Note that the difference between Equations 7.18 and 7.19 is the objective function to optimize, while the constraint remains the same.

The quadratic optimization problem as posed in Equation 7.19 can be solved using a standard optimization method, called Lagrangian multipliers. This strategy finds local optima of a function under some equality constraints and is widely implemented by many standard programming libraries. More information on the technical details of Lagrangian multipliers can be found in a related book by Bertsekas (1982), while Jordan's lecture notes (Jordan and van Greunen, 2004) provide excellent details on how this method works in solving *SVMs*. One important detail worth noting is that solving *SVMs* only requires the computation of pairwise dot products $(x_i \cdot x_j)$, between all data points x_i, x_j belonging to dataset D.

Once the optimal values of β and β_0 are obtained, at classification time, given a new data point x, if $f_{SVM}(x) = \beta^\top x + \beta_0 > 0$, we will output class value 1, otherwise, output -1; f_{SVM} is the function representing the learnt decision boundary.

Practical Note: Lab 7.6

Lab 7.6

Please see the supplemental materials for the book.

Goal of Lab 7.6

The lab shows how to use *SVMs*, without the kernel trick, to predict a discrete target variable. For this lab, we continue to use the *DOTA* dataset courtesy of *DOTAlicious* Gaming and the Game Trace Archive (Guo and Iosup, 2012).

7.3.5.2 KERNEL METHODS WITH SVMS

The *kernel method*, or kernel trick, allows *SVMs* and other linear classifiers, such as *logistic regression*, to learn nonlinear decision boundaries. This is particularly useful as it makes *SVMs* applicable even in cases when the data is not linearly separable. It accomplishes this by seeking a linear decision boundary, not on the original data, but on the data projected into a higher dimensional space that could then become linearly separable.

Figure 7.5 demonstrates a situation like that. On the left side, you have the data, originally in two-dimensional space, that is, clearly not linearly separable, as points from one class (represented as blue squares) completely surround those of the other class (red circles). However, if the data is appropriately projected onto a three-dimensional space as depicted in the right chart, there now exist hyperplanes in this new space that can linearly separate the data. When projected back to the original vector space, such hyperplanes take the form of a nonlinear separating boundary.

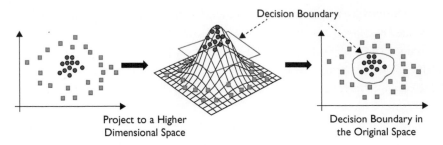

Figure 7.5 Data projected into a higher dimensional space (right figure) may become linearly separable.

The challenge with this approach is that the computational process can be expensive, as the process now includes a data transformation step, in which the data needs to be projected into the higher space, before an *SVM* can be applied.

The algorithm proceeds as follows:

Step 1: Training data D is projected onto a higher dimensional space using a mapping function ϕ, resulting in the new data D'.

Step 2: Solve the optimization problem with training data D', as discussed in Section 7.3.5.1 (Equation 7.19), to obtain the decision function f'_{SVM} in the new space. This step is just ordinary *SVM* or *logistic regression* applied on D'.

Step 3: Given a new data point x to classify, obtain the projected datum $x' = \phi(x)$.

Step 4: Return the label determined by $f'_{SVM}(x')$.

In this process, Steps 1 and 3 are overhead, incurred due to the projection step. The issue with this approach lies not only in the computation power and time required to execute the transformation but also in the additional space needed to store the new data. For instance, suppose d is the original dimensionality, and d' is the new one. In practice, d' could be exponentially larger than d for the data to become linearly separable, which implies an exponential overhead on the storage space as well.

Fortunately, as we already noted, solving the optimization problem for *SVMs* only requires the pairwise dot product of the data vectors. Therefore, as long as we have some magical function that computes such products without the explicit data transformation, we can ignore Steps 1 and 3 above and directly solve for f'_{SVM}. Kernels are those magical functions, each of which takes the form of $K(x_i, x_j)$— with x_i, x_j being two data points in the original training set—and returns the dot product of the images of x_i, x_j projected onto a higher dimensional space (Jordan and Thibaux, 2004). Specifically, $K(x_i, x_j) = \phi(x_i) \cdot \phi(x_j)$ for some mapping function ϕ.

SVMs with the kernel trick are the same as the original *SVM* method, but all dot products are replaced by a kernel instead—that is, replacing $(x_i \cdot x_j)$, with x_i, x_j being data points in D, by $K(x_i, x_j)$ with K being a kernel function. Each kernel corresponds to a projection represented by the mapping function ϕ, which can be non-obvious in some cases. That said, as discussed above, there is no need to know the explicit form of ϕ to apply the kernel trick, so this is by no means a deal breaker.

Some popular kernels include:

- Quadratic kernel:s $K(x_i, x_j) = (x_i \cdot x_j)^2$. Returns the square of the dot product.
- Polynomials of degree k: $K(x_i, x_j) = (x_i \cdot x_j + c)^k$. This is a generalization of the quadratic kernel, with c as some selected constant and k as the selected degree.
- Radial kernel (also referred to as Gaussian kernel): $K(x_i, x_j) = exp\left(-\frac{\|x_i - x_j\|^2}{2\sigma^2}\right)$, where σ is the standard deviation of the selected Gaussian.

In Lab 7.7, you will learn to use the kernel trick to find nonlinear decision boundaries.

7.3.5.3 HYPERPARAMETER TUNING

There are no hyperparameters to tune for *SVM*. Normal data preprocessing procedures, such as scaling, are required for vanilla *SVM*, that is, linear *SVM* without the kernel trick, to ensure that no input feature dominates the computation. With the kernel trick, parameters related to the chosen kernel may need tuning. For example, the standard deviation σ has to be tuned for the radial kernel.

Practical Note: Lab 7.7

Lab 7.7

Please see the supplemental materials for the book.

Goal of Lab 7.7

The lab shows how to use *SVM*, with and without the kernel trick, to predict a discrete target variable. For this lab, we continue to use the *DOTA* dataset courtesy of *DOTAlicious* Gaming and the Game Trace Archive (Guo and Iosup, 2012).

7.3.6 Decision Trees

Decision Trees (DTs) (Mitchell, 1997), as the name implies, is a family of algorithms whose goal is to build a tree that filters the data based on feature values of direct classification decisions to suitable leaf nodes, each of which denotes a single class output. Figure 7.6 depicts an example *DT*. As shown in the figure, there are two types of nodes in a *DT*, that is, internal nodes (e.g., number of games won > "1000") and leaf nodes (e.g., SkillLevel = "2"). An internal node in the tree has at least two children, while leaf nodes are childless. Each internal node corresponds to a value test on a single feature, with branches representing the subset of data that satisfies the corresponding test value. Each leaf node, on the other hand, contains a subset of instances that should belong to a single class. As you can see in this example, the tree is developed to use features to classify players' *SkillLevel*. Given an input, the output class is determined by traversing the tree from the root node to a leaf, following branches that match the features in the input. For instance, the input (Number games won = "500," Kills = "9," Deaths = "50") will land in the leftmost leaf, corresponding to the output SkillLevel = "1," while the input (Number games won = "900," Kills = "20," Deaths = "50") will end up at the second leftmost leaf, that is, output SkillLevel = "2."

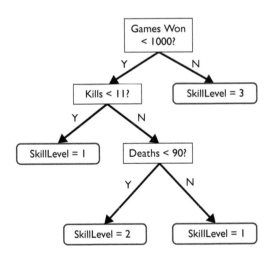

Figure 7.6 A decision tree that determines a player's skill level, given feature values of number of games won, number of kills, and number of deaths (DOTAlicious dataset). For each node, the left branch (labeled with "Y") is the branch taken when the result of the condition is true, and the right when it is false.

Given a training dataset, a large number of *DTs* could be constructed and yield high accuracy. For example, the simplest approach is to compute a *DT* in which each leaf node contains a single element in the training data. However, such trees would be gigantic in size, wasting precious resources in both space (for storage) and time (as classification requires traversal from the top to the bottom of the tree). Moreover, large trees are more likely to overfit the data.

Using principles from information theory, most *DT* algorithms aim to construct small-sized trees with leaf nodes as homogeneous (or *pure*) as possible. A group of data points in which all elements are similar, that is, belong to the same class, is said to be homogeneous. As such, the notion of homogeneity is crucial to *DT*. Homogeneous sets make classification straightforward, since all elements belong to a single class. A concept from information theory, namely entropy, is a commonly used measure of homogeneity for this purpose (see Chapter 4 for a worked-out example of this).

Given a set S, each member of which is assigned a label in $\{l_i, i = 1, 2, \ldots, n\}$, the entropy of this set is defined as

$$E(S) = - \sum_{i=1}^{n} p_i \log p_i \qquad \text{(Equation 7.20)}$$

with p_i being the probability a randomly selected element of S belonging to class l_i. Entropy is maximized when elements in S are equally distributed in terms of class labels and minimized (i.e., 0) when all elements belong to the same class, that is, homogeneous.

Entropy represents the amount of information contained in S and is used to quantify how homogeneous elements in S are. The smaller $E(S)$ is, the less information S contains, and the more homogeneous elements in S are.

With entropy as the measure for class homogeneity, a *DT* algorithm, namely *ID3* (i.e., Iterative Dichotomizer 3) uses information gain as the measure to rank different feature tests performed on current data and choose the best internal nodes to add to the tree. Information gain represents the increase in entropy after an attribute A is selected to split a dataset. Formally, information gain is computed as

$$IG\,(S, A) = E(S) - \sum_{j=1}^{k} \frac{|S_j|}{|S|} E(S_j) \qquad \text{(Equation 7.21)}$$

where

- A takes value $\{a_1, a_2, \ldots, a_k\}$
- S_j is the subset of S in which the attribute A takes on value a_j
- $|S|$ and $|S_j|$ refer to the number of elements in the set S and S_j

As depicted in Equation 7.21, information gain captures the change in entropy as the difference between the entropy values before splitting the data, the first $E(S)$, and after the weighted sum, $\sum_{j=1}^{k} \frac{|S_j|}{|S|} E(S_j)$.

Since entropy is minimized with highly homogeneous data, a test with higher information gain corresponds to partitioning the results in more homogeneous subsets, that is, subsets with most items belonging to the same class. Such a test should be placed as close to the root node as possible, since it does the most work in separating (or classifying) data, thus increasing the chance of having a small tree, as there is not much to do once data is properly separated into singly labeled subsets. Besides entropy, other measures of homogeneity prevalently used include Gini Index (implemented in CART algorithm), or misclassification rate. Similar to entropy, these measures take nonnegative values and are minimized (i.e., 0) in pure sets and maximized when all classes are equally distributed.

One thing worth noting is that DT has no fixed number of parameters. Its tree model can grow as much or as little as we desire, by adding more or less internal (test) nodes. As such, DT is known to be a nonparametric method with the power to fit any nonlinearity in the training dataset. However, its strength is also its weakness, due to the problem of overfitting. Generally, the more complex a model is, the more easily it suffers from overfitting. As the DT can grow freely, it can quickly become complex.

More advanced DT algorithms tackle this issue by trying to reduce the tree's fitness (i.e., performance) on training data, in exchange for more generalizability. The popular way to achieve this is through tree pruning, that is, remove subtrees whereby the branching is considered to be poorly applicable outside of the training data. Situations where a node X (thus the subtree rooted under X) may be pruned include

- When the data subset at X is too small (e.g., less than 10 records).
- When the data subset at X is reasonably homogeneous (e.g., its entropy is less than a certain threshold).

- When X is already too deep. A large tree tends to be more overfitting than a smaller one, so the rationale here is to keep the tree at a reasonable size and not to grow it beyond certain depth.

All these rules are heuristics that aim to stop expanding a tree too large.

7.3.6.1 METHOD

As explained above, the construction of a DT is an iterative process, in which internal decision nodes that drive data splits are selected one by one and added to the growing tree. The node selection criterion could be information gain or similar metrics that aim to maximize data purity at each split. Some tree pruning mechanisms can be in place during the process of construction to avoid overfitting.

Input

- Training dataset
- Attribute selection criterion E (e.g., information gain or Gini index).

The steps are as follows. Starting with an empty tree and a training dataset D with input attributes $X = \{X_1, X_2, \ldots, X_k\}$:

Step 1: Select attribute X^* that scores best with respect to the selection criterion E, computed on D
Step 2: Create an internal node with the test variable being X^* and branches being values of X^*. This node plays the role of a filter, splitting the data into subsets according to the test on values of X^*.
Step 3: Remove X^* from X
Step 4: At each branch of X^*, if

1. The data subset contains samples belonging to the same class,
2. X is empty, that is, there is no attribute available for selection, or
3. The data subset is empty,
   Then: Add a leaf node to this branch, taking the majority class value of the data subset, then stop expanding this branch.
   Otherwise, go to Step 1 with the computation of criterion E computed on the data subset, instead of D.

Once the tree is constructed, classifying a new data point is done by traversing the tree from the root node, conducting tests on the attributes along the way, until a leaf node is reached. The class value associated with the leaf node is then returned as the predicted value.

In Lab 7.8, we are going to see how to use rpart package in R to construct a *DT*.

7.3.6.2 HYPERPARAMETER TUNING

One hyperparameter that can be tuned to avoid overfitting is the threshold defining the minimum number of data records at leaf nodes. Intuitively, if a leaf node contains too few data points, it is likely that the compound conditions to reach that node only apply to an insignificant subset of the data, thus more prone to overfitting. This type of tuning will be discussed in Chapter 8.

Practical Note: Lab 7.8

Lab 7.8

Please see the supplemental materials for the book.

Goal of Lab 7.8

The lab shows how to use a *DT* to predict a discrete target variable. For this lab, we continue to use the *DOTA* dataset courtesy of *DOTAlicious* Gaming and the Game Trace Archive (Guo and Iosup, 2012).

7.3.7 Random Forests

Random Forests (*RFs*) (Breiman, 2001) are a family of ensemble methods, meaning they utilize collections of simple classifiers to make a collective decision on classification or prediction tasks. In *RF*, the simple classifiers collated are *DTs*. More specifically, *RF* aims to make the collection of trees as decorrelated as possible, through the use of (1) data bagging and (2) feature bagging. After the tree ensemble is built, the output of *RF* is computed by taking the average of the member trees' outputs in the case of regression, or their majority vote in the case of classification.

By keeping the trees decorrelated, *RFs* are known to be resistant to overfitting, which is one of the main reasons behind their popularity. Specifically, *RFs* avoid overfitting because of bagging and feature subsampling in tree building.

Bagging (bootstrap aggregating) is a technique that randomly generates training samples with replacements from the original training dataset to train the trees and thereby avoids fitting to any single training set. It also lets all models vote in the end and chooses the result that is most voted by the models.

Feature bagging refers to the technique that randomly selects a subset of features for consideration when selecting an internal node in the tree building process. This technique avoids the domination of features that have high predictive power in the collection of trees being built. Normally, without the limitation on feature selection, such features would tend to be picked more often due to their goodness, thus leading to trees highly correlated, defeating the purpose of learning multiple trees.

Readers are encouraged to check out the original paper on *RF* (Breiman, 2001) for a more thorough understanding of the technique's technical details.

7.3.7.1 METHOD

Given a training dataset D, the *RF* algorithm builds a collection of *DTs*, in which the number of trees is a controlled parameter T. Each tree is built in the following manner:

> **Step 1:** Generate a bootstrapped training sample set D_i by sampling with replacement from D: The size of the sampled set is a parameter to be set, keeping in mind that the larger the size, the closer to the full training set it gets. The most popular choice is to select $|D_i| = |D|$ (James et al., 2013).
>
> **Step 2:** Train a *DT* on D_i with one adjustment: The set of features to consider for each split is randomly selected anew from the original feature set p. The size of the feature subset m is another free parameter. The most popular choice is $|m| = \sqrt{|p|}$ for classification and $|m| = \frac{|p|}{3}$ for regression (Hastie, Tibshirani, and Friedman, 2009).

For classification, given an input datum x, the output is the majority voting of trees' predictions

$$c^* = argmax_{c \in C} \sum_{i=1}^{T} I_{f_i(x)=c} \qquad \text{(Equation 7.22)}$$

where

- C being the set of class values,
- T the number of trees,
- $f_i(.)$ the output of classifier (tree) i, and
- $I_{f_i(x)=c}$ being the Kronecker delta function (Spiegel and O'Donnell, 1997) of $f_i(x)$ and c, that is, 1 if $f_i(x) = c$ and 0 otherwise.

For regression, the output is the average of trees' outputs

$$f^* = \frac{1}{T} \sum_{i=1}^{T} f_i(x) \qquad \text{(Equation 7.23)}$$

In Lab 7.9, we are going to examine how to train a *RF* in R.

7.3.7.2 BY-PRODUCTS

Besides the main task of classification, one advantage of using *RF* is that it returns a ranking of input feature importance as a by-product—as you would have seen in the lab. An input features' importance represents the degree to which such feature contributes to the performance of the resultant *RF* model. Features with higher importance values are those that are crucial to the predictive power of the *RF* model, while those with low importance can be removed from the set of input features without significant impact.

The importance of feature values offers insights into the features' contribution to the classification and helps identifying important features from irrelevant ones. One direct application is feature selection and thus dimensionality reduction.

7.3.7.3 HYPERPARAMETER TUNING

There are four hyperparameters to be tuned: the number of trees, the sample size $|D_i|$, the maximum number of features to consider for each tree, and the minimum amount of data records at each leaf node in the trees. In practice, the sample size $|D_i|$ is often set to be equal to $|D|$, that is, the full data size.

While the last two hyperparameters are meant to obtain a set of trees that are as robust against overfitting as possible, the first parameter, that is, the number of trees, represents how extensive we want the forest to be. The barrier to stop us from having an infinitely large number of trees is the training time. The more trees we have, the more time it takes to train the model. In general, a few thousand trees should suffice.

Practical Note: Lab 7.9

Lab 7.9

Please see the supplemental materials for the book.

Goal of Lab 7.9

The lab shows how to use *RFs* to predict a discrete target variable. For this lab, we continue to use the *DOTA* dataset courtesy of *DOTAlicious* Gaming and the Game Trace Archive (Guo and Iosup, 2012).

7.4 Final remarks

In this chapter, you learned regression and classification methods to help you predict some class value given input features.

Some important takeaways:

- Many techniques assume interdependencies among independent variables. If independent variables are correlated, this may cause undesirable effects such as inflating coefficients in *linear regression*, or rendering the method inapplicable, such as *NB*. It is, therefore, important that during data preprocessing, you identify and eliminate such correlations from the data, for example, by removing correlated features from the data.
- Despite appearing rather naive in its assumption, *NB* classifiers perform reasonably well in practice when dealing with many input features, so they are a good method to try first when analyzing a new dataset.
- *Logistic regression* and *SVM* are very similar techniques that try to find a decision boundary that linearly separates data points of different classes. Generally, *logistic regression* and *linear SVM* (i.e., traditional *SVM* with linear kernel) perform similarly in terms of running time and output quality. However, in cases where the decision boundary is nonlinear, *SVM* with a nonlinear kernel (such as Gaussian) would be the preferred method.
- While being extremely interpretable, *DTs* are sensitive to and easily overfit training data—that is, relatively small changes in a few data points could lead to significant changes in the final tree's structure. Ensemble methods such as *RFs* are designed to address this shortcoming, at the expense of interpretability, as we lose the ability to transform the model into human-readable rules.
- Some models (i.e., white-box) are more transparent than others. As such, they would be more suitable in cases when the model will be examined and interpreted by nonexpert users—such as producers, artists, or designers.

● ●

EXERCISES

1. List all the features in the *DOTAlicious* dataset and determine which variables are discrete, and which are continuous, and explain why? Also, look at correlations between the variables and discuss them.

2. Using the *DOTAlicious* data, train a *linear regression* model that predicts "KillsPer-Min." What are your observations of the new model?

3. What is regularization in *linear regression*? Explain its role (e.g., what issue it tries to fix).

4. Explain the intuition behind *KNN*.

5. In setting *K* for *KNN*, what issue could you face if *K* is too small? What issue could you face if *K* is too large?

6. Train a regression model using *KNN* that predicts "KillsPerMin."

7. What assumptions underlie *NB*? How do these assumptions help the *NB* approach?

8. What is a key difference between *logistic regression* and *SVMs*?

9. *DTs* are considered to be interpretable models. Why?

10. How do *RFs* avoid the problem of overfitting?

11. Using *DOTAlicious* data, do some research on the variables and build a model that predicts the number of deaths based only on in-game performance statistics. Compare different classification methods in this exercise.

12. Using the *VPAL* data, described in Chapters 2 and Appendix, compare and contrast the different classification methods for predicting personality variables from game play data. To do this, make up your own hypothesis concerning what personality variable you would like to predict. Then, explain why and what features you will be using for this task.

● ●

BIBLIOGRAPHY

Adadi, A., and Berrada, M. (2018). Peeking inside the black-box: A survey on Explainable Artificial Intelligence (XAI). *IEEE Access*, 6, 52,138–60.

Bayes, M., and Price, M. (1763). An essay towards solving a problem in the doctrine of chances. By the Late Rev. Mr. Bayes, F. R. S. Communicated by Mr. Price, in a Letter to John Canton, A. M. F. R. S. *Philosophical Transactions of the Royal Society of London*. Royal Society. https://doi.org/10.2307/105741

Bertsekas, D. P. (1982). *Constrained optimization and Lagrange multiplier methods*. Academic Press. https://doi.org/10.1002/net.3230150112

Bishop, C. M. (2006). *Pattern recognition and machine learning. Pattern recognition*. New York, New York, USA: Springer-Verlag. https://doi.org/10.1117/1.2819119

Breiman, L. (1984). *Classification and regression trees*. New York: Routledge.

Breiman, L. (2001). Random forests. *Machine Learning*, 45(1), 5–32. https://doi.org/10.1023/A:1010933404324

Guo, Y., and Iosup, A. (2012). The game trace archive. In *Annual Workshop on Network and Systems Support for Games*. https://doi.org/10.1109/NetGames.2012.6404027

Han, J., Kamber, M., and Pei, J. (2011). *Data mining: Concepts and techniques*. Waltham, MA: Elsevier Science.

Han, J., Micheline, K., and Jian, P. (2011). *Data mining: Concepts and techniques*. Waltham, MA: Elsevier Science.

Hastie, T., Tibshirani, R., and Friedman, J. (2009). *The elements of statistical learning. The mathematical intelligence.* New York, NY: Springer. https://doi.org/10.1007/b94608

Hofmann, T., Schölkopf, B., and Smola, A. J. (2008). Kernel methods in machine learning. *Annals of Statistics, 36*(3), 1171–220. https://doi.org/10.1214/009053607000 000677

Hosmer, D. W., Lemeshow, S., David, W., and Hosmer, S. L. (1989). *Applied logistic regression. Applied logistic regression.* https://doi.org/10.1002/0471722146

James, G., Daniela, W., Trevor, H., and Robert, T. (2013). *An introduction to statistical learning. Springer texts in statistics.* New Jersey: Wiley.

James, G., Witten, D., Hastie, T., and Tibishirani, R. (2013). *An introduction to statistical learning.* New York, NY: Springer. https://doi.org/10.1007/978-1-4614-7138-7

Jordan, M. I., and Thibaux, R. (2004). The Kernel Trick. Retrieved July 2, 2018, URL: https://people.eecs.berkeley.edu/~jordan/courses/281B-spring04/lectures/lec3.pdf

Jordan, M. I., and van Greunen, J. (2004). Maximal Margin Classifier. Retrieved July 2, 2018, URL: https://people.eecs.berkeley.edu/~jordan/courses/281B-spring04/lectures/lec2.pdf

Mitchell, T. M. (1997). Machine learning. *Annual Review of Computer Science, 4.* https://doi.org/10.1145/242224.242229

Muja, M., and Lowe, D. G. (2014). Scalable nearest neighbor algorithms for high dimensional data. *IEEE Transactions on Pattern Analysis and Machine Intelligence, 36*(11), 2227–2240.

Perrier, A. (2015). Feature importance in random forests. URL: https://alexis perrier.com/datascience/2015/08/27/feature-importance-random-forests-gini-accuracy.html

Tharwat, A., G. T., Ibrahim, A., and Hassanien, A. E. (2017). Linear discriminant analysis: A detailed tutorial. *AI Communications, 30*(2), 169–90. https://alexisperrier.com/datascience/2015/08/27/feature-importance-random-forests-gini-accuracy.html.

Rao, C. R. (1948). The utilization of multiple measurements in problems of biological classification. *Journal of the Royal Statistical Society. Series B (Methodological).* Royal Statistical Society. https://doi.org/10.2307/2983775

Spiegel, E., and O'Donnell, C. (1997). *Incidence algebras* (1st ed., Vol. 206). Marcel Dekker, Inc., New York, NY.

Kuhn, M. (2018). "The 'caret' Package," URL: http://topepo.github.io/caret/.

'createDataPartition' function, https://www.rdocumentation.org/packages/caret/versions/6.0–80/topics/createDataPartition

Available classification and regression models provided by 'caret', https://topepo.github.io/caret/available-models.html.

CHAPTER 8

Supervised Learning in Game Data Science: Model Validation and Evaluation

In the previous chapter, we discussed the technical details of classification and regression methods. In the machine learning pipeline, these methods are often referred to as model learning. The machine learning pipeline consists of several phases: learning (discussed in Chapter 7), validation, and evaluation. The latter two phases are the subject of this chapter. Also, in Chapter 7, we discussed how you can use classification and regression algorithms to develop a model from data. However, this model must be evaluated and validated to enable you to understand the model's success, predictive capabilities, and power.

To briefly recap, validation is the step used to tune the hyperparameters of the model. Here, we often integrate a cross-validation process, which we will discuss in more detail below. Evaluation, on the other hand, is the process of testing the performance of the model using unseen data, the test dataset.

In an environment where the model in question is intended for inclusion in a piece of software, you would also need to go through a productization process. Productization is a potentially complex development process and occurs following the data science process. We will discuss this process at the end of the chapter.

Game Data Science. Magy Seif El-Nasr, Truong Huy Nguyen Dinh, Alessandro Canossa, and Anders Drachen, Oxford University Press. © Magy Seif El-Nasr, Truong Huy Nguyen Dinh, Alessandro Canossa, and Anders Drachen (2021).
DOI: 10.1093/oso/9780192897879.003.0008

Similar to other chapters, the methods discussed here will be illustrated through practical labs in R. In particular, this chapter includes the following supplemental labs:

- **Lab 8.1:** Classification model evaluation using scalar metrics
- **Lab 8.2:** Classification model evaluation using AUC
- **Lab 8.3:** Regression model evaluation
- **Lab 8.4:** Model validation (specifically, cross validation)

8.1 Machine learning pipeline

Figure 8.1 shows a snapshot of the processes and datasets involved in the machine learning pipeline. Data is usually divided into several datasets: one for model training (called the training set), one for model selection or validation (called the validation set), and one for model evaluation (called the test set). Note that the training set usually contains most of the data, followed by validation, and the test set typically contains the least amount of data.

In Chapter 7, we discussed model training at length. Two other steps are necessary to develop successful and validated models. One of these steps is model validation. The goal of model validation is to tune the model's hyperparameters. Recall from the last chapter that hyperparameters are parameters that are taken by the algorithm as input, and thus they can be tuned to further enhance the model's performance. These parameters are often set before the training process begins. Examples of hyperparameters that you have seen before are *K* in *KNN* or *K-means* (see Chapters 6 and 7).

Note that, at the end of each section in the previous chapter, we have briefly identified the hyperparameters that you need to tune as you run that algorithm. We also discussed how you may want to set different values for these

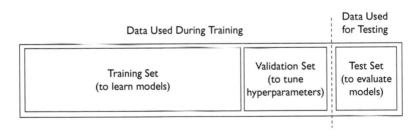

Figure 8.1 Data subsets for model learning, validation, and evaluation. Training set is used for learning, validation set for selection, and test set for evaluation.

hyperparameters and compare the models. Since each set of hyperparameters would impose different conditions within which the learning algorithm computes the best model, choosing the best set of hyperparameters is also referred to as model selection (see Chapter 7).

The second (and often last) step in the machine learning pipeline is model evaluation. This is where you assess how well the model performs on a set of data that it has not been seen before. You have already done this in the labs for Chapter 7.

In order to determine if a model is a good or a bad fit for the given data, you need to understand performance metrics, which are standardized measures that allow you to assess the fitness or effectiveness of a model. Such metrics can be used for both model selection and evaluation. We will discuss these performance metrics next.

8.2 Performance metrics

In this section, we discuss the methods used to assess the model fit. Most of these methods take the form of a scoring function with a single number (usually real number), while some are visualization-based. Due to their simplicity, scoring methods provide a very convenient and intuitive way to compare models. Below, we discuss examples of these.

On the other hand, for regression (continuous class values), most popular metrics include mean-squared error, mean-absolute error (MAE), and R-squared, defined in Section 8.3.2.

8.2.1 Classification metrics

In case of classification, the output can be one or more target class values. In the case where two class values exist, that is, binary classification, the class values are often referred to as positive and negative. These names are historically chosen due to the proliferation of classification tasks in medical settings, in which doctors label patients based on their medical record data as either positive (i.e., diagnosed as having the illness) or negative (i.e., not having the illness). As such, most popular metrics are computed based on ratios of false positive (FP) and true positive (TP) and true negatives (TNs). This means a model can have several outcomes:

- The model predicts a class as positive and it was positive (TP)

- The model predicts a class as positive and it was negative (FP)
- The model predicts a class as negative and it was negative (TN)
- The model predicts a class as negative and it was positive (false negative, FN)

This computes what is called the confusion matrix; see Table 8.1 for an example.

Table 8.1 shows an exemplary confusion matrix, where the class labels are win and loss. This matrix contains the following information (if we take Win to be positive and Loss to be negative):

- TP: Number of times data points with class Win are classified as Win, that is, positive data points correctly classified as positive
- FP: Number of times data points with class Loss are classified as Win, that is, negative data points incorrectly classified as positive
- TN: Number of times data points with class Loss are classified as Loss, that is, negative data points correctly classified as negative
- FN: Number of times data points with class Win are classified as Loss, that is, positive data points incorrectly classified as negative

Note that the computation of false and true positive/negatives can be generalized to other class labels beyond just positive and negative. In cases where there are more than two class values (for instance, $C_1, C_2, \ldots, C_n$), these measures are each associated with a class value. For example, TP with respect to C_i would represent the frequency with which the model correctly predicts a C_i data point as C_i, and FP the frequency with which the model wrongly predicts a data point not belonging to C_i as C_i.

From these values, we can compute several important scoring metrics:

- **True Positive Rate (TPR)**, or sensitivity (**also known as** *Recall*): Computed as the fraction of correctly assigned positive points, that is,

$$\frac{TP}{TP + FN}$$

(Equation 8.1)

Table 8.1 *An example confusion matrix.*

		Actual class	
		Class = Win	Class = Loss
Predicted class	Class=Win	True positive	False positive
	Class=Loss	False negative	True negative

Note that Recall represents the ability of the model to recall positive data points, that is, the rate at which positive data points are correctly identified. In many settings (such as medical), positive data are the relevant data, as opposed to negative data which are much more plentiful and less significant. Recall captures how well the model performs within the subset of positive data only.

Interpretation of recall: Ranging from 0 to 1 (0: bad, 1: good)

- **True Negative Rate (TNR) or specificity**: The fraction of correctly assigned negative points. This measure captures how accurately the model predicts the positive cases, computed as the rate at which a predicted positive is indeed a positive, as follows:

$$\frac{TN}{TN + FP} \qquad \text{(Equation 8.2)}$$

Interpretation of sensitivity and specificity: Ranging from 0 to 1 (0: bad, 1: good)

- **Accuracy.** Captures the overall accuracy of the model, computed as the rate at which the model makes good predictions, as follows:

$$\frac{TP + TN}{TP + FP + TN + FN} \qquad \text{(Equation 8.3)}$$

Interpretation of accuracy: Ranging from 0 to 1 (0: bad, 1: good)

- **Precision.** Captures how accurately the model predicts the positive cases, computed as the rate at which a predicted positive is indeed positive:

$$\frac{TP}{TP + FP} \qquad \text{(Equation 8.4)}$$

Interpretation of precision: Ranging from 0 to 1 (0: bad, 1: good)

- **F-measure.** As you can see, both precision and recall have their own merit, reflecting different goodness aspects of a model. F-measure is an attempt to combine both measures into a single value. Specifically, F-measure, also referred to as F_1, is computed as the weighted harmonic mean of precision and recall, as follows:

$$F_1 = \frac{2}{\frac{1}{precision} + \frac{1}{recall}} = \frac{2 \cdot precision \cdot recall}{precision + recall} \qquad \text{(Equation 8.5)}$$

Interpretation of F-measure: Ranging from 0 to 1 (0: bad, 1: good)

Practical Note: Lab 8.1

Lab 8.1

Please see the supplementary materials for the book.

Goal of Lab 1

The lab introduces how to compute the discussed evaluation measures for a decision tree model. As an exercise, you can perform the same evaluation methods on other models you produced in Chapter 7.

8.2.2 Area under the ROC Curve (AUC)

In cases in which the classifier does not directly assign discrete labels to test data, the model can also be evaluated using the *AUC* metric (a visualization-based method). The *AUC* metric does not use information from the confusion matrix; instead, it takes a visual form, meaning that it takes the form of, and should be interpreted from, a graphical chart.

The *AUC* represents the area under the curve plotting the model's sensitivity against sensitivity and specificity as defined above. Figure 8.2 depicts an AUC. Generally, classifiers like *Naïve Bayes* (*NB*) assign labels by first computing class probability estimation *P(positive)*; then, if *P(positive)* is greater than a threshold $T \in [0, 1]$, it will assign "positive" as the label of the data point. As

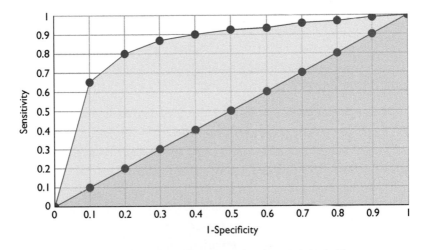

Figure 8.2 ROC (receiver Operating characteristic chart).

such, when the threshold T varies between "0" and "1," the model's sensitivity and specificity will also vary accordingly. Specifically, if T approaches "0," most data points will be assigned as "positive"; thus, sensitivity approaches "1" and specificity approaches "0." Increasing sensitivity usually comes at the cost of decreasing specificity. The perfect model is one that has both sensitivity and specificity close to "1," in which case the ROC curve resembles the unit square and AUC approaches "1." The less optimal model (e.g., by randomly assigning labels) tends to have a close-to-linear increment of sensitivity and decrement of specificity as T varies, resulting in the ROC curve looking like the diagonal line in the chart (drawn in blue Figure 8.2). Note that there are worse models than randomly selecting labels, at which point the model is less useful than a random model. This is not common but can happen.

Practical Note: Lab 8.2

Lab 8.2

Please see the supplementary materials for the book.

Goal of Lab 2

The lab introduces how to use AUC to assess the performance of an *NB* model. As an exercise, you can perform the same evaluation methods on other models you produced in Chapter 7.

8.2.3 Regression metrics

Unlike classification, regression models' outputs are continuous. This makes measures based on the confusion matrix not suitable for such models; however, there is a possible way to use the methods above to evaluate these models. This can be done if you convert the regression problem into a classification problem by using discretization, specifically by binning the target variable into nonoverlapping ranges. In such a case, the problem of approximating the target variable is transformed into one that aims to predict the range it will fall into. You can then use the metrics discussed above to evaluate such predictive models. We will leave this for you as an exercise and concentrate on other approaches here that are specifically developed for continuous models.

Note that the biggest issue with the discretization approach discussed above is the loss of precision due to the compression of the target variable into ranges. In some cases, such conversion is not desirable. For instance, predicting how much a player is willing to pay for a game item. In this case, it might make sense at first to divide the whole range of money spent into intervals and label them accordingly. For example, people who spent less than $10 can be labeled as non-spenders, those between $10 and $100 mild-spenders, and those more than $100 big-spenders. However, as money is a sensitive matter to deal with, even a small price difference can yield unexpected psychological effects that lead to significant reluctance to spend. Further, in such cases, it is also unclear how to set the thresholds properly. This prediction problem is, therefore, more suitably formulated as regression, with continuous target output, rather than classification. Therefore, we will need scoring metrics that can score such models.

Some popular regressions metrics include

- **Mean-Squared Error (MSE)** computes the average squared deviation of predicted values from the corresponding true values, that is,

$$MSE = \frac{1}{N} \sum_{i=1}^{N} (y_i - \hat{y}_i)^2 \qquad \text{(Equation 8.6)}$$

where $\hat{y}_i$ are predicted values of y_i. The rooted version of this metric, that is, root-mean-square error (RMSE), yields values in the same unit as the target variable, making it easier to perceive and interpret the overall deviation, thus is also highly popular.

$$RMSE = \sqrt{\frac{1}{N} \sum_{i=1}^{N} (y_i - \hat{y}_i)^2} \qquad \text{(Equation 8.7)}$$

- **Mean Absolute Error (MAE)** computes the average absolute deviation of predicted values from the corresponding true values, that is,

$$MAE = \frac{1}{N} \sum_{i=1}^{N} |y_i - \hat{y}_i| \qquad \text{(Equation 8.8)}$$

Where $\hat{y}_i$ are predicted values of y_i.

- **R-squared** (R^2) is one of the most used metrics in linear regression models, is also known as the coefficient of determination. It is computed as follows:

$$R^2 = 1 - \frac{\sum_{i=1}^{N} (y_i - \hat{y}_i)^2}{\sum_{i=1}^{N} (y_i - \bar{y})^2} \qquad \text{(Equation 8.9)}$$

where $\hat{y}_i$ are predicted values of y_i, and $\bar{y}$ is the mean of y_i. In this formula, the numerator represents the total individual errors made by the predictions, while the denominator represents variance of the data. As such, we can see that R^2 captures how good the predictions are, taking into account how hard the task is, as denoted by the data variance, as a normalization term. When R^2 approaches "1," the predictions are getting close to the actual data. When R^2 is smaller than "1" (usually close to "0" but it could also be negative), it means the model's predictions are not good. In reality, it is very rare that you get R^2 equal to "1," so values such as "0.9" or even "0.8" may already be considered good.

Interpretation of R^2: Ranging from $-\infty$ to 1 (negative to close to 0: bad, 1: good)

Practical Note: Lab 8.3

Lab 8.3

Please see the supplementary materials for the book.

Goal of Lab 3

The lab examines how to compute and interpret these evaluation measures for a linear regression model.

8.3 Model validation process

Recall that model validation or model selection refers to the task of selecting the most appropriate set of hyperparameters to learn a model from. The general process is as follows:

Step 1: Identify a finite set of hyperparameter candidates.

Step 2: For each of the hyperparameter candidate, develop a candidate model by running the algorithm using the hyperparameters and inputs using the training set as data (see Figure 8.1).

Step 3: Evaluate all candidate models on a validation set (see Figure 8.1), which may not overlap with the training data.

Step 4: Repeat for all set of hyperparameter candidates.

Step 5: Return the hyperparameter candidate associated with the best performing model resulted from Step 4.

Important Note

Difference between model selection/validation and evaluation

Note that model selection differs from model evaluation in that it only helps you to get the best possible structure of a model, and thus can be considered a part of the bigger phase of training a model. For example, you would use this process to decide the best number of neighbors K in KNN models that would yield the best result. Model evaluation, on the other hand, is used to test the model's performance against unseen data. It can also be used to compare different models, such as *KNN* vs. *decision trees*.

8.3.1 Cross validation vs. dedicated validation set

To select the dataset used for validation, there are two main approaches: using a dedicated validation set, as discussed before and depicted in Figure 8.1, a validation set is a subset of the original training data, set aside for validation. The other approach is to perform cross-validation. You may want to perform cross-validation in cases when you do not have enough data to have a dedicated validation set. In such a case, cross-validation is a better approach since it ensures that the model is trained on the whole training dataset, yet still validated on unseen data.

Cross-validation generates different pairs of training-validation sets, then repeatedly uses them to learn and validate multiple models in these sets. The validation performance is computed as the mean of all these iterations. Specifically, cross-validation involves the following steps:

Step 1: Partition the data used for training D into M disjoint, equal-sized subsets $D_1, D_2, \ldots, D_M$
Step 2: For M times ($i = 1 .. M$)
o Use the union of $D_1, D_2, \ldots, D_{i-1}, D_{i+1}, \ldots, D_M$ to learn a model
o Compute a performance metric value m_i of the resultant model on D_i
Step 3: Output the performance value as

$$m = \frac{1}{M} \sum_{i=1}^{M} m_i \qquad \text{(Equation 8.10)}$$

Note that due to the way the averaging is done, cross-validation is usually done with scalar, instead of visualization-based performance metrics.

The simplest form of cross validation is leave-one-out cross-validation, in which each D_i contains one single datum, that is, $M = |D|$. More sophisticated approaches may leave more than just one datum out for validation. One of the most popular cross-validation methods is called ten-fold cross-validation, in which M is set to 10.

Important Note

Using Cross Validation Technique

It is important to note that cross-validation is not only a process that is used for model selection but also for model evaluation (see later). In such a case, the training and test sets are split similarly as we do with the validation set, but (1) different models are learned instead of just changing the hyperparameters used and (2) the averaged performance value will be used to evaluate different models.

8.3.2 Automated algorithms for validation

As model validation requires the enumeration of hyperparameter values from a fixed set of candidates, it can be automated using algorithms. Such automated model selection algorithms typically navigate the parameter space to search for the best performing hyperparameter according to a predefined performance metric. Different algorithms differ in the way they navigate this space.

For instance, the simplest one of all, Grid Search, refers to the technique that navigates the space by exhausting the list of hyperparameter candidates, train one model for each configuration, and select the best performing one. As such, *Grid Search* allows users to have complete control over which parameters to examine and just automates the process of model training and evaluation. Due to its simplicity, this is the most popular method used nowadays.

Beyond *Grid Search*, there are other more sophisticated methods that readers are encouraged to explore, which are beyond the scope of this book, such as Bayesian optimization, random parameter optimization, and gradient-based optimization (Bengio, 2000; Bergstra and Bengio, 2012; Snoek, Larochelle, and Adams, 2012). We will leave these to you as further readings and exercises.

8.4 Model evaluation process

Model evaluation refers to the task of evaluating a learned model using one of the performance metrics described earlier. As depicted in Figure 8.1, evaluating a model needs to be conducted on a data subset that the model did not use for training (e.g., testing set). This is done for two reasons:

- To ensure fairness, especially when there are many competing models. Each model comes with its assumptions, and it may happen that the

---

Practical Note: Lab 8.4

Lab 8.4

Please see the supplementary materials for the book.

Goal of Lab 4

The lab examines how to tune hyperparameters of a model using cross-validation.

---

training data has some special characteristics that favor certain models over others. For example, if the training data is linear, just out of chance, it may give linear models an edge over others. As such, computing performance metrics on the training data will give high scores for these models.

- To ensure that our judgment of a model's performance is not influenced by overfitting. Models such as decision trees are known to be highly versatile, are able to model nonlinearity in the data, and thus, may also be prone to overfitting. Overfitting happens when a model captures the nuances of the training dataset so well that it fails to appropriately generalize outside of this set. Remember that our goal in training a model is to get one that can help us predict unseen values, not seen ones. Therefore, it is necessary to base the evaluation on a model's performance on a separate test set that does not overlap with the training set.

Model evaluation is usually adopted in the last step of the machine learning pipeline when multiple trained models are compared.

8.5 Debugging a learned model

The objective of classification is not just to model the training data, but to achieve adequate predictive performance on new, unseen data. Overfitting and underfitting are two problems we can encounter in training a classifier that can negatively impact the classification of unseen data.

8.5.1 Overfitting and underfitting

Overfitting refers to the problem that a learned model fits a training dataset too well, and thus fails to generalize beyond the training data. A classifier is said to be overfitting when it fits the training dataset overly well, that is, so well that it fails to generalize beyond this set and performs purely on test sets.

Overfitting can occur when

- The model selected is more complex than the data's underlying structure to be modeled, or
- The dataset used for training the model is too small

In both situations, the problem of overfitting arises when we are trying to learn too much from too little information. In the first case, a complex model is defined by a large number of parameters, which we are trying to learn from data, and whose degree of freedom is small, that is, a simple structure with few parameters. In the second case, even when we have selected a model with the right number of parameters, if the training data is too small in size, thus containing less information than needed to appropriately train the model, we would end up with an overfitting problem as well.

In contrast to overfitting, underfitting occurs when the classifier does not model the training data well enough. This is often caused by using models not complex enough to capture the structure and relationships in the data.

Underfitting is often simpler to solve than overfitting, as we can detect underfitting at the training phase when the model does not perform well on the training set. The solution is to simply use a more sophisticated model. For instance, vanilla *SVM* will suffer from underfitting if the data is not linearly separable. One solution, in this case, is to employ the kernel trick with *SVM* to relax the assumption of linear separability. Overfitting, on the other hand, can occur to even seemingly perfect models, thus it is harder to detect, especially with limited data.

Next, we will discuss some types of errors a model may suffer from, the basics of which can help guide the process of debugging a model to avoid underfitting and overfitting.

8.5.2 Bias, variance, and irreducible errors

A classification model aims to approximate a model that maps from the input features to the output, which allows it to predict unlabeled data. Such a classifier is prone to three types of errors: bias error, variance error, and irreducible error:

- Bias error is made due to the simplifying assumption that the learning algorithm has on the data. For example, in *linear regression*, the learning algorithm assumes that the relationship between the input and the output is linear. Although this makes the learning task easier due to the simplification, the resultant classifier is highly biased toward a model family that may be incapable of adequately capturing the complexity of the structure of data.

- Variance error is error due to using a different data on a learned model. This is a sign of overfitting, as the learned model fails to capture the structure of unseen data and thus failed to generalize.
- Irreducible error is inherent to the variability nature of the data, and thus unavoidable. In training a model, we, therefore, do not attempt to address this kind of error.

Both bias and variance refer to the prediction error a classifier makes on a dataset: the former refers to the error on the training data and variance on the test data.

High bias errors are therefore signs of the following issues:

- Too simple models
- Assumptions of the learning algorithm are not met

As such, classifiers prone to high bias error include a model that assumes a linear relationship governing the data, such as *linear regression* (assumption: linear relationship between input features and output), *logistic regression* (assumption: linear relationship between input features and the threshold value to decide the output label), and *linear discriminant analysis* (assumption: linear relationship between input features and the decision of output label). Further, parametric classifiers make assumptions on the targeted model structure and use parameters to tune that structure, as discussed in Chapter 7.

High variance errors are signs of:

- Overfitting
- Overly complex models

Classifiers prone to high variance error tend to be nonparametric models that can capture nonlinear structures, such as *decision trees,* or *neural networks* with many hidden layers.

8.6 Final remarks: Productization

As you have learned in this chapter, model selection and evaluation constitute important steps in machine learning. While model learning is what really turns data into models, validation and evaluation ensure that the model we obtained is the best given the parameters of the algorithm used (validation) and performance measures (evaluation). These processes ensure that any derived insights are as accurate as possible.

As discussed above, in an environment where the supervised learning model is intended for inclusion in a piece of software, you will also need to go through a productization process. This essentially means translating the model into a format where it can be part of a commercial product. This involves turning the model into a standardized, tested, packaged, and supported product or part of a product, which is ready for marketing and application. For a model to be relevant for productization, it has to provide value to a customer, whether that customer is internal (e.g., an analytics team) or external (e.g., the players).

For example, a churn prediction classifier could be integrated into the analytics pipeline of a company so that it automatically reruns at specific intervals and provides churn probabilities for new and existing players. There can be many advantages of a completely or partly productized machine learning model, but not all machine learning models in game data science should be productized and the decision to do so rests on a cost–benefit analysis.

Productization is generally viewed as a process that happens after the data science process (knowledge generation cycle) is completed, that is, it is a development and design task rather than an analytics task, and thus not covered in detail in this book. However, in reality, the best practice to adopt is to consider productization early on in the data science process (see later). It is very important to understand the context that commercial game data science operates in, and aspiring game analysts are recommended to build an understanding of this process.

Productization of machine learning models requires spanning and, sometimes, very substantial gap between a model and a production-ready application (Weber, 2018). There are far more models created than ever turned into a product. Productization is a very large topic in its own right and out of scope of this book, but a couple of key points to be aware of, if the goal is to productize a model, are:

(1) **Flexibility:** There is no perfect model, but the model should accommodate a certain set of real-life situations that may need redesign. This means redesigning the models to accommodate flexibility in terms of new inputs, variations in data regimes and quality, changes in sparsity, and so on. This requires that we use data that is available in the applied, productized situation. For a game, this means using data from that game or games as they would look and play

to the audiences. Cross-validation should also be carried out, especially with streaming data. Finally, ensemble models or combined models can often be usefully combined through aggregation, and give you more flexibility, rather than a single model.

(2) **Robust code:** The code for a model that is to be productized must be robust. This means specifically restructuring the code to adhere to good code quality. It is often the case that following the process of iterative validation and testing, discussed in this chapter, causes the code to be messy. Therefore, restructuring and refactoring the code may be necessary. Quality code must be kept in focus from the beginning. Data scientists work with data, and programmers with code. These are different jobs, and here they need to work together. To help alleviate these issues, always use a version control repository such as Github. Consider also whether the amazing open-source library you have found really has the quality needed for a product. Finally, always perform a thorough risk analysis and assume everything will go wrong in production. Further, allow for error detection within your code.

(3) **Performance:** Runtime is critical in the real world and often more important than precision. Whether we can predict churn for a cohort at 14 days with 91.8% or 92% makes minimal impact, but if runtime slows down so we cannot get predictions for new cohorts before those cohorts leave the game, we have a problem. Always check that runtime is shorter than the minimal required output frequency and understand the cost–benefit of different frequencies (if you have a runtime problem consider parallelization). This is notably important for applications where models are running continuously. Always consider what the balance is between the complexity of the model and needed accuracy. When you really think about this, you might find that traditional statistics in at least some situations can do the job sufficiently well.

(4) **Connectivity:** Your model does not live in a vacuum; it is part of a larger package. It is vital to think not only of the model and what it does but also where the data is coming from in real-life situations and where it goes. The data flow to and from the productized model is essential as broken data can lead to issues with models. To ensure such connectivity, use databases, APIs, and standardized formats for data files. File format should be very rigidly defined and well documented. And always validate data, see Chapter 2, in the operationalized space to avoid the kind of broken data issue mentioned above.

EXERCISES

1. What is model validation?
2. Why do we need to evaluate models?
3. What is the role of a validation set? Why cannot we use the test set for model validation?
4. Consider the following predictions of a classification model.

Ground Truth	T	T	F	T	F	F	T	F	T
Prediction	T	T	F	F	T	F	T	F	F

The two class values are T and F, with T representing the positive case, and F negative.

a Draw the confusion matrix depicting the performance of the model.

b Compute the following performance metrics.

i. Sensitivity

ii. Specificity

iii. Accuracy

iv. Precision

v. Recall

vi. F-Measure

5. Consider the following predictions of a regression model:

Ground Truth	2.5	7	3	5	4	3.5	6	4.5	3
Prediction	3	5	4	5	3	4.5	6	4	2

Compute the following performance metrics:

a Mean-squared error

b R-squared

c Mean absolute error

6. Consider the following receiver operating characteristic curves of three models trained on the same dataset (see Figure 8.3).

a Which model is better between models 1 and 2? Explain why.

b At a false positive rate of 0.3, which model performs the best? Explain why.

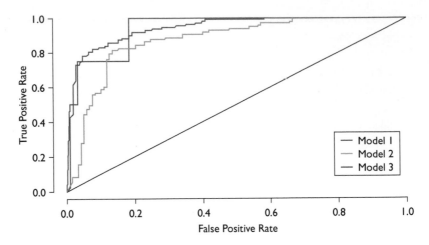

Figure 8.3 ROC of three models.

7. Starting with Lab 2 code:

    a Train a *logistic regression* model on the data from this lab.

    b Draw the ROC curve and compute AUC for this *logistic regression* model.

    c How does its performance compare to the *NB* model?

8. How does cross validation work?

9. Is *linear regression* more susceptible to overfitting or underfitting? Explain why.

10. Assume that you train a *decision tree* and get one with high variance. How should you adjust your model to fix this issue? Adjusting a model means to change the set of hyperparameters defining it.

11. Given the labs in Chapter 7, add a proper validation and evaluation procedures to each lab. Discuss the results compared to what was implemented in the original labs.

•••

BIBLIOGRAPHY

Bengio, Y. (2000). Gradient-based optimization of hyperparameters. *Neural Computation*, *12*(8), 1889–900.

Bergstra, J., and Bengio, Y. (2012). Random search for hyper-parameter optimization. *Journal of Machine Learning Research*, *13*, 281–305. https://doi.org/10.1162/153244303322533223

Breiman, L. (2001). Random forests. *Machine Learning*, *45*(1), 5–32. https://doi.org/10.1023/A:1010933404324

Hastie, T., Tibshirani, R., and Friedman, J. (2009). *The elements of statistical Learning*. New York, NY: Springer. https://doi.org/10.1007/b94608

James, G., Witten, D., Hastie, T., and Tibishirani, R. (2013). *An introduction to statistical learning. Springer texts in statistics*. New Jersey: Wiley. https://doi.org/10.1007/978-1-4614-7138-7

Snoek, J., Larochelle, H., and Adams, R. P. (2012). Practical Bayesian optimization of machine learning algorithms. *Advances in Neural Information Processing Systems, 25*, 2960–8. https://doi.org/2012arXiv1206.2944S

Spiegel, E., and O'Donnell, C. (1997). *Incidence algebras* (1st edition, Vol. 206). New York, NY: Marcel Dekker, Inc.

Weber, B. (2018). Productizing ML models with dataflow. Medium.com.

CHAPTER 9

Neural Networks

A rtificial neural networks (ANNs) and the larger family of neural network (NN)–based methods are important algorithms and tools used for prediction in the field of data science. Within game data science, these techniques are often applied to predict churn, customer lifetime value, in-game purchase, in-game behaviors, as well as to recommend items and discover player patterns. Good examples of the work done in this area are discussed through the work of Yokozuna—an up-and-coming company working on developing advanced predictive techniques for commercial games (http://yokozunadata.com/research/).

NNs, and especially deep NNs, outperform other machine learning models covered in the previous chapters. Recall that, in Chapter 6, we introduced unsupervised learning techniques, and in Chapter 7, we introduced supervised machine learning methods. NNs can be used for both supervised and unsupervised learning tasks due to their ability to model complex, nonlinear relationships in the data. Moreover, the use of deep learning models has reduced the necessity of time-consuming and hand-crafted feature engineering, as the models can make use of more information and can capture the underlying structure of input data. However, they also require more data and computational power. Nevertheless, the last few years have seen major advancements in computational power and an increase in the available datasets from games, specifically from e-sports titles. This then stimulated the growth and the use of NN and deep NN techniques within games.

It should be noted, however, that using an NN or a deep NN comes at a cost of getting results that are not interpretable due to the black box nature of the

Game Data Science. Magy Seif El-Nasr, Truong Huy Nguyen Dinh, Alessandro Canossa, and Anders Drachen, Oxford University Press. © Magy Seif El-Nasr, Truong Huy Nguyen Dinh, Alessandro Canossa, and Anders Drachen (2021). DOI: 10.1093/oso/9780192897879.003.0009

model. This may or may not be a problem given the company and the nature of the problem tackled with this approach. It should also be noted that there are many methods currently under research that explore developing tools to explain the NN and deep NN models; these are being developed within a growing area of research called explainable Artificial Intelligence. Therefore, this issue of interpretability may be resolved in the future. For now, however, you should note that interpretability is an issue when using any of the techniques discussed in the chapter.

Generally speaking, ANNs (Mitchell, 1997) are machine learning models developed to mimic the inner working of the brain. The brain is considered one of the most amazing natural computing systems. The inspiration behind ANNs comes from scientists' observation of how the brain operates using extremely simple processing units, such as neurons, which enables it to handle abstract tasks and discover sophisticated correlative relationships. An important element of this approach is the interconnectivity of neurons, which dictates how information is propagated and processed, a little at a time, through the network.

In this chapter, we will begin with a discussion on the fundamental concepts of NNs, such as the processing unit (also called neuron or perceptron) and a basic NN called *Feedforward Neural Network* (*FNN*), as well as how such networks can be trained from data. Next, we will briefly touch on some state-of-the art NN-based models used in deep learning, namely Convolutional Neural Networks (CNNs). In Chapter 11, we will discuss another class of neural networks that work with sequence data, which is called Recurrent Neural Network (RNN) and Deep Recurrent Neural Networks (deep RNNs). In this chapter, besides discussing the basics, we will also discuss some case studies of using these techniques with game data, and specifically with commercial game data, demonstrating the utility of the approach in today's industry and applications.

It should be noted that this chapter will not provide very deep details of NN techniques, as in some cases that may require a whole book to delve into—rather, this chapter will provide a high-level introduction of the subject. Interested readers should look up the resources in the bibliography section for more details.

Let us start by discussing what an ANN is. An ANN is a collection of artificial neurons that are organized in layers. The basic architecture of an ANN is shown in Figure 9.1. The circular shapes represent the neurons, and the neurons are organized in layers. Layers can have different numbers of neurons. The first layer is called the input layer, and the last one is called the output layer. All the layers

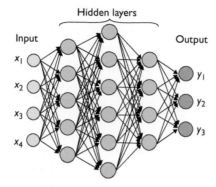

Figure 9.1 The basic architecture of an artificial neural network showing the input, hidden, and output layers.

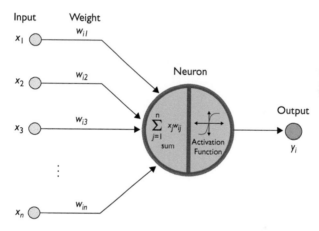

Figure 9.2 The general structure of a neuron: a weighted sum of the input features is computed before feeding into an activation function, which outputs a real number.

in between the input and output layers are called hidden layers. The signal flows from the input layer to the output layer through the hidden layers.

This network is built from small units called neurons. Neurons process data, which is in the form of a numeric vector, and return a single number as its output. As depicted in Figure 9.2, given the input data $x = (x_1, x_2, \ldots, x_n)$, the transformation at a neuron i comprises two steps:

- **First**, compute the weighted sum of the input: $z = w_{i0} + \sum_{j=1}^{n} x_j w_{ij}$, where $w_i = (w_{i0}, w_{i1}, w_{i2}, \ldots, w_{in})$ is the weight vector of neuron i. Each weight is associated with an inbound edge of the neuron (Figure 9.2). Note that w_{i0} is a special weight, called bias, that is not directly associated with the input. Its role is to account for the translation of the activation function, similar to the role of the value b in a linear function $y = ax + b$. Alternatively, this could be represented as the dot product of two vectors: w_i and the input vector $(1, x_1, x_2, \ldots, x_n)$.

- **Second**, the resulting weighted sum z is passed through an activation function ϕ. For example, if the sigmoid function is employed, the output of the neuron is computed as $\phi(z) = \frac{1}{1+e^{-z}}$.

One can use different types of functions for these neurons, some popular ones include linear, step function, sigmoid, tanh, rectified linear unit, and leaky rectified linear. Each activation function has its pros and cons related to the complexity of the data processed and the complexity of the parameter learning process. If a neuron suffers from the issue of the vanishing gradient, a common issue faced when training multilayer NNs that we will discuss in Section 9.1.4, its weights will be updated very slowly to correct the observed error, thus requiring a lot more data and time to train the network. This is one key concern that practitioners of NNs have in mind when designing such networks. We will discuss it in more detail below.

There are generally three types of NN: Feedforward Neural Networks (FNNs), Convolutional Neural Networks (CNNs), and Recurrent Neural Networks (RNNs). In the next sections, we will discuss these different types of networks. We will postpone the discussion of RNNs till Chapter 11, where we discuss advanced sequence analysis, as RNN is well known for handling sequence data.

This chapter is then divided into two sections:

- Feedforward Neural Networks (FNN) (Section 9.1)
- Convolutional Neural Networks (CNN) (Section 9.2)

Further, this chapter will not contain labs, unlike other chapters, since these are more advanced methods and require more setup to get them to work. Further, they also require a larger amount of data than what we made available with this book. However, interested readers should refer to the R manual for libraries and tutorials on the methods discussed here. Large game datasets can be obtained from Kaggle or specific title APIs, such as *League of Legends* and *DOTA 2*.

9.1 Feedforward neural networks (FNNs)

FNNs are a family of NNs in which data flows in one direction (i.e., forward) from the input layers, through the hidden layers, before ending up at the output layer (see Figure 9.1). This is in contrast to other networks, such as RNNs (Hochreiter and Schmidhuber, 1997), discussed in Chapter 11, in which data may propagate in the opposite direction toward the input layer. FNNs are used for supervised learning tasks, such as classification and regression, in which the goal is to model the relationship between input features and one or many output variables.

9.1.1 Structure of the network

In this network, there is an input layer, consisting of linear neurons, each of which is associated with one input feature. For example, consider the task of predicting a player's skill level: "novice," "beginner," "intermediate," or "advanced," based on three of the player's in-game statistics: the number of *deaths*, *kills*, and *assists*. In this case, one possible design for an FNN to tackle this task is to use three neurons in the input layer, each corresponding to one such statistics, several hidden layers, and a single node in the output layer that represents the skill level.

For such a network, hyperparameters to be tuned include the number of hidden layers and the number of neurons in each hidden layer. Note that different hidden layers may contain different number of neurons. Also, note that the connections between the nodes can also be a design choice. Figure 9.3 shows an example where we chose two hidden layers and a fully connected network, that is, each node is connected to all the other nodes in the subsequent layer.

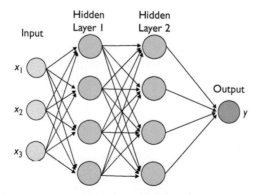

Figure 9.3 A feed forward neural network with two hidden layers. Each circle is a neuron, and the directed links represent the flow of processed data as the output of one node into the input of the nodes in the next layer.

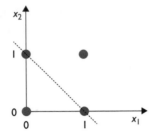

x_1	x_2	y
0	0	0
0	1	1
1	0	1
1	1	0

Figure 9.4 Two-variable XOR truth table and plot in 2D space. The red and blue dots represent two different output values of y, 0 and 1, respectively.

When there is no hidden layer, the resultant network is also called a single-layer perceptron, in which all input nodes are directly connected to a single output neuron. Such simple structures were shown to be capable of learning *only* linearly separable structures, that is, there exists a line separating data points of two classes in a binary classification task. More specifically, a single-layer perceptron cannot learn the XOR operator, which has a nonlinear relationship between the input and output (Minsky and Papert, 1969). Figure 9.4 shows a visualization of XOR and why such a function is hard to capture using a line. Since a perceptron is capable of only learning linearly separable classes, it is not able to classify such XOR example, because no straight line can cleanly separate the red and blue circles shown in the figure.

The power and flexibility of NNs lie in the synergy resulting from combining a large number of neurons, which lead to the successful and widespread use of deep networks. Deep networks refer to NNs that have a large number of hidden layers (thus deep) and nodes. They form the basis for what is commonly referred to as deep learning. In this context, the multilayer perceptron models or FNNs with multiple hidden layers are also considered general Deep Neural Networks (DNNs).

9.1.2 How does an FNN work?

An FNN aims to model the function F^* that maps input data x to output y by treating such learning task as an optimization problem. It defines a mapping $y = F(x, \theta)$, where x are the input parameters, and θ are parameters that it is trying to optimize, so that the approximate function F is as close as possible to the actual mapping function F^*, which is unknown.

During training, the network learns and updates the parameters in an itera-tive process to drive F to match F^* using training data. It must be noted here that, during this process, the NN does not adjust the architecture (i.e., number of hidden layers, number of neurons, activation functions) of the model, rather it adjusts the weights and biases associated with the neurons to try to get an optimal output given the training data. After training is over, the model can be used to generate outputs from the inputs. A good model would generate output that is close to actual values for the training data as well as for other data it has not seen before (e.g., test data).

To further understand what these weights are, consider the FNN shown in Figure 9.5. Each connection from a node to another has a weight, as shown in Figure 9.5, and in Tables 9.1 and 9.2. The entry $w_{ij}^{(l)}$ in this matrix is the weight associated with the link connecting the node i in the previous layer to node j in layer l. The superscript notation is used to denote the corresponding layer in the neural network. Notice that each layer's weights include a bias term $w_{0j}^{(l)}$, which is represented by the top node in the input and is used to anchor the computed weights. Corresponding to these terms at each layer is the dummy input valued 1 to be multiplied with the bias term in the neuron.

To follow how this works, let us take a specific example of the input $x = (x_1, x_2) = (2, 5)$, as shown in Figure 9.5 above. Note that we first append

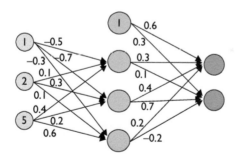

Figure 9.5 A sample feed forward network with weights.

Table 9.1 Parameters to the neural network shown in Figure 9.4.

Hidden layer's weights	Bias	Weight for input 1	Weight for input 2
Neuron 1	$w_{01}^{(1)} = -0.5$	$w_{11}^{(1)} = 0.1$	$w_{21}^{(1)} = 0.4$
Neuron 2	$w_{02}^{(1)} = -0.7$	$w_{12}^{(1)} = 0.3$	$w_{22}^{(1)} = 0.2$
Neuron 3	$w_{03}^{(1)} = -0.3$	$w_{13}^{(1)} = 0.1$	$w_{23}^{(1)} = 0.6$

Table 9.2 *Parameters to the neural network shown in Figure 9.4 (continued from Table 9.1).*

Output layer's weights	Bias	Weight for input 1	Weight for input 2	Weight for input 3
Neuron 1	$w_{01}^{(2)} = 0.6$	$w_{11}^{(2)} = 0.3$	$w_{21}^{(2)} = 0.4$	$w_{31}^{(2)} = 0.2$
Neuron 2	$w_{02}^{(2)} = 0.3$	$w_{12}^{(2)} = 0.1$	$w_{22}^{(2)} = 0.7$	$w_{32}^{(2)} = -0.2$

a dummy element of 1 to x, so it becomes $x = (x_0, x_1, x_2) = (1, 2, 5)$. Each of the neurons in the hidden layer receives data from the input layer. The net input for each neuron in the hidden layer is processed by multiplying the input attributes with the associated weights, as follows:

$$z_{n_1}^{(1)} = w_{01}^{(1)}x_0 + w_{11}^{(1)}x_1 + w_{21}^{(1)}x_2 = -0.5 \times 1 + 0.1 \times 2 + 0.4 \times 5 = 1.7$$

$$z_{n_2}^{(1)} = w_{02}^{(1)}x_0 + w_{12}^{(1)}x_1 + w_{22}^{(1)}x_2 = -0.7 \times 1 + 0.3 \times 2 + 0.2 \times 5 = 0.9$$

$$z_{n_3}^{(1)} = w_{03}^{(1)}x_0 + w_{13}^{(1)}x_1 + w_{23}^{(1)}x_2 = -0.3 \times 1 + 0.1 \times 2 + 0.6 \times 5 = 2.9$$

The output from each neuron is then calculated by feeding the z values into an activation function. For this example, let us use the sigmoid function ($\phi(z) = \frac{1}{1+e^{-z}}$) as the activation function for the neurons in the hidden layer.

$$a_{n_1}^{(1)} = \phi\left(z_{n_1}^{(1)}\right) = \frac{1}{1 + e^{-z_{n_1}^{(1)}}} = \frac{1}{1 + e^{-1.7}} = 0.8455$$

$$a_{n_2}^{(1)} = \phi\left(z_{n_2}^{(1)}\right) = \frac{1}{1 + e^{-z_{n_2}^{(1)}}} = \frac{1}{1 + e^{-0.9}} = 0.7109$$

$$a_{n_3}^{(1)} = \phi\left(z_{n_3}^{(1)}\right) = \frac{1}{1 + e^{-z_{n_3}^{(1)}}} = \frac{1}{1 + e^{-2.9}} = 0.9478$$

Now that we have calculated the output for each of the neurons in the hidden layer, these are then considered as inputs for the output layer $h = (h_{10}, h_{11}, h_{12}, h_{13}) = (1, 0.8455, 0.7109, 0.9478)$ vector with the additional feature $h_{10} = 1$, as shown in Figure 9.5. The calculation process is similar to what was shown in the previous step:

$$z_{n_1}^{(2)} = w_{01}^{(2)} h_{10} + w_{11}^{(2)} h_{11} + w_{21}^{(2)} h_{12} + w_{31}^{(2)} h_{13}$$

$$= 0.6 \times 1 + 0.3 \times 0.8455 + 0.4 \times 0.7109 + 0.2 \times 0.9478 = 1.3276$$

$$z_{n_2}^{(2)} = w_{02}^{(2)} h_{10} + w_{12}^{(2)} h_{11} + w_{22}^{(2)} h_{12} + w_{32}^{(2)} h_{13}$$

$$= 0.3 \times 1 + 0.1 \times 0.8455 + 0.7 \times 0.7109 + (-0.2) \times 0.9478 = 0.6926$$

Similarly, by applying sigmoid functions, we get the final output of the output layer neurons, as follows:

$$a_{n_1}^{(2)} = \phi \left(z_{n_1}^{(2)} \right) = \frac{1}{1 + e^{-z_{n_1}^{(2)}}} = \frac{1}{1 + e^{-1.3276}} = 0.7904$$

$$a_{n_2}^{(2)} = \phi \left(z_{n_2}^{(2)} \right) = \frac{1}{1 + e^{-z_{n_2}^{(2)}}} = \frac{1}{1 + e^{-0.6926}} = 0.6665$$

In this example, we have shown how a forward pass happens in an FNN in detail. In reality, these calculations are done using matrix multiplication, which can be represented and implemented more efficiently.

It is worth mentioning that we have shown one activation function for all hidden layers as well as the output layer, whereas it is possible to use different activation functions for different nodes or layers. For instance, in classification problems, it is a very common practice to use the *softmax* function at the output layer rather than using activation functions as shown earlier.

9.1.3 Training an FNN

Training an FNN refers to the task of estimating the parameters associated with all the neurons in the network. Each neuron i is characterized by its input weights $w_i = (w_{i0}, w_{i1}, w_{i2}, \ldots, w_{in})$, so training here means estimating these weight vectors for all the neurons so that the values coming out of the output layer match the corresponding output values in the data.

Note that when training an FNN, we do not try to determine or tune the parametric forms of the neurons, that is, whether they should be a *sigmoid*, *tanh*, or *rectified linear* function, etc. Determining the parametric forms of the neurons is part of a larger task called structure learning, in which both the neurons' types as well as how links are connected between layers. Usually, the structure needs to be fixed before the model training step. Different structures can lead to different networks that process the data in different ways. In

Section 9.2, we will discuss some of these commonly used networks, such as CNNs, that make up the state-of-the-art in deep learning.

The process of training an FNN net follows the same principles as that of training classification models, which was discussed in Chapters 7 and 8. Essentially, the available data is split into three disjoint sets for training, validation, and testing. The parameters of a network are learned using the training set through a learning algorithm, such as backpropagation, which we are going to discuss in detail below. Training stops when the prediction error is lower than a desired small threshold, indicating that the model learned is already good enough. The validation set is then used for structure learning, that is, picking the best structure for the network, while the test set is used for comparing the model with other algorithmic approaches. In cases when data scarcity is a concern, cross validation is used instead of maintaining fixed, disjoint training and validation sets. Note that due to the high complexity of FNNs specifically and neural networks generally, overfitting is a real issue that often needs addressing. Approaches to tackle overfitting, discussed in Chapter 8, are applicable here as well.

One of the most widely used algorithms to train an FNN is called *backpropagation* (abbreviated to *backprop*), which is short for "the backward propagation of errors." *Backpropagation*, in general, proceeds by first assessing the error from the output layer then propagating that error backward in the network adjusting the weights as it goes. The idea behind *backprop* is to first initialize some random weights to the whole network, then let the data flow through the network to produce a predicted output. When the predicted output is obtained (at the output layer), it will be compared to the ground truth (output values from the data). The amount of mismatch (error), if any, will then be used to update the weights, layer by layer, starting from those closest to the output layer toward those near the input layer. The updated values are directly related to the error, and where the neurons are. Usually, the closer they are to the output layer, the bigger the update. As such, the error can be said to propagate backward through the network. This is why the method is called *backpropagation*.

The amount of numerical mismatch between the ground truth and the network output is called Loss ($\mathcal{L}$), which is a function of input x and output $\hat{y}$. The objective of the NN is to optimize the weights of the network so that $\mathcal{L}$ is minimized for both the training data and the future unseen data. Training a NN is similar to training any other machine learning model using gradient-based learning. NNs are usually trained by iterative, gradient-based optimizers.

Computing the gradient is complicated in NNs because of the complex architecture as well as the nonlinearity of the network. However, gradients can be calculated efficiently using the *backpropagation* algorithm. Note here that *backpropagation* only refers to the method for computing the gradient. Training of the network by updating the weights is done by standard *gradient-based* algorithms (e.g., *gradient descent* or *stochastic gradient descent*).

The weights are updated using the gradient of the *Loss* function with respect to the weights. In general, this update can be represented by the following equation (which is similar to the definition of *gradient descent* optimizers):

$$W = W - \alpha \nabla_W \mathcal{L}$$

where α denotes the learning rate, W is the weight matrix for all the layers, and $\mathcal{L}$ is the *loss* function, which is calculated using the actual target value y and the network output $\hat{y}$. The gradient $\nabla_W \mathcal{L}$ is the derivative of the *loss* function $\mathcal{L}$ with respect to the weight matrix W.

The calculation of $\nabla_W \mathcal{L}$ is done layer by layer starting from the final layer. First, $\nabla_{W^{(L)}} \mathcal{L}$ is calculated for the final layer L which is then used to calculate subsequent gradients $\nabla_{W^{(L-1)}} \mathcal{L}, \ldots, \nabla_{W^{(2)}} \mathcal{L}, \nabla_{W^{(1)}} \mathcal{L}$.

More formally, the algorithm comprises the following steps:

- **Step 1:** Calculate $\frac{\partial \mathcal{L}}{\partial W^{(L)}}$. The first step is to calculate the gradient for the final layer, which means to take the derivative of the loss function $\mathcal{L}$ with respect to the weight matrix $W^{(L)}$ of the final layer $\mathcal{L}$. To calculate this, the chain rule of the derivative is applied. As shown in Figure 9.6, first, the derivative of $\mathcal{L}$ is taken with respect to activation $a^{(L)}$. Next, the derivative of $a^{(L)}$ is taken with respect to the net input $z^{(L)}$ to layer L.

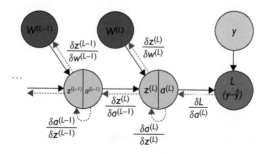

Figure 9.6 Back propagation steps are shown in red dotted arrows for the final layer L and blue dotted arrows for layer $(L-1)$.

Finally, the derivative of $z^{(L)}$ is taken with respect to the weight matrix $W^{(L)}$ of the final layer L. The backpropagation of the gradients is shown in red dotted arrows in Figure 9.6.

- **Step 2:** Calculate $\frac{\partial \mathcal{L}}{\partial W^{(l)}}$ for all the other layers $l = L - 1, \ldots, 2, 1$. The calculation is similar to Step 1. This value is represented by the blue dotted arrows in Figure 9.6. The calculated values for layer L from Step 1 are also used for the layer $L - 1$, as the derivative is taken for the loss function $\mathcal{L}$. Similarly, for layer $L-2$, the values calculated for layer $L-1$ are used, and so on for all other layers.

- **Step 3:** At the end of the calculation for all the layers, the values $\frac{\partial \mathcal{L}}{\partial W^{(1)}}, \frac{\partial \mathcal{L}}{\partial W^{(2)}} \cdots, \frac{\partial \mathcal{L}}{\partial W^{(L)}}$ are returned from the algorithm.

The overall learning of an FNN is an iterative process between forward-pass and backpropagation. The initial step is to randomly (in most cases) set the weights of the neurons. After the forward-pass, the algorithm calculates the loss and uses *backpropagation* to propagate and update the weights. This process is repeated, up to several iterations, generally called epochs. We stop when the error is minimal when tested with the testing set, which means the network can generalize on unseen data.

9.1.4 Advantages and disadvantages of FNNs

Feedforward neural networks can be used to learn highly complex nonlinear relationships between the input data and the output. However, such flexibility comes at a cost, as NNs can overfit very easily, see Chapter 8 for more discussion of overfitting. As such, it is important to properly evaluate NNs and compare their performance to other simpler models to ensure that the resulting model did not overfit.

Another challenge faced when training NNs is called the vanishing gradient problem, which occurs when *gradient-based optimization* techniques are used with certain activation functions. Specifically, during *backpropagation* as we move backward through the hidden layers, the gradients tend to get smaller and smaller (vanishingly small) preventing the weight from changing its value. This means that the neurons in the earlier layers learn very slowly because of the very small updates in their weights as compared with the neurons in the later layers of the network. As a result, the training time increases, and in the worst case, this may completely stop the NN from further training in the layers near the input. This problem makes it challenging to learn and tune the parameters of the earlier layers in the networks, especially if the network has large numbers of layers.

9.1.5 DNN in game data science

There are several examples within the games industry and research that use NNs and specifically DNNs for different types of predictions and item recommendations.

Bertens et al. (2018) show a great example where they were concerned with developing a model that can predict the next item that a player would purchase in a game. In modern games, the performance and strategy of players depend on the types of items they use. Most games allow players to buy a wide range of virtual items with real money. Due to this open market of items, sometimes, players may be overwhelmed by the variety and the capability of different items they are presented. Therefore, the industry has produced many techniques for item recommendation. Correctly predicting items of interest for different players would result in a good recommendation system. To predict items players would purchase next, Bertens et al. proposed two different approaches: *Extremely Randomized Tree (ERT)* and *Deep Neural Network.*

The data used in this work is collected from a Japanese card game called *Age of Ishtaria* published by Parade Game in 2014. The idea is to use user data up to time *t* and then predict the next purchase after time *t*. The user data contains a time series of the number of purchases per item and the total sales per item for each user. These are then converted into general statistics, producing a fixed size vector that is used as an input to a NN. Bertens et al. used an FNN of two hidden layers of 2,048 units followed by dropout layers after each one. Dropout layers do not perform any computation, but randomly drop some neurons from training, which helps in alleviating issues faced with deep networks, such as overfitting and vanishing gradient. Dropout can also apply to input layers to reduce overfitting on single features. The output of the model is the probability of items that the player will buy on the next purchase.

They evaluated the model based on three categories: the predicted item was purchased on the next purchase action, the predicted item was purchased, and the predicted item was purchased within a predefined time window. The resulting model shows that users have different purchase probability for each item. Capturing such information allows the game to personalize its predictions per user and provides a more successful recommendation system for the game. Their results show that the *ERT* model was slightly better than the *DNN* in predicting the item with the highest probability. However, both models performed similarly considering top 2 and top 3 items on the next purchase.

While the authors of this paper did not compare the results to any other models, it is a good example showing the use of deep NNs in the games domain. However, with the discoveries and the work in deep learning with convolutional and recurrent networks, NN-based methods are gaining more popularity and predictive power with game data. Therefore, the results produced by the paper may be better enhanced with these new models. We will discuss these new types of NNs in the next section.

9.2 CNNs

CNNs are a type of NNs most frequently used in image processing and computer vision when the input is an image, and therefore, the input is a matrix-like structure rather than a single dimension vector. CNNs are a special kind of NNs that can remember spatial information by processing an image as a whole and analyzing groups of pixels at a time. Similar to other NNs, CNNs have an input layer, hidden layers, and an output layer of neurons associated with weights and biases. Linear or nonlinear functions are applied within the neurons as discussed earlier.

One of the factors that differentiates CNNs from other NNs is that the input is a grid-like topology rather than a 1D input vector. A simple example of such input is an image that is generally represented in the grid-like topology of a 3D matrix. The first two dimensions of the 3D matrix represent the width and height of the image, and the third dimension represents the color channel (red, green, and blue for color image) of the image. Each element of the 3D matrix is the pixel value of the image for a certain color.

The term convolution refers to the linear mathematical operation that operates on two functions to produce a third function that expresses how one function is modified by the other. CNNs use convolution instead of general matrix multiplication in at least one of the layers. This is why they are called CNNs.

9.2.1 CNN's architecture

The basic architecture of a CNN is similar to the ordinary neural networks with the addition of three new types of layers: convolutional layer, pooling layer, and normalization layer. As mentioned previously, CNNs take 3D matrix as input, and every matrix element is considered as a neuron in the input layer, thus making it a 3D volume of neurons. Similarly, as the input layer, the hidden layers are also a 3D matrix of neurons. As a result, each layer has its width, height, and depth irrespective of the depth (number of layers) of the network as a whole. However, the output layer is generally a 1D vector just as an ordinary NN and the conversion from the input 3D layer to output 1D vector is generated by using subsequent hidden layers.

The convolutional layer is the key to preserving the spatial information of the previous layer. A convolutional layer applies a series of image filters to the input from the previous layer. The image filters are known as convolutional kernels. The resulting filtered images are expected to extract features like edges of different objects or distinguish colors of different classes or other information that are vital to the desired output of the network.

The pooling layer employs a pooling function that generates a summary statistic of the nearby outputs at certain locations in the input to the pooling layer, and hence reduce the number of parameters and computations in the network. It is a common practice to insert a pooling layer in-between two successive convolutional layers. The pooling layer operates independently on every depth slice across the width and the height of the input volume using a pooling function. For example, the max pooling function operates on a rectangular region reporting the maximum output within it.

One of the most common forms of pooling is to use max pooling with a rectangle (also called pooling filter) of size 2 × 2 applied along with a stride of 2, as shown in Figure 9.7. Using this operation, the input is down sampled by 2 along both width and height. The max operation reports the maximum activation over 4 numbers within each 2 × 2 rectangle for every depth slice of the input volume.

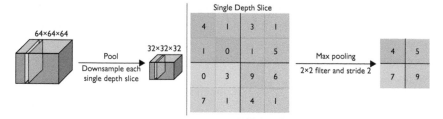

Figure 9.7 Pooling layer down samples each depth slice independently and reduces the size of the input volume across width and height (left). Max pooling of filter 2 × 2 with stride 2 generates output by taking the maximum of each 2 × 2 rectangle.

The intuition behind using pooling layers is to down sample the input image across width and height keeping the desired activations depending on the pooling function. The pooling layer helps make the network indifferent to small changes in the input.

Other popular pooling functions include average, weighted average, or L^2 norm of a rectangular neighborhood. There are relevant research works that suggest using different pooling functions in various situations. In practice, max pooling works better in many cases.

Another common practice is to use a normalization layer in a convolutional neural network which normalizes the values of the output volume from the previous layer. A normalization layer is typically used immediately before activation layers. It accelerates convergence and improves the performance of the model, especially when saturating sigmoids are used. It also makes the model less sensitive to higher learning rates and initialization. Further, it acts as a form of regularization. However, recently normalization layers have fallen out of favor in complex networks because of their minimal contribution.

9.2.2 How does the convolutional layer work?

The convolutional kernel (or the filter) is applied to the input image or data from the previous layer. The filter has a fixed size of width and height a depth which is the same as that of the input data from the previous layer (i.e., 4 × 4 × 3 for an input data of size 32 × 32 × 3). A filter is a 3D matrix which is applied to the data by sliding across the width and the height and performing the convolution operation. The convolution operation is essentially the dot product between the entries of the filter and the input at any position. Applying a filter by sliding across the width and height of the input data would generate a 2D activation map that gives responses of that filter at every spatial position. In practice, a set of filters is used instead of just one filter in each convolutional layer. Each filter in the set generates a separate 2D activation map which is stacked along the depth dimension to produce the output data from the convolutional layer. As stated previously, each of the filters is expected to extract features from objects and colors that would help the subsequent layers to differentiate the classes. The network can learn the filters that can extract useful features through training.

Figure 9.8 shows the results of two convolutional filters applied to an input image. The convolutional filters detect edges of the image in different directions. The upper filter detects the horizontal edges, and the lower one detects the vertical edges in the image.

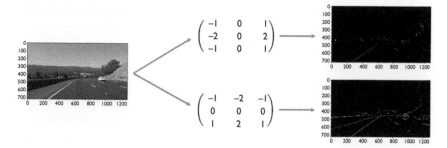

Figure 9.8 Applying two 3 × 3 convolutional filter detects the horizontal and vertical edges in the image.

There are three hyperparameters related to each convolutional layer: (i) number of filters, (ii) stride, and (iii) padding. The number of filters used in each convolutional layer determines the depth of the output data volume. Stride determines how much the filter slides each time across the width and the height. Stride 1 means the filter is moved 1 pixel at a time, stride 2 means the filter is moved 2 pixels, and so on. Using stride value of more than 2 is uncommon in practice. Note that, increasing the stride decreases the width and the height of the output volume from the convolutional layer. Padding means to pad the input data with some value around the border. Generally, zero-padding is used because padding with zero does not introduce additional information to the actual data. Padding can be to preserve the spatial size of the input so that the output width and height are the same as the input.

Now, as we have discussed how the convolutional layer works, we will discuss the benefits of using convolutional layers. We have already discussed that the filters are learned because they capture the features that are useful to differentiate the classes. Two other motivations for using convolutional layers are (i) local connectivity and (ii) parameter sharing. The convolutional layer preserves the local connectivity of the input volume. Each entry of each 2D activation map of the output volume corresponds to the local information of the input volume which is called the receptive field. The receptive field is of the same size as the filter. The local information extends only to the width and height of the input volume, but the full information is preserved along the depth dimension. The intuition behind this is that part of the image that represents a specific feature is important in identifying the class, whereas the depth of the image determines the color of the part as a whole.

Parameter sharing refers to the use of the same parameters across different positions of the input data, which in turn reduces the total number of parameters of the network. In ordinary NNs, the entry of the weight matrix is different for each position of the input, whereas, in CNN, one filter is a matrix of weights and this filter is applied to different positions of the input data, and hence, the filter shares the parameter for different positions of the input. As a result, instead of learning different parameters for different positions, the network learns a fixed set of parameters for each filter for every location of the input. Though this does not affect the runtime of the forward propagation, it reduces the storage requirement significantly.

Besides saving storage issues, parameter sharing also captures the same features throughout the image. Suppose a human face can be anywhere in the image rather than the face in the center. Using the same parameter for a filter would capture the same information for a feature present anywhere in the image.

9.2.3 An example of CNN: AlexNet

Different CNN architectures have been used for a long time. *LeNet-5* architecture (LeCunn et al., 1998) was introduced in 1998; however, constrained by the availability of computing resources, it was not popular. With the advent of technology, Graphics Processing Unit (GPU) use, and the use of deep architectures, *AlexNet* (Krizhevsky et al., 2012) significantly outperformed all the prior competitors on an image dataset called *ImageNet* (Deng et al., 2009). Due to its popularity and use nowadays, we will discuss it next.

Figure 9.9 shows the architecture of *AlexNet*. The network is split into two pipelines as shown and was trained on two NVIDIA GeForce GTX 580 GPUs.

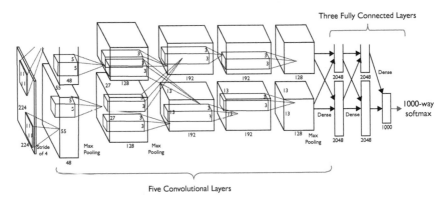

Figure 9.9 AlexNet architecture adapted from Krizhevsky et al. (2012).

There are some interconnections between the two pipelines; however, we will focus on one pipeline here to understand the architecture. *AlexNet* contains five convolutional layers and three fully connected layers followed by *ReLU activation* function after each layer. The input image has three channels for RGB image with the size = 224 × 224 in width and height. It uses a convolution filter of size 11 × 11 at the first convolutional layer, 5 × 5 in the third convolutional layer, and 3 × 3 filter in other convolutional layers. A different number of filters are used in convolutional layers, as shown in the figure. Max pooling of filter size 3 × 3 with a stride of 2 is used after the first, second, and fifth convolutional layers, which reduces the input volume across the width and the height. After the convolutional layers, there are three fully connected layers where dropout is also applied. The final output layer uses *softmax* which consists of 1,000 neurons, which is the same as the number of classes in the dataset.

Some other renowned CNN architectures include *VGGNet* (Simonyan and Zisserman, 2014), *GoogleNet* (Szegedy et al., 2015), *ResNet* (He et al., 2016), *Inception v4* (Szegedy et al., 2017), and *DenseNet* (Huang et al., 2017). Common datasets for image classification used to benchmark these networks include Caltech-101 (Fei-Fei et al., 2007), Caltech-256 (Griffin et al., 2007), CIFAR-10 (Krizhevsky and Hinton, 2009), CIFAR-100 (Krizhevsky and Hinton, 2009), and ImageNet (Deng et al., 2009).

9.2.4 CNN in game data science

CNNs have been used in game data science, and recently, there have been many applications of deep learning in games research due to the availability of game data and the increase in computational capability. CNN can be very useful in game data science. CNNs have shown great success with image analysis. Game frames and image analysis have been heavily used for procedural content generation, gameplay analysis, as well as player modeling, and therefore CNNs are an obvious choice. There are other algorithms and techniques (e.g., *SVM* and *KNN*) that can be used for image classification or analysis. However, in general, they need feature engineering, which includes designing handcrafted features, feature selection, and extraction. CNNs can be thought of as an automatic process for feature extraction inside the model. Furthermore, CNNs have shown better accuracy and performance over other models. One disadvantage of using CNN is the need for a large amount of training data and computational power to train the model. However, this may not be an issue for many games and game companies nowadays. Below, we will discuss two projects that leveraged a CNN-based architecture for analysis of game data.

9.2.4.1 CASE STUDY 1: PLAYER EXPERIENCE EXTRACTION FROM GAMEPLAY VIDEO

Obtaining and analyzing gameplay data has now become an important part of the game design and development process, as discussed in Chapter 1. However, gameplay data logs may not always be available due to the lack of instrumentation of a particular game. To recreate this data log, one idea is to automatically generate game logs based on recorded gameplay videos, which can be done through deep learning as demonstrated by Luo et al. (2018).

Luo et al. proposed two approaches, both of which employ CNNs, but one uses it as a supervised learning method while the other uses transfer learning (a variant of NN learning technique). The first approach, called the paired approach, uses CNN as a supervised learning algorithm. The game videos were first parsed into frames. These frames were paired with labels for active game events happening in each frame to generate a dataset. As a result, the dataset is composed of labeled game frames. This dataset was next used to train a CNN (*AlexNet* architecture) so that it can predict which game events are happening given the input frame. As a result, this becomes a multiclass classification problem, where the input is a game frame, and the output is a prediction that one or multiple game events have occurred in the input frame. This approach was evaluated on *Gwario*, a clone of *Super Mario Bros* (Miyamoto et al., 1985). The process is depicted in Figure 9.10. The problem with this approach is that it requires a large, well-labeled dataset, while taking a significant amount of training and computation power to train the network before it could appropriately start to recognize the events.

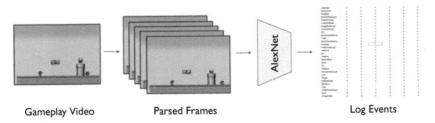

Gameplay Video   Parsed Frames   Log Events

Figure 9.10 Visualization of the procedure used to generate log events using CNN from gameplay video. Luo, Z., Guzdial, M., Liao, N., and Riedl, M. (2018, September). Player experience extraction from gameplay video. In *Fourteenth Artificial Intelligence and Interactive Digital Entertainment Conference*. © 2018, Association for the Advancement of Artificial Intelligence.

The second approach, called the transfer approach, addressed the issues identified in the previous approach by leveraging a technique called transfer learning,—a machine learning method where one model is trained on one task and later used as a pretrained model for a different task. In their work, Luo et al. demonstrated how a specific transfer learning paradigm, called student–teacher learning (Wong and Gales, 2016), can be used to take a classification network trained on one game dataset (e.g., *Gwario* in this case) to "teach" another (called *student*) network to carry out a similar task in another game (e.g., *Megaman*). The student network is the same as the teacher network, except for the last output layer, which directly turns learned features in hidden layers into predictions. The intuition here is that such hidden layers may capture some important structures that can generalize beyond the original training set. They evaluated this approach in two games: *Megaman* (Capcom, 1987) and *Skyrim* (B. G. Studios, 2011). Their results demonstrate the utility of this approach.

As for *Megaman*, the teacher network is set to be the one trained with *Gwario* data as obtained from the paired approach. Since *Megaman* and *Gwario* are both side-scrollers and fairly similar in nature, the authors were able to obtain decent performance, beating the strongest baseline (called domain adaptation, in which all data is adapted to match the target domain before training) just by a single training epoch on the student network. The improvement is, however, fairly modest—that is, only 0.8% better.

With *Skyrim*, they trained the teacher network using a readily available dataset called *UCF-101* (Soomro et al., 2012), which comprises images of daily life human activities, such as crawling, applying lipstick, bowling, etc. Since *Skyrim* is a photorealistic game and the pretrained network was trained on actual photos with similar actions in the real world, the transferred knowledge proves to be quite effective again, outperforming baselines that do not utilize transfer learning. The accuracy of prediction on *Skyrim* with this method was close to 100%, while the learning was faster with a smaller dataset.

This case study shows the power of CNNs and their use in game image analysis and prediction.

9.2.4.2 DEEP CONVOLUTIONAL PLAYER MODELING ON LOG AND LEVEL DATA

In another example, Liao et al. (Liao, Guzdial, and Riedl, 2017) propose an approach to predict players' experience based labeled measures of challenge, creativity, design, frustration, and fun. The goal of this analysis is to predict these measures using game logs and game level structure information. The game logs contain game events. The game-level information contains blocks, collectibles, or enemies present in the level.

They first used CNN to model players using only game logs. These logs are represented as a matrix where each row is an event or action happening in the level and the column is the number of time steps. To make the matrices of the same shape, the time step was normalized to a predefined size for each level. The input to CNN is two game logs of the same player playing two different levels. A CNN was then trained for each feature using this data and the labels.

Another approach used was *a* hybrid network, which combined both the game log CNN and level information CNN to build a final fully connected layer. In previous work, Guzdial et al. (2016) used only the game-level information to predict player experiences, which inspired the use of level information along with the game log, as player experience depends on the performance as well as how the level is structured. The intuition of using game logs is that the two players may play through the same levels but rank them differently in terms of experience.

Liao et al. evaluated these techniques using two games: *Super Mario Bros* (Miyamoto et al., 1985) and *Gwario* (a derivative of *Super Mario*). Players were asked to label each possible pair, and labels were then used to generate the dataset. They then compared the performance of the models with log data only, level data only, and both. Their results showed that using the level and logs separately achieved similar performances, but using both of them together achieved significantly better performance in terms of prediction accuracy: around 10% increase in accuracy with both vs. with level or log data alone. This showed that the level of information, as well as the set of events happening in the game, is complementary to predict the player experiences.

A similar approach can be used with other game data to assess the gameplay experiences. The process is to convert the game log and the level information into a 2D matrices, which can then be used as the CNN input. This work showed how CNNs can also be used with variables other than the images.

9.3 Summary and conclusive remarks

Due to the availability of game data and the increase in computational power, the use of NNs and deep networks is on the rise in data science in general, and specifically within the field of game data science. Complex deep networks are used as they can generalize to highly complex relationships over unseen data and, as a result, provide better performance than traditional models. Such networks have been used to serve many purposes within the game production cycle, including churn predicting, predicting and measuring customer lifetime value, recommending items, as well as discovering and forecasting player behavior patterns. Deep learning has shown good performance and results on these problems.

Despite the good performance shown with this approach, the issue of interpretability discussed above is still a big concern. While it is true that the final model and prediction output is important for games, why such results are obtained is also important for different stakeholders, including design, marketing, or production teams. This issue discourages the use of deep NNs for problems where such interpretability is important. In such situations, approaches and techniques discussed in previous chapters are often used. However, it can sometimes be beneficial to use multiple approaches with the same problem to assess which approach would work best for your problem and dataset.

While interpretability has been a problem, there are several new studies looking into the development of interpretability tools and techniques for NNs. We believe this area will continue to expand in the future. Therefore, due to the accelerated research work within this area, we advise the reader to read on more current resources, as the discussion in this chapter can become too basic or obsolete at the given time.

• •

ACKNOWLEDGMENTS

This chapter was written in collaboration with Sabbir Ahmed. His work and analysis done on the NN techniques are an invaluable contribution to this chapter.

• •

BIBLIOGRAPHY

Bertens, P., Guitart, A., Chen, P. P., and Periáñez, Á. (2018, August). A machine-learning item recommendation system for video games. In *2018 IEEE Conference on Computational Intelligence and Games (CIG)* (pp. 1–4). IEEE, Maastricht, Netherlands.

Deng, J., Dong, W., Socher, R., Li, L. J., Li, K., and Fei-Fei, L. (2009, June). Imagenet: A large-scale hierarchical image database. In *2009 IEEE Conference on Computer Vision and Pattern Recognition* (pp. 248–55). IEEE, Miami, FL.

Fei-Fei, L., Fergus, R., and Perona, P. (2007). Learning generative visual models from few training examples: An incremental Bayesian approach tested on 101 object categories. *Computer Vision and Image Understanding, 106*(1), 59–70.

Goodfellow, I., Yoshua, B., and Aaron, C. (2016). *Deep learning*. Cambridge, MA: MIT Press.

Griffin, G., Holub, A., and Perona, P. (2007). Caltech-256 object category dataset. URL: https://resolver.caltech.edu/CaltechAUTHORS:CNS-TR-2007-001

Guitart, A., Chen, P., and Periáñez, Á. (2019). The winning solution to the IEEE CIG 2017 game data mining competition. *Machine Learning and Knowledge Extraction*, *1*(1), 252–64.

Guzdial, M., and Riedl, M. (2016, September). Game level generation from gameplay videos. *Proceedings of the AAAI Conference on Artificial Intelligence and Interactive Digital Entertainment*, *12*(1). Retrieved from https://ojs.aaai.org/index.php/AIIDE/article/view/12861

He, K., Zhang, X., Ren, S., and Sun, J. (2016). Deep residual learning for image recognition. In *Proceedings of the IEEE Conference on Computer Vision and Pattern Recognition* (pp. 770–8).

Hochreiter, S., and Schmidhuber, J. (1997). Long short-term memory. *Neural Computation*, *9*(8), 1735–80. https://doi.org/10.1162/neco.1997.9.8.1735

Huang, G., Liu, Z., Van Der Maaten, L., and Weinberger, K. Q. (2017). Densely connected convolutional networks. In *Proceedings of the IEEE Conference on Computer Vision and Pattern Recognition* (pp. 4700–8).

Kosko, B. (1988). Bidirectional associative memories. *IEEE Transactions on Systems, Man and Cybernetics*, *18*(1). https://doi.org/10.1109/21.87054

Krizhevsky, A., and Hinton, G. (2009). Learning multiple layers of features from tiny images (Vol. 1, No. 4, p. 7). Technical report, University of Toronto, Toronto, Canada.

Krizhevsky, A., Ilya, S., and Geoffrey, E. H. (2012). Imagenet classification with deep convolutional neural networks. *Advances in Neural Information Processing Systems*, *1*, 1097–105.

Lample, G., and Chaplot, D. S. (2017, February). Playing FPS games with deep reinforcement learning. In *Thirty-First AAAI Conference on Artificial Intelligence*, AAAI, Menlo Park, CA.

LeCun, Y., Bottou, L., Bengio, Y., and Haffner, P. (1998). Gradient-based learning applied to document recognition. In *Proceedings of the IEEE86.11* (pp. 2278–324).

Liao, N., Guzdial, M., and Riedl, M. (2017, August). Deep convolutional player modeling on log and level data. In *Proceedings of the 12th International Conference on the Foundations of Digital Games* (p. 41). ACM, pp. 1-4.

Luo, Z., Guzdial, M., Liao, N., and Riedl, M. (2018, September). Player experience extraction from gameplay video. In *Fourteenth Artificial Intelligence and Interactive Digital Entertainment Conference*.

Minsky, M., and Papert, S. (1969). *Perceptrons: An introduction to computational geometry*. Cambridge, MA: MIT Press. https://doi.org/10.1007/978-3-540-32360-0

Mitchell, T. M. (1997). Machine learning. *Annual Review of Computer Science*. 4. https://doi.org/10.1145/242224.242229

Miyamoto, S., Yamauchi, H., and Tezuka, T. (1985). *Super Mario Bros.* Nintendo Entertainment System, Nintendo.

Mnih, V., Kavukcuoglu, K., Silver, D., Graves, A., Antonoglou, I., Wierstra, D., and Riedmiller, M. (2013). Playing Atari with deep reinforcement learning. *arXiv preprint arXiv:1312.5602*.

Simonyan, K., and Zisserman, A. (2014). Very deep convolutional networks for large-scale image recognition. *arXiv preprint arXiv:1409.1556*.

Snodgrass, S., and Santiago, O. (2015). A hierarchical MDMC approach to 2D video game map generation. In *Eleventh Artificial Intelligence and Interactive Digital Entertainment Conference*.

Soomro, K., Zamir, A. R., and Shah, M. (2012). UCF101: A dataset of 101 human actions classes from videos in the wild. Report No. CRCV-TR-12-01. *arXiv preprint arXiv:1212.0402*.

Summerville, A., and Mateas, M. (2016). *Super Mario* as a string: Platformer level generation via LSTMS. *arXiv preprint arXiv:1603.00930*.

Szegedy, C., Liu, W., Jia, Y., Sermanet, P., Reed, S., Anguelov, D., . . . and Rabinovich, A. (2015). Going deeper with convolutions. In *Proceedings of the IEEE Conference on Computer Vision and Pattern Recognition* (pp. 1–9).

Szegedy, C., Ioffe, S., Vanhoucke, V., and Alemi, A. A. (2017, February). Inception-v4, inception-resnet and the impact of residual connections on learning. In *Thirty-First AAAI Conference on Artificial Intelligence*.

Wong, J. H. M., and Mark, J. G. (2016). Sequence student-teacher training of deep neural networks. *Interspeech*, San Francisco, CA.

CHAPTER 10

Sequence Analysis of Game Data

A ll behavioral telemetry from players can be understood as sequences of actions and game state changes. You can think of games as state machines: a player performs an action, and the game calculates a response. These responses trigger an update to the game state (describes the environment variables of the game), and the player is then confronted with new choices to perform a new action. We can envision game playing as a cyclical process of players performing actions, followed by updates to the game state. For example, in a Role-Playing Game (RPG), users talk to Non-Player Characters (NPCs), and when presented with a dialog option, they make a specific selection. They are then given an answer and a range of possible other actions to take. This prompts a further selection, and so on. Each decision the player makes is informed by the state of the game at the time that an action was taken. This state is a description of a situation or context, which includes the options available to the player at the time of action selection, what the NPC has told the player in the past, the NPC's state, etc. Figure 10.1 shows a depiction of this cycle/loop.

While the reasons players make certain choices at any given point in a game can be difficult to clarify due to the vast number of psychological and social game-external factors, as well as in-game factors, the game state as it is expressed within the confines of the game is directly measurable and trackable. Here, we will refer to the in-game state as the virtual context when we talk about the factors inside the game that directly or indirectly relate to the choices that players can make in games.

Game Data Science. Magy Seif El-Nasr, Truong Huy Nguyen Dinh, Alessandro Canossa, and Anders Drachen, Oxford University Press. © Magy Seif El-Nasr, Truong Huy Nguyen Dinh, Alessandro Canossa, and Anders Drachen (2021). DOI: 10.1093/oso/9780192897879.003.0010

Figure 10.1 The basic game state loop (player actions in black, and system actions in grey): Player performs an action. This action is perceived by the game engine, and a response is calculated. The execution of the response updates the state of the game. This change is perceived by the player, who cognitively processes the change and makes a decision about how to react. This eventually leads to the next action in the cycle.

10.1 Data representation: sequences, events, and actions

For sequence analysis and the discussion within this chapter, we can think of a play session as a long string of choices and responses. We will call this sequence a sequence of events (see Figure 10.2). The fundamental building block of such a sequence is an event, more specifically, a game event or a player action. What comprises an event is defined by the analyst and is based on the purpose of the analysis. For example, a click of a button can be an example of a player action. Similarly, completing a quest or creating a character are also examples of player actions. In this way, our definition of "what an event is" is purpose-dependent and can be anything from the most minute motoric motion to aggregate or abstracted events covering large sections of gameplay.

A common baseline for sequence analysis of player behavior is a basic action defined as the activation of a single function in a game. For example, running in a straight line from point A to B, opening a menu, attacking another character, etc. Executing a basic action can require multiple motoric motions by the player (e.g., several button presses), but there is one mechanism activated. When our

Figure 10.2 An example of a sequence of player actions. In this instance, the actions comprise groups or sets of fine-resolution actions (e.g., "play mission 1" can represent minutes or more of gameplay time). The level of abstraction used in sequence analysis in game data science is determined by the analyst based on the purpose of the analysis.

level of resolution for actions requires the combination of multiple basic actions (e.g., completing a mission, having a conversation with an NPC, or designing a character), we then refer to these as abstracted actions or aggregated actions (see Figure 10.2).

The level of abstraction for actions is usually defined by the analyst or designer, or both. This type of abstraction is very important and must be done with care because it can help uncover many things within your data if done right. For example, in *Tom Clancy's The Division*, you could abstract the actions to represent the fires shot, enemies hit, and cover moves (micro loops). But you could also develop an abstraction that represents the types of activities and game modes chosen (PVP (player vs. player), PVE (player vs. environment, solo, or groups) (macro loops). It is important to understand that both abstraction level and the use of sequences rather than aggregate data can shed different light on your data, facilitating different levels of analysis than what we have seen in previous chapters. Now back to sequence analysis.

Sequence analysis treats such abstract events as units of analysis— irrespective of how many actions are represented within these events.

Many data science methods specifically consider sequences. Sequence mining, for example, is a data mining method applied to sequential data. Time-series data can also be viewed as one type of sequence. Such sequence analysis is incredibly common, not only for evaluating human behavior but also in any situation where measurements are taken as a function of time, distance, or some other dimension.

Our discussion of game data science is not complete without a chapter on sequence analysis within the context of an actual game. This chapter will focus on introducing sequence analysis methods and showcasing their use through analysis of *DOTA 2* player behaviors. We will not discuss the application of these methods to churn or player modeling. However, it is possible to extrapolate from examples in this chapter and apply these findings to churn or player modeling or other applications of this nature. Extending these methods toward such topics is still an active area of research.

For this chapter, we will introduce standard techniques for analyzing sequence data, which can be roughly categorized into four types:

- Explorative sequence data analysis methods are methods that allow you to gain an understanding of player behavior by visualizing different sequences, inspecting transitions and frequencies of particular sequences, inspecting entropy of particular states or actions occupying specific times, and analyzing variations between sequences or within particular time points.
- Sequence pattern mining methods are a set of algorithms concerned with identifying all frequent patterns (events that co-occur with varying lengths) within sequence data or time-series data. In this section, we will discuss one such algorithm called *Sequential Pattern Discovery using Equivalence* (*SPADE*).
- Sequence clustering methods are methods that allow clustering over sequence data. In this chapter, we will discuss *Optimal Matching (OM)* as an example method.
- Recurrent Neural Networks (RNNs) are deep learning methods developed to model sequence data. Several methods have been proposed, such as *LSTM (Long Short-term Memory)*. RNNs will be discussed in more detail in Chapter 11.

To practice the methods used, the chapter includes the following labs:

- **Lab 10.1:** Focuses on explorative sequence data analysis. We will use the TraMinerR package in R.
- **Lab 10.2:** Focuses on sequence pattern mining. We will use the arulesSequences package in R.
- **Lab 10.3:** Focuses on sequence clustering techniques using *OM*. For this lab, we will use the TraMinerR package.

Before we discuss these topics, we will first discuss the differences between sequence and aggregate data to show you the advantages and disadvantages of using sequence data for your analysis. We will then introduce the dataset we will use in this chapter. We will also discuss the different data formats we will be using for the algorithms discussed in the chapter. It is important to understand that each algorithm will require the data in a different format, and that you will need to develop a script that transforms the data into a format that you can use as input for the algorithms discussed. For such scripts and transformations, you can consult earlier chapters, especially Chapter 2, as well as online tutorials.

10.2 Why sequence data analysis?

As you can imagine, sequence data usually takes up more space than aggregated data, because it contains individual actions a player took in chronological order rather than a total count of the number of times a single type of action was taken. This means that when you work with sequence data, you will inevitably end up with large datasets.

Handling complex and large data is an active area of research that is still in its infancy, and thus we believe that more resources will be available to handle such data as the field continues to grow. We will not discuss methods for handling big distributed data in this book. Interested readers should consult other resources for big data storage and processing. Some good places to start include survey papers summarizing relatively recent works in the field such as Chen and Zhang (2014) and Kambatla et al. (2014).

10.2.1 Understanding sequence data

To help you understand the differences between sequence data and aggregate data, we will use an example of data collected from the multiplayer game *DOTA 2*, depicted in Table 10.1.

As you can see, this data looks very different from what you have seen in the previous chapters. Let us take a closer look. The columns in this table are *profileid*, *segment*, and a list of operations [1, . . . ,*n*] entitled *op_num.1*, *op_num.2*, etc. Each row represents a specific player (identified as *profileid*) during a specific portion of gameplay: early game, mid game, or late game (the three segments of gameplay that a *DOTA 2* match can be divided into), and each operation *op_num.** in that row corresponds to an action or behavior that the player exhibited in the logged data.

As a whole, the sequence represents an abstraction of all the actions taken by the player during the gameplay session. For example, imagine you played *DOTA 2* and made the following actions during the game: roamed the map collecting gold on your own, met up with your teammates, encountered and fought the enemy team, killed an enemy, and finally got killed. The data of such a sequence may be represented as follows: [*your profileid*] [*solo*] [*solo*] [*solo*] [*teaming*] [*teaming*] [*harrassed_by_opponents*] [*fight_intensifies*] [*kill_hero*] [*death*].

To give you a better look, let us compare this to a dataset similar to what you have been working with, as shown in Table 10.2. This is similar to other data

Table 10.1 Sequential data of DOTA 2.

profileid	segment	op_num.1	op_num.2	op_num.3	op_num.4	op_num.5	op_num.6	op_num.7	op_num.8	op_num.9
herodisruptor_2500916535_2	early_game	solo	solo	solo	solo	solo	solo	fight	fight	solo
herodisruptor_2500916535_2	mid_game	solo	solo	solo	solo	solo	teaming	solo	solo	teaming
herodisruptor_2500916535_2	late_game	death	harrassed_by	fight_diminis	solo	solo	solo	solo	solo	solo
herorubick_2500811393_3	early_game	solo	solo	solo	kill_hero	teaming	teaming	solo	solo	solo
herorubick_2500811393_3	mid_game	solo	solo	solo	teaming	teaming	solo	solo	solo	solo
herorubick_2500811393_3	late_game	death	teaming	teaming	solo	solo	teaming	solo	solo	solo
herosven_2501342105_3	early_game	solo	solo	solo	solo	solo	solo	kill_hero	solo	solo
herosven_2501342105_3	mid_game	solo	solo	solo	solo	solo	solo	solo	solo	solo
herosven_2501342105_3	late_game	kill_hero	fight	solo	solo	solo	teaming	solo	solo	solo
heroemberspirit_2501098786_3	early_game	teaming	solo	solo	solo	solo	solo	fight	solo	solo
heroemberspirit_2501098786_3	mid_game	solo	solo	teaming	fight	solo	solo	kill_hero	kill_hero	kill_hero
heroemberspirit_2501098786_3	late_game	teaming	solo	solo	solo	solo	solo	solo	solo	solo
heromirana_2501294293_2	early_game	solo	kill_hero	kill_hero	solo	teaming	teaming	death	kill_hero	kill_hero
heromirana_2501294293_2	mid_game	kill_hero	kill_hero	solo	solo	teaming	solo	solo	kill_hero	kill_hero
herokeeperofthelight_2501088650_2	early_game	solo	teaming	solo	teaming	solo	solo	solo	solo	solo
herokeeperofthelight_2501088650_2	mid_game	solo	solo	teaming	teaming	solo	teaming	teaming	teaming	teaming
herokeeperofthelight_2501088650_2	late_game	fight	fight	solo	solo	solo	solo	solo	solo	solo
herobatrider_2500632973_2	early_game	teaming	solo	solo	solo	solo	solo	solo	solo	solo
herobatrider_2500632973_2	mid_game	solo	solo	kill_hero	solo	solo	solo	solo	solo	solo

Table 10.2 Aggregated data of DOTA 2.

profileid	fight_inter	fight_dimi	team_fight	full_team_	teaming	harrassed_	fight	solo	kill_hero	death
herodisruptor_2500916535_2	0	0	0	0	0	0	1	17	1	0
herodisruptor_2500916535_2	0	0	0	0	4	0	2	11	0	2
herodisruptor_2500916535_2	0	1	0	0	0	1	0	9	0	1
herorubick_2500811393_3	0	0	0	0	2	0	0	21	2	3
herorubick_2500811393_3	0	2	0	0	14	1	1	35	3	9
herorubick_2500811393_3	0	1	0	0	5	1	0	15	0	3
herosven_2501342105_3	0	0	0	0	0	0	2	9	1	0
herosven_2501342105_3	0	1	0	0	5	0	2	40	7	2
herosven_2501342105_3	0	0	0	0	9	0	3	16	8	1
heroemberspirit_2501098786_3	0	0	0	0	1	0	4	20	2	0
heroemberspirit_2501098786_3	0	0	0	0	8	0	6	27	8	1
heroemberspirit_2501098786_3	0	0	0	0	1	0	0	10	0	0
heromirana_2501294293_2	0	0	0	0	6	0	2	10	3	2
heromirana_2501294293_2	0	0	0	0	9	0	2	34	8	1
herokeeperofthelight_2501088650_2	0	0	0	0	2	0	1	25	1	4
herokeeperofthelight_2501088650_2	0	0	0	0	6	0	1	26	0	1
herokeeperofthelight_2501088650_2	0	0	0	0	8	0	2	32	1	1
herobatrider_2500632973_2	0	0	0	0	2	0	2	11	1	0
herobatrider_2500632973_2	0	0	0	0	11	0	3	46	2	3

you used throughout the book, where every row corresponds to a player, and every column an aggregated count of times that action was exhibited by that player. This table, instead of showing the sequences of actions each player took, displays aggregated data of the number of times a specific action was taken.

Representing data in terms of sequences provides us with information concerning how actions occurred in relation to each other—that is, what actions were performed as setup for others, what actions were performed as a response or reaction, whether actions (or subsequences of actions) were more likely to occur early or late in gameplay, and what patterns of actions occurred repeatedly vs. sparingly.

10.2.2 Sequence data enables temporal and spatial analysis

To understand the benefits of sequence data more clearly, let us take a look at another example. Tables 10.3 and 10.4 show sequence and aggregated data from the same match for two players: Herorubick and Herosven.

From the aggregated data, we can see that Herosven died less than Herorubick and that Herorubick spent more time teaming up than Herosven. However, these numbers do not tell us much in regard to the temporal or sequential relationships between these actions. It is, therefore, hard to interpret strategies or decision-making tactics. For example, it is hard to tell if Herorubick's teaming behavior was due to protection because he was dying more or whether these were unrelated events.

In contrast to such aggregated data, the sequence data displayed in Table 10.3 gives us a better picture. During the late_game segment, Herorubick partakes

Table 10.3 *Sample sequences.*

ProfileID	Segment	op_num.1	op_num.2	op_num.3	op_num.4
Herorubick	late_game	Fight	death	teaming	teaming
Herosven	late_game	Fight	death	solo	solo

Table 10.4 *Sample aggregated data.*

ProfileID	fight	death	teaming	solo
Herorubick	4	5	6	5
Herosven	5	3	3	6

in the sequence [fight] [death] [teaming] [teaming]. This sequence shows that the player chose to stay near teammates, possibly for protection, after his death. In contrast, Herosven exhibits the sequence [fight] [death] [solo] [solo], which implies that he chose not to team up after his death. These two sequences display two different strategies: one player choosing to stay close to the team to gain strength in numbers, and the other choosing to go solo.

Many of the examples of data analysis and modeling in previous chapters concentrated on aggregated statistics across time or sessions, where we ignored the sequences of actions or temporal factors. In this chapter, we focus on analysis methods that take spatial and temporal factors into consideration. This can be beneficial for many reasons. For example, understanding sequences of player actions may help explain why players decided to stop playing or why and how they changed play styles (Valls-Vargas et al., 2015). Understanding temporal progression of player movement can help answer questions about how players learn the game and can allow us to develop an informed method of player profiling in order to adapt the game to their interests or play patterns.

10.2.3 Sequence mining enables player profiling: A case study

To further exemplify the use of sequence data, we will use a case study to show the benefits of sequence analysis for *Tom Clancy's The Division*, a game from Ubisoft Massive. The case study was described by Canossa et al. (2018). We focus on why Ubisoft Massive chose to integrate action sequences in their player profiling work and the benefit of using such an approach. For a more detailed discussion on the methods used, readers are referred to Canossa et al. (2018).

In modern game development, it is crucial that we place our players into groups or clusters that share specific traits. If we do not do this, our ability to understand who the players are, and how they play our games, is hampered. The ability to profile players is important because different groups of players react differently to the same stimulus and behave differently within the confines of the same game. We, hence, need to understand these differences so we can deliver the best possible user experience.

Today, major commercial titles can track hundreds, if not thousands, of behavioral metrics from each player on a continuous basis as they progress in a game. Such behavior trails can then be used to group players. Behavioral profiling has, thus, been introduced in recent years as a means for building an accurate and actionable grouping of players. Currently, a wealth of different models are being employed across academia and industry to establish such clusters based on behaviors.

In Chapter 6, we discussed different segmentation and clustering techniques to understand different player groupings. At the time of writing this book, creating groupings of players is still largely based on aggregated data (discussed in the introduction of this chapter). Such aggregate measures, from the perspective of the designers of contemporary major commercial titles, are almost meaningless. These statistics become actionable *only if* they are delivered for a specific group. For example, it could be expected that a population of risk-taking players have a high death rate. If the same happens to conservative players, it can be symptomatic of imbalances in the game.

Furthermore, such aggregate data captures only snapshots of players' behaviors. These are not always useful to design teams. While much more complex and information-rich profiling techniques exist, including psychological information about players, for example, these are much less integrated in the industry and much less investigated in academia. That said, behavioral profiling is attractive as a means for building a better understanding of players and finding out what they are interested in. This is because these techniques allow us to consider the players in a quantifiable way by using telemetry data.

10.2.3.1 OVERVIEW AND RESEARCH APPROACH

The central questions of Canossa et al.'s work with the Ubisoft team is framed as follows: can we use sequence analysis for behavior profiling, and if so, what are the advantages of using sequence data over aggregate data for this problem? To answer these questions, a case study was spearheaded by the analytics team at Massive Entertainment, a part of Ubisoft, with additional help from the Ubisoft Montreal team in collaboration with researchers from the University of York and New York University. Together, they developed a methodologically simple framework for investigating behavior profiling. The work was published in Canossa et al. (2018).

The case study considers *Tom Clancy's The Division*, a Massive Entertainment flagship title, with over 20 million players. It is an online shooter game with a persistent world and an ongoing history. The gameplay is complex, and players have agency in determining how to play the game. As something fairly unique in games research, the team had analysts, researchers, and designers of the game working closely together. This gave analysts and researchers the ability to not only develop models in collaboration with the design team of a major commercial title but also to validate proposed models and ensure the usefulness of the developed profiles.

The current standard in behavioral profiling is to do snapshot profiling. Snapshot profiling focuses on the game as it is at the time of study and is commonly reliant on aggregated variables over players' lifetimes, or for a short temporal window, as discussed in Chapter 6. Snapshot profiling is useful in understanding the state of the player and how the game is being played at a given moment. However, snapshot profiles have limited shelf life, because players change their behavior over the course of their play sessions. In other words, we do not play the same game in the same way throughout our whole interaction timelines with the game. To solve this problem, Canossa et al. (2018) adopted dynamic profiling. Dynamic profiling takes into account the historical information of the players. In the current case, the idea was to integrate ordering of player actions while also trying to condense the massive differences in how players play the game into more manageable profiles.

As discussed above, the level of abstraction of what events to represent is important. To determine the level of abstraction, the research team worked with the design team of *The Division*—across game, level, and system designers—to identify the kinds of player activities or events that were meaningful to them. A workshop was organized to identify what kinds of activities could be useful for the design team when the activities were examined as sequences. Through the workshop, a list of 22 player activities was identified. This was expanded by including modifiers, such as whether the activity was carried out in groups or alone, as well as the difficulty setting at the time. They then ended up with 52 activities. Metrics were then engineered for each of these, and the relevant data from about 10,000 randomly selected players who played across March–April 2017 was extracted. Next, sequential pattern mining (via the *CM-SPAM* algorithm) was used to identify frequent sequences. Unlike *SPADE* (discussed above), researchers imposed the rule that subsequences be consecutive—that is, when identifying a subsequence, no gaps between events were accepted. This resulted in 826 sequences.

The team then applied Shannon entropy (see Section 10.4.2) to identify the most information-rich sequences. This is a step that can be ignored but helps identify potentially useful sequences. Additionally, cross correlation was used to detect sequences that were similar. Furthermore, the results were checked with the design team to verify that similarity measures between sequences made sense to them.

Finally, different cluster models were applied on the sequences, resulting in six behavioral profiles, characterized by these sequences. As discussed in Chapter 6, cluster analysis on player behavior has to be approached carefully, as the choice of the model can have implications on what results we end up with. In this case, *Ward*'s method (see Chapter 6) provided a reasonable approach. Confidence for the chosen number of clusters was generated using elbow plots (as discussed in previous chapters).

10.2.3.2 RESULTS

Both sequence-based and traditional aggregate-based behavioral profiles were presented to *The Division*'s team. Sequence-based models proved highly popular. Below, we will discuss the results and why sequence analysis was more popular.

The cluster analysis resulted in six clusters (or behavior profiles): Strategizer, Social Farmer 1, Social Farmer 2, All-Rounder, Solo Wanderer, and Lone Street Bandit. These profiles are characterized by specific sequences of behavior. For example, the Lone Street Bandits engage in the sequence of (rogue solo, extraction, solo, and rogue solo), which represents a specific form of solo play. The Social Farmers, on the other hand, move from random hostile encounters to side missions and occasionally main missions, but always as a group. The Strategizer tends to follow a loop of behavior sequences: safe area, inventory operation, loadout operation. The loadout operation is usually difficult and requires a high degree of intentionality and planning. The other clusters are self-explanatory.

Using this analysis, the team found several indicative behavioral loops—that is, patterns of behavior that repeat themselves over and over, such as the one discussed above by Strategizer. These were deemed particularly useful in informing design, as they allow designers to understand how players move between favorite activities, not just the frequency of these activities, which is provided by aggregate based approaches.

10.2.3.3 BENEFITS OF SEQUENCE-BASED METHODS

Sequence-based profiles are useful in understanding how users play the game and whether that behavior matches what the designers intended. Sequence-based analysis is also important for understanding the sequences and loops leading up to desired or undesired events—for example, a player buying an item or stopping to play the game. Furthermore, such models can be used to inform matchmaking between players, by showing us their preferred activities. It is also worth noting that the domain knowledge of the design team was crucial to the usefulness of the result.

In summary, while sequence data may be large and therefore difficult to handle, they are beneficial as they give you a much more granular look into players' decisions that may help you when developing hypotheses or further studies with players. Now let us dive into how one would perform sequence analysis. Let us take a look at the *DOTA 2* data that we will be using for this chapter.

10.3 *DOTA* 2 data

As we start to look into how to do sequence analysis in more detail, we will use data from *DOTA 2* for this chapter, which is similar to the DOTAlicious game data you have worked with in the past chapters. In *DOTA 2*, each game pits two teams of five players, referred to as *Radiant* and *Dire*, against each other in combat. The game, similar to "Capture the Flag," is won when one team destroys the other team's "ancient," which is located in their base on the opposite end of the map. The game map consists of three lanes with forested areas between them, a river, and several NPC entities ranging from monsters, such as Roshan, to structures, such as barracks. Each lane is populated by a set of towers that fire beams at enemy entities that get too close. In order to reach the enemy's base, players must destroy these towers.

The data we are using in labs and as examples within the chapter includes data from approximately 200 players, split into 550 sequences based on game segments (described below). The *DOTA 2* dataset prepared contains the following fields:

- *ProfileId:* Unique per user.
- *PlayersessionId:* Unique ID for each session played in the game.
- *Segment:* A *DOTA 2* game can be divided into three segments of gameplay, early, mid, and late games. We divided each player's total sequence into three sequences (one for each segment). There is some ambiguity with regard to when a game segment begins and ends within a game; for our purposes, we mark the end of the "early game" as the moment when the first tower falls, and the end of the "mid game" as the moment when the first tier 3 tower falls. Note that not all matches make it to "late game."

- *Sequence of actions for each player:* We defined 10 different types of actions based on what the player is doing and whether other team members are in the vicinity. These are:
  - o "solo": A player has no allied players in their vicinity
  - o "fight": A player has encountered at least one enemy player
  - o "kill_hero": A player secures a kill against an opponent
  - o "teaming": A player has allied players (at least one) in their vicinity
  - o "death": A player dies
  - o "harrassed_by_opponents": A player encounters at least two enemies
  - o "fight_diminishes": The number of opponents in a player's vicinity decreases
  - o "fight_intensifies": The number of opponents in a player's vicinity increases
  - o "team_fight": A player has more than one ally and more than one opponent in their vicinity
  - o "full_team_assembly": A player's entire team is in their vicinity

These events were abstracted from the game's low-level telemetry using a script that we developed. This is similar to the approach described in Chapter 4 in terms of feature engineering. In other words, the features above were developed from raw data through the process of scripting. We identified that these features are important for our analysis. However, depending on your question, you may want to define different features from the raw data.

It should be noted that the *VPAL* data, which we used in earlier chapters, can also be converted into sequence data that can be used with the methods discussed in this chapter. However, we will keep this process aside as an exercise.

10.4 Representation of sequence data

There are several ways that a sequence can be represented, as discussed in Gabadinho et al. (2011); see Table 10.5. Sequences can be represented in the form of STS (STate Sequence), in which each state is an action, and thus all actions are represented as $A_1, A_2, \ldots, A_n$, with commas or other delimiters separating them. Some implementations of algorithms, such as sequence mining algorithms, require a -1 after every state to denote the end of a state and a -2

Table 10.5 *Representation of sequence data.*

Format	Data Example
STS	P1, P1-1, EarlyGame, solo, solo, fight, death
	P1, P1-2, MidGame, solo, teaming, teaming, kill_hero, fight, fight, fight, death, solo
SPS	P1, P1-1, EarlyGame, (solo,2), (fight,1), (death,1)
	P1, P1-2, MidGame, (solo,1), (teaming,2), (kill_hero,1), (fight,3), (death,1), (solo,1)

TimeStep	Player ID	Session ID	Time Step	State
	P1	P1-1	1	solo
	P1	P1-1	2	solo
	P1	P1-1	3	fight
	P1	P1-1	4	death
	P1	P1-2	1	solo
	P1	P1-2	2	teaming
	P1	P1-2	3	teaming
	P1	P1-2	4	kill_hero
	P1	P1-2	5	fight
	P1	P1-2	6	fight
	P1	P1-2	7	fight
	P1	P1-2	8	death
	P1	P1-2	9	solo

to denote the end of a sequence, for example, $S_1 - 1 \, S_2 - 1 \, S_3 - 1 \ldots S_n - 2$. Other formats discussed by (Gabadinho et al., 2011), including State-Permanence-Sequence (SPS), are not used in this chapter but are used by algorithms you may encounter in your analysis or libraries you use, and therefore, we included it in the representations discussed in Table 10.5.

Table 10.5 shows examples using STS, SPS, and TimeStep formats. In the table, STS represents information as *playerID*, *sessionID*, *GameSegment*, and then the sequence of actions or states. Similarly, SPS representation is as follows: *playerID*, *sessionID*, *GameSegment*, and then the sequence of actions or states. However, the way that sequences are represented is different from STS. Instead of a stream of actions or states separated by commas or spaces, each action or state is represented with a "()" followed by a count of how many times this state or action is repeated. For example, player P1 repeated solo two times, so instead of repeating the term two times, we are representing it as (solo, 2). The TimeStep format represents a time step in a new row. It then shows the states or actions associated with the time step in that row.

As you can see, the SPS format is more compact. The algorithms we use in this chapter will mostly be able to convert data from one format to another given enough information. However, you will need to process the data into one of these standard formats. The current dataset we will use in this chapter is already represented in the STS format.

10.5 Explorative sequence data analysis

For explorative sequence data analysis, we will use an R package called TraMineR (Trajectory Miner: A Toolbox for Exploring and Rendering Sequences). This is an open-source package that comes with a lot of functionality to perform analysis on sequential data. Using this package, you can create a sequence using the *seqdef* function. The function takes the following inputs: the data containing the sequence, the format, and the alphabet, which represents the states or actions. It then creates a sequence that we can use to perform some operations on. In this section, we will discuss these functions, using *DOTA 2* data, to help you understand how to use this package and explore the sequences in your data. It should be noted that Lab 10.1 goes into the functions in much more depth and shows how to apply them to the data.

Practical Note: Lab 10.1

Lab 10.1

Please see the supplemental materials for the book.

Goal of Lab 10.1

The lab goes over how you can use TraMineR to upload data, create a sequence, and perform some simple analyses and visualizations of the sequence data.

10.5.1 Plotting sequences and frequent sequences

Most often, you would like to start by plotting the sequences in your data to see how they vary. Once a sequence has been created (using the process discussed above), the *seqIplot* function can be used to plot all of the sequences in the data. Further detail on how each function works and step-by-step instructions on how to use it to create and plot sequences can be seen in Lab 10.1. Once we have processed the *DOTA 2* data and split it into segments based on early, mid, and late game, we have 550 player sequences. Using this dataset, we plot the graph of all the sequences (see Figure 10.3).

10.5.1.1 EXAMINING OVERALL PATTERNS

The value of beginning with a graph of the entire dataset is that it gives an at-a-glance view of the data and allows you to quickly scan for patterns. Looking at Figure 10.3, the x-axis represents the operation number, which is a temporal measure of exactly when in a given sequence a specific action occurred. All of

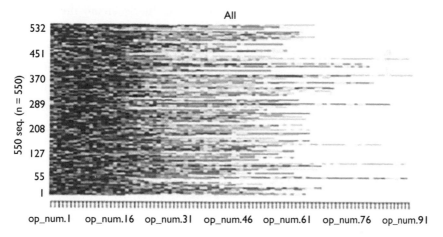

Figure 10.3 The data of 550 early-, mid-, and late-game sequences.

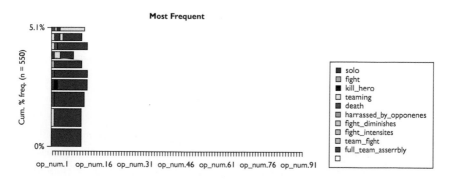

Figure 10.4 The most frequent sequences of the 550 sessions.

the sequences are organized along the y-axis. The positioning of a sequence on the y-axis is determined by its row in the table that was provided to TraMineR. Recall that we split the *DOTA 2* data by game segments. Therefore, *op_num.1* is not the first action in the game for all the sequences displayed. If this sequence is in mid or late game, then *op_num.1* will be the first operation in that segment. To demonstrate how this visualization can be used to extract behavioral patterns, we will walk through a sample exploratory analysis of the visualization in Figure 10.3.

Once you have your data organized and visualized like this, you can scan the graph for any sequence patterns that are indicative of noteworthy trends in player behavior. For example, an immediate observation is the frequency of the "solo" behavior, exhibited in every sequence and especially in the longer ones. From this high-level observation, we can thus identify a behavioral pattern that applies to the data Solo Oriented Early Game by visualizing the different sequences by segment: we found early *DOTA 2* gameplay is characterized by a predominant focus on individual goals, such as "farming" (killing nonplayer entities to acquire more gold), and some focus on team goals, such as "ganking" (the act of teaming up to surprise attack an unsuspecting enemy). Thus, the early game sequences displayed above begin mostly with instances of the "solo" state, broken up by the occasional multiplayer-oriented behavior.

Such a visualization illustrates how displaying all the sequences in this manner allows for quick, at-a-glance analysis. Although the patterns extracted at this stage may be high level, they can act as guides for further analysis by giving analysts an idea of what patterns they are likely to see as they zoom in further, and where in the data they may specifically want to focus. It can also provide quick feedback as to whether or not the processing of the data was sufficient to the analysts' needs. For example, perhaps, the abstraction chosen is leading to sequences that are too similar to each other. Iteratively displaying the entire set of sequences can be used to fine-tune the abstraction such that the information needed to extract behaviors of interest is sufficiently visualized.

10.5.1.2 EXAMINING MOST FREQUENT PATTERNS

While looking at the entire set of sequences can be helpful, it can also be a lot of information to visualize, and when dealing with large datasets, it may be difficult to see what is happening in the sequences. One possible avenue to resolve this is to focus on the most frequent patterns in the sequences, rather than all of them. We can single out the most frequent patterns using the *seqfplot* function, presented in lab 10.1. Using this function, we created the plot seen in Figure 10.4, which shows only the most frequent patterns. The function considers both completely segmented sequences (such as an entire early game sequence) and subsequences. The x-axis remains the same as in Figure 10.3; however, this time the y-axis represents a percentage. The value at the top of the y-axis (5.1% in Figure 10.4) is the percentage of the entire set of sequences that are represented by the ten most frequent sequences. The width of each sequence in the graph is determined by how much of that overall percentage is represented by that specific sequence. Therefore, in Figure 10.4, the most frequent sequences make up 5.1% of the entire dataset indicating that, overall, sequences were fairly different from each other.

To demonstrate the benefit of looking at sequences in this manner, we will go through an example analysis. Using the *DOTA 2* data visualized in Figure 10.4, we can identify frequent sequences of interest that can be used to derive generalized behavioral patterns that apply across the entire dataset. For our purposes, we will discuss one such pattern and how it was extracted from the visualization: Situational Teamwork: Two sequences, the second from the top, (a), and the fourth from the top, (b), alternate between "teaming" and "solo." These imply different styles of gameplay in which players' behaviors varied based on situational needs. When players needed to work with teammates, they did, otherwise they operated on their own. The sequence (b) has a particularly long "teaming" segment, perhaps indicating a single extended period of teaming up to apply pressure on the enemy and perhaps try to achieve an objective. The other sequence (a) displays two fairly short "teaming" segments, indicating what are likely shorter bursts of a team grouping up to harass or threaten an enemy, but not committing to staying together for an extended period to work toward an objective.

Although we only discuss one strategic pattern in our example, this discussion illustrates how looking at the most frequent sequences, rather than the entire dataset, can be used to derive behavioral patterns; and the same type of analysis as the one we have demonstrated can be used to extract other patterns. The advantage of using *seqfplot* is that it presents a smaller, more focused set of data for analysis, alleviating risks of information overload, and focusing on common patterns, while still providing information about how these patterns relate to the data in its entirety. The disadvantage is that when the frequent sequences are only a small percentage of the entire set (as they are in our example) patterns identified through this approach may not generalize to the rest of the data.

10.5.1.3 INSPECTING FREQUENT PATTERNS PER IMPORTANT GAME ELEMENTS (E.G., LOCATION AND GAME SEGMENT)

Another disadvantage of looking at only the most frequent sequences is that some temporal information is lost. As it was discussed earlier, we included the game segments, "early," "mid," and "late," in our *DOTA 2* data, so we could see how gameplay changed as the game progressed. Thankfully, this information can be used to preserve some of the temporal contexts while focusing the analysis on frequent sequences. Using the same functions, but with *group=playerData$segment* added to the function parameters, we can produce the most frequent sequences in each game segment, as can be seen in the scripts in Lab 10.1. Figure 10.5 shows these groupings.

Again, the x-axis is the operation number, and the y-axis is the percentage of the entire set represented by the 10 most frequent sequences. But now, instead of a single graph, we have three (one for each game segment), displaying the most frequent sequences in that segment specifically. Not only does this maintain temporal context but it also allows us to see how sequences vary and converge at different points in gameplay. Looking at the example in Figure 10.5, the most frequent sequences in the early and mid-game are 6.5% and 5% of the entire set of sequences for those segments. This indicates that at these points in gameplay, player action varies quite a bit. However, the most frequent sequences in the

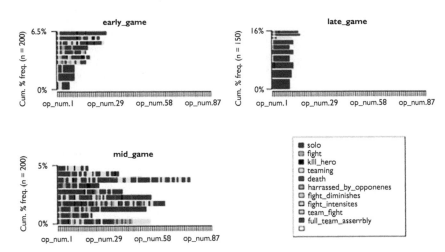

Figure 10.5 The most frequent sequences by game segment of the 550 sessions.

late game segment are 16% of the entire set of late game segment sequences, indicating that late game segment behavior is a little bit more uniform overall.

Separating the sequences by segment also allows for the type of exploratory analysis done previously in Section 10.5.1.2 to be applied to each segment in order to facilitate the extraction of behaviors based on a more defined temporal context. We will walk through an example of how this can be done to extract player behavioral patterns. For this purpose, we will discuss one pattern per game segment and how this can be seen in the visualization in Figure 10.5.

Early Game Behavior: Push to Early Win: In the early game plot, we can see several sequences that contain more frequent transitions between behaviors, containing frequent "fight," "death," "kill," and "teaming" visits. For example, the fourth sequence up from the bottom of the early game graph starts with soloing, before transitioning into a series of "teaming," "fight," and various other fight-related events. What we are likely seeing here is that the player's team or enemy team has engaged in aggressive early game strategy. Unlike the previously discussed approach, this strategy involves engaging the enemy in combat early to try and end the game fast. As a result, players' early game sequences will display more state transitions, and more states that involve other players, enemy or ally, as they are spending more time fighting and harassing opponents. Of note is the fact that this sequence does not include the "kill_hero" event, instead it contains the "death" event. Further, the "teaming" event frequently comes after fighting events. Thus, it is possible to theorize that this sequence represents players who were defending against an aggressive early game strategy, rather than the ones enacting it.

Mid Game Behavior: Focusing a Threat: The bottom sequence in the mid-game graph is characterized by early "solo" behavior eventually displaying an instance of "kill hero." After this, the sequence contains an instance of "death" followed by drastically different, team-oriented actions, including "teaming," "fight," and "harrased_by_opponents." What may be represented by this sequence is that players were allowed, by the opponent, to gain eXperience Points (XP) and gold, until they became a threat, by killing an opponent, at which point the focus turned to blocking these players' advancement. As a result, these players teamed up for safety. Thus, the sequence reflects this with instances of action states that involve the presence of nearby allies and enemies.

Late Game Behavior: Power Dynamics: The top two sequences in the late game graph are interesting. They are nearly identical, but one contains an instance of "kill_hero" while the other displays an instance of "death." It is possible that one of the sequences represents heroes who became powerful late in the game. These heroes were able to easily secure kills on their own. The other stream represents heroes in the opposite position, who remained killable targets up until the end of the game. It is even possible that these sequences correspond to each other in some way, with one representing players on teams that lost to the players represented by the other.

This example demonstrates the benefit of visualizing the sequences based on segment, such that the analyst can see and consider how the timing of a sequence pattern reflects and influences player behavior. Although we focus on *DOTA 2* in the example, such a temporal split can be applied to most games. For example, in a basic RPG game, there may be a segment of gameplay that takes place in a dungeon, then a town, then an overworld map. Thus, the data could be split based on the order in which the locations were visited.

10.5.1.4 EXAMINING FREQUENCIES OF STATES OVER TIME

Another way to display the sequence information is based on state distribution by time points. This can be presented in two ways: via a plot of the state distribution (Figure 10.6) created using the *seqdplot* function or via the raw numbers (Figure 10.7) created using the *seqstatd* function.

Both approaches present the same information, but they visualize it in different ways, thus it is up to you to decide which visualization technique you want to use (or if you would like to use both). The advantages of the plot (Figure 10.6) are much the same as the advantages of plotting the entire dataset (Figure 10.3) in that the plot allows for a quick "at-a-glance" analysis. Here, the y-axis represents the frequency of the indicated event appearing at that operation number in the sequence; thus, an analyst can quickly draw

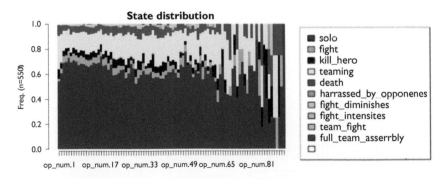

Figure 10.6 The state distribution by time point as a plot.

[State frequencies]

	op_num.1	op_num.2	op_num.3	op_num.4	op_num.5	op_num.6	op_num.7	op_num.8	op_num.9	op_num.10
solo	0.5436	0.6109	0.6927	0.7036	0.7345	0.6945	0.7145	0.7049	0.6746	0.6858
fight	0.0200	0.0327	0.0527	0.0455	0.0509	0.0491	0.0509	0.0474	0.0588	0.0628
kill_hero	0.0764	0.0509	0.0418	0.0582	0.0273	0.0327	0.0473	0.0474	0.0423	0.0444
teaming	0.2673	0.2291	0.1618	0.1436	0.1509	0.1418	0.1255	0.1311	0.1562	0.1479
death	0.0355	0.0655	0.0455	0.0436	0.0273	0.0655	0.0473	0.0546	0.0515	0.0499
harrassed_by_opponenes	0.0000	0.0055	0.0000	0.0036	0.0036	0.0055	0.0036	0.0055	0.0037	0.0000
fight_diminishes	0.0018	0.0018	0.0055	0.0018	0.0036	0.0073	0.0091	0.0073	0.0092	0.0055
fight_intensifies	0.0036	0.0036	0.0000	0.0000	0.0018	0.0036	0.0018	0.0018	0.0018	0.0018
team_fight	0.0018	0.0000	0.0000	0.0000	0.0000	0.0000	0.0000	0.0000	0.0018	0.0018
full_team_asserrbly	0.0000	0.0000	0.0000	0.0000	0.0000	0.0000	0.0000	0.0000	0.0000	0.0000

	op_num.11	op_num.12	op_num.13	op_num.14	op_num.15	op_num.16	op_num.17	op_num.18	op_num.19
solo	0.6834	0.6705	0.6608	0.6761	0.6934	0.6857	0.692	0.7427	0.6667
fight	0.0503	0.0460	0.0451	0.0405	0.0412	0.0464	0.061	0.0361	0.0516
kill_hero	0.0540	0.0460	0.0510	0.0567	0.0494	0.0380	0.061	0.0609	0.0423
teaming	0.1546	0.1743	0.1627	0.1498	0.1420	0.1624	0.046	0.1219	0.1573
death	0.0484	0.0421	0.0569	0.0506	0.0494	0.0549	0.148	0.0361	0.0728
harrassed_by_opponenes	0.0019	0.0077	0.0059	0.0081	0.0021	0.0000	0.052	0.0023	0.0023
fight_diminishes	0.0037	0.0057	0.0098	0.0101	0.0144	0.0084	0.000	0.0000	0.0000
fight_intensifiesintensifies	0.0019	0.0057	0.0020	0.0061	0.0082	0.0042	0.000	0.0000	0.0070
team_fight	0.0000	0.0019	0.0039	0.0000	0.0000	0.0000	0.000	0.0000	0.0000
full_team_asserrbly	0.0019	0.0000	0.0020	0.0020	0.0000	0.0000	0.000	0.0000	0.0000

	op_num.20	op_num.21	op_num.22	op_num.23	op_num.24	op_num.25	op_num.26	op_num.27	op_num.28
solo	0.6750	0.6371	0.6785	0.5938	0.5951	0.6084	0.6354	0.6360	0.570
fight	0.0600	0.0470	0.0381	0.0540	0.0521	0.0615	0.0278	0.0294	0.044
kill_hero	0.0525	0.0679	0.0627	0.0739	0.0675	0.0550	0.0694	0.0551	0.066
teaming	0.1375	0.1593	0.1526	0.1818	0.1994	0.2039	0.1979	0.1875	0.245
death	0.0575	0.0731	0.0490	0.0795	0.0736	0.0453	0.0417	0.0809	0.068
harrassed_by_opponenes	0.0075	0.0052	0.0054	0.0028	0.0031	0.0162	0.0035	0.0037	0.000
fight_diminishes	0.0100	0.0052	0.0082	0.0114	0.0061	0.0065	0.0174	0.0000	0.008
fight_intensifies	0.0000	0.0026	0.0054	0.0028	0.0031	0.0032	0.0069	0.0037	0.004
team_fight	0.0000	0.0026	0.0000	0.0000	0.0000	0.0000	0.0000	0.0037	0.000
full_team_asserrbly	0.0000	0.0000	0.0000	0.0000	0.0000	0.0000	0.0000	0.0000	0.000

Figure 10.7 The state distribution by time point as numbers (the first 28 states, cut off for space).

conclusions about where certain actions are more likely to occur. However, it does not display the exact values, which is the primary advantage of the numbered distribution (Figure 10.7). However, this visualization may take longer to analyze, as frequencies will need to be checked and compared one by one.

Again, we will provide an example of the type of information that can be extracted from this visualization, using the *DOTA 2* data as an example. In Figure 10.6, we can see that the frequencies become more erratic toward the ends of the sequences. Because we are working with the segmented data, the ends of the sequences represent player responses to some impending gameplay segment transition. Thus, we can define a behavior pattern from the visualization.

Team-Combat-oriented Transitions: For our purposes, we marked the beginning of mid-game as the moment when the first tower falls and the beginning of late game as the moment when the first T3 (defined above) tower falls. Both of these events are characterized by combat. As a result, the ends of the segments in our data (which mark the time period leading up to these transitions) are characterized by combat-oriented action states, such as "teaming," "kill_hero," "death," and "fight." The state distribution graph below reflects this in a straightforward way. The frequency of the "death" state, for example, is far greater right at the end, which also reflects the fact that mid-game sequences tend to begin with death. In many cases, a team's attempt to destroy a tower will be contested by the defending team meaning the ensuing team fight will likely result in at least one death. If the defending team loses more players than the attacking team, this will likely cost them the tower, leading to the state transition, hence the pattern we see above.

Although we base this analysis largely on the plot in Figure 10.6, the same information could be extracted by looking at the frequency numbers (Figure 10.7) if one were to visualize them for entire sequences. This information benefits an analyst by allowing them to clearly and concisely see exactly when during gameplay certain actions occurred more often, in the context of the entire dataset. Similar information can be gained by looking at the plot of the entire set (Figure 10.3); however, the plot of the entire set becomes increasingly difficult to extract information from, as the number of sequences grows while these visualizations remain legible.

10.5.2 Entropy of states over sequence positions

In some cases, you may want to understand the diversity of states seen at a particular position. In this case, the measure of Shannon entropy would be of interest. Entropy, as an information measure, has been discussed in earlier chapters; thus, we will not define it again here; please see Chapter 7 for a definition. In this section, we want to see how to derive entropy for sequence data. Representing the sequences in this way can provide high level, easy-to-interpret insight into how player behavior shifts between moments of highly uniform action to moments of highly varied action. This, in turn, can provide insight into how a game environment may be influencing player behavior, as highly uniform behavior is likely the result of some constant factor in the design of the game.

To demonstrate, if we apply the function *seqHtplot* (see Lab 10.1) to the *DOTA 2* data, we get the plot in Figure 10.8. As you can see from this figure, the entropy measure fluctuates quite a bit. *DOTA 2* is a highly situational game, requiring players to work independently and coordinate as a group in various ways depending on the circumstances. Thus, the degree to which events are diverse or not at a given position in the sequence will depend on the context. Further, as our abstraction is based on spatiotemporal location of teammates, members of a team who have chosen to team up will all bear the event "teaming"

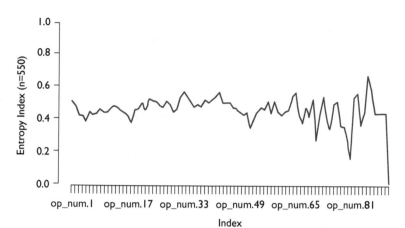

Figure 10.8 Shannon entropy for each position in the sequence.

for that position in the sequence, resulting in a lower Shannon entropy at that point. Note the high amount of fluctuation toward the end of the graph. This happens at the end points of the various sequences, which, as discussed above, correspond to either an impending transition to the next game segment or the end of the game (if it is a late game sequence). This fluctuation indicates more variety in behavior among players who are likely attempting to gain an advantage or stop an opponent during a crucial point in gameplay and are thus acting in a more varied, situational manner rather than following a widely acceptable strategic pattern. This also reflects what was seen in the state distribution graph above.

10.5.3 Transition probabilities

Transition probability from one state to another can be valuable in understanding the most probable sequence and useful further in explaining how much deviation different players have from the norm. Knowing the likelihood that any given action will be followed by another action can provide insight into popular strategies (often referred to as a *meta* in online gaming communities) and help guide the analysis of how the design of a game may influence player behavior. Probabilistic transitions are foundational to the development of more advanced techniques, which we will see in Chapter 11.

For now, we will just explore how probabilities can be used to draw conclusions about players' strategic behaviors, using the *DOTA 2* example. As shown in Lab 10.1, we can calculate the probabilities of transitions between

events using the *seqtrate* function. We calculated this transition matrix for the
550-session data. The matrix for the states is shown in Figure 10.9. As you
can see, the highest transitions are from "solo" to "solo," "fight_diminishes"
to "solo," "team_fight" to "fight_diminishes," "harrassed_by_opponents"
to "fight_diminishes," and "fight_diminishes" to "fight diminishes." The
transitions from other events to "solo" are also reasonably high and higher
than most of the transitions from any state into any other state.

The relatively high frequency of any state transitioning to the "solo" event is
likely due to players ending up alone on the map after disengaging from other
activities. For example, after a team fight, the surviving players on the losing
team may flee the area to escape death. In doing so, it is likely that they would
scatter as well as avoid areas likely to have enemy activity, thus ending up in

	[-> solo]	[-> fight]	[-> kill_hero]	[-> teaming]	[-> death]
[solo ->]	0.77	0.03	0.04	0.12	0.04
[fight ->]	0.53	0.19	0.06	0.12	0.09
[kill_hero ->]	0.33	0.08	0.18	0.26	0.13
[teaming ->]	0.43	0.02	0.07	0.39	0.08
[death ->]	0.55	0.21	0.02	0.13	0.04
[harrassed_by_opponenes ->]	0.00	0.01	0.05	0.01	0.07
[fight_diminishes ->]	0.72	0.04	0.00	0.23	0.00
[fight_intensifies ->]	0.00	0.10	0.00	0.14	0.00
[team_fight ->]	0.00	0.00	0.08	0.00	0.17
[full_team_asserrbly ->]	0.25	0.00	0.25	0.25	0.00
[->]	0.00	0.00	0.00	0.00	0.00

	[-> harrassed_by_opponenes]	[-> fight_diminishes]	[-> fight_intensites]
[solo ->]	0.00	0.00	0.00
[fight ->]	0.00	0.00	0.00
[kill_hero ->]	0.01	0.00	0.00
[teaming ->]	0.00	0.01	0.01
[death ->]	0.05	0.00	0.00
[harrassed_by_opponenes ->]	0.08	0.77	0.00
[fight_diminishes ->]	0.00	0.00	0.01
[fight_intensifies ->]	0.08	0.61	0.00
[team_fight ->]	0.00	0.75	0.00
[full_team_asserrbly ->]	0.00	0.00	0.00
[->]	0.00	0.00	0.00

	[-> team_fight]	[-> full_team_asserrbly]	[->]
[solo ->]	0.00	0.00	0
[fight ->]	0.00	0.00	0
[kill_hero ->]	0.00	0.00	0
[teaming ->]	0.00	0.00	0
[death ->]	0.00	0.00	0
[harrassed_by_opponenes ->]	0.00	0.00	0
[fight_diminishes ->]	0.00	0.00	0
[fight_intensifies ->]	0.08	0.08	0
[team_fight ->]	0.00	0.00	0
[full_team_asserrbly ->]	0.00	0.25	0
[->]	0.00	0.00	0

Figure 10.9 The probability of transitions between states.

the solo state. Similarly, "fight_diminishes" indicates a decrease in the number of nearby enemies. The high transition probabilities listed above indicate that when players take actions in which they are engaged with the opponents, such as "team_fight" or "harrassed_by_opponents," they are more likely to disengage the enemy than go for a kill or allow themselves to be killed. Strategically speaking, this is the right choice to make, as allowing the enemy team to get more kills will hurt one's chances of victory.

A higher transition probability between two events means that it is more common for the second event to follow the first. This information, when applied to a large dataset, can shed light on common strategies. These common strategies are of interest to those who wish to gain insight into how a player base at large is approaching problem solving and gameplay. These insights can be used to inform design changes, or to model player behavior.

10.5.4 Summary of exploratory analysis

In this section, we demonstrated the various ways you can use the TraMineR library for an exploratory analysis of players' action sequences. We identified some interesting gameplay patterns and behavioral trends from the data by applying various visualization techniques on sequence data. Approaching the data using these methods allows you to identify player strategies in terms of what actions players take, when they take them, and what actions they are likely to take next. It is important to note, however, that different visualizations have different advantages and disadvantages and provide different kinds of insights, such as the most common trends or how trends change over time. The best technique depends on the data available and the research questions you are exploring. Next, we will explore other techniques to analyze sequence data, such as sequence mining and clustering.

10.6 Sequence pattern mining

Sequence pattern mining is an area of data mining concerned with extracting frequently occurring patterns from sequence data. This approach has been applied in several domains with great success. In marketing studies, the approach is known as *item set mining*, and it is used for market analysis. Once extracted, these frequent patterns can tell us what items one person is likely to buy given that he bought item *x*. A good example is: if someone buys a car, then they are more likely to buy insurance next. For software applications such as web search, it is beneficial for the system to account for such frequent sequences so it can optimize or dynamically adjust website content.

Similarly, one can think of many different uses of such functionality in games. If we know frequent patterns and can identify what the player is doing, then we can predict the probability of subsequent actions and optimize the game design accordingly. This can help us with many important design problems, such as churn, difficulty adjustment, content tuning to maximize engagement or interest, and segmentation of players according to their in-game activity.

In the previous section, we explored sequences through visualizations. Sequence pattern mining is another approach where we can use frequency to develop a set of patterns of different lengths. For each pattern identified, we can identify the level of support from the data. This is calculated as the frequency of the pattern given the data. Intuitively, this means we can output a set of patterns and determine how frequently these patterns will appear in the data.

10.6.1 What is sequence pattern mining?

There are several methods developed to deduce frequent patterns in a given dataset. In order to understand how these methods work, let us see an example. Table 10.6 shows three sessions from the *DOTA 2* dataset. Notice that the format in this table is different from the formats we discussed above. Here, we have a

Table 10.6 *Sequence structure for sequence mining.*

SID	EID	Sequence in time EID for Sequence No. SID
1	1	Solo
1	2	Solo
1	3	Fight
1	4	Solo
2	1	Solo
2	1	Solo
3	2	Solo
3	1	Teaming
3	2	Death

SequenceID (*SID*), which is mapped to *player id* in our data. *Event ID* (*EID*) denotes the order of events in sequence (*SID*). Therefore, each player, *SID*, will have a sequence of events ordered by *EID*. In the table above, *SID* 1 has four events: "solo," "solo," "fight," and "solo."

From the table, we can see that the event "solo" is most often followed by another "solo" event at some point in its event sequence. Therefore, we say that (solo, solo) is a co-occurring pattern or subsequence. Similarly, ("solo", "death) is also a possible co-occurring pattern.

It is important to note that co-occurring patterns or subsequences do not need to happen consecutively for them to be considered subsequences or patterns. As long as event *b* comes after event *a,* the pattern (a, b) is considered a valid subsequence, even if the occurrence in the data was: a, c, c, and b. This makes the search space very large, because you must iterate over all possible co-occurrences and see how well such co-occurrences are supported by the data.

The objective of the sequence pattern mining algorithm is to find all subsequences that can occur given the dataset and how much support (the strength of the probability of such a subsequence occurring) they have. For example, given the sequences in Table 10.6, the subsequence ("solo," "solo"), which appears in two different sequences, has a higher level of support within the dataset than the subsequence (solo, teaming), which appears in only one sequence.

The topic and very first algorithm developed to tackle this problem was proposed by Argwal and Srikant (1995) in 1995. The first algorithms include *AprioriAll* and *GSP*. A popular and more efficient algorithm proposed by Zaki (2001) is *SPADE* classes. In the following subsections, we will use *SPADE*. It should be noted that *SPADE* is one of the most efficient algorithms in this area up to this point in time. Since introducing all algorithms within this area is beyond the scope of the book, interested readers can consult the references and review bibliography for more information about the other algorithms in this area.

10.6.2 SPADE

SPADE uses a lattice-theoretic approach to decompose the search space, which allows the algorithm to search independently through each sublattice. This reduces the database scans needed as well as operations, and thus delivers a more efficient solution.

Input to SPADE:

- Dataset, D
- *Min_Support*, a variable indicating the threshold by which a co-occurring pattern is considered. A *min_support* of 0.5 means that only patterns that have 50% support (i.e., occur 50% of the time within the data) are considered.

The algorithm then grows the subsequences one at a time, keeping all generated patterns or subsequences that have a minimum support, *Min_Support*, or higher. It then outputs these patterns.

10.6.3 Applying SPADE

To apply this algorithm to our data, you will need to transform the data into an input structure that *SPADE* can use. Different implementations of *SPADE* require different formats. We will be using R and the arulesSequences package (see Lab 10.2). For this implementation of *SPADE*, you will need to transform the data to the TimeStep format shown in Table 10.6. The *SPADE* algorithm will then iterate over all possible sequences and return the most frequent sequence patterns exceeding or equal to the *min_support* threshold. Any patterns with smaller support than the *min_support* will not be collected or shown in the output.

You may want to treat *min_support* as a hyperparameter (as we have done with other machine learning algorithms in previous chapters) and run the algorithm several times with different numbers and inspect the sequences. If you set *min_support* too high, *SPADE* will return a small number of patterns. On the other hand, if you set it too low, *SPADE* will produce many patterns that are not really as frequent as you may want. To get an intuition on this, let us try an example.

Using the *DOTA 2* data, we ran the *SPADE* algorithm with a very low min_support of 0.1 because we wanted to see all patterns and their support. This search resulted in well over 100,000 subsequences. As you can see in Table 10.7, this total number of subsequences returned by the algorithm is extremely large; thus, we can run the algorithm again with a higher *min_support* (e.g., "0.5"), and the output size, seen in Table 10.7, is now significantly smaller, consisting of 269 subsequences in total. Raising *min_support* to "0.7" results in even fewer subsequences, a total of 37 subsequences, and setting it to "1" results in only 1 sequence. This illustrates the way in which manipulating the *min_support* will

Table 10.7 *Number of subsequences in the output of SPADE run on the sequence data—using a min_support of 0.1, 0.5, 0.7, and 1.*

Min-Support	0.1	0.5	0.7	1
# of Subsequences in Output	189,907	269	37	1

Table 10.8 *Four most frequent subsequences of lengths 2, 3, 4, and 5 output by SPADE run with a min_support of "0.7."*

Length:	Top 4 Sequences:	Support:
2	< {solo},{solo} >	0.9963
	< {teaming},{solo} >	0.885
	< {solo},{teaming} >	0.811
	< {teaming},{teaming} >	0.767
3	< {solo},{solo},{solo} >	0.993
	< {teaming},{solo},{solo} >	0.875
	< {solo},{teaming},{solo} >	0.785
	< {solo},{solo},{teaming} >	0.758
4	< {solo},{solo},{solo},{solo} >	0.993
	< {teaming},{solo},{solo},{solo} >	0.869
	< {solo},{teaming},{solo},{solo} >	0.769
	< {solo},{solo},{solo},{teaming} >	0.725
5	< {solo},{solo},{solo},{solo},{solo} >	0.993
	< {teaming},{solo},{solo},{solo},{solo} >	0.856
	< {solo},{teaming},{solo},{solo},{solo} >	0.765
	< {teaming},{teaming},{solo},{solo},{solo} >	0.715

affect the output size of the algorithm. As suggested, figuring out the correct *min_support* requires tuning, as it depends on the kind of information you are looking for. For example, once you have these subsequences, you will probably either run qualitative or quantitative analysis on them. Therefore, you will need to set the threshold to a number that is practical given your next phase of studies, the research questions, and hypotheses.

Table 10.8 demonstrates *SPADE's* output. This table contains the four most frequent sequences of lengths 2, 3, 4, and 5, from *SPADE* run with a *min_support* of "0.7." As a subsequence gets longer, its support naturally goes down. All of the subsequences presented consist solely of the solo and teaming action states. Regardless of length, the most common subsequences involve only the solo event. This tells us that the solo event frequently occurs after a previous instance of the solo event in a given sequence. This is consistent with what we can see in the previous section.

You should note from Table 10.8 that the frequency with which solo events come after teaming events. Specifically, for all lengths, the second most frequent sequence was a single instance of the teaming event followed by one or more instances of the solo events. This indicates that players are likely to perform a solo event numerous times, as indicated by (solo, solo) subsequences after performing the teaming event. This is also true of sequences of players who performed the teaming event after previously performing a solo event, as is represented by the third most frequent subsequence shown in Table 10.8.

Lab 10.2 goes through the example in more detail showing you how to apply the function on a dataset.

Practical Note: Lab 10.2

Lab 10.2

Please see the supplemental materials for the book.

Goal of Lab 2

The lab applying concepts discussed in this section on the player dataset we used with TraMineR. In this lab, we will be using the arulesSequences package, which implements the SPADE algorithm.

10.6.4 Summary of sequence pattern mining

In this section, we demonstrated how *SPADE* can be used to perform sequence pattern mining on game data. Sequence pattern mining can be used to find frequent sequences and subsequences of actions that can provide insight into what players are likely to do after performing a given action. This information can be used to predict different behaviors, such as churn or spending money on a game, all of which are critical to a game's success and longevity. Please see the references included in the bibliography section (e.g., Bosc et al., 2013, Cavadenti et al., 2016, Canossa et al., 2018) if you are interested in reading more about the current state of the art of sequence pattern mining in game data science.

10.7 Clustering of sequences

In the previous sections, we looked into how to visualize sequence data and how to find the most frequent sequences. However, these methods do not give us a way to understand differences between players or ways to group them based on their behaviors. In this section, we look into methods for clustering sequences. This is important because you can profile players by grouping them based on their actions. Further, you can understand more about how players exhibit similar problem-solving strategies if you can group them based on their behaviors.

To cluster sequences, you can use any of the clustering algorithms discussed in Chapter 6. However, as discussed in Chapter 6, clustering algorithms require a distance function in order to perform cluster analysis and output clusters. Previous research resulted in several methods that can help you develop a good distance metric for sequences. In this section, we will discuss some of these methods but focus on *OM*, which we have found to be the most effective. If you are interested in learning more about the state of the art of such methods see the bibliography section (e.g., Canossa et al., 2018; Drachen et al., 2014 and Saas et al., 2016).

It should be noted that we are assuming that states and actions are discrete, or that any continuous data has been turned into discrete values through binning, as discussed earlier. If we are dealing with continuous time-series data, the development of distance metrics can be done using *Dynamic Time Warping (DTW)* provided by the DTW library in R. *DTW* is a mathematical method used to calculate similarity between continuous streams of data given a set of constraints and costs. An example of data types one can use *DTW* for is biometric data, such as EEG. Since most game data can be turned into discrete values, we will discuss *OM* instead of *DTW* in this chapter. If you want to read more on the topic, please consult the excellent article by Giorgino (2009).

Lab 10.3 contains a walkthrough of the functions that can be used to perform *OM*, clustering on the sequence data and distance measures produced by

OM. We will discuss some of the results from this lab here to give you an understanding of the method and its value.

Practical Note: Lab 10.3

Lab 10.3

Please see the supplemental materials for the book.

Goal of Lab 3

The lab goes over how you can use the TraMineR package to perform Optimal Matching and clustering.

There are two ways to develop a similarity measure between sequences: (a) by counting the dissimilar attributes and (b) by calculating the amount of effort required to edit one sequence to match the other. In the next two subsections, we will discuss these methods in more detail.

10.7.1 Simple distance measures based on counts

One way to calculate the similarity or distance between two sequences is based on common attributes between a sequence s_1 and s_2. There are standard ways of calculating this measure, Table 10.9 shows these techniques. In order to grasp these techniques, you should consult Lab 10.3.

Table 10.9 *Representation of distance measures for sequence data.*

Measure	How it is calculated
Hamming distance (HAM)	$D_H = \sum_{i=0}^{n} l_i (s_1, s_2) - n$, where l is defined as: $l_i = \{ 1 \; s_1^i \neq s_2^i, 0 \; otherwise \}$ and n is the length of the sequence s_1 or s_2, it is assumed that the sequences are of equal length
Longest Common Prefix (LCP)	It is the longest consecutive subsequence that matches given sequences s_1 and s_2, counted from the beginning of the sequences.
Reversed Longest Common Prefix (RLCP)	It is the longest consecutive subsequence that matches given sequences s_1 and s_2, counted from the end of the sequences.
Longest Common Subsequence (LCS)	Same as LCP but the subsequence does not have to be consecutive.

10.7.2 Optimal Matching (OM)

If you apply the distance measures in Table 10.9, you will see that the resulting distances do not really differentiate between the sequences in a meaningful way, where meaningful here is judged qualitatively. For example, running *Longest Common Prefix* (LCP) on the first 11 sequences from *DOTA 2* results in the output displayed in Figure 10.10. This can be created using the *seqdist* function provided in Lab 10.3.

The numbers tell us what the longest consecutive subsequence is between each pair of sequences. While this gives us an idea of the degree to which two sequences differ, it does not tell us much about what the differences are.

Another method developed in the social sciences is called *OM. OM* measures similarity between sequences based on the cost of transforming one sequence to match another. This technique was discussed in Levenshtein (1966) and Abbot and Forrest (1986). There are two types of operations that can be used to transform one sequence to another: (a) insertion or deletion and (b) substitution. *OM* considers the costs of these two operations to determine the minimum cost to transform one sequence to another. The costs are set by the analyst, and therefore they can control how these measures are biased toward one operation vs. the other by setting the costs accordingly. In addition, one can adjust the cost of each substitution, insertion, or deletion based on the frequency of specific events within the sequence.

For example, if we use the *TRATE* cost script in Lab 10.3, we can set the cost for insertions based on frequency. Here, the cost to substitute event, *a,* with event, *b,* is based on the probability of transitioning from event, *a,* to event, *b.* Setting the costs in this way favors transitions with high frequencies and penalizes those that are uncommon.

	[,1]	[,2]	[,3]	[,4]	[,5]	[,6]	[,7]	[,8]	[,9]	[,10]	[,11]
[1,]	0	175	194	176	206	172	157	192	205	126	131
[2,]	175	0	195	177	207	173	158	193	206	139	132
[3,]	194	195	0	194	216	186	167	202	223	158	151
[4,]	176	177	194	0	206	172	157	192	203	140	133
[5,]	206	207	216	206	0	198	179	214	235	170	163
[6,]	172	173	186	172	198	0	149	184	201	136	129
[7,]	157	158	167	157	179	149	0	157	186	121	114
[8,]	192	193	202	192	214	184	157	0	221	156	149
[9,]	205	206	223	203	235	201	186	221	0	169	162
[10,]	126	139	158	140	170	136	121	156	169	0	95
[11,]	131	132	151	133	163	129	114	149	162	95	0

Figure 10.10 Longest common prefix output for the first 11 sequences.

10.7.3 Clustering based on optimal matching distances

Once a distance measure is developed between sequences, we can then use any of the clustering techniques we discussed in Chapter 6. In Lab 10.3, we use hierarchical clustering to create the clusters. In particular, we perform clustering using the distance measure produced by *OM*, as described in the previous section.

If we perform this operation on the *DOTA 2* dataset, we will get four distinct clusters discussed in Table 10.10.

Cluster 1: These sequences likely belong to players who gave up or quit the game early or who were simply members of games that were over more quickly. Several of these sequences display frequent presence of the "kill_hero" event, indicating that they may belong to players on teams with distinct advantages over their opponents, leading to a high number of kills in a short time, and the opposing team's quick defeat.

Clusters 2 and 3: These sequences are similar but have a few noteworthy differences. Cluster 2 sequences have a higher frequency of "solo" events toward the beginning, gradually transitioning into a high frequency of team-oriented action states toward the latter middle sections and then finally returning to "solo" events toward the end. By contrast, Cluster 3, which is also the largest cluster in the set, presents a relatively stable mix of team and solo action-oriented events throughout, without any obvious changes in the frequency of certain states appearing at any given part of the sequence.

Cluster 4: This cluster is the most different one from other clusters, characterized by sequences similar to Cluster 3, with a mix of states toward the

Table 10.10 *The four clusters produced by the OM clustering method.*

Cluster No.	Description
Cluster 1	49 sequences, all of which are notably shorter in length than the sequences of the other clusters.
Cluster 2	41 sequences, characterized by a high frequency of solo behavior toward the beginning and end with team behavior in the middle.
Cluster 3	95 sequences characterized by a consistent frequency of team and solo behavior throughout.
Cluster 4	15 sequences characterized by a high concentration of "teaming" toward the end.

beginning, but a high frequency of "solo" events. However, unlike the sequences of Cluster 3, which return to the high frequency of "solo" events at the end, Cluster 4 sequences consist almost exclusively of the "teaming" event at the end. There are two possible explanations for this pattern. One possible explanation is that we are seeing sequences that belong to a special type of supporting hero in *DOTA 2*, sometimes referred to as a "babysitter support." Their role is to accompany another hero early game and support them in interactions against opponents by providing shields or healing, which could explain the higher frequencies of teaming up actions early in the game. As the game goes on, these heroes' presence becomes increasingly important for their teammates to gain an advantage against the opposing team; this means that their mid and late game behavior is characterized by supporting other team members. These heroes never become truly self-sufficient, as they do not have the damage output necessary to take out opponents before they are killed themselves, thus they remain with teammates for protection. This explains the dominance of the teaming action at the end of their sequences.

Further, there are several possible explanations for the variances between Clusters 2, 3, and 4. One possible way to explain the clusters is through character roles. *DOTA 2*'s team, as in other MOBA or RPG games, consists of five players, each controlling a different hero who is designed to fulfill various roles, including: "carry," "support," "tank," or "jungler." Tanks, junglers, and similar heroes tend to have high defense, crowd control abilities, such as stuns, and movement abilities that make them difficult to catch, thus making them suitable characters for roaming solo around the map, harassing enemies, and helping teammates in need of assistance. It is possible that Cluster 3 is indicative of players in this role. In addition, carries are powerful damage dealers with low defense who are easily killed in early game. A carry will probably spend time farming, killing NPC entities for gold and XP (experience points). Once they accumulate enough XP and gold, they will begin to engage more with enemies. Such patterns are indicative of players in Cluster 2.

This example and discussion demonstrate how sequence analysis combined with *OM* and clustering techniques can be a powerful tool for deriving meaning from player data. By examining the data in this way, we can see patterns that allow us to glean contextual information and hypothesize about what may have been occurring during gameplay. This process allows analysts and designers to gain insight into players' styles of teamwork and their strategic considerations.

10.8 Summary and takeaways

Games are played and experienced sequentially, with players taking actions and the games calculating responses to those actions. When we aggregate behavioral telemetry data, we lose the sequential information and context of the action. In many situations, such loss is not a problem, but there are other instances where studying the sequence of player actions can be useful or even necessary. In this chapter, we introduced the idea of looking at sequences of player behavior and covered some of the basic methods for analyzing sequential data.

Specifically, we discussed different methods to explore sequence data using the TraMineR and arulesSequences packages in R. We also explored the use of the frequent sequence pattern mining algorithm, *SPADE*, on game data. In addition, we discussed clustering techniques—particularly *OM*—and showed how to apply it using the TraMineR package.

Different techniques present various pros and cons. Using *SPADE* to mine frequent subsequence patterns allows for a clear and granular observation of common behavior patterns, but it loses the big picture due its focus on subsequences without taking continuity into account. Without continuity, we lose some aspects of temporal sequences that may be important for the question being examined.

Using TraMineR to examine frequent sequences allows for at-a-glance analysis of game data and facilitates the identification of high-level trends. However, it does not provide any quantitative measures of similarity between sequences. Clustering alleviates this problem by combining sequences into clusters based on their similarity to one another. However, as discussed in Chapter 6, clustering is always dependent on the actual distance measure. As discussed above, there are various ways to derive distance measures for sequences, but these can be biased and require human input for encoding domain and game knowledge. Through our experience, we often found it helpful to develop our own similarity or distance measures based on what we believe are important differences between states.

While in this chapter we mostly focused on sequence action analysis, Chapter 11 will introduce more advanced techniques that allows you to construct probabilistic graphical methods and add more information about the game state rather than simply the sequences of actions that occurred.

EXERCISES

1. Transform the VPAL data to STS and SPADE formats.

2. Using the VPAL data in STS format and the TraMineR library, plot the sequence graphs discussed in Section 10.5. What can you say about the sequences in the data based on these plots?

3. Using the VPAL data in the format for *SPADE*, apply the *SPADE* algorithm following the steps in Lab 10.2. What can you say about the sequences based on the output of the algorithm?

4. Using the VPAL data in STS format, use the operations discussed in the optimal matching section (Section 10.7) to cluster the dataset. How many clusters does the data produce? What do these clusters represent? Do these clusters match with personality or other demographic data provided with the dataset?

5. Using the TraMineR library and the operations discussed in the explorative analysis section, perform explorative sequence analysis on the character role datasets provided: Carries_Segmented.csv, Initiators_Segmented.csv, and Support_Segmented.csv. What differences do you see in the frequent sequences between roles? By game segment? What differences do you see in the transition probabilities? What conclusions can you draw from this?

6. Follow the operations discussed in Section 10.7 and apply *SPADE* to each of the role datasets provided: Carries_Segmented.txt, Initiators_Segmented.txt, and Support_Segmented.txt. What differences do you see in the outputs between roles? What conclusions can you draw from this?

7. Using the unsegmented role datasets and TraMineR library, follow the operations discussed in Section 10.7 to cluster each role's dataset: Carries_Complete_Seq.csv, Initiators_Complete_seq.csv, and Support_Complete_Seq.csv. How many meaningful clusters does each dataset produce? What are the differences between the clusters within each role and between roles? What conclusions can you draw from this?

ACKNOWLEDGMENTS

This chapter was written in collaboration with Erica Kleinman. Her work and analysis performed on the DOTA 2 data was an invaluable contribution to this chapter.

BIBLIOGRAPHY

Agrawal, R., and Srikant, R. (1995). Mining sequential patterns. In *11th Intl. Conf. on Data Engineering.*

Abbott, A., and Forrest, J. (1986). Optimal matching methods for historical sequences. *Journal of Interdisciplinary History*, 16, 471–94.

Blei, D. M., Ng, A. Y., and Jordan, M. I. (2003). Latent Dirichlet allocation. *Journal of Machine Learning Research*, 3(Jan), 993–1022.

Blei, D. M. (2012). Probabilistic topic models. *Communications of the ACM, 55*(4), 77–84.

Bosc, G., Kaytoue, M., Raïssi, C., and Boulicaut, J. F. (2013, November). Strategic patterns discovery in RTS-games for E-sport with sequential pattern mining. In *MLSA@ PKDD/ECML* (pp. 11–20).

Canossa, A., Makarovych, S., Togelius, J., and Drachen, A. (2018). Like a DNA string: Sequence-based Player Profiling in *Tom Clancy's The Division*. In *Artificial Intelligence and Interactive Digital Entertainment Conference*. York. URL: https://aaai.org/ocs/index.php/AIIDE/AIIDE18/paper/view/18125

Cavadenti, O., Codocedo, V., Boulicaut, J. F., and Kaytoue, M. (2016, October). What did I do wrong in my MOBA game? Mining patterns discriminating deviant behaviors. In *2016 IEEE International Conference on Data Science and Advanced Analytics (DSAA)* (pp. 662–71). IEEE, Montreal, QC, Canada.

Chen, C. P., and Zhang, C. Y. (2014). Data-intensive applications, challenges, techniques and technologies: A survey on Big Data. *Information sciences, 275*, 314–47.

Chen, Z., Seif El-Nasr, M., Canossa, A., Badler, J., Tignor, S., and Colvin, R. (2015, September). Modeling individual differences through frequent pattern mining on role-playing game actions. In *Eleventh Artificial Intelligence and Interactive Digital Entertainment Conference, AIIDE*.

Drachen, A., Yancey, M., Maguire, J., Chu, D., Wang, I. Y., Mahlmann, T., Schubert, M., and Klabajan, D. (2014, October). Skill-based differences in spatio-temporal team behavior in *Defense of the Ancients 2 (DOTA 2)*. In *2014 IEEE Games Media Entertainment* (pp. 1–8). IEEE, Toronto, Canada.

Gabadinho, A., Ritschard, G., Muller, N. S., and Studer, M. (2011). "Analyzing and visualizing state: Sequences in R with TraMineR." *Journal of Statistical Software, 40*(4), 1–37. URL: http://www.jstatsoft.org/v40/i04

Gabadinho, A., Ritschard, G., Studer, M., and Muller, N. S. (2011). *Mining sequence data in R with the TraMineR package: A user's guide*. University De Geneve, Geneva, Switzerland. URL: http://mephisto.unige.ch/pub/TraMineR/doc/TraMineR-Users-Guide.pdf

Giorgino, T. (2009). Computing and visualizing dynamic time warping alignments in R: The dtw package. *Journal of statistical Software, 31*(7), 1–24.

Harrison, B., and Roberts, D. L. (2013). Analytics-driven dynamic game adaptation for player retention in Scrabble. *Proceedings of Computational Intelligence in Games*, Niagra Falls, Ontario, Canada.

Hornik, K., and Grün, B. (2011). Topicmodels: An R package for fitting topic models. *Journal of Statistical Software, 40*(13), 1–30.

Kambatla, K., Kollias, G., Kumar, V., and Grama, A. (2014). Trends in big data analytics. *Journal of Parallel and Distributed Computing, 74*(7), 2561–73.

Koller, D., and Friedman, N. (2009). *Probabilistic graphical models: principles and techniques*. Cambridge, MA: MIT Press.

Levenshtein, V. (1966). Binary codes capable of correcting deletions, insertions, and reversals. *Soviet Physics Doklady, 10,* 707–10.

NGram. Package in R. URL: https://cran.r-project.org/web/packages/ngram/ngram.pdf. Accessed 2017.

Orkin, J., and Roy, D. (2007). The restaurant game: Learning social behavior and language from thousands of players online. *Journal of Game Development, 3*(1), 39–60.

Saas, A., Guitart, A., and Periánez, A. (2016, September). Discovering playing patterns: Time series clustering of free-to-play game data. In *2016 IEEE Conference on Computational Intelligence and Games (CIG)* (pp. 1–8). IEEE, Santorini, Greece.

Valls-Vargas, J., Ontanón, S., and Zhu, J. (2015, September). Exploring player trace segmentation for dynamic play style prediction. In *Proceedings of the Eleventh AAAI Conference on Artificial Intelligence and Interactive Digital Entertainment* (pp. 93–9). Santa Cruz, California.

Zaki, M. J. (2001). SPADE: An efficient algorithm for mining frequent sequences. *Machine Learning, 42*(1), 31–60.

CHAPTER 11

Advanced Sequence Analysis

A s you have seen in the previous chapter, analyzing and using sequence data can be very powerful. You also learned how to use simple visualization techniques, frequent pattern mining, and sequence clustering techniques to make sense of sequence data. In this chapter, we will look at more advanced techniques.

We will specifically discuss examples of how advanced techniques can be used to uncover players' strategies and problem-solving patterns as well as to predict churn. While it may be very obvious why predicting churn is important, it may not be as obvious why one would want to uncover or understand players' strategies. In Chapter 10, we presented a case study that sheds some light on the utility of such analysis. Further, understanding what players are trying to do in their gameplay can allow us to uncover issues in the design, such as puzzles that are too hard or scenarios where players are not on the right path. We can also develop adaptive strategies to balance a game's complexity or difficulty by building more accurate predictive models of play behavior. The methods discussed in the previous chapter, including frequent sequence mining, exploratory sequence analysis, and sequence clustering, cannot directly predict churn or player strategies. Frequent sequence mining only outputs a list of sequences that occur frequently. It is then up to the analyst to discern behavioral patterns from such output. Sequence clustering methods output sequence groupings; however, they do not model latent structures or hidden processes, such as risk taking or conservative attitudes. This is only possible if you specifically develop such features (see Chapter 4).

Game Data Science. Magy Seif El-Nasr, Truong Huy Nguyen Dinh, Alessandro Canossa, and Anders Drachen, Oxford University Press. © Magy Seif El-Nasr, Truong Huy Nguyen Dinh, Alessandro Canossa, and Anders Drachen (2021).
DOI: 10.1093/oso/9780192897879.003.0011

In order to uncover players' strategies and behaviors from logs of game actions, we will need to use more advanced techniques. These techniques allow us to model the probability of what might be happening in players' minds as they take a given action, uncovering intent, goals, and plans from action streams. Note that there are many possible reasons a player has for performing certain actions in a game environment. We thus need to use probabilities to model such uncertainty to be able to develop models that can include and reason about latent variables—inferred variables that are not directly observable in the data.

Different approaches have been proposed in the area of artificial intelligence to understand a person's plans from their low-level action streams. This area is called *plan recognition* (see Sukthankar et al., 2014; Carberry, 2001), and the techniques used within the area are called probabilistic graphical models (Koller and Friedman, 2009). In this chapter, we will introduce several advanced techniques and topics within the area of probabilistic graphical models, such as Bayesian Networks (BNs), Markov Logic Networks (MLNs), Hidden Markov Models (HMMs), and grammar-based techniques—as example techniques that can be used by researchers to infer users' goals and strategies from activity data.

Note that plan recognition is an area of active research. The techniques currently proposed work on toy problems and have not seen much success yet in fully complex game environments. Therefore, this chapter will read very differently from other chapters. We will review previous work in the field of plan recognition and how they were applied to games outlining their limitations and challenges that currently exist in this area. We wanted to outline some open problems for interested readers who would like to take on these challenges and build on previous work.

This chapter is divided into the following subsections examining different approaches of advanced sequence analysis with the goal of modeling players' goals, intent, strategies, and plans:

- Probabilistic planning-based approach (Section 11.1)
- Bayesian Networks (BNs) or Dynamic Bayesian Networks (DBNs) (Section 11.2)
- Hidden Markov Models (HMMs) (Section 11.3)
- Markov Decision Process (MDP) (Section 11.4)
- Markov Logic Networks (MLNs) (Section 11.5)
- Recurrent Neural Networks (RNNs) and Deep Recurrent Neural Networks (Section 11.6)

With the exception of RNNs, most of the probabilistic methods discussed in this chapter have been published and used extensively in research with very few example adoptions by the industry. Therefore, in this chapter, we will highlight the techniques with simple examples and show how they have been applied. However, as mentioned above, most of these techniques were used and developed for very constrained scenarios, and thus may not work for complex games like the ones out in the market today.

This chapter will focus mostly (with the exception of Section 11.6) on methods that perform advanced sequence analysis to produce interpretable models, such as graphical models. Remember at the end of Chapter 9 we discussed the issue of interpretability with black-box classification methods used in machine learning. Interpretable models show clear structures and probabilities that a nonexpert can understand and inspect. This also has the added advantage of being used as a way to communicate results to stakeholders within a company. The exception to this is black-box methods, such as Recurrent Neural Networks (RNNs), which we will discuss in the last section. RNNs are not easily interpretable, although there is current work examining the development of explainable models to explain the results of RNNs or other black-box methods. Interested readers are urged to investigate this topic further as the field progresses.

11.1 Probabilistic planning-based approach

11.1.1 The approach

In the earliest formulations of plan recognition, the problem was studied as a question of recognizing a single goal or strategy, assumed to be the only one pursued, from a sequence of observed actions. To this end, the techniques use a plan library—a library of possible strategies or plans that a person can pursue in a given situation. This is typically built by hand, as a set of potential sequences of actions that might achieve each goal. The plan recognition problem is formulated to determine which plan in the library is most similar and maps to the observed actions (Carberry, 2001). To give you a concrete example of what that may look like for a game like *DOTA*, consider a "Gank." To achieve a gank, a player can team up with others and go toward an enemy player and kill them, or they may trap the enemy together each player taking a different side in the map. A plan library here will need to include all plans (i.e., the different ways and sequences of actions) that a team may take to achieve such a gank. This would need to account for all different placements of teammates and enemies.

As you can see from the example above, such simple formulation of the problem does not work with current games, because:

1. Every plan has to be specified manually, which is infeasible and unscalable for current games, and,

2. The method assumes that each observation sequence could unambiguously correspond to only one goal/strategy, which is almost impossible in complex games, where players may take many routes to achieve each goal, including suboptimal ones, and may switch goals repeatedly or pursue several goals at once.

Fortunately, modern work addresses these restrictions. Instead of using a hand-constructed plan library, Ramírez and Geffner (2009) developed a plan recognition system based on a modification of this classical planning problem (see sidebar: "What is Classical Planning?"). By performing a search using a planning algorithm, rather than through a predefined library of manually specified plans, they sought to mitigate the expense of hand constructing such a library. Since existing off-the-shelf planning algorithms already computed the optimal paths to goals, and the plan recognition problem could be specified as a planning problem for the conjunction of several goals, they were able to use off-the-shelf planners to experiment with this approach.

They then evaluated their approach on several standard planning benchmark problems. They tested both optimal and suboptimal planners and found a very large speedup for using suboptimal planners, at the cost of a small accuracy loss of 5–15% on most of the problems they tested. In one planning domain, however, they found a more significant accuracy loss of 15–42%. They sought to mitigate this by using a heuristic to break ties in the suboptimal planner toward actions that would achieve more goals. This did not fully resolve the inaccuracies, but it did mitigate them to a limited extent in most cases.

What is Classical Planning?

Classical planning is a set of algorithms whereby a plan is developed given a particular goal. Many algorithms exist to address this problem. An example is HTN (Hierarchical Task Networks) (Nau et al., 1999).

HTN is a planning algorithm that relies on decomposing a task into a set of subtasks. Most implementations of HTNs use formal logic as a representation mechanism. An HTN is composed of:

- Primitive tasks (actions to be executed)
- Compound tasks (can be seen as tasks that are composed of other subtasks)
- Goal tasks (goals to be accomplished, which include the success conditions)

Within HTNs, one can also represent constraints (preconditions for each task/subtask that make these tasks/subtasks applicable). For example, a compound task will require several subtasks to be accomplished before it can be completed. HTNs also allow the definition of further constraints on the compound tasks and subtasks, such as order preservation constraints, postconditions, and preconditions.

Shop is an HTN algorithm (Nau et al., 1999) described in Figure 11.1. As you can see from the figure, the algorithm continuously finds tasks that are applicable given the state S, task list T, and the knowledge base D.

procedure SHOP (S, T, D)

1. **if** T = nil **then return** nil **endif**
2. t = the first tak in T
3. U = the remaining tasks in T
4. **if** t is primitive (i.e., there is an operator for t) **then**
5.   nondeterministically choose an operator 0 for t
6. P = SHOP $(o(S), U, D)$
7.   if P = FAIL then return FAIL **endif**
8.   **return** cons (p, P)
9. **else if** there is a method applicable to t whose
    preconditions can all be inferred from S **then**
10.   nondeterministically let m be such a method
11.   **return** SHOP(S, append(m(t,S), U), D)
12. **else**
13.   **return** FAIL
14. **endif**
end SHOP

Figure 11.1 Shop—a hierarchical task network algorithm. Figure used with permission from AAAI. Original appeared in Nau, D., Cao, Y., Lotem, A., and Munoz-Avila, H. (2001). The SHOP planning system. *AI Magazine, 22*(3), 91–91.

HTNs can then be seen as constructing an AND-OR tree, where each task is composed of several subtasks to be completed (AND), but each of these subtasks may further have a number of subtasks that can achieve them (OR). Since the introduction of the *Shop* algorithm, there have been several other algorithms proposed, such as *Shop 2* (Sirin et al., 2004). Readers are encouraged to consult the bibliography section for a more up-to-date discussion on planning algorithms.

Unfortunately, the problem of having to assign each sequence to a strategy is not addressed by Ramírez and Geffner's (2009) approach. To resolve this problem, Ramírez and Geffner (2010) proposed a modification of their original approach using a probabilistic formulation of plan recognition that was still based on classical planning. With this approach, they tried to find the probability of a goal given some observations, formulated as follows: $P(G|O)$, where P is the probability, G is the goal, and O is a set of observations. You can refer to the paper by Ramírez and Geffner (2010) for full details of the derivation of this probability and the rest of the implementation details of their approach.

Another similar approach was developed by Geib and Goldman (2009), who developed a probabilistic plan recognition algorithm, called *PHATT*. *PHATT* was developed to create and compare the likelihoods of possible explanations of an observed action sequence, given a plan library using a HTN representation (see sidebar: "What is Classical Planning?"). In particular, Geib and Goldman (2009) described their approach as an algorithm that steps through the observation trace assigning sets of observations to possible hypothesized plans or goals. These sets can then be used as explanations of the observations.

They defined the problem as finding the probability of particular plans and goals given the observations *obs*, and a plan library defined by several expressions *exp* specifying the sequence of actions needed to be fulfilled for a plan. Next, they solved the following equation:

$$p\left(exp \wedge obs\right) = P(goals)P\left(plans|goals\right) P\left(obs|exp\right) \qquad \text{(Equation 11.1)}$$

where *P(goals)* is the prior probability of the user adopting some *goals*, which can be calculated from given probabilities of each goal in the plan library. *P(plans|goals)* is the probability that these *goals* would lead to the *plans* for this observation (the selection of the OR nodes in the generated plan tree). *P(obs|exp)* is the probability that the observed sequence of actions, *obs*, are executed by the user given the plans in *exp*. In their work, they did not assume that there is one clear sequence of actions per plan, and thus this probability is more complex; it accounts for partial order and interleaved or overlapping plans. For more information on the formalization of probability and its derivation, please see the paper (Geib and Goldman, 2009).

Using the plan library, starting with an initial set of empty hypotheses, they iterated over the possible changes to the hypotheses as they observed actions, adding new tree instances into existing or new goals as necessary where the associated plans are suggested by the actions that they observed. They also calculated the probabilities of these explanations for the player's plans and goals, based on the formalization above.

11.1.2 What does this mean for current commercial games?

The use of a classical planner to solve the problem of defining a plan library by hand provides several important benefits. One can take advantage of extensive, ongoing research in optimally solving (or approximately solving) planning problems, which are also used to build AI agents in the industry. This approach also obviates the need to pre-specify every possible approach a player could take to achieve a goal, instead it enables designers to focus on specifying the available actions, their required preconditions, and their effects on the game world. For complex games, in which a large number of possible approaches could achieve the same goal, this may be necessary to make the specification of the problem tractable.

However, the basic use of planning requires several assumptions and conditions. Using a planner in a game environment requires that the world state, potential actions, and their consequences be efficiently and concretely simulated. For games with no existing forward model of actions and their consequences, where the only existing way to simulate the effects of an action is to try it, this may be difficult to achieve. Many games, for instance, incorporate complex physics simulations that are too computationally intensive to run at high framerates, and that would need to be replaced with an approximation to build a fast forward simulation. Significant rebuilding or duplication of game logic may be necessary to specify a game as a planning domain. Moreover, such a specification may be prohibitively complex for a game with many potential actions, and the search space for a planner may grow to the point where even approximate, suboptimal planners become too expensive to use in real time.

The advantage of *PHATT* or similar probabilistic approaches is in the flexibility of these methods; they can account for missing observations, support multiple concurrent goals, and handle partially ordered plans. As *PHATT* creates many possible explanations for the observations, including explanations with multiple goals, and it ranks and assigns probabilities to those explanations, it is applicable to more complex problems than the original, one-goal-at-a-time formulations of plan recognition.

However, the proliferation of explanations can also be seen as a drawback for *PHATT*. The probabilistic ranking of many explanations may be acceptable for some situations, but it may be difficult to determine the true explanation when several are competing to be the most probable. Additionally, the probabilistic ranking of explanations requires certain assumptions and prior probability decisions, such as deciding how strongly to prefer simpler explanations with a single goal over more complex explanations with multiple simultaneous goals. If these assumptions are incorrect for a particular domain or a problem, they may lead to inaccurate results. Finally, generating and ranking many explanations requires significant processing time. *PHATT* may have trouble running in real-time when applied to modern games. Work that builds on *PHATT* often attempts to reduce these computational costs.

11.1.3 Applying this approach to games

While there are many planners developed for games, such as Goal-Oriented Action Planning in *F.E.A.R.* (Orkin, 2006), the main obstacle to using these planning approaches to uncover players' strategies from data as discussed above is the computational cost of performing planning. The tests from Ramírez and Geffner (2010) showed times ranging from half a second to over 50 seconds for the suboptimal planner on domains with under 200 actions and around 20 goals, which is considered mediocre for real-time processing. The largest times were seen in domains with a high number of possible combinations of actions, due to a lack of ordering constraints. With more processing power, parallelization, or further improvements to planners, this time–cost may decrease. At the moment, however, this technique may be difficult to apply to games with highly open action spaces or many potential goals, such as open-world role-playing and action games or complex real-time strategy games.

Therefore, instead of using classical planners, current approaches use plan libraries constructed by the game design expert. This was the case for researchers who extended *PHATT* into a new system called *Hostile Intent, Capability, and Opportunity Recognizer* (*HICOR*), built to uncover player strategies from Real-Time Strategy (RTS) games. To enable the use of this system, they extended it to add resource management and influence maps as a way to establish utility for particular plans given the dynamic nature of RTS games. In addition, they added the ability for the HTN to account for delayed and concurrent actions that are important for RTS, such as sending a scout but continuing with the plan until they hear back, or a scout waiting till a behavior is observed before they continue their plan. They formulated two different plan libraries, one at the strategic level and the other at the tactical level. Their results were very promising, showing that the system made wrong predictions only 11% of the time. Furthermore, the system always converged to the correct plan before the plan was finished.

However, up to now, this approach required a lot more research before it can be used practically within the industry. The approach results in low accuracy of prediction rates and is intractable for most complex games. In the next sections, we will discuss other approaches that are more promising.

11.2 Bayesian Networks (BNs) or Dynamic Bayesian Networks (DBNs)

11.2.1 The approach

Another approach for creating structured probabilistic models for plan recognition employs BNs. BNs are a type of probabilistic graphical model that represent the probabilistic relationships between variables as a directed graph. The nodes within the graph contain conditional probability tables for a variable, based on the information flow into that node from other nodes in the network (the "parent" variables). BNs compactly and efficiently represent a probabilistic model, because they use Bayes' rule and conditional probability to avoid storing the entire joint probability distribution for all the variables. For a more detailed description of BNs, please see the sidebar "Theory: What are Bayesian Networks (BNs)?"

Theory: What are Bayesian Networks (BNs)?

Bayesian Networks (BNs) (Pearl, 1988) are a graphical probabilistic representation of variables and their dependencies. Imagine you want to deduce if a player is highly ranked or not. To deduce this, four variables come into play, as shown in Figure 11.2. *High Rank* depends on the variable *Score* which in turn depends on both *Champion* and *Role*. The probability of *High Rank* depends on *Score*.

Figure 11.2 An example of a Bayesian Network.

Based on expert knowledge, we can then deduce prior probabilities for these variables. Given these probabilities, we can calculate the probability of some variables occurring given the occurrence of specific variables—for example, probability of *Score* given that *Role* and *Champion* match some specific values. Using probability theory, we can deduce these probabilities given the network using the Chain Rule. The chain rule describes the probability distribution of random variables composed in the BN in terms of products of conditional probabilities that describe the relationship between these variables. Thus, given the network in this example, we define the following:

---

continued

Theory: What are Bayesian Networks (BNs)?

$$P(C, R, S, H) = P(C)P(R)\,P(S|C, R)\,P(H|S)$$ (Equation 11.2)

where $P(C, R, S, H)$ is the probability of the champion, C, role, R, score, S, and high rank, H. $P(C)$ is the prior probability of champion, C. $P(R)$ is the prior probability of role, R. $P(S|C, R)$ is the prior probability of score, S, given, champion, C and role, R. Finally, $P(H|S)$ is the prior probability of high rank, H, given, score, S.

Given the BN and some observed variables, such as the C and R, we can then deduce information about unobserved variables, such as S and H. This process is called probabilistic inference. BN researchers have proposed several inference methods. The most widely used is the *Variable Elimination* or the *Loopy Belief Propagation algorithm*. For more information, refer to Koller and Friedman (2009).

When using a BN approach for gameplay action sequence analysis or player modeling, most solutions use Dynamic Bayesian Networks (DBNs). This is an extension of BNs that model relationships between variables over different time steps or sequences.

There are several implementations of algorithms for BN and DBN in R and Python that you can use. A good book to use for BN understanding within R is Nagarajan et al. (2013).

A good example of the use of BNs is Horvitz et al.'s (1998) work at Microsoft research on a project called *Lumiere*. The project aimed to develop an assistive AI system for computer software users based on observations or logs of their behaviors. To determine whether intent and goals can be deduced from users' actions when using a software package, like Microsoft Excel, they first constructed a Wizard of Oz interface, whereby experts could see users' actions and then try to help them. They asked different users to perform spreadsheet tasks. Experts observed the users' actions from a separate room. They were able to see all the mouse movements and activities. Using expert interaction and deduced users' plans, Horvitz et. al. (1998) could extrapolate a model to predict the times when users needed help as well as the topics they needed help with. Through this process, they identified various features that are important for the identification of issues and help strategies. They also found that timing between pauses can be an important clue that a user is ready for assistance. Note that these can also be great insights for player modeling within the context of games.

Given these experimental results, they developed an instrumentation system to collect user activity data. This is similar to the telemetry process in game analytics as discussed in Seif El-Nasr et al. (2013). They developed their own language for deducing metrics or important features from activity data, based on their Wizard of Oz experiment. An example of this is the feature *Dwell (t)*, where the user paused without any actions for a certain amount of time. These features are similar to the high-level metrics we discussed in Chapters 2 and 4.

Using the experimental results, and working with experts, Horvitz et. al. (1998) then developed a BN (see the sidebar "Theory: What are Bayesian Networks (BNs)?" for an introduction to the subject) that would allow them to infer the probability of a specific goal given the sequence of actions or features observed in the data. Due to the importance of timing and temporal inference, they later adjusted their BN approach and adopted a DBN to model users' goals and actions, or lack thereof. DBNs are an extension of BNs to handle templates or time-series data, as discussed above.

11.2.2 What does this mean for current commercial games?

BNs and DBNs are attractive probabilistic modeling approaches because they are structured, visual, and transparent. They are easy to inspect, with clear probabilistic relationships, and they can be tweaked in many ways: adding and removing variables, changing how they relate, modifying prior and conditional probabilities, and so forth. Whenever a prediction is made using a BN, it is relatively straightforward to inspect which variables contributed to the probability of the results, and how. The interpretability and designability of this approach make it attractive for games, as it allows game designers to inspect and adjust probabilities and the resulting models.

As with *PHATT*, modeling plan recognition with a BN or DBN requires a significant manual effort. Albrecht et al. (1998) described the intensive user testing and expert assistance that went into building their model. When designing a BN, you need to define the observed variables, their relationships to other observed and latent variables, their prior probabilities, and possibly their conditional probabilities based on other variables. The conditional probabilities may be learned from existing data, but that requires sufficient annotated training data. While there are some methods developed for learning the structure of a BN itself, they are not always successful in building effective networks. BNs can take significant processing time to make predictions when they grow larger, especially if there are few cases of conditional independence among the variables.

11.2.3 Applying this approach to games

BN-based plan recognition has been applied to games by Albrecht et al. (1998), who used a DBN to build a plan recognition system for adventure games. They used the term "keyhole plan recognition" to signify plan recognition algorithms that use an incomplete view of information about a user's plans (as if someone is looking at a user through a keyhole from another room). They applied this technique to a text-based virtual MUD (Multi-User Dungeon) game called *Shattered Waters*. The MUD has over 4,700 locations, and 20 different quests. In the dataset, there were over 7,200 actions observed.

As with other games, players' goals were not concrete and were hard to determine. While there were quests that had specific goals, the users could join the game with their own goals, such as socializing with other players or beating the game system. In their work, Albrecht et al. (1998) assumed that players had no other motives except those dictated by the game. They then developed a method to infer player's goals from their actions, and thus were able to infer what future actions the players would pursue based on these goals and this assumption.

Using actions, quests, and locations as variables, they developed multiple DBN structures where they varied the dependencies between the variables and the previous time step's variables. They used a learning algorithm to learn the probability parameters and used inference algorithms (belief propagation) to infer future actions, quests, and locations given the observed actions, quests, and locations. Next, they ran several tests at each time step, asking if the player took action a_1 at time 1, can we predict the next action, quest, and location. The model's prediction of quests and locations tend to be higher in accuracy than next actions, where the next actions mostly range from 20% to 40%, while locations tend to range from 40% to 60% and quests range around 80%. Of course, the prediction rates are higher as the player progresses through the game.

Another good example of using BN for plan recognition in games is the work by Conati et al. (1997 and 2002). This work aimed to develop a user model for tutoring physics. They developed a BN that represents all possible solutions of a given physics problem set. The solutions were derived from a rule-based system developed to solve physics problems, which they constructed based on expert knowledge. They used the BN to identify students' problem-solving strategies, which were then used as input to the tutoring system for a model of the user. We can see a similar approach used in commercial games, where a designer can help develop a rule-based problem solver for the given game levels, and then a BN can be developed to represent the likelihoods of these solutions given observed actions. Using the BN, we could then reason about the players' strategies and recognize their goals and plans, and thus adapt the game based on that player model.

11.3 Hidden Markov Models (HMMs)

11.3.1 The approach

Another popular approach to modeling users' goals, intentions, and plans through sequence data is a Hidden Markov Model (HMM). HMMs have been used in many domains and have seen a lot of success in speech recognition as well as in modeling activities and intent. For a review of what HMMs are, please see the sidebar: "Theory: What are Hidden Markov Models?".

Theory: What are Hidden Markov Models?

Markov Networks (MNs) are similar to BNs but where the edges are nondirectional. Thus, their inference and learning algorithms are different to accommodate the difference in how knowledge is propagated through the network. HMMs are MNs but with hidden nodes denoting latent variables.

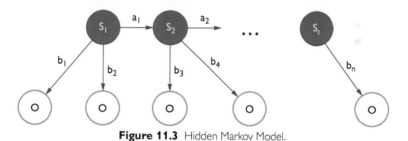

Figure 11.3 Hidden Markov Model.

An HMM is a generative probabilistic model of time-series data, mainly used for analyzing and recovering a sequence of internal hidden states generated by a sequence of output observations (Rabiner and Juang, 1986). An HMM is characterized by parameters shown in Figure 11.3, and given by the formula:

$$\lambda = (s_t, o_t, A, B, \pi) \qquad \text{(Equation 11.3)}$$

where s_t represents the finite set of the hidden states; o_t is the finite set of observed outputs; $A = \{a_1, a_2, \ldots a_n\}$ is the state transition probability matrix that defines the probability of going from one state to another, where n is the number of states; $B = \{b_1, b_2 \ldots b_n\}$ is the emission matrix (i.e., observation probability matrix) that defines how each observation contributes to each state; and π is the initial state probability matrix that represents the probability of being in a given state at the start of the sequence.

Various algorithms exist that estimate or learn the parameters of the model based on the data.

As shown in the sidebar, developing and using an HMM requires us to develop a model that is composed of a number of states, s, and state transitions, a, between the states that can then explain the observable output. Further, we also need some variables b_i that determine the impact of each state on observables. HMM can be used as both supervised and unsupervised methods. Most often, the *Viterbi* algorithm (Forney, 1973) is used to determine the most probable or correct path of hidden states given a sequence of observables. For player behaviors, for example, this algorithm can be used to uncover the optimal path of the most probable behavioral sequence that caused the observations.

When solving a supervised problem, we assume that the hidden states, s, correspond to labels that an expert produces for the data. For example, for players, we can label strategies in the data, high-level behaviors, or whether the player churned or not.

When labeled data is not available, HMM can be used in an unsupervised fashion. To do so, we will have to do more computation to determine the number of states and develop some estimations of the probabilities or parameters of the model. Without labeled data, it is uncertain how many hidden states exist or what these states are. To determine the number of hidden states, s, and infer the labels from the data, one can use the *Baum-Welch* algorithm. This algorithm is an *Expectation-Maximization (EM)* algorithm which learns the best parameters from the data that best fits the observations. Thus, it optimizes the likelihood of getting the observed output. The algorithm iteratively adjusts the parameters of the model to maximize the likelihood of the sequence of observed data, where the paths of hidden states are determined via the *Viterbi* algorithm. The algorithm uses a gradient search in the parameter space to optimize the likelihood, and thus it converges in local optima.

This process, however, assumes that we know how many states exist in the model. Sometimes, this information is unknown, or such information cannot be inferred by experts. In such cases, we can treat the number of states as hyperparameters, where we iteratively use the process above with different numbers of states, and then assess the fitness of the model using a scoring measure, such as *Bayesian Information Criterion (BIC)*. For more information on how these models work mathematically, readers are referred to Boussemart et al. (2011).

11.3.2 What does this mean for current commercial games?

As discussed above, one can use HMMs in unsupervised and supervised fashions. Further, there are well-defined methods for defining an HMM, since the only hyperparameter is the number of states. This makes them suitable for predictions in environments with several observed and unobserved variables, where the precise probabilistic relationships between those variables are not necessarily known ahead of time but can be discovered through training data. Similar to other probabilistic graphical models, HMMs are highly interpretable and can handle uncertainty through probabilistic output. These advantages make them very promising to use for games because we can relatively easily train and develop an HMM without having too much expert knowledge or work, and we can produce a model that can be interpretable by many stake-holders within the game development teams.

However, this approach does come with drawbacks. HMMs make a lot more assumptions than BNs, which may constrain their ability to model different and complex structures from data. They assume that the current state is entirely independent of all historic data other than the immediate previous state. In games where players may enter the same game state along several paths or for several reasons, or where long-term memory of prior states is necessary to predict the player's future actions, this Markov assumption may significantly limit the accuracy of an HMM model.

It is unclear whether HMMs would be suitable for predictions and differentiation of many hypotheses of particular plans and goals. This is an active research area.

11.3.3 Applying this approach to games

There have been few works that use HMMs to model players' actions and plans given sequence data. Matsumoto and Thawonmas (2004) presented an approach to classify players into different types based on sequence action data using HMMs. Recently, Bunian et al. (2017) used HMMs to uncover individual differences between players using Virtual Personality Assessment Lab (VPAL) data, which you used in the previous chapters.

However, there are not many works that used HMMs to deduce strategies. We will instead discuss an example that used HMMs to predict churn (Tamassia et al., 2016). In their work, they used HMMs to predict churn in a very popular game called *Destiny*. *Destiny* is an AAA title game that combines game mechanics from shooter games and Massively MultiPlayer Online Role-Playing Games (MMORPG). According to PCGames, the game hit 6 million monthly active players in late 2018. The business model of the game relies on its online content, including downloadable content, micro-transactions on emotes, weapon packs, and other in-app purchases. Similar to many free-to-play models, churn is an important element to predict and model.

As a hybrid game, *Destiny*'s data will naturally include player behaviors from shooter and MMORPG mechanics, such as "run," "jump," "crouch," "shoot," "melee combat," and "kills," as well as RPG type mechanics, such as "XP," "attributes," "class," and an "inventory" system. These elements of massive multi-player actions add further complexities, similar to the ones found in Multiplayer Online Battle Arena (MOBA) games, such as group activities including raids, which require coordination and multiple players collaborating in action.

Tamassio et al. (2016) used this game to model churn using a time-series data and an HMM approach. They collected data over 17 months (September 2014– January 2016) with a total of 10,000 players with 24,118 characters randomly sampled, culminating in 1,809,564 of total playtime hours, with 158 hours as the average number of hours for a player.

To develop the HMM for the data, they defined a churn window of C, where C is the number of weeks with null (or no) activity. They then defined some features given the data. The features were aggregated across weeks as follows:

- Mean lifespan: Average lifespan of a player in seconds, calculated based on life vs. killed events.
- Kill-death ratio
- Activities completed ratio given what they entered into
- Current absence: This is calculated as the number of weeks since they last played.
- Current absence to mean absence ratio
- Weeks present ratio: Calculated as the number of weeks a player has been active given when they registered for the game.

Using these features, they created an HMM model with output values as "churned" or "not churned."

They then compared the HMM's performance to other classification methods in terms of *precision, recall, F1 score*, and *AUC* (described in Chapter 8). HMM seems to outperform other classifiers, including *Bagging, Naïve Bayes, Nearest Neighbor, Gradient Boosting, Decision Tree, Discriminant Analysis, AdaBoost, Logistic Regression*, and *Random Forest*, in *precision* and *AUC* (see Chapter 7 for a review of these classifiers). However, *Random Forest* seems to outperform all other classifiers in terms of *recall and F1 Score*. Further, in terms of *F1 score, Discriminant Linear Analysis, Logistic Regression*, and *Random Forest* seem to score best. This shows mixed results of the use of HMM. However, there are many advantages to using HMM, including interpretability, which is important for reporting analysis results to stakeholders.

11.4 Markov Decision Process (MDP)

11.4.1 The approach

Markov Decision Processes (MDPs) are a way to formulate problems that are characterized by actions to maximize rewards in a fully observable situation or environment. An MDP consists of a set of world states, S, and available actions from those states: A. The MDP may be probabilistic, in that the actual result of taking an action (the next state, s') may depend on a probabilistic transition model $P(s'|s,a)$. Each time the agent acts, it receives a reward r, though that reward may be zero or negative. That reward may be the same whenever an agent enters a particular state, or it may depend on the state and action that led there. An optimal policy for solving an MDP would be to take any world state, s, and an output action, a, that maximize the future expected rewards (usually discounted over time, to prioritize more immediate rewards). For more details on MDPs, see Russell and Norvig (2009), Chapter 17.

An MDP is commonly used as a problem formulation in reinforcement learning, because an optimal policy for an MDP can be found by repeated simulation and iteration, without prior human-labeled data, as long as the world state is clearly defined, the action space is limited, and the reward function is known.

An interesting approach for plan recognition using MDPs was proposed by Oh et al. (2014). In a nutshell, their technique can be summarized as follows: first, they use MDPs to develop a set of stochastic policies, which represent the behaviors users adopt when pursuing hidden goals. Each of these policies is a function $P_g(s, a)$: $S \times A \rightarrow R$ that returns the probability that a user will take action, a, in state, s, with the intent of maximizing the long-term reward when pursuing goal, g. The assumption here is that human users are more or less rational, thus, the optimal policies of such MDPs can be used to approximate their behavior. Next, using this set of policies, they can leverage Bayes' theorem to update the assistant agent's belief on the user's implicit goal given observed actions. Now let us take a look at these two steps in more detail. We will discuss Step 2 (plan recognition) first to understand what pieces of information are needed for the task before showing how we can get them from Step 1 (MDP formulations of user behaviors).

Oh et al. (2014) formalized the plan recognition approach as follows: Suppose that there are m possible states $S = \{s^1, s^2, \ldots, s^m\}$. At each time step, t, the user can take one of n actions $A = \{a^1, a^2, \ldots, a^n\}$. Naturally, the probability of a sequence of action and state transitions would depend on the action and sequence of previous states. The probability distribution of a goal given observed states and actions $O_t = (s_1, a_1, s_2, \ldots, s_t)$, where t is time, can be computed, using Bayes' theorem, as:

$$P(g|O_t) = \frac{P(s_1, a_1, \ldots, s_t|g)\ P(g)}{\sum_{g' \in G} P(s_1, a_1, \ldots, s_t|g')\ p(g')} \qquad \text{(Equation 11.4)}$$

The observed sequence $O_t = (s_1, a_1, s_2, \ldots, s_t)$ can be expanded as follows:

$$P(s_1, a_1, \ldots, s_t|g) = P(s_1|g)\ P(a_1|s_1, g)\ P(s_2|s_1, a_1, g) \ldots$$
$$P(s_t|s_{t-1}, a_{t-1}, \ldots, s_1, g)$$
$$= P(s_1|g)\ P(a_1|s_1, g)\ P(s_2|s_1, a_1, g) \ldots$$
$$P(s_t|s_{t-1}, a_{t-1}, g) \qquad \text{(Equation 11.5)}$$

where g is the list of all goals. Note that the Markov principle (stating that future state depends only on the current state) allows us to simplify the conditional probabilities in Equation 11.5 by disregarding past states and actions, and only keeping the most recent state-action pairs, and the targeted goal:

$$P(s_t|s_{t-1}, a_{t-1}, \ldots, s_1, g) = P(s_t|s_{t-1}, a_{t-1}, g) \qquad \text{(Equation 11.6)}$$

In Equation 11.5, note that there are two types of conditional probabilities. The first are probabilities of states $P(s_i|*)$, given the goal and most recent pair of states and actions. The second are probabilities of actions $P(a_i|*)$, given the goal and current state. These two pieces of information can be obtained by formulating the users' behaviors as MDPs.

An MDP is represented as a tuple: $\langle S, A, r, T, \gamma \rangle$, where S and A are, as defined above, the sets of states and actions, r is reward, T is state transition function $S \times A \times S \rightarrow R$, which takes as input the current state s and action a and returns the real value representing the probability of landing in a next state s', and γ is the discount factor for reward/penalty received in a future state. This formulation is frequently used in reinforcement learning (Sutton and Barto, 1998), where solving an MDP will result in a policy that maps each state to an optimal action in the deterministic case, and each state to a distribution of actions in the probabilistic case.

To solve an MDP (i.e., compute the optimal policy that leads to the highest expected long-term reward), a common approach is to use *Value Iteration*. In

Value Iteration, the value of each state $V(s)$ is defined to be the maximum accumulated reward that can be achieved from that state, mathematically formulated as follows:

$$V(s) = max_{a \in A} \left[r(s, a) + \gamma \sum_{s' \in S} V(s') T(s'|s, a) \right] \quad \text{(Equation 11.7)}$$

The value of each given state is obtained by maximizing the value of a chosen action given the reward at the next state and the expected rewards from future transition to other states. You can see that Equation 11.7, when formulated for all states in S, provides an equation system that can be solved to obtain $V(s)$, $\forall s \in S$. *Value Iteration* is simply the iterative algorithm that solves this recursive equation system, starting from some random initialization and terminating when the changes in value are smaller than a negligible threshold.

Once the value function V is obtained, a deterministic optimal policy, π, that maps each state to an action, can then be computed by selecting the actions that maximize the value given the current state, s, defined as follows:

$$\pi(s) = argmax_{a \in A} \left[r(s, a) + \gamma \sum_{s' \in S} V(s') T(s'|s, a) \right] \quad \text{(Equation 11.8)}$$

While deterministic policies work well for Reinforcement Learning when we want to optimize the action for an autonomous character, it is not suitable for plan recognition, as we cannot assume that users will always choose the action that would maximize their rewards. To address this, Oh et al. (2014) opted for obtaining stochastic policies that output a probability distribution for each given state, computed based on expected reward, as follows:

$$P(a|s) = \pi(s, a) \; \alpha \left[r(s, a) + \gamma \sum_{s' \in S} V(s') T(s'|s, a) \right] \quad \text{(Equation 11.9)}$$

Given such MDP formulations as discussed above, you can see that we obtain crucial pieces of information to infer the user's hidden goal given observations in Equation 11.4 by getting (1) probabilities of states $P(s_i|*)$ from the transition function T, and (2) probabilities of actions $P(a_i|*)$ from the optimal stochastic policies after solving the MDPs (Equation 11.9).

11.4.2 What does this mean for current commercial games?

Oh et al. (2014) constructed this algorithm for developing assistants in scenarios where goals and plans may be known a priori, or where the number of goals is constrained, and where planned protocols exist describing how to act in each given situation. For instance, they posited that this could be used in emergencies, with codified response protocols. The question is: how does this technique fare in games where the users come in with many different goals and optimize on a larger set of rewards, and where plans may not be known a priori? The approach may seem too simplistic for current commercial games as it assumes a small state and action spaces. Current games are usually far too complex with thousands of states and actions or more. Further, we have investigated using a similar approach with a very simple game with mixed results. The results do not show great accuracy for prediction of strategies due to players' variation and opportunistic behaviors, which tend to be situational. And even a game with very simple state space can be intractable. We will discuss such an example below.

11.4.3 Applying this approach to games

We used this approach to understand players' strategies and problem-solving patterns as they played a game called *WuzzitTrouble*. *WuzzitTrouble* is a commercial game developed by BrainQuake and released in 2013. The game is designed to teach arithmetic by providing symbolic and narrative-based arithmetic puzzles. The goal of the game is to free creatures called Wuzzits from traps by collecting all the keys in a level. Players can collect keys by moving cogs to the right position on the large wheel as shown in the screenshot. For example, the game starts with the marker is at number 0. It needs to be moved to number 20 and also to number 50 to obtain both the keys needed to free the trapped Wuzzit. Players accomplish this by rotating the large wheel clockwise or counterclockwise using the gears below. The distance, or the number of units, moved by the large wheel depends on the gears. Each small cog can be turned up to five times to generate a five-step turn of the wheel, offering up to five opportunities to collect a key (or another item) with a single move. This is a critical gameplay mechanic to learn in order to free the Wuzzit with the smallest number of moves.

WuzzitTrouble has been instrumented to collect data on each move the player makes. In addition to action data, the logs also include information about players' performance, such as the number of points and stars earned. However, the data collected does not include *player ids*, just *session ids*. Therefore, we cannot uniquely follow players across sessions, but we can identify that a player played one session, since this will have a one-to-one mapping. We have around

100,000 levels completed, 5,000 sessions of varying lengths; 700 sessions played 15 levels or more. For analysis purposes, since we need long sessions for analysis, we chose to limit the analysis to sessions with 15 levels, so our analysis included only 700 sessions.

We used a similar process to the one discussed by Oh et al. (2014). In particular, we were interested in understanding how players learned and progressed through the game. Did they optimize on specific strategies or explore different strategies? Did they struggle to come up with a strategy to solve puzzles in the game? To answer these questions, we used an MDP to generate value functions for different rewards that players might have been optimizing on given the scores that the game uses.

We postulated that players might be optimizing on a score, where the score is the reward. Or they might be optimizing on just passing the level with any score, in this case the reward is just finishing the level. Each of these behaviors can be depicted as following a respective action policy π. For each behavior, we then generated the Value V and Q functions using the following formulae:

$$V^{\pi}(s_0) = E_T \left[\sum_{t \in T} \gamma^t R(s_t, \pi(s_t)) \right] \qquad \text{(Equation 11.10)}$$

$$Q^{\pi}(s_0, a) = R(s_0, a) + E_{s^t \sim T(s_0, a)} \left[V^{\pi}(s^t) \right] \qquad \text{(Equation 11.11)}$$

for all $s_0 \in S$, and $a \in A$, where

- s_0 and s_t are states in the state space S, and $a \in A$ is an action
- R is the reward function, T is the transition function, and γ is the discount factor.
- V^{π} and Q^{π} are functions used to measure the long-term utility (E_T is the expected value computed over all possible outcomes as dictated by transition function T) of following policy π, similar to what was discussed above.

Note that our Q function allows us to compute a rank order of actions, given a state and a hypothetical policy π they may be following. Such a rank, thereafter, referred to as *Q-rank*, would be small—that is, close to "0," for actions that are optimal according to policy π, and far from "0" otherwise. Assuming that players act optimally if they chose a policy π to follow, we can infer which policy, and thus goal, they are pursuing by tracking the Q-ranks of the action sequence players take over time.

Next, to make it easier to track a player's strategies and goals using the afore-mentioned insight, we visualize the player's actions' Q-ranks to see how much he/she deviated from the zero line, which represents the optimal strategies. This can be useful for designers to see how much the player fluctuates from optimal strategies to see if the levels need tuning.

To do this type of comparison, we used simple visualizations (see Figure 11.4). The figure shows how much a player deviated from the two goals, we identified and modeled *Level Passing* (LP) and *Score Maximization* (SM). The way we would read these images is: if the player approaches "0" rank in any of these graphs, it means that the player adhered to that optimal strategy for that goal. The height of a point in the graph represents the amount of deviation from optimal strategy. Therefore, the images show that this player sometimes prioritized SM moves over LP, but at other times prioritized LP moves over SM. Consequently, there was a lot of variance and deviations from ideal patterns. Overall, we see that the player attempted exploration by deviating away from LP's optimal moves, but eventually gave up and fell back to LP before quitting the game. Furthermore, we can aggregate these numbers (by taking the mean of all exhibited actions' Q-ranks in a level) and see variances across levels as shown in Figure 11.5. As we can see from this figure, the player goes back and forth between different optimal behaviors and actions and the variance for each level is high, showing variance within levels as well.

11.4.4 An extension of this approach—POMDP

As previously mentioned, MDPs require a fully observable world state. They assume that the agent has all the information necessary to make its decisions, without any ambiguity in the current situation. They allow probabilistic results

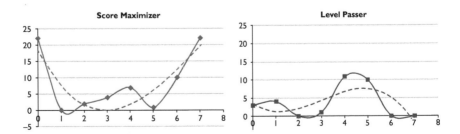

Figure 11.4 Two images showing the Q-ranks of one player as a score maximizer vs. level passer. The graph shows 0 as the optimal for each goal; each action is plotted based on how far it is from the optimal.

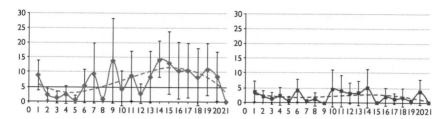

Figure 11.5 Two images showing average Q-ranks in each level where error bars are standard deviations; dotted lines are respective trend lines of the graphs.

of actions but not probabilistic inputs. Partially Observable Markov Decision Processes (POMDPs) relax this assumption. They require only that the world state be consistently defined, such that it is explorable and discoverable, not that it is fully available to the agent in all situations. POMDPs are, therefore, more complex and can find good policies (better than MDPs) for more difficult problems. However, there are currently no general purpose methods for perfectly "solving" POMDPs in a reasonable amount of time.

Baker and Tenenbaum (2014) developed a plan recognition system that uses POMDPs. Because POMDPs can explicitly represent incomplete knowledge about other agents, Baker and Tenenbaum considered reasoning using POMDPs as a form of Theory of Mind[1], which in turn implies that other agents are acting according to a particular internal logic that reflects their current mental state—that is, their beliefs about the world and their desires. Specifically, Baker and Tenenbaum defined Bayesian Theory of Mind (BToM) to be a formal version of Theory of Mind, in which other agents are assumed to act to satisfy their own internal goals according to their own beliefs, but in a way that may not be perfectly optimal or based on unerring rational decision-making. BToM uses probabilistic modeling (with POMDPs) to represent approximate adherence to a rational decision-making process with room for variation and error.

Baker and Tenenbaum (2014) represented the observed agent's beliefs and desires using a DBN, solving forward and backward inference with standard POMDP solution-approximation methods, where the forward modeling of a POMDP represents finding a policy and inferring the agent's plan. This inverse planning approach is common in plan recognition, and in this case, it also naturally incorporates probabilistic uncertainty. Specifically, desires in their model are represented as objects or events. Beliefs are represented as possible

---

[1] It is the idea of ascribing mental states to ourselves and others. This idea is very important for simulating teammates or coordinating agent-human or agent-agent systems.

world states that may be true, associated with probabilities of their truth. The observer agent explicitly tracks the observed agent's likely beliefs and desires, according to a Bayesian model that incorporates uncertainty about both.

Testing this approach in a relatively simple domain, a simulation of a student looking for and choosing between three food trucks, Baker and Tenenbaum (2014) found that their model was more effective in predicting the agent's goals and plans than two simplified models. One of these alternate models assumes that the agent has full knowledge of the world state before beginning its search, essentially treating their reasoning approach as an MDP instead of a POMDP. In the baseline model, the agent's modeled beliefs are fixed, based on a prior distribution of the possible world states, and are not updated as the agent explores the environment. Compared to both simplified models, the BToM model was more successful in describing the internal beliefs and desires of the observed agent in a way that matched manual human judgments.

11.4.5 Can we apply POMDP in current commercial games?

The technique relies on a precise formulation of the problem space as a POMDP. Thus, limitations similar to the ones discussed when using MDP-based techniques apply here. Specifically, there must be a compact world state and a clearly defined forward simulation. Moreover, the prior probability distributions or tables for player beliefs and desires must be set, either by expert determinations or by learning from data. In the case of the simple food truck domain, this is relatively easy: the agents can be expected to travel reasonably short paths towards their desired food truck once they see it. In other games, with more complex decision-making, the problem formulation may not be nearly as easy. Moreover, POMDPs are known to be significantly more computationally complex than MDPs, and inverse planning is more computationally intensive than planning (Baker and Tenenbaum, 2014). In terms of computational hardness, POMDPs are known to be in the class of PSPACE-complete problems (Papadimitriou and Tsitsiklis, 1987), which are much harder than NP-problems with no efficient solution known to exist.

It is unclear whether it is currently computationally feasible to even approximate an inverse planning solution to POMDPs for complex games. Therefore, no wonder we have *yet* to see more examples of this approach used for commercial or modern games. In the future, however, better inverse planning solvers and increased computing power may help to alleviate these concerns, and we may see these approaches become more viable for today's games.

11.5 Markov Logic Networks (MLNs)

11.5.1 The approach

Ha et al. (2014) presented another approach using MLNs to recognize players' goals in an open-ended game. Before we discuss their approach, we will first introduce MLNs. Please note that we assume that you have a fundamental knowledge of first-order logic. If you need a refresher on that, please consult Russell and Norvig's book (2009).

MLNs are similar to BNs, which we discussed earlier in this chapter. The main difference is that MLNs do not have directed edges that represent conditional probability relationships. Instead, they use first-order logic, with weights to represent the probability of each logical statement. For more information about MLNs, see the sidebar "Introduction to Markov Logic Networks."

Introduction to Markov Logic Networks

Markov Logic Networks (MLNs) was proposed as an approach for combining First-Order Logic and probabilistic graphical models (Richardson and Domingos, 2006). Using First-Order Logic, you can represent knowledge in a database, which we can call the knowledge base. The knowledge base represents the state of the world. This is usually represented in the form of predicates, such as $Shot(Jim)$, which can be true or false. We can then define rules such as: $\forall x, Shot(x) \rightarrow Killed(x)$, which means that all people who are shot are killed in the game. Using unification and resolution or logic procedure, we can deduce the fact $Killed(Jim)$, by unifying x/Jim.

MLNs are represented as a knowledge base in first-order logic as discussed above, but with weights attached to each predicate or knowledge clause. This weight then adds flexibility to the logic representation, adding uncertainty; the predicate has a probability of being true or false. This representation can then be viewed as a template for constructing an MN. MNs are similar to BNs, as described above, but are undirected networks—that is, the relationship between variables does not have a specific direction. Similar to BNs, they represent relationships between variables $A \in \{a_1, a_2, \ldots, a_n\}$, where there is a defined joint probability distribution over the variables. Similar to BNs, MNs also have been a subject of research for a long time. The research community has developed various standard algorithms for inference and learning using them. Discussion of the representation and algorithms involved with MNs is out of the scope of this book, but readers are referred to Koller and Friedman (2009).

A first-order knowledge base can be thought of as a representation of possible worlds, where each of these rules is a hard constraint. A world does not exist where one of these rules is violated. With MLN, weights are introduced to relax this assumption and add probability to the mix. Thus, while there can exist a world that violates one of the constraints, it will have a smaller probability than the one that satisfies all constraints. This then introduces the fact that being shot may not always result in death, but being shot and dying are connected with some probability y.

11.5.2 What does this mean for current commercial games?

This approach presents a good possibility for modeling complex relationships within games in a logical fashion, enabling us to reason about players' actions using this model. However, like other approaches discussed above, this approach relies on a large amount of authoring from developers or designers that may render it infeasible with current complex games.

11.5.3 Applying this approach to games

Ha et al. (2014) applied this method to recognize player goals within an open-ended game. The group developed a game that teaches 8th grade microbiology, called *Crystal Island*. Their goal was to recognize players' goals so that they can develop an AI-based coaching or tutoring system within the game.

In order to do that, they formulated the goal recognition problem as a classification problem whereby they try to predict players' goals given a sequence of actions and states using a labeled dataset. They formulated the behavior modeling problem within the game into a set of predicates and rules. These predicates are as follows: $action\,(t, a)\,, loc\,(t, l)\,,$ *and state* (t, s), which denote a player taking action a at time t, while at location l at time t, and the game is in state, s, at time, t, respectively. Each action, location, and state predicate is observable. They defined the predicate *goal* (t, g), which denotes that the player is pursuing goal g at time t. This predicate is the target that needs to be predicted.

They then used MLNs to define relationships and probabilities between these predicates and rules. They used MLNs for two reasons. First, in an open-ended game, players' goals may not be independent of one another. Thus, a technique that can model goal recognition by modeling the relationships between goals, rather than treating them as independent variables, would be important. The second reason is very important—most often, players approach a game without a set goal. Their goal emerges through their interaction. Therefore, there is not necessarily a direct causality between behaviors and goals. Using MLNs, with their undirected graphical representation, is appropriate given this issue.

Using MLNs, Ha et al. (2014) formulated the rules above into the network as shown in Figure 11.6. Using a standard inference algorithm called *Cutting Plane Inference (CPI)*, which provides an efficient method based on Maximum A Posteriori (MAP) inference. Inference here is used to deduce the target *Goal* given the observed predicates of action, state, and location at different time steps and the rule set as described above.

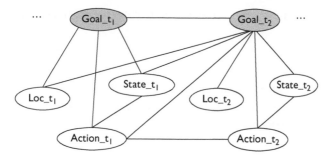

Figure 11.6 Markov logic network used by Ha et al. (2014) in their Goal Recognition Solution. Figure used with permission from Elsevier. Original appeared in Ha, E. Y., Rowe, J., Mott, B., and Lester, J. (2014). Recognizing player goals in open-ended digital games with Markov logic networks. *Plan, Activity and Intent Recognition: Theory and Practice*, 289–311.

Using this example, they evaluated the use of MLN against a baseline and against n-gram model. An n-gram model is a type of probabilistic model that attempts to predict the next item using a sequence of N-1 items preceding it. Ha et al. calculated the F1 value using the confusion matrix, showing that MLNs seem to produce a far better result than n-grams and the baseline. Using their dataset, they showed that MLNs produce 82% improvement over the baseline, producing a 0.484 F1 score compared to 0.266 for the baseline and 0.33 for bigrams. However, such scores are still too low for application in games.

11.6 Recurrent Neural Networks (RNNs) and Deep Recurrent Neural Networks (DRNNs)

11.6.1 The approach

One common difficulty of the approaches discussed above is that they often require significant manual content creation using expert knowledge. For instance, MLNs require expert knowledge of the game design to define a complex set of predicates and rules, and then to construct a network structure to properly form relationships between them. Other approaches described in the previous chapter require manual construction of various forms, including plan libraries, network structures, probability tables, and so forth. Some researchers, therefore, are looking to obviate some of this manual processing using machine learning to automatically extract information from existing game data. Recurrent Neural Networks (RNNs) are used for this purpose.

RNNs are Neural Networks (see Chapter 9) that are designed for processing a sequence of variables and can handle variable length sequences, which would not be practical for ordinary neural networks. The sidebar titled "Introduction to RNNs" gives an overview of the technique.

Introduction to RNNs

Recurrent Neural Networks (RNNs) are Neural Networks with loops in them to allow retention of history information (see Figure 11.7). In this figure, x is the input sequence of vectors, which is represented as $\langle \ldots x_{t-1}, x_t, x_{t+1}, \ldots \rangle$. The output sequence y is represented as $\langle \ldots y_{t-1}, y_t, y_{t+1}, \ldots \rangle$. Note here that each value of x_i and y_i itself can be a vector. The primary differences between RNNs, NNs, and CNNs are the links between the neurons in the hidden layer. Each neuron h_t in the hidden layer takes input from two sources: x_t and h_{t-1}. The links from the previous timestep make the subsequent timesteps dependent on the data that was seen previously in the sequence.

Each rectangular box (in blue) in the network shown in Figure 11.7 is a hidden layer at timestep t, and each holds a number of neurons. The output of a neuron h_t is a function of the input and the output from the previous neuron. $U, V,$ and W represent weight matrices that are to be learned by training the neural network.

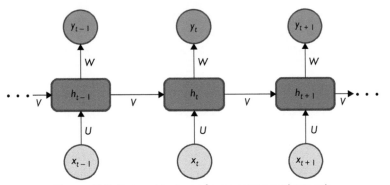

Figure 11.7 Basic architecture of a recurrent neural network.

Training an RNN is similar to ordinary NNs. As discussed in Chapter 9, feedforward networks use *backpropagation* as an algorithm for updating the weights of the network. Similarly, for RNNs, *real-time recurrent learning* and *backpropagation* through time are two of the most popular algorithms used to calculate the weights of the network.

One interesting thing to note here is that the same matrix V and U are applied repeatedly to each timestep. Due to this parameter sharing, the network has fewer parameters to learn and at the same time, it helps to generalize the network. This is also important for information that can occur at different positions of the sequence. Having the same weight matrix would treat the same information at different positions with the same importance.

There are several variations to RNNs based on how the network is configured. The capability of retaining information makes RNNs highly suitable for representing and reasoning about sequence data. However, standard RNNs face a major issue, which limits the amount of information retained due to decays in the network.

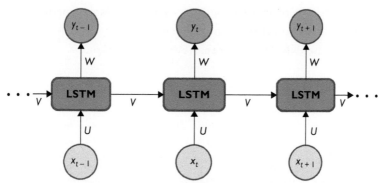

Figure 11.8 Basic architecture of a long–short-term memory model.

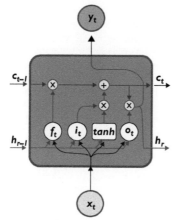

Figure 11.9 The insides of a long–short-term (LSTM) memory block.

Deep Recurrent Neural Networks (DRNN) are similar to the basic RNNs, but where hidden layers are stacked on top of each other or where the RNN layers are interleaved. *LSTM* (Long Short-Term Memory) is a kind of deep RNN proposed by Horchreiter and Schmidhuber (1997). *LSTMs* have memory blocks within its architecture to enable it to store long-term data. The basic architecture is shown in Figure 11.8, as you can see, instead of the hidden units in Figure 11.7, *LSTMs* have *LSTM* blocks. Each of these *LSTM* blocks or cells (shown in Figure 11.9) act as memory cells with gates that decide what old information to forget, what new updates need to happen, and what to output from that layer to the next.

Figure 11.9 shows an *LSTM* cell in detail and the gates inside it. Each gate in the *LSTM* cell has its weight and bias matrices. Each gate inside the *LSTM* cell at timestep t gets the same input h_{t-1} and x_t. The gates use these inputs to generate the cell state which holds the memory of the *LSTM* cell. The following equations show the formulation of *LSTM* cells for each gate during the forward pass.

continued

Introduction to RNNs

$$\text{Forget Gate}: f_t = \sigma\left(V_f h_{t-1} + U_f x_t + b_f\right) \qquad \text{(Equation 11.12)}$$

$$\text{Input Gate}: i_t = \sigma\left(V_i h_{t-1} + U_i x_t + b_i\right) \qquad \text{(Equation 11.13)}$$

$$\text{Cell State}: c_t = f_t \circ c_{t-1} + i_t \circ \tanh\left(V_c h_{t-1} + U_c x_t + b_c\right) \qquad \text{(Equation 11.14)}$$

$$\text{Output Gate}: o_t = \sigma\left(V_o h_{t-1} + U_o x_t + b_o\right) \qquad \text{(Equation 11.15)}$$

In these equations:

- f_t, i_t, o_t are, respectively, activation functions at the forget, input, and output gates of cell t. Notice how these gates process both the current input x_t and the prior cell's hidden state h_{t-1}
- c_t is the state of cell t
- V_k, U_k, b_k with $k \in \{f, i, o\}$ are weight matrices and bias terms of the respective gates
- σ is a sigmoid function

Here, the cell state c_t stores information of data depending on the output from the *forget* and *input* gates. Both *forget* and *input* gates are mathematically similar with distinct weight and bias parameters. Each of them transforms h_{t-1} and x_t, uses the sigmoid function, and outputs a number between "0" and "1," inclusive. To calculate the cell state, there are two parts: first, the output from the *forget* gate is multiplied by the previous cell state. This decides how much previous information needs to be forgotten by the cell. Second, the output from the *input* gate is multiplied by a new candidate value calculated by $\tanh\left(V_c h_{t-1} + U_c x_t + b_c\right)$. As a result, the cell state stores a weighted sum of previous state information and new candidate information. Finally, the output gate behaves similarly to the input and forget gates.

The hidden state and the final output values are similarly calculated using the following equations (Equation 11.16 and 11.17).

$$\text{Hidden State}: h_t = o_t \circ \tanh\left(c_t\right) \qquad \text{(Equation 11.16)}$$

$$\text{Output}: y_t = f\left(W_y h_t + b_y\right) \qquad \text{(Equation 11.17)}$$

The hidden state h_t is calculated using the output from the output gate o_t and the cell state through a **tanh** filter. The final output y_t is calculated using h_t with weight matrix W_y and bias term b_y followed by a softmax function f.

The first RNN-based approach focused on looking into deducing strategies from data was proposed by Bisson et al. (2015). This work builds on the HTN-based model of plan recognition from *PHATT* (Geib, Maraist, and Goldman, 2008; Geib and Goldman, 2009), described above whereby a plan library defined as an HTN is used. An RNN was then used to learn to represent plan hypotheses and determine their probabilities based on particular play-traces.

The training dataset for the RNN consists of a set of pairs *(H, y)*, where *H* is a set of possible hypotheses and *y* is the index of the hypothesis in that set that corresponds to the one the agent is following. Through training, the RNN processes each hypothesis in the set, gives it a score, and predicts the highest scoring one to be the right candidate. Negative log likelihood loss is used to learn the weights that best fit the data and cause it to provide the correct hypotheses for the training examples. This is essentially a multinomial logistic regression or choosing the correct category (the correct hypothesis for the plan and goal) from a set of possible hypotheses.

Bisson et al. (2015) tested this RNN-based prediction for HTN plan libraries against the original approach on different domains, including on the problem of unit navigation in the real-time strategy game *StarCraft*. In all three problem domains, the RNN-based prediction algorithm outperformed the original at nearly all stages of plan completion.

11.6.2 What does this mean for current commercial games?

This approach is very attractive for modeling players' behaviors within game environments, especially when trying to deduce strategies or predict the next action. This is due to the technique outperforming previous work mentioned in this chapter as well as alleviating the expense of using expert knowledge to manually define planning domains and probability distributions. Though the approaches described above do not fully eliminate all the manual work, they reduce some aspects of it. Bisson et al. (2015) increases accuracy relative to nonmachine-learning-based techniques while automatically determining probabilities and vectorized feature representations for their HTN hypotheses. Using RNN, Min et al. (2016) avoided the need for a plan library and manually transforming the world state to extract important features, instead they allowed the *LSTM* to automatically determine the relevant actions and world state features.

However, in spite of these advantages, there are some disadvantages that make the use of RNNs for games problematic. Specifically, as is the case with many machine learning methods, a considerable amount of data is required to train the model. Additionally, the approach lacks an explanation or understanding of the learned strategies or of how the sequences of action data pertain to the goals. For instance, Bisson et al. (2015) provide no clear method for manually interpreting or inspecting the feature vectors or plan to determine why certain replays lead the algorithm to conclude that particular hypotheses are more likely than others. Min et al. (2016) predict goals, but they do not describe a method for expanding their system to predict full plans. Though other researchers are working on improving the interpretability of neural networks, they often rely on visual information to depict the networks' decisions (Olah et al., 2018), which may not apply naturally to plan recognition problems. If you found cases where the RNN-based plan recognition algorithms failed to predict the correct goals or plans, it would be difficult to tweak them to fix those specific cases without gathering additional data and re-training the algorithm, which might introduce other unforeseen problems. For this reason, many game designers currently prefer more interpretable approaches, except in cases where they can review the output manually before it is shown to players.

In other words, while the technique seems to be more feasible to use for commercial games and provides great results compared to other methods discussed in this chapter, it may lack the explainability that may be needed for different stakeholders.

11.6.3 Applying RNN to games

RNNs have been used in game data science for some time. Since RNNs can remember a long sequence of information, it performs better in handling time-series data than other techniques. RNN-based techniques have also been used for procedural content generation as well as AI agent generation (Summerville and Mateas, 2016; Summerville et al., 2016; Lample and Chaplot, 2017). To give an example of using RNN in game data science, we will focus on the work of Guitart et al. (2019), where they devised a method based on RNN to predict churn. Their work won the IEEE CIG 2017 Game data mining competition. An example of churn prediction was discussed above using HMM. Here, we will discuss RNN as an alternative approach.

As with the study discussed above, the goal of this work is to predict if a player will stop playing the game as well as their remaining game lifetime. This was divided into two problems:

1. Predicting if a player would stop playing or not
2. Predicting the time when the player would stop playing

The data used for this work is taken from a multiplayer online game called *Blade and Soul* (NCSoft, 2012). In this work, *tree-based ensemble learning* and RNN, specifically *LSTM*, have been used to solve the two problems.

The datasets consisted of one training and two test datasets. The datasets contained logs of game actions and events with associated information. The first step was to preprocess the data and use some feature engineering techniques. The data contained more than 3,000 variables that included time-series data as well as static features. The two test datasets were of different business models for the game. The first dataset was collected with the game following a subscription-based business model, and the second one was collected with the game following a free-to-play business model. The training dataset contained data for both business models.

LSTM was used to solve the problem of predicting if the player would stop playing. The model was a combined structure of an *LSTM* and a Deep Neural Network (DNN). Figure 11.10 shows the structure of the model used. The intuition behind using the combined model is the nature of the data. The time-series data was given as input to the *LSTM* part, and the static features were given as input to the fully connected layer. Output from both parts were merged into a representative vector which worked as an input layer to another fully connected network with the final output. The final output of the model was to predict a binary result whether the user would churn or not.

The training data was partitioned into training and validation splits to perform cross validation (as discussed in Chapter 8). The parameters were tuned, and the best model was selected from the performance on the validation splits. The evaluation for the binary prediction was done using *F1 score*. The combined *LSTM* and *DNN* model performed best for the second test dataset (the one with the free-to-play games). However, for the first test dataset (the one with the subscription model) *tree-based ensemble learning*, specifically *extremely randomized tree*, worked better for predicting if the player would churn than the combined model.

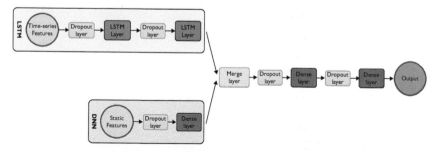

Figure 11.10 *Neural network* architecture to predict whether the user would churn or not.

11.7 Summary

In this chapter, we discussed several advanced techniques used for dealing with sequence data. Specifically, we discussed how such techniques can be used to model, identify, or predict players' strategies, next actions, and churn. We introduced and showed the use of various techniques including:

- Probabilistic methods using classical planning
- BNs and DBNs
- HMMs and POHMMs
- MLNs
- MDP
- RNNs and deep RNNs, specifically *LSTM*

It is important to note that all these techniques have their advantages and disadvantages. We outlined some of these in this chapter. In general, it is important for you to understand whether an interpretable model is necessary for the communication chain in your company or for your research. If it is, then that will eliminate the use of techniques like RNN or deep RNNs in favor of other more white-box approaches. If the prediction rate and accuracy are more important and you have tons of data, then deep RNNs are an option. Moreover, if you are in a domain that is hard to model and you have been modeling by hand in the past, it might be a relief to use RNNs and HMMs as such techniques can learn the structure of the problem automatically with few hyperparameters to tune.

It is also important to note that most researchers or data scientists will use different algorithms, when feasible, as we did in the previous chapters, and compare the results.

Of course, all these techniques are within an area of open research, where new modeling techniques are being proposed that may lead to deeper and better models. Therefore, readers should be up to date with techniques proposed through various forums in the machine learning community, such as NeurIPS (Neural Image Processing Systems) and ICML (International Conference on Machine Learning).

• •

ACKNOWLEDGMENTS

This chapter was written in collaboration with Nathan Partlan, Madkour Abdelrahman Amr, and Sabbir Ahmad, all PhD students at Northeastern University. Nathan's and

Madkour's work and analysis done on the algorithms presented, their application to games, and the example game research work presented are invaluable to this chapter. Further, Sabbir's work on recurrent neural networks is also an important contribution to the work presented. We would also like to thank Profs. Yusuf Pisan, Professor at University of Washington Bothell, and Foaad Khosmood, Professor at Cal Poly at San Luis Obispo, for providing invaluable feedback on this chapter.

BIBLIOGRAPHY

Albrecht, D. W., Zukerman, I., and Nicholson, A. E. (1998). Bayesian models for keyhole plan recognition in an adventure game. *User Modeling and User-Adapted Interaction*, 8(1), 5–47.

Baker, C. L. and Tenenbaum, J. B. (2014). Modeling human plan recognition using Bayesian theory of mind. In Sukthankar, G., Geib, C., Bui, H. H., Pynadath, D., and Goldman, R. P. (eds). *Plan, Activity, and Intent Recognition: Theory and Practice* (Chapter 7, pp. 177–204). USA: Morgan Kaufmann.

Bisson, F., Larochelle, H., and Kabanza, F. (2015). Using a recursive neural network to learn an agent's decision model for plan recognition. In *Proceedings of IJCAI*, pp. 918–24.

Boussemart, Y., Las Fargeas, J., Cummings, M. L., and Roy, N. (2009). Comparing learning techniques for hidden Markov Models of human supervisory control behavior. In *AIAA Infotech Aerospace Conference and AIAA Unmanned. Unlimited. Conference*.

Boussemart, Y., Cummings, M. L., Fargeas, J. L., and Roy, N. (2011). Supervised vs. unsupervised learning for operator state modeling in unmanned vehicle settings. *Journal of Aerospace Computing, Information, and Communication*, 8(3), 71–85.

Bunian, S., Canossa, A., Colvin, R., and Seif El-Nasr, M. (2017). Modeling individual differences in game behavior using HMM. *AIIDE*.

Carberry, S. (2001). Techniques for plan recognition. *User Modeling and User-Adapted Interaction*, 11(1), 31–48.

Conati, C., Gertner, A. S., VanLehn, K., and Druzdzel, M. (1997). On-line student modeling for coached problem solving using Bayesian Networks. In *UM97—Proceedings of the Sixth International Conference on User Modeling* (pp. 231–42). Sardinia, Italy.

Conati, C., Gertner, A., and Vanlehn, K. (2002). Using Bayesian networks to manage uncertainty in student modeling. *User Modeling and User-Adapted Interaction*, 12(4), 371–417.

Domingos, P., and Richardson, M. (2006). Markov logic networks. *Machine Learning*, 62(1–2), 107–36.

Forney, G. D. Jr. (1973). The Viterbi algorithm. In *Proc. IEEE*, 61(3).

Ghallab, M., Nau, D., and Traverso, P. (2004). *Automated planning: Theory and practice*. San Francisco, CA: Morgan Kauffman.

Gers, F. A., Schmidhuber, J., and Cummins, F. (1999). Learning to forget: Continual prediction with LSTM. *In proceedings of International Conference on Artificial Neural Networks (ICANN)*, Edinburgh, UK.

Geib, C. W., and Goldman, R. P. (2009). A probabilistic plan recognition algorithm based on plan tree grammars. *Artificial Intelligence, 173*(11), 1101–132.

Geib, C. W., Maraist, J., and Goldman, R. P. (2008). A new probabilistic plan recognition algorithm based on string rewriting. In Proceedings of *Eighteenth International Conference on Automated Planning and Scheduling (ICAPS)*, pp. 91–8.

Graves, A. (2012). *Supervised sequence labelling with recurrent neural networks. Studies in Computational Intelligence.* UK: Springer.

Guitart, A., Chen, P., and Periáñez, Á. (2019). The winning solution to the IEEE CIG 2017 game data mining competition. *Machine Learning and Knowledge Extraction, 1*(1), 252–64.

Ha, E. Y., Rowe, J., Mott, B., and Lester, J. (2014). Recognizing player goals in open-ended digital games with Markov logic networks. In Sukthankar, G., Geib, C., Bui, H. H., Pynadath, D., and Goldman, R. P. (eds). *Plan, Activity and Intent Recognition: Theory and Practice* (Chapter 7, pp. 289–311). USA: Morgan Kaufmann.

Hochreiter, S. and Schmidhuber, J. (1997). Long short-term memory. *Neural Computation, 9*(8), 1735–80.

Horvitz, E., Breese, J., Heckerman, D., Hovel, D., and Rommelse, K. (1998, July). The Lumiere project: Bayesian user modeling for inferring the goals and needs of software users. In *Proceedings of the Fourteenth Conference on Uncertainty in Artificial Intelligence* (pp. 256–65). Morgan Kaufmann Publishers Inc.

Hovland, G., Sikka, P., and McCarragher, B. (1996). Skill acquisition from human demonstration using a hidden Markov model. In *International Conference on Robotics and Automation* (pp. 2706–11), Minneapolis, MN.

Kabanza, F., Bellefeuille, P., Bisson, F., Benaskeur, A. R., and Irandoust, H. (2010). Opponent behavior recognition for real-time strategy games. In Proceedings of *5th AAAI Conference Workshop on Plan, Activity and Intent Recognition*, pp. 29-36.

Koller, D. and Friedman, N. (2009). *Probabilistic graphical models: principles and techniques.* Cambridge, MA: MIT Press.

Lample, G. and Chaplot, D. S. (2017, February). Playing FPS games with deep reinforcement learning. In *Thirty-First AAAI Conference on Artificial Intelligence*, pp. 2140–6.

Matsumoto, Y. and Thawonmas, R. (2004). MMOG player classification using hidden Markov models. In *Entertainment Computing–ICEC 2004*.

Min, W., Mott, B. W., Rowe, J. P., Liu, B., and Lester, J. C. (2016, July). Player goal recognition in open-world digital games with long short-term memory networks. In *IJCAI* (pp. 2590–6).

Nagarajan, R., Marco, S., and Sophie, L. (2013). Bayesian networks in R. New York: Springer.

Nau, D., Cao, Y., Lotem, A., and Munoz-Avila, H. (1999, July). SHOP: Simple hierarchical ordered planner. In *Proceedings of the 16th International Joint Conference on Artificial Intelligence-Volume2* (pp. 968–73).

Nguyen, T. H. D., Subramanian, S., Seif El-Nasr, M., and Canossa, A. (2014). Strategy detection in Wuzzit: A decision theoretic approach. ICLS Workshop.

Oh, J., Meneguzzi, F., and Sycara, K. (2014). Probabilistic plan recognition for proactive assistant agents. *Plan, Activity, and Intent Recognition* (p. 10, 23). The Netherlands: Elsevier, Amsterdam.

Ogawara, K., Takamatsu, J., Kimura, H., and Ikeuchi, K. (2002). Modeling manipulation interactions by hidden Markov models. In *International Conference on Intelligent Robots and Systems* (pp. 1096–101).

Olah, C., Satyanarayan, A., Johnson, I., Carter, S., Schubert, L., Ye, K., and Mordvintsev, A. (2018). The building blocks of interpretability. *Distill*, 3(3), e10. https://doi.org/10.23915/distill.00010

Orkin, J. (2006). Three states and a plan: The AI of F.E.A.R. In *The Game Developers Conference*. San Francisco, CA, USA.

Papadimitriou, C. H. and Tsitsiklis, J. N. (1987). The complexity of Markov decision processes. *Mathematics of Operations Research*, 12(3), 441–50.

Pearl, J. (1988). *Probabilistic reasoning in intelligent systems: Networks of plausible inference*. San Mateo, CA: Morgan-Kaufmann.

Rabiner, L., and Juang, B. (1986). An introduction to hidden Markov models. *IEEE ASSP Magazine*, 3(1), 4–16.

Ramírez, M. and Geffner, H. (2009). Plan recognition as planning. In *Proceedings of the 21st International Joint Conference on Artificial Intelligence* (pp. 1778–83).

Ramírez, M. and Geffner, H. (2010). Probabilistic plan recognition using off-the-shelf classical planners. In *Proceedings of the Conference of the Association for the Advancement of Artificial Intelligence (AAAI 2010)* (pp. 1121–6).

Richardson, M. and Domingos, P. (2006). Markov logic networks. *Machine learning*, 62(1), 107–36.

Russell, S. and Norvig, P. (2009). *Artificial intelligence: A modern approach*. Third Edition (p. 25, 27). Egnlewood Cliffs: Prentice-Hall.

Seif El-Nasr, M., Draken, A., and Canossa, A. (Eds.). (2013). *Game analytics: Maximizing value of player data*. UK: Springer.

Sirin, E., Parsia, B., Wu, D., Hendler, J., and Nau, D. (2004). HTN planning for web service composition using SHOP2. *Web Semantics: Science, Services and Agents on the World Wide Web*, 1(4), 377–96.

Stratonovich, R. L. (1960). Conditional Markov processes. *Theory Prob. Appl.*, 5(2), 156–78.

Sukthankar, G., Geib, C., Bui, H. H., Pynadath, D., and Goldman, R. P. (Eds.). (2014). *Plan, activity, and intent recognition: theory and practice*. USA: Morgan Kaufmann.

Summerville, A. and Mateas, M. (2016). *Super Mario* as a string: Platformer level generation via lstms. *arXiv preprint arXiv:1603.00930*.

Summerville, A., Guzdial, M., Mateas, M., and Riedl, M. O. (2016, September). Learning player tailored content from observation: Platformer level generation from video traces using lstms. In *Twelfth Artificial Intelligence and Interactive Digital Entertainment Conference*.

Sutton, R. S. and Barto, A. G. (1998). *Reinforcement learning: An introduction* (Vol. 1, No. 1). Cambridge: MIT Press.

Tamassia, M., Raffe, W., Sifa, R., Drachen, A., Zambetta, F., and Hitchens, M. (2016, September). Predicting player churn in destiny: A hidden Markov models approach to predicting player departure in a major online game. In *2016 IEEE Conference on Computational Intelligence and Games (CIG)* (pp. 1–8). IEEE, Santorini, Greece.

Torkaman, A. and Safabakhsh, R. (2019). Robust opponent modeling in real-time strategy games using Bayesian networks. *Journal of AI and Data Mining, 7*(1), 149–59.

Toy, D. (2017). *Improving companion AI behavior in Mimica.* San Luis Opispo, Thesis.

CHAPTER 12

Case Study

Social Network Analysis Applied to In-game Communities to Identify Key Social Players

A s discussed in Chapter 1, the games industry has been experiencing a paradigm shift turning games from products sold on a store shelf to services distributed online and continuously managed and refined to increase customer retention. In the past few years, player retention has become one of the most important metrics, sometimes surpassing player acquisition; entertainment value is measured in hours of playtime. In order to accommodate for this shift in values, commoditization strategies have begun revolving around subscription-based models, free-to-play games with premium content, free updates, premium DLC, and season passes. That shift from a product to a service can be seen in many discussions within the games industry. For example, in an interview, Anne Blondel-Jouin, vice president of Live Ops at Ubisoft, explained: ". . .games as a service, or live games, refer to games that offer an evolving long-term, entertaining experience for our players. They often have a focus on online competitive multiplayer experiences, such as *Tom Clancy's The Division*, but they can also include other types of game experiences like *The Crew* (Wong, 2017)."

As shown by the success and longevity of games such as *World of Warcraft*, *League of Legends*, *Overwatch*, and *Destiny*, social connections foster prolonged retention. One of the most important tools that the industry uses to investigate social connections, especially in online games, is Social Network Analysis (SNA). Examples of SNA methods in game analysis are included in the works of Ang and Zaphiris (2010), Ducheneaut, Yee, Nickell, and Moore (2006), Ho

Game Data Science. Magy Seif El-Nasr, Truong Huy Nguyen Dinh, Alessandro Canossa, and Anders Drachen, Oxford University Press. © Magy Seif El-Nasr, Truong Huy Nguyen Dinh, Alessandro Canossa, and Anders Drachen (2021). DOI: 10.1093/oso/9780192897879.003.0012

and Huang (2009) and Park and Kim (2014). Similar to the literature on online communities (Kraut et al., 2012), studies within the games' domain suggest that there are as few as 1% of the members who can be coined as key contributors who keep the community alive. Pirker et al. (2018) utilized SNA to investigate play patterns of players who play with the same people and those who play with random groups, and how such patterns impact performance in the game *Destiny*. There is much more work within this domain; interested readers are encouraged to search for more fascinating research.

In this chapter, we will discuss an example to illustrate how SNA is applied to address the problem of retention using *Tom Clancy's The Division* (*TCTD*) as a case study. The hypothesis driving this research was that players' behaviors are influenced by social contagion: "we do what our network does." This means that players interacting with influential individuals will tend to play longer, and thus increase the players' playtime and social play, and eventually they will in turn become influential individuals.

SNA tools can help understand who the most influential players are in a live online social game using methods that were briefly introduced in Chapter 1, but will be detailed here, specifically: modularity, centrality, and prestige measures.

There is no agreement on what an influential person is (Riquelme and Gonzalez-Cantergiani, 2016). However, two types of influencers can be distinguished in previous work: (1) an individual who impacts the spread of information or behavior—people who influence people (Weimann, 1991) and (2) an individual who exhibits some combinations of desirable attributes, such as trustworthiness and expertise, or network attributes—connectivity or centrality (Keller and Berry, 2003). For this work, we will define influential players as players who make exceptional use of social features, such as creating groups for multiplayer sessions. They have a marked impact on the community, which can be measured in terms of both increased length and frequency of play-sessions for all members of the sub-community that they helped establish.

Centrality measures have been proven to be relevant indicators in the analysis and comprehension of influencers in a social network (Knoke and Bert, 1983; Bonacich, 1987). The most utilized measures of centrality are in- and out-degree, betweenness, eigenvector, and closeness; they are all measures of an actor's prominence in a network (Wasserman and Faust, 1994). For an in-depth overview of these measures, please check Chapter 1.6.2.1.

We have not included labs in this chapter. However, in this chapter, you should expect to learn about the game *TCTD*, the dataset we used, and how SNA was used to determine influential players. Datasets recommended for this type of analysis must contain nodes representing IDs of players and edges representing actions performed by one player on another player. As an exercise, you can try to apply these methods on the datasets available publicly or elsewhere in the book.

12.1 The game: *Tom Clancy's The Division (TCTD)*

TCTD is an online-only open-world RPG shooter game, set in a near-future New York City in the aftermath of a smallpox pandemic. Two screenshots of the game are shown in Figure 12.1. The player, an agent of Strategic Homeland Division, must help the group rebuild its operations in Manhattan, investigate the nature of the outbreak, and combat criminal activity in its wake. Released in March 2016, *TCTD* accumulated more than 20 million players, becoming the fastest selling new IP (Intellectual Property) of all times. As of September 2017, there were almost 2 million active monthly players.

TCTD combines elements of role-playing games with collaborative Player versus Environment (PvE) and Player versus Player (PvP) online multiplayer activities. It is possible to play and replay all the story missions and side missions with up to four real players in co-op (PvE). Alternatively, it is possible to enter a PvP area called the *Dark Zone* and challenge other players. In PvE, the activities are completing any of the main or side missions, engaging in search and destroy

Figure 12.1 Screenshots of group play and group management in *Tom Clancy's The Division*: (a) group play; (b) group management. Copyright Ubisoft; figures published with permission from Ubisoft.

and high-value target missions, encountering random hostiles, and participating in the incursions. In PvP, the activities are going rogue, extracting newly acquired loot, stopping an extraction in progress, and clearing landmarks[1].

All activities, in both PvP and PvE, can be completed solo or in groups. Groups are composed of the group creator and up to three other players. Groups can be created through "quickmatch" with random players or with players already connected as friends through Xbox Live, PlayStation Network, or Uplay accounts. Uplay is a multiplayer and communications service for PC, used exclusively by first-party Ubisoft games. Groups can be created or joined at safe houses and social hubs scattered around the game area or right before beginning any given activity. Ubisoft maintains official forums for all the games published, which are, amongst others, used to find and connect with players for group activities. In fact, the group discussion channel is the third most popular out of eight channels on the *TCTD* official forums.

Churn here is defined as a period of at least one month without logging in. A playtime segmentation report showed that active players spent more than 60% of their time playing in groups, while players who churned the game spent less than 37% of their time in groups. Based on that and the existing literature, we hypothesize that social dynamics have a big impact on player retention. Therefore, SNA is the exact analysis tool needed to identify influential players. Let us start looking into this by first looking at the type of data collected through the game.

---

[1] There are several types of missions that can be described as follows: *Search and Destroy missions*: challenging tasks catering to players in the later stages of the game. Players will need to take out various groups of level 30 enemies, and once they do, they can gain access to *High Value Target missions*, which are missions where players are tasked with taking out elite enemies at level above 30. These missions are more difficult, so players may need to team up with other players, but the reward consists of high-end weapons and gears. *Incursions* are a type of mission only available after the last mission is complete. They are considered among the most difficult PvE content in the game. Going rogue: it is the act of behaving maliciously toward another player in the Dark Zone; it causes the player that went rogue to become target of regular players by rewarding the kill of a rogue with rare loot. *Extraction*: all the loot collected in the Dark Zone (PvP) is contaminated. When players pick this loot up, they will be marked with a flag that makes them a target for other players. If players want to keep the loot, they need to extract it by navigating to specific points in the Dark Zone and calling in for an helicopter extraction, wait 90 seconds and then attach the loot to the rope that will be unrolled from the helicopter. Extractions can be stopped by any player at any time. *Clearing landmarks*: There are 25 recognizable buildings or locations in New York's Dark Zone that have been taken over by gangs and killing the gang leader is rewarded with loot.

12.2 The dataset

Since the original authors of this work are employees at Ubisoft, they had access to data collected by both the Uplay platform and the *TCTD* game. But to reduce the computational time for this analysis, instead of working with the whole dataset from more than 14 million players, an initial random sample of 200,000 PC players was polled from *TCTD*, and we then included all their friends on Uplay who also own *TCTD*, which led to a sample of 246,041 players; this will be referred to as the initial sample. This initial sample was polled in April 2017 of PC players only, because our access to account data was limited to the Uplay service. Including PS4 and Xbox players would have required special permission from Sony and Microsoft. In addition, we made sure to include the friends of the sampled players as we were interested in exploring communities, and thus, not including their friends would impose an incomplete network. The total population at the time of polling was 14,716,507 players, making the initial sample account for 1.7% of the population.

The dataset consists of two tables. The first table has the IDs of the group creators, the time of group creation, the IDs of players invited to each group, and their status (friend on Uplay or quickmatched). The second table has various statistics for each player in the group, such as their total and daily playtime and number of friends.

12.3 Data analysis

We used conventional SNA techniques to identify influencers in our dataset. Given that there is no agreement on which individual measure to utilize when identifying influencers, we used six different measures of centrality: closeness, betweenness, eigenvector, in-degree, out-degree, and page rank. All the sets of players identified by each centrality measure are intersected with each other to identify the players that are considered central for each of the six measures. In this work, we define influencers as players who satisfy all these six conditions.

We then plotted the resulting influencers onto a network graph where the nodes represent the players and the color of a node indicates the community (module) the node belongs to. The resulting super graph is depicted in Figure 12.2. The size of the nodes is proportional to the importance of a player. Hence, influencers display a much bigger size than normal players.

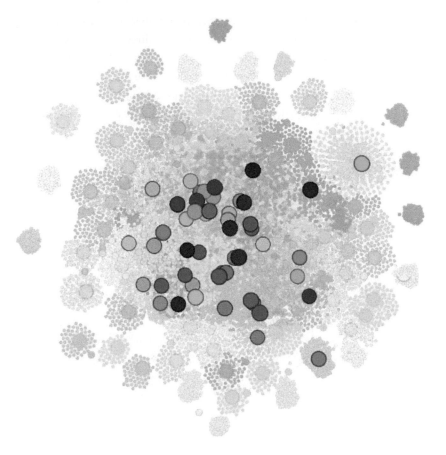

Figure 12.2 The 49 identified influencers mapped on the super-graph using conventional SNA techniques.

12.3.1 Identifying influencers

We first computed centrality measures, which aim to quantify the "influence" of a particular node within a network. Our aim was to identify communities using modularity, and then within each community, point out which player may be more influential. To accomplish this, we considered the following measures:

1) Closeness centrality: How easily accessible a node is to all other players, represented as the length of the shortest path. The average farness (inverse distance) by which a player accesses all other players ranges between 0 (not connected) and 1 (shortest distance). We selected all nodes with values > 0, resulting in 182 players.

2) Betweenness centrality: It represents the number of shortest paths to other players, or how likely a player is the most direct route between two other players. A score of 0 means that the node is not on any shortest paths. We selected all nodes with values > 0; resulting in 78 players.

3) In-degree (prestige): Number of connections to a node from others. These are players invited most often to groups. The range is between 0 and 5; we selected all nodes with values => 2, resulting in 371 players.

4) Out-degree: number of connections from a node to other nodes. These are group creators that frequently invite other players. Values range between 0 and 630, and we selected all nodes with values > 0, resulting in 165 players. In- and out-degree together tell us how many players a certain player can reach directly.

5) Eigenvector centrality: While degree centrality (defined above) counts all connected nodes equally, eigenvector centrality treats connected nodes differently based on their "importance," or how well a player is connected to others. The range is between 0 and 1. We selected all nodes with values > 0.05, resulting in 198 players.

6) Pagerank: What fraction of players can be reached via directed paths. It uses links as a measure of importance. Each node is assigned a score based on its number of incoming links (its "in-degree"). These links are also weighted depending on the relative score of its originating node. The result is that nodes with many incoming links are influential, and nodes to which they are connected share some of that influence. The scores range between 0.000063 and 0.000059. We selected all nodes with values > 0.00006, resulting in 178 players.

As is shown in Figure 12.3, we are interested in the intersection between the sets of players meeting the threshold criteria for each measure. This intersection returned 49 players. These 49 players will be referred to as influencers from now on. It is important to note how intersecting across the six measures of centrality gives us a very conservative selection of players, since in order to be considered influencers, they must satisfy all six criteria.

Figure 12.2 shows the network divided into communities using modularity measures (color coded); there are three types of communities, entangled (at the center of the network), peripheral (at the edge of the network but still connected to other communities), and floating (disconnected from other communities). In all, 47 out of 49 influencers map onto the entangled sub-communities that form the heart of the network, indicating a high level of overlap where players are members of several communities.

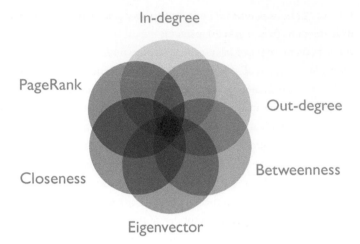

Figure 12.3 Intersection among players with the highest centrality regarding closeness, eigenvector, betweenness, in/out-degree, and pagerank.

12.3.2 Sampling comparison players: Power users and baseline players

After we identified the influential players, we sampled a group of comparison players to get a better understanding of who these influencers are and what characteristics they possess that differentiates them from other players. Because we hypothesized that playtime and/or social play alone cannot explain the effect on other players, for this comparison group, we selected the most engaged players in the whole population—generally known as power users. It is important to note that power users belong to an already existing category of players; within Ubisoft, they are known as star players[2]. Ubisoft routinely invites star players to special events and sees them as an important resource for community building. With this in mind, it is legitimate to wonder whether power players could count as another influencer type (e.g., the "celebrities, evangelists, or experts," the traditional social media influencers). There may be some overlap between these categories. However, as our data offers no good, easy indicator of popularity and status within the player community, we cannot test this assumption. In the context of *TCTD*, *power users* are defined as players with:

---

[2] Star Player Official Page. https://www.ubisoft.com/en-gb/community/star-players

- At least 70 hours playtime. The whole player population has an average playtime of 67 hours and 20 minutes.
- At least 10 friends on Uplay. On average, players have 8.60 friends.
- *Gearscore* in the top 5%. *Gearscore* is an indicator for how well-equipped players are. Every weapon or piece of gear found after reaching level 30 (the level cap) has a *Gearscore* value. The higher an item's *Gearscore*, the stronger the item is, making it a more valuable field asset. The overall *Gearscore* of players defines their progression after the "end-game" (i.e., completing all the story missions).
- At least played twice in groups in the week before we polled the sample. We added this criterion to ensure that the power users made extensive use of the multiplayer functionalities of the game.

Applying these criteria to our initial sample led to 2,102 power users (less than 1% of the sample). It is interesting to compare influencers to power users because we made no effort to remove influencers from the initial sample, yet no influencer was found amongst the power users group. A third comparison was carried out with a baseline population, and so from the initial sample of 246,041 players, we removed the 49 influencers and the 2,102 power users, leaving 243,890 baseline players.

Additionally, we intended to longitudinally compare the impact that influencers, powers users, and baseline players may have on others. For that purpose, we needed to extend our samples. First, we selected all players who engaged with the 49 influencers ($n = 16,742$), all players who engaged with 49 power users randomly selected from the 2,102 initial power users sample ($n = 1,346$), and all players who engaged with the 49 baseline players randomly selected from the initial sample ($n = 560$). For the latter sampling, we excluded players with less than 1 week of total playtime. This sample will be used in Section 12.4.2.

Lastly, we examined if there was behavior transfer from influencers to the players they interacted with by re-running the influencer identification method from Section 12.3.1 after a year had passed. For this, we needed to extend the three samples. We selected all players who interacted with the 49 influencers and who were still active a year later ($n = 3,901$) and added all players that interacted with them ($n = 99,672$); we also selected all players who interacted with the 49 power users and who were still active a year later ($n = 390$) and added all players that interacted with them ($n = 8,725$); and finally we selected all players who interacted with the 49 baseline players and who were still active a year later ($n = 28$) and added all players that interacted with them ($n = 302$).

12.3.3 Constructs and measures

As discussed before, to evaluate our hypotheses, we focused on two constructs: playtime and social play. Both constructs are measured as follows:

- Playtime: Average daily playtime calculated only for days of activity.
- Social play: Ratio of solo vs. group play.

Playtime is used as a proxy for retention. Social play is also used as an indicator of how long a player will be engaged with a game, as we hypothesize that players will value the social dimension of play most.

Both measures were chosen in the context of *TCTD*. For example, we chose to use playtime and not days played because it fits better with the game's monetization model: players need to play "enough" every day to see value in buying upgrades or subscriptions. Days played would not offer this level of granular information.

12.4 Results

12.4.1 Descriptive statistics

Table 12.1 shows an overview of the three groups: influencers, powers users, and the total population. The comparison is based on the whole lifetime of players. On average, it turns out that the powers users are indeed the powers users we would expect; they have more sessions played, more daily playtime, but especially far more playtime, kills, skill kills (i.e., killing enemies with particular abilities), and items extracted compared to the influencers and the total population. For example, power users (454 hours) played almost four times more than the influencers (119 hours) and seven times more than the baseline population (67 hours). The influencers, on the other hand, have on average far more friends (208) compared to the power users (26.5) and baseline population (8.60), but especially interact with others (342) more in group play than power users (27) and the baseline population (11). Interestingly, both influencers and power users spent about two-thirds of their time in group play, whereas this is the reverse for the baseline population. Another interesting observation is that for performative measures (e.g., kills, skill kills, and items extracted), influencers perform similar to the baseline population. As for group play, power users spent only marginally more time than influencers (61%) and power users (67%) in group vs. solo play and competitive vs. cooperative play, but especially

Table 12.1 *Comparison of the three populations: Influencers, power users, and total population.*

	Influencers	Power users	Total population
Total # players	49	2,102	243.890
# Sessions M(SD)	178.27 (313.94)	213.71 (258.13)	44.54 (442.5)
# Kills, M(SD)	7,353 (5,286)	26,937 (55,374)	6,849 (10,738)
# Skill kills, M(SD)	1,172 (1,719)	5,385 (4,261)	1,041 (3,247)
# Items extracted, M(SD)	437 (328)	1,561 (3,566)	513 (1,895)
# Friends M(SD)	208.07 (104.59)	26.51 (32.42)	8.60 (36.35)
# Groups created M(SD)	87.94 (90.82)	205.03 (301.12)	22.36 (138.46)
# Groups joined M(SD)	47.19 (148.42)	173.40 (137.21)	20.38 (52.17)
# Players interacted with M(SD)	341.89 (229.47)	27.05 (274.69)	10.72 (306.43)
Tot. playtime (hours) M(SD)	119.63 (98.51)	454 (172.37)	67 (217.38)
Daily playtime (hours) M(SD)	2.56 (1.64)	3.39 (1.96)	1.56 (1.47)
Time spent in group/solo play	61%–39%	67%–33%	38%–62%
Time spent in coop/competitive play	53%–47%	46%–54%	49%–51%
Official forum posts (<10 posts)	22%	8%	0.2%
Official forum posts (>10 posts)	8%	2%	0.03%

they created (205) and joined (173) many more groups compared to influencers and the average players.

However, these numbers are somewhat deceiving. When we consider their total playtime, it turns out that on average power users create 0.45 and join 0.38 groups per hour; the average player creates 0.38 and joins 0.30 groups per hour; and influencers create 0.74 and join 0.39 groups per hour. Therefore, it shows that power users are only marginally more engaged per hour than the average player and that influencers take far more initiative in creating groups.

In terms of group play, it is also interesting to consider with whom both influencers and power users played. On average, power users play with 27 other players in their lifetime. This is interesting because the number of players that power users interact within groups (27) is very close to the number of friends

(26.5), indicating that power users tend to play almost exclusively with their friends. At the same time, each influencer plays on average with 342 other players, a larger number compared to the already large number of their friends (208), indicating that influencers play in groups with considerably more players than just their friends.

Therefore, while power users spend on average about equal amounts of time in group play, they are more likely to play with friends rather than strangers.

Additionally, we aimed to explore non-game-related behaviors such as posting on official *TCTD* forums. The success of a game, and thereby the well-being of the community, depends in part on meta-gaming activities, that is, activities that take place outside of the game itself but are about the game, such as discussing strategies, providing tips and suggestions, or sharing experiences. Meta-gaming also relies on the effort of certain individuals (Salovaara, Johnson, Toiskallio, Tiitta, and Turpeinen, 2005), and forums are the prototypical form of meta-gaming. Therefore, if the identified influential players are very active on forums, it will strengthen our findings.

For this effort, we only considered the official Ubisoft forum called *The Division forums*, which at the time of consideration had a population of 26,632. This means that less than 1% of the total population of *TCTD* players is active on this site. There are many other dedicated *TCTD* forums; however, it would have been more difficult, if not impossible, to match people posting on these forums with their play stats. We extracted data from the official Ubisoft forum because users will have to login using their Uplay account, and therefore, we were able to match forum-posting behavior with their player statistics. It is not surprising to find out that for our small sample of 49 for each group, 22% of the influencers posted between 1 and 10 times on the official forums, while that number decreased to 8% for the power users and to 0.2% for the baseline population. This pattern is exacerbated when examining the ratio of the three populations that posts more than 10 times on the official forums.

Figure 12.4 shows a direct comparison of the measures that distinguish the influencers, namely playtime, number of friends, and reach, defined as the number of people that players interacted with in multiplayer.

12.4.2 Evaluation of impact

Once we explored the superficial differences between the three populations, we wanted to see the impact of interacting with each one. First, we isolated all players who played with the 49 influencers (16,742), all players who played

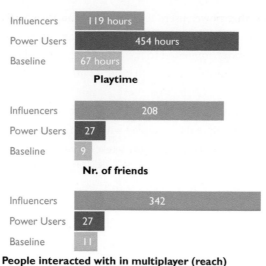

Figure 12.4 Direct comparison for the three measures that set the influencers apart.

with 49 randomly selected power users (1,346), and all players who played with 49 randomly selected baseline players (560) at least twice in the week before polling the data. Next, we split the data based on their communities in two: data regarding play behavior corresponding to the two weeks before joining the community (operationalized as being added as friends on Uplay) and data regarding play behavior for the two weeks after joining the community. Finally, we compared daily playtime and social play ratio two weeks before and two weeks after joining the communities of the influencers, power users, and baseline players, respectively.

Results are shown in Figure 12.5. There is a clear change and impact on the behavior of players who join the community of the influencers: the daily playtime increases considerably, from a number very close to the average of the baseline population to a number very close to the influencers themselves; the amount of time spent in groups increases from the total population average to almost the same amount of the influencers. In contrast, for players who played with power users, both the daily playtime and social play do not change drastically. The numbers are also similar to the powers users themselves, suggesting that not only do power users play together with their (limited) group of friends (see Table 12.1) but they are also likely to play together with other power users. Engaging with random players does not change behavior and, as expected here, the statistics are similar compared to the total population.

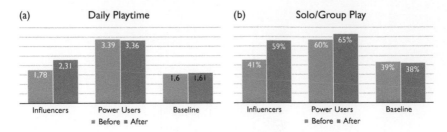

Figure 12.5 Examining changes in behavior (two weeks before and two weeks after) in players engaging with influencers, power users, and the baseline. The behaviors examined are (a) daily playtime and (b) social play.

Paired-samples t-tests were conducted to compare daily playtime (DV1) and social play (DV2) two weeks before joining a community (condition1) and two weeks after (condition2); see Table 12.2.

As for the playtime (DV1), there was a significant difference for the daily playtime of players interacting with influencers before ($M = 1.78, SD = 1.41$) and after ($M = 2.21, SD = 1.36$) they joined the influencers' community; $t(16,741) = 28.83, p = .001, r = .22$. No significant effect on daily playtime was witnessed for players interacting with power users two weeks before ($M = 3.39, SD = 2.43$) and after ($M = 3.36, SD = 2.35$) joining their community; $t(1345) = -0.26, p = .796, r = .007$. For the random sample of players, there was also no significant effect on daily playtime, two weeks before ($M = 1.6, SD = 1.49$) and after ($M = 1.61, SD = 1.42$) joining their community; $t(559) = 0.14, p = .885, r = .005$. These results support the hypothesis that joining a group with an influencer did, in fact, increase the daily playtime of players, at least in the first two weeks after joining, while the same could not be stated of power users or a random sample of players during the same period.

As for social play (DV2), joining an influencer's community significantly changed the ratio from two weeks before ($M = 0.41, SD = 0.27$) to after ($M = 0.59, SD = 0.16$); $t(16,741) = 74.32, p = .001, r = .50$. This ratio change was also significant for players joining a power user's community compared to their situation two weeks before ($M = 0.6, SD = 0.23$) and after ($M = 0.65, SD = 0.27$) joining them; $t(1,345) = 4.79, p = .001, r = .13$. For a random sample of players, two weeks before ($M = 0.39, SD = 0.29$) and after ($M = 0.38, SD = 0.27$) joining groups, it did not significantly change their social play ratio; $t(560) = -0.54, p = .588, r = .002$. These results support the hypothesis that the ratio of playing in groups significantly increased for players

Table 12.2 Changes in the influencers', power users', and random players' communities two weeks before (condition 1) and two weeks after (condition 2) engaging with influencers, power users, and random players.

	Influencers		Power users		Random players	
	Condition1	Condition2	Condition1	Condition2	Condition1	Condition2
DV1—Daily playtime (hours), M (SD)	1.78 (1.41)	2.21 (1.36)	3.39 (2.43)	3.36 (2.35)	1.60 (1.49)	1.61 (1.42)
DV2—Social play (ratio, group/solo)	41%–59%	59%–41%	60%–40%	65%–35%	39%–61%	38%–62%

joining an influencer's community, at least in the first two weeks after joining. While a significant increase in group play happened with joining power users as well, their impact is less. The effect size for influencers is large (.50) resulting in an average increase of 18% in group play, whereas the effect size for power users is small (.13) resulting in an average increase of only 5% of group play.

12.4.3 Retention and conversion to influencer

Lastly, we wanted to see what kind of impact influencers may have on other players beyond this period. For this analysis, we first considered if players are still actively playing *TCTD*. In our previous analyses, we used playtime and social play as measures because these can indirectly tell us about retention: more engaged players and players engaged in the multiplayer aspects of a game tend to stick around longer. But we can also directly measure retention. To calculate it here, we looked at which of the players who joined the communities of the influencers, power users, and baseline players were still active after one year. Figure 12.6 shows the retention results. After one year, 23% of the influencers' community is still active, whereas this is true for 29% of the power users' community and only 5% of the baseline players' community.

We also incorporated a second more ambitious consideration: which of the players from these communities may have become influencers themselves. As we have demonstrated, influencers have an impact on other players. Therefore, if these players are converted into influencers, they, in turn, can influence others—and thereby keep the community alive, even if certain influencers decide to leave the game. For this analysis, we first applied the same method for identifying the original 49 influencers except a year later (see Section 12.3.1). Then, we considered which of the newly identified influencers mapped onto the players from the initial population that the original influencers, power users, and random players engaged with. Figure 12.7 shows the conversion results, which are remarkable. From the community of the random players, only two

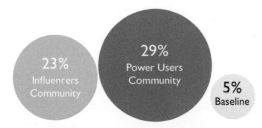

Figure 12.6 Retention rate of the community of the three populations after one year.

Figure 12.7 Conversion rate of players to influencers.

players were identified as an influencer a year later, which is a conversion rate of 1% based on the still active players in that community. The influence of power users is greater than that of random players: from their community, 22 players are identified as an influencer resulting in a rate of 6%. In contrast, as we hypothesized, the influence of influencers is far greater than the random players and power players; from the community of influencers, we identified a staggering number of 1,002 influencers, which corresponds to a rate of 26%.

12.5 Discussion and conclusion

We discussed an example use of SNA to identify influencers. As you can see from this example, SNA is a very powerful method to identify key members who are heavily engaged (as expected) both in number of friends and groups created and in the number of forum posts. In addition, it is interesting to see the comparison between influencers and power users.

Please note that you can use many other metrics to identify influencers using forum posts. For example, with text mining and sentiment analysis, a novel metric can be defined that uses the influential responses in online health community forums (e.g., Zhao et al., 2014).

In this chapter, however, we used conventional SNA techniques to identify key members who are very engaged with the game but also with other players. The question we investigated is whether these so-called influencers really influence other player's behavior, as measured by their playtime and social play, and if they do so more than other players. Our results provide supporting evidence that influencers do indeed impact other players, and more so than others.

Homophily is always a possible confound in social contagion work (Christakis and Fowler, 2013). For this reason, we ran a quasi-experimental analysis comparing playtime and social play ratio pre/post joining the team of an influencer vs. power player vs. normal player (Figure 12.5 a and b). Homophily (i.e., influencers attract already-social and already-active players) would predict higher overall playtime and social play ratio among influencer team members, but not the significant changes we observed. This makes us confident in claiming causality that influencers are socially contagious.

Retention is a key measure for success in the games industry. Our results suggest that not only are influencers socially contagious but they are also important for retention. While the retention is higher for power users, it should be kept in mind that influencers are able to retain 10 times the number of players and that power users tend to engage only with similar users, so their influence is more of a reinforcing feedback loop than having an impact on the community at large. What is most striking, however, is that players who have interacted with influencers may become influencers themselves after a year (26% chance). Such influence is not as noticeable with power users (6%) or random players (1%). This data suggests that the social contagion effect of influencers may go as far as converting a significant portion of the players they interact with into influencers. Because we did not (quasi-)experimentally test this or observe whether these new influencers exhibit the same kind of impact, we cannot claim causality here, neither can we fully illustrate what impact this has on the community. However, these results provide further evidence of the important role that influencers play in online game communities, especially with the issue of retention in mind. In fact, as the sustained lifetime of a game depends in large measure on a healthy, lively community of players engaged with the multiplayer aspects of the game, these players seem to form the invisible social backbone of a game community.

It is important to observe that the selected power users are indeed power users: compared to the average player, they have far more kills (four times more), skill kills (five times more), and items extracted (three times more), and play more competitively (3%). Interestingly, the statistics for influencers on these performative metrics are fairly similar to the average player. Therefore, what defines influencers in contrast to power users is that they have a wide-reaching and solid network of friends and an active engagement with the multiplayer aspects of a game rather than an elite performance in the game. Influencers are the social butterflies. Although these metrics highlight the differences between influencers vs. power users vs. average players, it is important to note that these metrics are not sufficient to identify influencers. When applying one or a combination of metrics, it was impossible to achieve the same result. Therefore, SNA seems to be required to identify influencers. The approach we have taken here is to define influencers on the basis of combining six centrality measures and then inspecting the results visually for verification. Future research is needed to further refine this approach and examine how it generalizes to other contexts.

As the industry adopts more of this kind of analysis, we expect to see new methods emerging. Therefore, you are encouraged to continue reading papers from industry and academia if you are interested in this topic.

● ●

ACKNOWLEDGMENTS

This chapter was written as an extension to a paper that received an honorable mention at CHI (Canossa et al., 2019). Therefore, we would like to acknowledge the help of Casper Harteveld (professor, Northeastern University), Sebastian Deterding (professor, York University), and Ahmad Azadvar (User Research Lead at Ubisoft Massive). Further, this research has been accomplished with the support of Ubisoft, the Games Lab, and the Live Ops team at Massive Entertainment.

● ●

BIBLIOGRAPHY

Ang, C. S., and Zaphiris, P. (2010). Social roles of players in MMORPG guilds: A social network analytic perspective. *Information, Communication & Society, 13*(4), 592–614.

Barbieri, N., Bonchi, F., and Manco, G. (2012, December). Topic-aware social influence propagation models. In *2012 IEEE 12th International Conference on Data Mining* (pp. 81–90).

Bartle, R. (1996). Hearts, clubs, diamonds, spades: Players who suit MUDs. *Journal of MUD Research, 1*(1), 19.

Bastian, M., Heymann, S., and Jacomy, M. (2009). Gephi: An open source software for exploring and manipulating networks. *ICWSM, 8*, 361–2.

Bhagat, S., Goyal, A., and Lakshmanan, L. V. S. (2012). Maximizing product adoption in social networks. In *Proceedings of the Fifth ACM International Conference on Web Search and Data Mining* (pp. 603–12). New York, NY, USA: ACM.

Bi, B., Tian, Y., Sismanis, Y., Balmin, A., and Cho, J. (2014). Scalable topic-specific influence analysis on microblogs. In *Proceedings of the 7th ACM International Conference on Web Search and Data Mining* (pp. 513–22). New York, NY, USA: ACM.

Blondel, V. D., Guillaume, J.-L., Lambiotte, R., and Lefebvre, E. (2008, 9 October). Fast unfolding of communities in large networks. *Journal of Statistical Mechanics, 2008*(10), P10008.

Boellstorff, T., Nardi, B., Pearce, C., and Taylor, T. L. (2012). *Ethnography and virtual worlds: A handbook of method*. Princeton, New Jersey: Princeton University Press.

Bonacich, P. (1987). Power and centrality: A family of measures. *American Journal of Sociology*, *92*(5), 1170–82.

Brown, D., and Hayes, N. (2008). *Influencer marketing: Who really influences your customers?* New York: Routledge.

Canossa, A., Azadvar, A., Harteveld, C., Drachen, A., and Deterding, S. (2019, April). Influencers in multiplayer online shooters: Evidence of social contagion in playtime and social play. In *Proceedings of the 2019 CHI Conference on Human Factors in Computing Systems* (p. 259). Glasgow, Scotland: ACM.

Calleja, G. (2007). Revising immersion: A conceptual model for the analysis of digital game involvement. In *Proceedings of DiGRA Conference*, Volume 4, Tokoyo, Japan.

Christakis, N. A., and Fowler, J. H. (2013). Social contagion theory: examining dynamic social networks and human behavior. *Statistics in Medicine*, *32*(4), 556–77

Chen, W., Wang, C., and Wang, Y. (2010). Scalable influence maximization for prevalent viral marketing in large-scale social networks. In *Proceedings of the 16th ACM SIGKDD International Conference on Knowledge Discovery and Data Mining* (pp. 1029–38). New York, NY, USA: ACM.

Chen, W., Wang, Y., and Yang, S. (2009). Efficient influence maximization in social networks. In *Proceedings of the 15th ACM SIGKDD International Conference on Knowledge Discovery and Data Mining* (pp. 199–208). New York, NY, USA: ACM.

The Division Forums. (n.d.). URL: http://forums.ubi.com/forumdisplay.php/498-The-Division (Accessed: 2017-9-17).

Ducheneaut, N., Yee, N., Nickell, E., and Moore, R. J. (2006). Alone together? Exploring the social dynamics of massively multiplayer online games. In *Proceedings of the SIGCHI Conference on Human Factors in Computing Systems* (pp. 407–16).

Hadiji, F., Sifa, R., Drachen, A., Thurau, C., Kersting, K., and Bauckhage, C. (2014, August). Predicting player churn in the wild. In *2014 IEEE Conference on Computational Intelligence and Games* (pp. 1–8).

Hamari, J., and Tuunanen, J. (2014). Player types: A meta-synthesis. *Transactions of the Digital Games Research Association*, *1*(2).

Ho, S.-H., and Huang, C.-H. (2009, 1 May). Exploring success factors of video game communities in hierarchical linear modeling: The perspectives of members and leaders. *Computers in Human Behavior*, *25*(3), 761–9.

Home.Kred. (n.d.). URL: http://kred.com. (Accessed: 2017-9-19).

Keller, E., and Berry, J. (2003). *The influentials: One American in ten tells the other nine how to vote, where to eat, and what to buy.* New York: Simon and Schuster.

Knoke, D., and Burt, R. S. (1983). *Applied network analysis.* Newbury Park, CA: Sage.

Klout, I. (n.d.). Klout—be known for what you love. URL: https://klout.com/home. (Accessed: 2017-9-19).

Kraut, R. E., Resnick, P., Kiesler, S., Burke, M., Chen, Y., Kittur, N., . . . Riedl, J. (2012). *Building successful online communities: Evidence-based social design.* Cambridge, MA: MIT Press.

Lambiotte, R., Delvenne, J. C., and Barahona, M. (2008, 9 December). Laplacian dynamics and multiscale modular structure in networks. arXiv.

Lee, C.-S., and Ramler, I. (2017). Identifying and evaluating successful non-meta strategies in league of legends. In *Proceedings of the 12th International Conference on the Foundations of Digital Games* (pp. 1:1–1:6). New York, NY, USA: ACM.

Newman, M. E. J. (2006, 6 June). Modularity and community structure in networks. *Proceedings of the National Academy of Sciences of the United States of America*, *103*(23), 8577–82.

Park, H., and Kim, K.-J. (2014, 10 November). Social network analysis of high-level players in multiplayer online battle arena game. In *Social informatics* (pp. 223–6). Cham: Springer.

Pearce, C. (2011). *Communities of play: Emergent cultures in multiplayer games and virtual worlds*. Cambridge, MA: MIT Press.

PeerIndex + brandwatch. (n.d.). URL: http://www.peerindex.com/. (Accessed: 2017-9-19).

Pirker, J., Rattinger, A., Drachen, A., and Sifa, R. (2018). Analyzing player networks in Destiny. *Entertainment Computing*, *25*, 71–83.

Riquelme, F., and González-Cantergiani, P. (2016). Measuring user influence on Twitter: A survey. *Information Processing & Management*, *52*(5), 949–75.

Salovaara, A., Johnson, M., Toiskallio, K., Tiitta, S., and Turpeinen, M. (2005). Playmakers in multiplayer game communities: Their importance and motivations for participation. In *Proceedings of the 2005 ACM SIGCHI International Conference on Advances in Computer Entertainment Technology* (pp. 334–7). New York, NY, USA: ACM.

Sotamaa, O., and Karppi, T. (2010). *Games as services-final report* (Tech. Rep.). Finland: Tampere University.

Srivastava, J. (2008, June). Data mining for social network analysis. In *2008 IEEE international Conference on Intelligence and Security Informatics*.

Subbian, K., Aggarwal, C. C., and Srivastava, J. (2016, 8 February). Querying and tracking influencers in social streams. In *Proceedings of the Ninth ACM International Conference on Web Search and Data Mining* (pp. 493–502). ACM.

Subbian, K., Sharma, D., Wen, Z., and Srivastava, J. (2013). Social capital: The power of influencers in networks. In *Proceedings of the 2013 International Conference on Autonomous Agents and Multi-Agent Systems* (pp. 1243–4). Richland, SC: International Foundation for Autonomous Agents and Multiagent Systems.

Taylor, T. L. (2009). *Play between worlds: Exploring online game culture*. Cambridge, MA: MIT Press.

Tondello, G. F., Wehbe, R. R., Orji, R., Ribeiro, G., and Nacke, L. E. (2017). A framework and taxonomy of videogame playing preferences. In *Proceedings of the Annual Symposium on Computer-Human Interaction in Play* (pp. 329–40). New York, NY, USA: ACM.

Wasserman, S., and Faust, K. (1994). *Social network analysis: Methods and applications* (Vol. 8). Cambridge, UK: Cambridge University Press.

Weimann, G. (1991). The influentials: Back to the concept of opinion leaders? *Public Opinion Quarterly*, *55*(2), 267–79.

Williams, D., Ducheneaut, N., Xiong, L., Zhang, Y., Yee, N., and Nickell, E. (2006). From tree house to barracks: The social life of guilds in World of Warcraft. *Games and Culture*, *1*(4), 338–61.

Wong, S. (2017, 10 January). How Ubisoft keeps "The Division" and "Rainbow Six Siege" ahead of the competition. URL: http://www.alistdaily.com/strategy/ubisoft-keeps-division-rainbow-six-sieg (Accessed: 2017-9-19).

Yee, N. (2006, December). Motivations for play in online games. *Cyberpsychology Behavior*, *9*(6), 772–5.

Zhao, K., Yen, J., Greer, G., Qiu, B., Mitra, P., and Portier, K. (2014, October). Finding influential users of online health communities: a new metric based on sentiment influence. *Journal of the American Medical Informatics Association*, *21*(e2), e212–18.

CHAPTER 13

Conclusions and Remarks

A s you come to the end of this book, we hope you have been able to gain more knowledge about the game data science process to help you start exploring, analyzing, and extracting actionable insights from game data. In this chapter, we will summarize the different parts of the game data science process we introduced in Chapter 1. We will then share some notes and words of hard-earned experience when embarking on using the methods discussed in this book. Further, we will open up the topic of ethics, as it is an important topic when you deal with player data. We will then introduce some issues that we did not address in this book, including how to deal with distributed big data, how to build bots from game data, how to use probabilistic models, and what are the overall applications of game data science within the production process.

In conclusion, this book should only be the beginning of your journey. There will always be new algorithms and methods developed that you can try with your game data. Always be on the lookout for these new methodologies. Hopefully, the book gave you enough of a foundation to allow you to explore and understand more advanced techniques proposed and discussed within the games industry and academic research.

13.1 Summary of the game data science process

The book focused on several stages of game data science discussed in Chapter 1 (see Figure 13.1). As you start with any data, remember data

Game Data Science. Magy Seif El-Nasr, Truong Huy Nguyen Dinh, Alessandro Canossa, and Anders Drachen, Oxford University Press. © Magy Seif El-Nasr, Truong Huy Nguyen Dinh, Alessandro Canossa, and Anders Drachen (2021).
DOI: 10.1093/oso/9780192897879.003.0013

Figure 13.1 Applied process of Knowledge Discovery through game data. The figure is reproduced from Seif El-Nasr et al. (2013) with permission from Springer.

preprocessing (discussed in Chapter 2) is an important first step to clean and prepare your data for analysis. It is a tedious process but an important one.

After you clean the data, you want to spend time understanding your data by perhaps going into an exploratory step. For this type of process, you may want to use statistical techniques (Chapter 3), visual analytics (Chapter 5), clustering (Chapter 6), sequence analysis (Chapter 10), or social network analysis (Chapter 12). As you play around with the data, you start to gather an understanding of your data, which will enable you to formulate some hypotheses that you can then evaluate.

When you move from exploration to hypothesis generation and testing, you start to formulate abstractions over your data that can help you address the questions or hypotheses you have formulated (Chapter 4). You can then use several methods from classification and regression (Chapters 7 and 8) to probabilistic graphical models (Chapter 11). These techniques will help you develop predictive models or test a hypothesis.

The final step is usually reporting and productization, which we discussed throughout the book chapters. This requires good confidence in the results and good visualizations to tell a coherent story using the data and results you have gathered to your stakeholders.

As you can see, the chapters in the book focused on all these topics in great detail. Further, the labs and practical examples discussed in each of these chapters helped ground you on how these techniques are applied. Hopefully, through the labs and exercises, you gained enough insights on these foundational techniques. As you move forward with your practice, there are several important points to remember, which we will discuss next.

13.2 Few words of advice on validity and reliability of your results

13.2.1 Ensure correctness

First, you want to make sure your analysis is done correctly. Make sure to validate your results as discussed in each chapter. Also, make sure you use standard methods with a good understanding of the assumptions behind these methods. Throughout the book, we made sure to discuss assumptions of each method, specifically when it comes to the type of data or measures the method uses. As discussed in the chapters throughout the book, some methods assume that the data is normalized, some methods assume that the data is of a certain format or of certain measurement type, and some methods are sensitive to the scales of the variables used. Therefore, you want to make sure you understand and are aware of these assumptions, otherwise your results will not be valid.

Another good practice is to check your results with a colleague. This is often good to establish reliability or correctness. Further, the process of explaining your process or comparing models with another person can help you uncover issues that may not be obvious without reflection.

13.2.2 Replicability and reproducibility

You may be aware of the so-called reproducibility crisis—a methodological crisis that has hit many academic fields, especially psychology and social science, but also many scientific disciplines, such as medicine, biology, and physics. Reproducibility is defined as the ability to obtain results that are consistent with the original study given all the procedures and data are the same. While the percentages reported, on how many published experiments were found to be problematic, varies per field, Baker (2016) stated that 70% of researchers have tried and failed to reproduce other scientist's experiments and 50% have failed to reproduce their own experiments. See Figure 13.2 for more results surveyed per field.

Figure 13.2 shows the factors reported by scientists concerning what they thought affects reproducibility. As you can see, some are caused by the pressure to publish. But some are also avoidable, such as poor experimental design, poor analysis, or insufficient mentoring. This is important to note. As we advised, working with a colleague can help increase the reliability of your results. This can be invaluable in making sure your results are reproducible and correct. We understand that sometimes the pressure of time may be insurmountable within industry and even within academia as deadlines push the team for quick results. However, it is really important to take the time and do the analysis correctly. Having a mentor or partner who works with you in parallel can help keep you on track to avoid these issues.

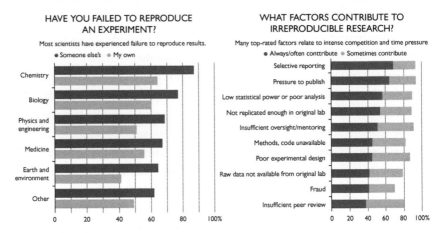

Figure 13.2 Reproducibility issue per field, and what scientists believe the factors affecting such reproducibility crisis is. Figure is reproduced with permission from Springer; the original appeared in Baker, M. (2016). 1,500 scientists lift the lid on reproducibility. *Nature News, 533*(7604), 452.

13.3 Ethics, biases, and data

Ethics is an important topic that has recently gained much attention with books, such as O'Neil's (2016) book *Weapons of Math Destruction*, describing the proliferation of big data in many sectors of our lives. The book describes many issues with using statistical models as measures or scoring mechanisms. Some of these issues, which we will discuss below, are: biases of the results due to imbalance in the amount of data from minorities and lack of trust in the models produced due to lack of transparency.

An important issue that O'Neil's book illuminates is how statistical models developed from big data can disadvantage certain populations. This is due to the elimination of individual differences as an important part of the analysis. For example, imagine you are looking at churn as a variable for your game, if you are building a statistical model from all players in your game, depending on the population you are sampling from, you may be disadvantaging your female players, or novice players, or LGBTQ players, or players of color. If you think about it, statistical models are usually drawn from data, and thus if you have very little data for specific types of players, you will tend to disadvantage this population if you lump them into the same dataset with everyone else. The best way to address this issue is to divide your population and develop models based on the different types of players you have. This way, you do not lump everyone in the same model.

Another important point made in O'Neil's book is the lack of transparency of the models used or developed. For example, let us take Netflix's recommendation system. The system uses specific parameters to recommend some movies for you based on what you have seen before, your ranking, and what other viewers who had similar rankings liked. This is similar to other recommendation systems used in games to recommend items or other games for you to play on Steam, for example. The inner workings of such algorithms are typically unknown to users. However, using transparent models could allow users to tune the recommendation to their own taste. Furthermore, lack of transparency often gives rise to unfounded suspicions or conspiracies. It is in fact common to hear that the Netflix recommendation system mainly suggests shows and films that maximize Netflix revenue rather than users' enjoyment.

This consideration leads to another important repercussion of the use of data: its connection with monetization. It is true that many companies now use data to figure out how to engage users more in the game or to turn unpaying users to paying users. This is not a secret, and in fact it is in most game user agreements. While it is most often the case that increasing user engagement will lead to an increase in sales, such alignment is not always true (Canossa, 2014). Game companies follow a business model to increase or maximize profits, and thus all design decisions made need to lead to monetary gain.

Addiction has also been discussed in the media. In fact, the DSM-5 recognized game addiction as a disorder calling it Internet Gaming Disorder (American Psychiatric Association, 2013). But according to Hodent (2019), there is a lack of scientific consensus that games are addictive. In fact, some other researchers have shown that games have been used as a way to escape from other underlying psychological issues, such as depression (see Rigby and Ryan, 2016). Hodent, in her talk at the Game Developers Conference in 2019, posed the question and made some suggestions of what the industry can do in the face of such ethical issues. Specifically, she discussed working with psychiatrists if addiction may be an issue for the game or working with researchers to define gaming disorders. She also discussed looking into further regulation especially for lootboxes (or skinner boxes) and gambling. As an example, China has put together an oversight committee, the "online games and ethics committee," to oversee the approval of new games in its territory.

Another important aspect of ethics here is user data, privacy, and sharing. While it is great to share data for scientific research and educational purposes, sharing identifiable data is problematic, including chat data that can reveal names of users. While health data is heavily regulated, game user data is not yet. Smith and Browne (2019) discussed some of these issues that the tech industry faces as a whole. They recommended further regulation to help mitigate some of the legal and privacy issues that companies face with such data. We believe such practice needs to also be discussed and imposed on game data as well. As an example, the EU General Data Protection Regulation (GDPR) has laid out some steps toward improving data privacy rights guaranteed by EU law. This is a great first step toward increasing users' privacy.

Additionally, privacy is becoming even more important due to the possibility of uncovering an individual's identity from streams of data, as shown by De Montjoye et al. (2013). Therefore, it is not enough to just anonymize the data anymore, and more work is needed to understand how to protect users' identity and privacy.

There is a lot of information that can be gleaned from game data, including, for example, how someone solves a particular problem or how they behave within risky situations. Is it okay to share this information publicly or even just use this to derive or change the game design? Should not the user be able to opt in or out of this? These are all important questions that you should consider and think about.

13.4 Other topics in game data science

There are several topics that are important to game data science that have not been discussed in this book. However, the book would not be complete without at least mentioning these areas of interest and discussing their implications on game data science.

13.4.1 Distributed big data

With game data now reaching millions and millions of data points collected from millions of users, see *DOTA 2* API as an example, techniques for dealing with big data become important. In terms of data storage and analytics architecture, there have been several advancements over the architecture we used in this book. In the book, for the sake of simplicity, we chose to use log files or CSV files containing all user sessions and information. However, this is not how the games industry is now storing its data. The games industry has also been innovating on the ways data is stored by moving to cloud and serverless computing, where there is a separation between the hardware where data is stored and the software by which the data is accessed and analyzed. A great resource discussing the evolution of the analytics architecture is Weber (2018).

Beyond storage, modeling is also impacted by issues of scale. Most often, with such data, it is hard to upload the whole data into memory, let alone do processing or visualize the whole dataset. There are many techniques for dealing with this issue developed by the data science community. These include distributed processing over distributed databases. One approach currently in practice is to distribute the data; algorithms are then developed to update parameters based on their share of data. Another approach is to distribute the model and allow access to the entire data as each model updates its own parameters. Synchronization happens only when necessary.

However, distributed processing poses many important challenges that we would like to discuss here. First, not all the techniques discussed in this book can be used in a distributed-based architecture. Most often, to parallelize such algorithms, one will need to summarize data or aggregate along the way. Second, there are many questions pertaining to how one can do exploratory data analysis with such distributed architecture.

A great example of how this is done is discussed by Weber (2019). In his article, he discusses how his team developed a distributed serverless platform for analyzing millions of user data through the use of Python and Spark, a fast-general-purpose cluster computing system developed by Apache. He discussed the development of a pipeline composed of several processes, including data extraction, feature engineering, feature application, model training, and model publishing. While these seem similar to what we discussed in the book, the process of dealing with big data involves more abstraction and summarization as data is moved from one process to the other. Further, using Python and Spark enabled them to apply many of the data processing functions, which are usually done on a dataframe (as the ones we discussed in this book), to distributed dataframes. Interested readers should consult the article for more details. It should be noted that R also has libraries to handle distributed databases; please see Parallel and Future packages.

13.4.2 Spatio-temporal analysis

Another important area that we did not discuss in the book is the concept of spatio-temporal analysis. While the discussion provided in Chapter 5 shows how a visualization system can be used for spatio-temporal analysis of game data, there is more that has been done in this area.

Spatio-temporal analytics is vital in game data science for the simple reason that playing games involve action in both of these dimensions, that is, time and space. How our players experience our games occur within these dimensions? Games user research, specifically, has to work with this understanding, and some of the most famous examples of game data science work have been developed via user testing, because user researchers needed to harness the utility of telemetry data (e.g., Kim et al., 2008). It is, therefore, very important to consider them, and we encourage the reader to investigate the references provided in this section.

To begin with, many games involve spatial operations. Whether simple point-and-click vector mechanics, navigation in 2D environments like side-scroller games, or fully-fledged 3D avatar-based movement. The spatial component often forms one of the basic elements in the playing experience. Therefore, the analysis and evaluation of spatial behaviors are important. A good example is discussed by Ubisoft in their analysis of players' paths through the *Assassin's Creed* series; see Dankoff's work (2011).

Similarly, the component of time is important. All game play occurs over time, and it is, therefore, common to consider this dimension. Indeed, many of the basic metrics like daily active users and user lifetime revenue, discussed in Chapter 1, are computed using temporal measures. We know time is important also from churn prediction, progression analysis, time spent analysis, and similar problems that are everyday bread-and-butter in game data science.

Time takes a special meaning when combined with space, because this brings us about as close as we can get to the experience of the player, while still operating in pure telemetry space. Despite this, spatio-temporal analytics remains a topic under-researched in academic research (Drachen and Schubert, 2013). There are only a few works on this topic within esports and visualization. Within the area of esports, this topic has gained attention recently, including papers such as the work of Schubert et al. (2016), which used spatio-temporal data to detect and identify encounters within the game. They developed an algorithm that uses this encounter data to predict win/loss. Further, within the area of visualization, many methods for spatio-temporal analysis have been proposed; see Chapter 5 for examples.

Spatio-temporal analytics generally has the goal of extracting patterns which are statistically correct and useful. A pattern in this context ranges from simple rules (e.g., "players will follow the road") to complex behaviors or models. The knowledge that can be extracted from spatio-temporal data is often more complex than nonspatial information, and the bandwidth requirements associated with capturing spatial information can be substantial (Aung et al., 2019). Thus, specialized methods may be required to consider spatial relations. Spatial data mining methods explicitly consider the spatial component of the data, like movement, often in addition to nonspatial components, such as time or entity/object features. Thereby, it is possible to distinguish information about which entities or objects are located close/far from each other on a map, and which objects are similar based on nonspatial, spatial, and/or temporal attributes. This can be incredibly important when analyzing player behavior, especially in 3D environments (e.g., open-world games and team-based games). In these situations, being aware of the players' behaviors in terms of navigation is not nearly as useful as understanding that navigation behavior in relation to objects and entities in the world. If we want to understand why players navigate the way they do, we need to look at the contextual aspects of behaviors, including players' goals, nearby players, objects and map design, and so forth.

Finally, in addition to modeling and accounting for contextual details, spatio-temporal data mining also models the change of all of such information over time. Techniques commonly used in the spatio-temporal analysis of player behavior include sequence mining or neural nets, see, for example, the work of Katona et al. (2019). In their work, the authors used spatio-temporal data to predict death (kill) events in *DOTA 2*. The model presented would not have worked without both spatial and temporal information, as *DOTA 2* is a highly complex team-based MOBA.

13.4.3 Probabilistic models

One way to address the issue of modeling players' behaviors within a dynamic complex environment such as today's games is to use probabilistic models. As discussed in Chapter 11, there is much work done, and is currently being done, in the field of machine learning and artificial intelligence on probabilistic models, such as Bayesian Networks (BN) or Markov Models. As discussed in the chapter, these methods are still an open area of research, especially when applied to complex games such as the ones in today's market. OpenAI Five explored the use of deep learning and reinforcement learning in this domain producing interesting and promising results (see https://openai.com/projects/five/). This field is still growing, and if you are a student looking for a PhD topic, this may be a good topic to take on. There are many opportunities to work on the use of these models within the game analytics pipeline.

13.4.4 Applications of game data science

As discussed in Chapter 1 and shown throughout the case studies discussed in this book, there are many applications to using data in the game development pipeline, including business, development workflow analysis, as well as design. From a design perspective, for example, it is important to use data to understand players' preferences, interests, and skills so that one can fine-tune the design for the players involved. Churn prediction is another important application of game data science, where companies are interested in predicting which players will churn. This is important to increase retention for the success of the business. Monetization is yet another important application. This is where companies can use insights about players' behavior patterns to convert nonpaying players to paying players. But there are also other uses of game data science, such as assessing game systems' performance, ensuring rapid and robust quick matching of players, or assessing workflow and production within the game development lifecycle. These types of data science systems operate on data that we did not discuss in this book due to inaccessibility of such data. This includes workflow and production data as well as system performance data. If you are running your own company, you can gain access to such data and run similar data analysis processes to what we discussed in this book. This can be helpful to assess the business and development side of your company and to tune company resources and policies accordingly.

13.5 Conclusion

In conclusion, we hope you enjoyed reading this book and going through the lab exercises. This book is a good place to start in this field because it discusses the fundamentals. You now have a basic foundation from which you can begin to do your own research or use these methods within your own game development and production practices.

Be sure to consult the various forums for games research and data science work. In the paper by Melcer et al. (2015), the authors discussed the many venues that publish game research and the trends of game research and innovation. Among these venues are Game Developers Conference, Gamasutra, ACM CHI Play conference, Foundations of Digital Games Conference, and Entertainment Computing Journal and IEEE Transactions on Games, to mention a few. Interested readers are advised to consult the paper and these venues.

● ●

BIBLIOGRAPHY

American Psychiatric Association. (2013). *Diagnostic and statistical manual of mental disorders (DSM-5˚)*. American Psychiatric Pub.

Aung, M., Demediuk, S., Sun, Y., Tu, Y., Ang, Y., Nekkanti, S., Raghav, S., Klabjan, D., Sifa, R., and Drachen, A. (2019): The Trails of Just Cause 2: Spatio-Temporal Player Profiling in Open-World Games. In *Proceedings of Foundations of Digital Games 2019*.

Baker, M. (2016). 1,500 scientists lift the lid on reproducibility. *Nature News*, *533*(7604), 452.

Canossa, A. (2014). Reporting from the snooping trenches: Changes in attitudes and perceptions towards behavior tracking in digital games. *Surveillance & Society*, *12*(3), 433–36.

Dankoff, J. (2011). Game Telemetry with Playtest DNA on *Assassin's Creed*. The Engine Room, September 12, 2011. URL: http://engineroom.ub

De Montjoye, Y. A., Hidalgo, C. A., Verleysen, M., and Blondel, V. D. (2013). Unique in the crowd: The privacy bounds of human mobility. *Scientific Reports*, 3, 1376.

Drachen, A., and Schubert, M. (2013) Spatial game analytics. In *Proceedings of IEEE Computational Intelligence in Games 2013* (pp. 1–8).

Hodent, C. (2019). Ethics in the game industry. *Game Developers Conference*.

Katona, A., Spick, R., Hodge, V. J., Demediuk, S., Block, F., Drachen, A., and Walker, J. A. (2019). Time to die: Death prediction in *Dota 2* using deep learning. In *Proceedings of the IEEE Conference on Games (CoG)*.

Kim, J. H., Gunn, D. V., Schuh, E., Phillips, B., Pagulayan, R. J., and Wixon, D. (2008, April). Tracking real-time user experience (TRUE) a comprehensive instrumentation solution for complex systems. In *Proceedings of the SIGCHI conference on Human Factors in Computing Systems* (pp. 443–52).

Melcer, E., Nguyen, T. H. D., Chen, Z., Canossa, A., El-Nasr, M. S., and Isbister, K. (2015). Games research today: Analyzing the academic landscape 2000–2014. *Network*, 17, 20.

O'Neil, C. (2016). *Weapons of math destruction: How big data increases inequality and threatens democracy*. New York: Broadway Books.

Rigby, C. S., and Ryan, R. M. (2016). Time well-spent? Motivation for entertainment media and its eudaimonic aspects through the lens of self-determination theory. In *The Routledge Handbook of Media Use and Well-Being* (pp. 52–66). New York: Routledge.

Schubert, M., Drachen, A., and Mahlman, T. (2016): Esports analytics through encounter detection. In *Proceedings of the 10th MIT Sloan Sports Analytics Conference*.

Smith, B., and Browne, C. A. (2019). *Tools and weapons: The promise and the peril of the digital age*. United States: Penguin Press.

Weber, B. (2018). A history of game analytics. *Gamasutra*.

Weber, B. (2019). Portfolio-scale machine learning at Zynga. *Gamasutra*.

Yang, P., Harrison, B., and Roberts, D. L. (2014). Identifying patterns in combat that are predictive of success in MOBA games. In *Proceedings of the Foundations of Digital Games*. Miami, Florida, USA.

Games Used in the Book

VPAL Game

The VPAL (Virtual Personality Assessment Lab) game (screenshot shown in Figure A.1) was developed as a modification of the Fallout: New Vegas (FNV) game, which is a role-playing 3D game.

Using the Fallout Las Vegas editor, we were able to build a game that includes the following interactions:

- Conversational Interactions: dialogue on personal topics, collaboration, positive emotes;
- Navigation: free movement, movement to areas preferred
- Interaction with the World: collection, crafting, interacting with pets;
- Combat Behaviors: confrontational dialogue, combat with players, combat with creatures;
- Narrative Compliance: compliance to main and/or taking side quests.

The game takes place in a generic town, in an unnamed country at an unspecific time. The player awakens and is not given any information about her identity or why she is there. This is a design choice. By leaving out details of the story, the game itself is less likely to influence specific behaviors.

The story of the game goes as follows. The small town is taken over by bikers and the player is asked to do something about the situation. The player can take action to solve this issue or not. The story encourages players to deal with the

Figure A.1 Screenshot from VPAL Game

bikers, but it does not mandate it, leaving the selection of actions open. The story is developed to be very generic in the hope that the players would recognize it as a trope and feel familiar with it allowing players to fill the gaps in the story.

The game environment was developed as an open-world to encourage exploration. However, to constrain players to a defined game arena while at the same time providing a rich environment consistently offering a multitude of options, the game environment consisted of a large valley circumscribed by natural borders such as mesas, mountains and high slopes.

The game also contains three classes of NPCs: characters that can initiate formal quests, characters that provide precise information about interesting locations in the world but without initiating a formal quest, and characters that provide opportunities for social interaction, offering details about themselves and their stories with no implications for the game world.

Intro House

The starting location is in a guestroom in the house of the mayor of a small town. Here the player awakens from a shock that caused memory loss, furthering a trope often seen in games. As soon as the game starts, a dialogue is triggered with Tracy, the mayor's daughter, initiating the tutorial, consisting of retrieving some clothing before Tracy will open the door of the guestroom to the rest of the house. This was done to ensure that players have minimal understanding of the controls for navigation, observation of the environment and basic interaction, such as collecting objects.

The mayor's house was designed to provide players with the opportunity to meet Mrs. Walker, the mayor's wife, who asks the player to help her get rid of a rat in the cellar. This quest is optional, as is the opportunity to talk to Mrs. Walker. There are two additional rooms, providing no rewards, a note is in one of the rooms has additional content to the backstory. From a design perspective, however, the rooms were mostly designed to offer a chance to wander or explore.

Towards the exit players will meet Mr. Walker, the mayor. Interacting with him triggers the dialogue that sets the player on the main quest, informing him/her about the disappearance of the sheriff and the gang of bikers who came from out of town. The mayor asks the player to speak to a character in the town for further details, but when exiting the house, players are free to disregard the suggestion and can avoid any quest and NPCs, with no penalties. This starting location affords behaviors, such as socializing with the family, accepting a side quest, combat by killing a rat in the cellar, and the chance to pick up a melee weapons: the baseball bat.

Outside

The valley is divided into two parts: the area where the town is located, and another small valley containing the Hotel. The town and the hotel are connected by a main road and separated by a chokepoint. The purpose of separating the hotel from the rest of the map is to give the hotel the relevance and focus deserved by the final showdown for all players following the main quest, setting it apart from players who are just wandering aimlessly in the town and the locations in its periphery. Only three buildings can be entered in town: the mayor's house, the bar, and the sheriff's office.

The Sheriff's Office

The sheriff's office is a small, deserted and dark environment, offering players the chance to pick up a gun and a stack of money that are clearly visible over a safe. As the main quest, can be solved both by paying off the bikers at the hotel or shooting them, this location provides instruments for both alternatives. This gives the player the choice of being either accommodating or aggressive when dealing with the bikers.

The Bar

The bar offers a spacious environment, several tables, plenty of objects, and a cramped back room. It accommodates two NPCs sitting and eating, both are generic characters with a few lines of dialogue about themselves and the town. There is also a shotgun hidden in the back. There are many objects to collect, catering for hoarding behaviors, several areas to sit, and an interactive jukebox. By offering several options to interact both with unanimated objects and characters, it becomes possible to gauge whether players are more oriented towards people or things. The shotgun in the back is only available to players who are willing to explore the space.

Abandoned house

An abandoned, dilapidated house, spacious and illuminated but cluttered with objects of no importance and no creatures. There is no reason for players to spend any time here, yet players who are very curious or dutiful might spend a long time trying to uncover something of value.

Silver mine

Along the road leading out of town there is a signpost pointing towards a mine, and a clearly marked path takes players directly to its entrance, making it an easy location to find. As soon as players enter the mine they are approached by Ann, who asks for help in locating and liberating her husband, who was captured by the bikers who invaded the town. This is the beginning of a structured, self-contained side quest.

The mine is a large and confusing albeit illuminated space structured in two levels. In the upper mine the bikers have taken residence. The leader of the pack, if approached, will ask for some silver as ransom to free the prisoner, alternatively it is possible to engage him and the gang in combat and free the prisoner after the fight.

The lower mine is a large and complex space, where players have to look for a suitcase full of silver, the only means to liberate the prisoner in a peaceful manner. As soon as the prisoner is free, he will ask the player to report his new condition to Ann, if the player chose to do so the quest will be considered complete.

The Hotel

The hotel is a spacious and brightly illuminated log cabin organized in two floors. Upstairs are eight rooms, where several bikers are resting. The lower floor is organized around the reception desk; on the left, we find the billiard room, with several bikers playing pool, while on the right is a bar lounge. Behind the reception are more rooms guarded by bikers, here the sheriff is kept prisoner. Players entering the hotel are confronted with the gang's leader. The leader instantly engages aggressively with the player indicating how the confrontation should play out. One option is paying the bikers money retrieved in the sheriff's office; this would free the sheriff and liberate the town from the gang peacefully. Another option is to engage in combat and defeat the gang. Last option is to avoid immediate confrontation evading the bikers, and accessing the rooms behind the desk and free the sheriff. At this point it is possible to decide whether to join the sheriff in a gunfight or provide him with a gun and let him take care of the gang alone.

Data Collected through the Game

All action data for the game which includes all player actions and game actions was logged. This data is available to you through the labs, see labs in Chapter 2 as an example.

The data collected is as follows:

- **Movement:** Name of location, subject number, time stamp (every 1/5th of a second/or 20 milliseconds, so steps proceed from 0.0, 0.2, 0.4 etc.), position in x, y, z, orientation of the camera in x, y, z, and *health*.
- **Quest:** Quest keyword, subject number, time stamp, name of quest, number of steps within the quest or whether it is started/ended.
- **Dialogue:** Dialogue keyword chosen, subject number, time stamp, name of the character the user is talking to and what the user said.
- **Object Interactions:**
  - Activate, object name, time step
  - Interaction, place, subject no., object, position

○ InteractionDoor, place, subject no., position

○ InteractionNPC, place, subject no., NPC name, position

- **Attack:** Attack, subject no., time step, object attacked, quest related/ unmotivated/self defense
- **Take hit:** take hit, subject no., time step
- **Shot:** shot, subject no., time step, object used to shoot
- **Looted:**

    ○ LootedDead, subject no., time step. the dead

    ○ Looted item, subject no., time step, item

Defense of the Ancients (DOTA) Game

Starting as a mod for World of WarCraft, *Defense of the Ancients*, better known via its acronym DOTA, has emerged as one of the major team-based strategy games. The current version of DOTA, i.e., DOTA 2, together with League of Legends (LOL), is considered the state-of-the-art in the genre of MOBA (Multiplayer Online Battle Arena) games (Minotti 2015).

The gameplay of DOTA and DOTA 2 includes two teams of 5 players each; each player controls a game character (referred to as a *hero*). The two teams fight each other on a common virtual battlefield. As the players advance in the game through successful completion of in-game achievements, such as killing of opponent characters or in-game creeps, they level up, becoming more powerful and able to perform more advanced attacks. Each team's ultimate goal is to defend their base from being destroyed by the other team. Once the base collapses, the game is over and the team whose base was destroyed is considered defeated. The outcome of a game match will affect how the involved players' skill stats are changed, with winning teams most likely seeing their stats increased and the losing teams seeing their stats decreased. Detailed information on the game can be found on the game website (http://www.dota2.com/).

In this book, we will use different datasets for DOTA, particularly: DOTAlicious and DOTA 2. When data from this game is used, they will be introduced more extensively in the chapters they are used. Also, data files will be available in the labs.

It has become a common practice for game companies, especially esports companies, to release their data through an online API (Application Programming Interface), which allows collection and usage of players' game play data. This opens new doors for data scientists, especially those aspiring in understanding the player experience, to tackle real-life problems through analyzing these data sets, and there is, for example, in esports a wealth of publications that utilize publicly available telemetry data to solve specific problems in and around esports. That said, usually data collected through this means is only allowed for non-shared, non-commercial, and personal use. You are highly recommended and encouraged to download data from these online APIs and apply what you have learned in this book to analyze it.

Games with public data API that we are aware of include:

- DOTA 2: https://docs.opendota.com/
- League of Legends: https://developer.riotgames.com/
- Heroes of the Storm: https://hotsapi.net/

Further, game data services, such as tracker.gg, provide additional examples of games with API access.

• •

BIBLIOGRAPHY

Guo, Yong, and Alexandru Iosup. 2012. "The Game Trace Archive." In *Annual Workshop on Network and Systems Support for Games*. https://doi.org/10.1109/NetGames.2012.6404027.

Minotti, Mike. 2015. "Comparing MOBAs: League of Legends vs. Dota 2 vs. Smite vs. Heroes of the Storm." VentureBeat. 2015.

INDEX